"*Dangerous Visions and New Worlds* offers a bir[d]
period when we were most passionate—about lit
and the sciences—and when we let the rockets expiore the s
while we turned to explore the multiverse in terms of the human
psyche. Powered by a faith that fiction—especially speculative
fiction—could change the world, the New Wave allied with the
underground press, the left, and the world of rock 'n' roll to create
a cultural explosion. This book recalls the highly individualistic
writers, with their often radically different approaches."

—Michael Moorcock, multi-award-winning author,
musician and former editor of *New Worlds* magazine

"Critics and general readers of science fiction have been struggling
to define, assess, and, in some cases, dismiss the New Wave era
since its inception. This entertaining volume offers a fresh, twenty-
first-century reappraisal of the major New Wave SF authors, along
with a concise history of the movement's significant publications.
Additional essays diversify the discussion to include less well-
known progressive authors and wide-ranging historical topics,
effectively placing the New Wave in a broader radical context.
Both an excellent introduction to the groundbreaking SF of
the period and an insightful critique of its continuing impact.
And having all the vintage covers in one place is very cool."

—Allan Kausch, original Lucasfilm Star Wars continuity
editor, preproduction editor of *The Selected Letters of
Philip K. Dick*, coeditor, with Michael Moorcock, of *London
Peculiar and Other Nonfiction* (PM Press, 2012)

## CONTRIBUTORS

Scott Adlerberg

Cameron Ashley

Rebecca Baumann

Kirsten Bussière

Kat Clay

Daniel Shank Cruz

David Curcio

Rjurik Davidson

Michael A. Gonzales

Molly Grattan

Brian Greene

Rob Latham

Nick Mamatas

Maitland McDonagh

Iain McIntyre

Andrew Nette

Kelly Roberts

Erica L. Satifka

Mike Stax

Lucy Sussex

Nicolas Tredell

Donna Glee Williams

# Dangerous Visions and New Worlds

## Radical Science Fiction, 1950 to 1985

Edited by **Andrew Nette** and **Iain McIntyre**

*Dangerous Visions and New Worlds: Radical Science Fiction, 1950 to 1985*
Edited by Andrew Nette and Iain McIntyre
All text copyright © 2021 the individual authors
This edition © 2021 PM Press

The editors and the publishers wish to thank all those who supplied images and gave permission to reproduce copyright material in this book. Every effort has been made to contact all copyright holders, and the publishers welcome communication from any copyright owners from whom permission was inadvertently not obtained. In such cases, we will be pleased to obtain appropriate permission and provide suitable acknowledgment in future editions.

ISBN: 978–1–62963–883–6 (paperback)
ISBN:  978–1–62963–932–1 (hardcover)
ISBN: 978–1–62963–902–4 (ebook)
Library of Congress Control Number: 2020947296

Cover by John Yates / www.stealworks.com
Interior design by briandesign

10  9  8  7  6  5  4  3  2  1

PM Press
PO Box 23912
Oakland, CA 94623
www.pmpress.org

Printed in the USA

# Contents

# Dangerous Visions and New Worlds

## An Introduction

The "long sixties," an era which began in the late 1950s and extended into the 1970s, has become shorthand for a period of trenchant social change, most explicitly demonstrated through a host of liberatory and resistance movements focused on class, racial, gender, sexual, and other inequalities. These were as much about cultural expression and social recognition as economic redistribution and formal politics. While the degree to which often youthful insurgents achieved their goals varied greatly, the global challenge they presented was a major shock to the status quo.

Science fiction, with its basis in speculation, possibilities, and the future, became the ideal vessel for expression in an era in which the focus of many was on the questioning and refusal of established power and social relations, on the one hand, and the exhortation and exploration of radical scenarios, on the other. The genre intrinsically reflected upon both lived and alternative realities—past, present, and future. A "New Wave" of writers who captured the utopian and dystopian zeitgeist leapt to prominence in the 1960s, coming to largely dominate the field by the 1970s.

Resistance to change came from authors, fans, and editors, often dubbed the "Old Guard," who were wedded to the conventions of the so-called "Golden Age" of science fiction. This was the period, generally recognized to stretch from 1938 to the late 1940s, when the genre first began to attract major public attention. Despite some important exceptions, key examples of which can be found in this book, the strictures and censorship of long-running science fiction magazines, such as well-known conservative John Campbell's *Astounding*, dominated the field during the high sales period of the 1950s and continued on into the 1960s. A focus on scientific progressivism, prim sexual morality, and linear narratives resulted in tales focused upon technological breakthroughs and space-conquering male heroes.

In their place came a flood of new work that challenged and destabilized the conservative norms of narrative and expression, as well as outlook and belief. Chafing at the way in which past conventions continued to weigh upon the present, some authors sought to distance themselves altogether by defining their innovative work as "speculative" rather than "science" fiction. This shift in focus was as much aesthetic as political. Influenced by modernist prose and poetry, William S. Burroughs and the Beats, New Journalism, psychedelics, and the quest for consciousness expansion, modes of expression became more disjointed and

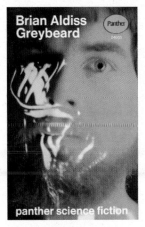

*Greybeard* (Panther, 1968)

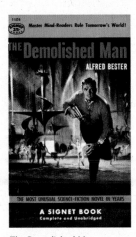

*The Demolished Man* (Signet, 1954)

*Bug Jack Barron* (Avon, 1973)

*What Entropy Means to Me* (Signet, 1973)

experimental and topics shifted to the state of inner rather than outer space. The New Wave still had its astronauts and interstellar explorers, but now they could be found psychologically crumbling under the physical and mental pressure of space flight and the directives of the oppressive military bureaucratic apparatus behind it. Elsewhere, the brave heroes of the past gave way to a new range of characters: genocidal antiheroes, cynical or conflicted over their role in imperial power games and corporate domination; overworked (or underworked) drones strung out on psychotropic or other mind-altering substances; those left in a deep state of confusion by the all-encompassing spectacle of modern mass media culture or made paranoid by pervasive political and corporate surveillance; and individuals left in despair at the commodification and destruction of the natural world.

The internal and external revolt expressed in the genre was in part facilitated by changes in the publishing industry. As we have detailed in our previous two works, *Girl Gangs, Biker Boys, and Real Cool Cats: Pulp Fiction and Youth Culture, 1950 to 1980* and *Sticking It to the Man: Revolution and Counterculture, 1950 to 1980*, the postwar period saw the paperback displace the pulp magazine and, even with the increasing presence of television, novels were hugely popular. This allowed a growing number of authors to make it into print, including some of those previously excluded from mainstream publishing, such as people of color and LGBTIQ writers.

In terms of science fiction, Michael Moorcock's rise to the editorship of the long running *New Worlds* magazine in 1964, the increasing popularity of genre novels, and the publication of groundbreaking anthologies such as *Dangerous Visions* and *England Swings*, all provided writers with new opportunities. Alongside the inclusion of radical commentary, experimental poetry, and other forms of expression previously foreign to SF magazines, *New Worlds* provided primarily British and American writers with the freedom to produce groundbreaking work. One of its admirers, the established yet highly controversial Harlan Ellison, subsequently helped to emphatically mark the New Wave's arrival with the aforementioned hefty and influential 1967 anthology *Dangerous Visions* and to further underscore its importance with 1972's *Again, Dangerous Visions*. Lauded by the critics and commercially successful, the two books included seventy-nine stories, five of which won major awards, and featured almost all of the key writers of the period, as well as detailed headnotes from Ellison regarding their work. The significant role that both *Dangerous Visions* and *New Worlds* played is acknowledged and honored by the title of the collection you are reading.

The rise of the New Wave was controversial. Because of the entrenched role of fandom and critique in SF, issues regarding form and substance were debated to a much larger degree than in other literary genres. Throughout the 1960s and 1970s, these arguments raged in the pages of fanzines and magazines, in letters between authors and readers, and at conferences, forums, and social events. The split between Golden Age right-wingers and New Wave left-wingers was exemplified by the pro– and anti–Vietnam War advertisements, replete with lists of endorsees, taken out in the June 1968 edition of *Galaxy Science Fiction* magazine, a pivotal moment in the genre covered in this volume. While some experimental authors leaned to the right and some conventional ones to the left, for the most part, those whose work was skeptical, if not an outright rejection, of the political status quo were also more likely to question the nature of reality more broadly and engage in nonconformist prose.

In keeping with the New Left in general, few, if any, of the New Wave writers looked to the Soviet Union for answers, except where it emerged in the form of Eastern Bloc dissidence, such as in the work of writers like Stanisław Lem and Arkady and Boris Strugatsky. Although some Western revolutionaries turned to Maoist China, Guevarist Cuba, and new and/or refreshed variants of Trotskyism, state socialism appears to have had little appeal to the majority of science fiction authors who believed in a radical restructuring of society. Although some took part in public demonstrations and other overt organized political action, most opted to undertake activism and sedition via literary expression. In keeping with the antiauthoritarianism of the counterculture, visions for real-world reform and revolution were either relatively fuzzy or aligned most strongly with anarchism and radical forms of feminism.

Not all of the writers covered in this collection believed that such widespread change was desirable or feasible. Some iconoclastic creative types, like Philip K. Dick, refused to align with any ideology or literary movement. Nevertheless, almost all were focused on shaking things up and testing the limits of morality and critical tolerance within and beyond the genre. The

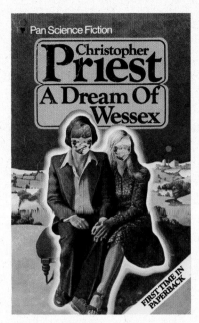

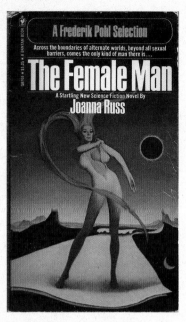

*A Dream of Wessex* (Pan, 1978)

*Memoirs of a Spacewoman*
(Four Square, 1964)

*The Female Man* (Bantam, 1975)

promise of science fiction, in its ability to transcend and travel beyond the limits of the present, was met not only by authors but also illustrators and designers. The influence of psychedelia, surrealism, and experimentation in general on book cover art during the period can arguably be seen most strongly in the science fiction field.

Literature always reflects the values, experiences, hopes, and fantasies of its creators, as well as the society and groupings they are a part of. Within speculative and science fiction genres the boundaries expanded rapidly to include pansexuality, communal lifestyles, hallucinogens, and radical politics. Changing, indeed, often reversing, conceptions of heroes and evildoers, and a blurring, if not complete demolition of the binary between them, were a regular feature of stories regarding near and far-future revolution and utopian societies. Alongside this came a renewed focus on dystopia. Living under the shadow of the destruction of Hiroshima and Nagasaki and the escalating Cold War superpower nuclear standoff, which had come close to global conflict with the US/Cuban missile crisis of 1962, and ever more cognizant of ecological and other issues, writers such as Brian Aldiss, Chelsea Quinn Yarbro, Kate Wilhelm, and John Brunner produced disturbing apocalyptic works that reflected upon existing threats and warned of far worse to come.

For some, the end of the world was less terrifying than the continuance of it. The anomie, ennui, and spectacle of technologically drenched modern life was harshly depicted in many 1960s and 1970s works by J.G. Ballard, Barry Malzberg, Norman Spinrad, Thomas M. Disch, and others. Such visions often reflected the end of various dreams of the long sixties, in terms of a better, more fulfilling world to come, be it via a dazzling array of new consumer goods or communal revolution. As the 1970s progressed, the postwar economic boom faltered, and achieving social change, where it had not been reversed or fought to a standstill, became an ever harder and less glamorous slog. The cynicism and weariness that this engendered, as well as the impact of events such as Watergate on those who clung to faith in democratic institutions, became ever more extant in science fiction.

Despite setbacks and a growing backlash from the privileged, the 1970s remained a period of social challenge and change. Just as women's liberation had pushed back against misogyny and the continuing second-class status of women within the New Left and counterculture, so it did within science fiction, with authors such as Ursula K. Le Guin, Joanna Russ, and Marge Piercy challenging the Old Guard and New Wave alike with their fiction and commentary. While science fiction emerging from and catering to the burgeoning feminist and gay and lesbian movements of the period often focused upon and channeled the inequities of the present into utopian and dystopian visions, writers

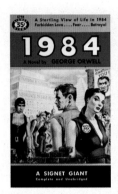

*1984* (Signet, 1955)

*Brave New World* (Chatto & Windus, 1932)

*Motherlines* (Berkley, 1978)

*More Than Human* (Penguin, 1965)

*The Primal Urge* (Sphere, 1967)

such as Judith Merril and Alice Sheldon, writing under the moniker James Tiptree Jr., offered implicit critique through settings that involved a future in which liberation and equality were a long accepted and unremarkable fact.

Racism and allied issues, such as anti-colonialism, structural poverty, and changing patterns of immigration—as well as declining imperial power, in the case of the UK, and imperial overreach, in the case of the US—were regularly explored by radical SF authors during the 1960s and 1970s. Relatively few works by people of color were published, however, until the 1980s. Beyond towering contributions from Octavia Butler and Samuel Delany, the impact of science fiction was arguably felt more among a select range of African American musicians, such as Sun Ra and Parliament/Funkadelic, rather than authors. Although a number of near-future insurrectionist novels from black authors, including Samuel Greenlee and the little-known Joseph Denis Jackson, were published, they were generally marketed as thrillers rather than sci-fi.

*New Worlds and Dangerous Visions* details, celebrates, and evaluates many aspects of this influential period of speculative fiction through twenty-four chapters written by contemporary authors and critics. New angles on key novels and authors are presented alongside excavations of topics, works, and writers who have been largely forgotten or undeservedly ignored. Interspersed between these chapters are short essays and cover spreads that serve to highlight the diversity of the field, as well as innovation in book cover illustration. With the exception of the Soviet Union's Strugatsky brothers, whose work appears here to demonstrate how radicals were pushing the aesthetic and political limits in a very different context—and whose books were published to considerable acclaim in the West—the authors and books covered in this collection are primarily those published in the US and UK or by writers based in those two nations. This is partially for reasons of space, but also because these two countries' milieus and book industries dominated the SF field in the period under review.

As with most movements proposing radical transformation, partisans of the New Wave sometimes portrayed the field as a decisive break with the literary and political conventions of the past. Such a focus on what was new tended to erase the work of those who had been advocating for change and practicing it in their work for some time. The legacy of George Orwell, Aldous Huxley, H.G. Wells, and other writers, as well as pioneering utopian and dystopian writers in the nineteenth and early twentieth century, was in many ways carried forward in the 1960s and 1970s. Although such early work falls largely outside the purview of this collection, the influence and continuing role of progressive authors who had an impact during the conservative 1950s, including Judith Merril, John Christopher, Mordecai Roshwald, Leigh Brackett, and John Wyndham, is scrutinized and given its due.

The impact of New Wave science fiction has, in turn, extended long beyond its heyday of the 1960s and 1970s. Although an explicit and heavy focus on technology returned with cyberpunk in the 1980s, the literary, thematic, and stylistic challenges and innovations presented in the preceding period were largely absorbed and refined rather than removed and rejected. While broader society has significantly changed and moral attitudes shifted, many of the social issues addressed by New Wave authors either remain or have been intensified, giving this body of work a continuing relevance.

**Iain McIntyre and Andrew Nette**

# Imagining New Worlds

## Sci-Fi and the Vietnam War

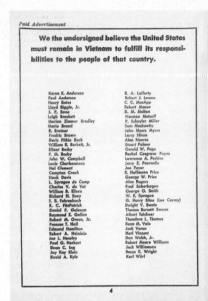

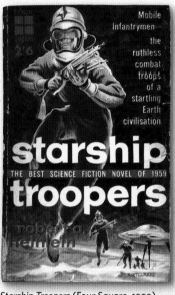

*Starship Troopers* (Four Square, 1959)

For those interested in the relationship between politics and literature, the "New Wave" of science fiction from the 1960s provides a useful example of the intersection where the reshaping of a genre goes hand in hand with a radical politics. That makes the story worth retelling, as we ask what a new political literature might look like and how we might reconsider our own practice today.

In June 1968, the well-known American magazine *Galaxy Science Fiction* published two advertisements, each containing a long list of science fiction writers, illustrators, and editors. The first read: "We the undersigned believe the United States must remain in Vietnam to fulfil its responsibilities to the people of that country." On the facing page, the second list began: "We oppose the participation of the United States in the war in Vietnam."

The anti-war ad had been organized by the writers Judith Merril and Kate Wilhelm. Merril had been in the Trotskyist movement during World War II and was both politically and personally radical. A member of the Futurians, a predominantly left-wing science fiction group, she'd led a colorful personal life and believed in women's right to sexual liberation and "free love."

As she and Wilhelm collected names, they were shocked—somewhat naively, perhaps, when other science fiction writers refused to sign. They had assumed that because the science fiction field was generally liberal and "forward-thinking," there would be widespread support for their advertisement. In fact, they had misread the situation entirely.

The pro-war signatories were—with some exceptions—writers of an older generation, from science fiction's self-proclaimed "Golden Age" of the late 1930s and 1940s, including John W. Campbell, the most influential editor of that time, and Robert Heinlein, an ex-leftist who had become a cold warrior for the right. Heinlein, who responded to Merril's list with declarations of "America first" and "US must win," expressed a far-right militarism in anti-communist novels like *The Puppet Masters* (1951) and *Starship Troopers* (1951). His *Glory Road* (1963) tells of a soldier who fights in Vietnam and brags about disemboweling a "Marxist" in the jungle.

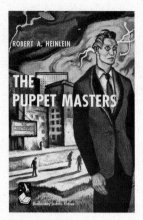

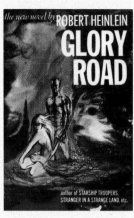

The Puppet Masters
(Doubleday, 1951)

Glory Road
(G.P. Putnam's Sons, 1963)

Other Golden Age writers were more liberal. Nevertheless, their work shared many characteristics. In the typical Golden Age SF story, the protagonist—almost always white and male—faced a plot puzzle created by some science-fictional dilemma, to be solved by either intelligence and scientific knowledge (the more liberal Golden Age writers) or through action (Heinlein and others from the right). For Golden Age writers, science was to lead us in a glorious progress from the suburbs to the stars. The Golden Age authors could, thus, ask: What kind of worlds will we be engaging with? What sort of alien environments and inhabitants exist there? At the center of many of the Golden Age texts—such as in Isaac Asimov's *Foundation* series—was empire.

In its elevation of science, its technological determinism, and its belief in progress, the Golden Age was thus an expression of the dominant postwar American liberalism, itself born from the moment when the US moved to center stage politically and economically. As the Marxist economist Ernest Mandel argued in *Late Capitalism* (1976), somewhat overstatedly, postwar ideology was "accompanied by a generalised proclamation of the advantages of organization.... Belief in the omnipotence of technology is the specific form of bourgeois ideology in late capitalism."

The anti-war signatories were, on the other hand, mostly of a younger generation: part of the New Wave, a term first used by Merril in 1966. As a movement, the aim of the New Wave was, as one of its members, Thomas M. Disch, explained, "to elevate SF to its true potential as the heir of Joyce and Kafka, Beckett and Genet." In doing so, it opened itself up to all kinds of radical content—New Left, feminist, countercultural.

The New Wave really began with the anarchist Michael Moorcock, who took over the English science fiction magazine *New Worlds* and edited it from Ladbroke Grove, a center of the "London Underground." Under Moorcock, *New Worlds* was transformed into an ambitious vehicle for a literary avant-garde within the genre. Moorcock aimed to revolutionize both science fiction and literary fiction by destroying the boundaries between the two, a task that included challenging all previous taboos, traditions, and norms. His first editorial proclaimed that *New Worlds* would publish "a kind of SF which is unconventional in every sense." The idea was, as he explained in a 1979 article in *Foundation: A Review of Science Fiction*, to "attempt a cross-fertilisation of popular SF, science and the work of the literary and artistic avant-garde." Thus, *New Worlds* "attacked the 'literary establishment' as well as social institutions and scientific orthodoxy." Later, Moorcock looked back on the project:

> During the sixties, in common with many other periodicals, *New Worlds* believed in revolution. Our emphasis was on fiction, the arts and sciences, because it was what we knew best. We attacked and were in turn attacked in the all-too-familiar rituals. Smiths [and Menzies, the book retailing company] refused to continue distributing the magazine unless we "toned down" our contents. We refused. We were, they said, obscene, blasphemous, nihilistic etc., etc. The *Daily Express* attacked us. A Tory asked a question about us in the House of Commons—why was public money (a small Arts Council grant) being spent on such filth. I recount all this not merely to establish what we were prepared to do to maintain our policies (we were eventually wiped out by Smiths and Menzies) but to point out that we were the only SF magazine to pursue what you might call a determinedly radical approach—and SF buffs were the first to attack us with genuine vehemence.

Playing the role of T.S. Eliot to Moorcock's Ezra Pound, as Disch once put it, was J.G. Ballard, a soft-spoken Englishman who had grown up in Shanghai. As a child during World War II, he had been incarcerated in a Japanese civilian detention center, an experience that formed the basis of his semi-autobiographical novel *The Empire of the Sun* (1984). The destruction of imperial certainties was to have a profound impact on Ballard, almost as much as the quiet respectability of suburban Shepparton, where he eventually settled after the war. For Ballard, the old science fiction was exhausted. In a 1962 piece for *New Worlds* titled "Which Way to Inner Space?" he wrote:

> I think science fiction should turn its back on space, on interstellar travel, extraterrestrial life forms, galactic wars and the overlap of these ideas . . . similarly, I think, science fiction must jettison its present narrative forms and plots.

He proclaimed a boredom with traditional science fiction, preferring an examination of "inner space" to outer space and gestured to surrealism and the unconscious. As he stated, "To attract a critical readership, science fiction needs to alter completely its present content and approach."

Ballard's own work reversed or inverted the central narrative strategies of Golden Age science fiction, replacing rational, cerebral protagonists with troubled, isolated antiheroes. His futures were not the spacefaring adventures of Asimov or Heinlein but crumbling worlds that were representations of the contemporary psyche, expressed in exotic and efflorescent language.

Ballard's rejection of the verities of science fiction set the foundations for the later works in the New Wave. Many American SF writers—Disch, Norman Spinrad, Harlan Ellison—began to send their most radical writing to Moorcock. Before long, the magazine had, in Ballard's words, "ceased to be an SF magazine at all, even within my elastic definition of the term, and became something much closer to *avant-garde* experimental writing." Ballard himself went on to write a series of brilliant experimental "condensed novels"—reflections on the media landscape, with titles like "Why I Want to Fuck Ronald Reagan" and "The Assassination of John Fitzgerald Kennedy Considered as a Downhill Motor Race." Among Ballard's notable acts was the curation of a show of crashed motorcars for a London art gallery, a precursor to his novel *Crash* (1973).

Very quickly, this experimentation brought all kinds of radical content into science fiction, into *New Worlds* in particular. Pamela Zoline's famous 1967 story "The Heat Death of the Universe" interspersed details of the everyday life of a housewife with other fragments, including an explanation of the second law of thermodynamics (that all closed systems lose energy and thus the universe will one day die). It was a brilliant story,

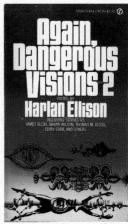

*Dangerous Visions*
(Doubleday, 1967)

*Again, Dangerous Visions*
(Signet, 1973)

but for many of the Old Guard one question remained: Was it science fiction?

The energy of the New Wave quickly spread to the US, with many of the US writers sending their most radical works to *New Worlds*. Merril lived for a year in England in 1967 and was so impressed that she edited the 1968 anthology *England Swings SF*. The American New Wave was probably most visible in the *Orbit* (1966) anthology edited by Damon Knight (Kate Wilhelm's husband) and, in particular, in Ellison's anthology *Dangerous Visions* (1967).

Ellison had marched with Martin Luther King and protested against the Vietnam War. His journalistic work, some of it printed in the countercultural *LA Free Press*, connected him with the New Journalism of the 1960s (Tom Wolfe, Norman Mailer, Hunter S. Thompson, and others), which, as cultural critic Morris Dickstein says, "included a broad spectrum of underground writing—political, countercultural, feminist, pornographic." In his introduction to *Dangerous Visions*, Ellison argued, "This book . . . was constructed along specific lines of revolution. It was intended to shake things up. It was conceived out of a need for new horizons, new forms, new styles, new challenges in the literature of our times."

The anthology contained many New Wave writers—Ellison himself, Brian Aldiss, Spinrad, Ballard, Philip K. Dick—while its sequel, *Again, Dangerous Visions* (1972), included Ursula K. Le Guin, whose "The Word for World Is Forest" was a consciously anti–Vietnam War story. Like Moorcock, Le Guin sympathized with the anarchist theorist Kropotkin. In one of the pieces in her 1989 collection *The Language of the Night: Essays*

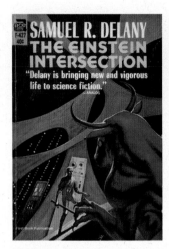

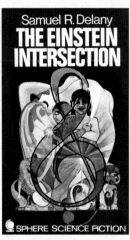

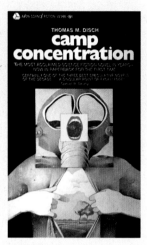

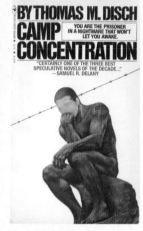

*The Einstein Intersection*
(Ace, 1967)

*The Einstein Intersection*
(Sphere, 1970)

*Camp Concentration*
(Avon, 1972)

*Camp Concentration*
(Bantam, 1980)

*on Fantasy and Science Fiction*, she rejected establishment science fiction:

> From a social point of view most SF has been incredibly regressive and unimaginative. All those Galactic Empires, taken straight from the British Empire of 1880. All those planets—with 80 trillion miles between them!—conceived of as warring nation-states, or as colonies to be exploited, or to be nudged by the benevolent Imperium of Earth towards self-development—the White Man's burden all over again. The Rotary Club on Alpha Centauri, that's the size of it.

Le Guin, along with Joanna Russ and others, introduced feminism into science fiction, with books like the former's *The Left Hand of Darkness* (1969) and the latter's *The Female Man* (1975). Le Guin was also involved in the civil rights and anti–Vietnam War movements, while Russ, a lesbian, was more combative in her challenge of male dominance in the field. But the writer in Ellison's anthology who most exemplified the radical impulse was probably Samuel R. Delany, whom Disch described as "the American New Wave's most brightly shining star." Delany's earliest novels share much of the imagery and symbolism of Ballard's disaster stories. Both writers depict decaying civilizations filled with empty cities and ruined technologies, but Delany concentrates on the cultural relativism of language and science, with an emphasis on the marginalized and on problems of identity. Delany himself is black and gay, and his story in *Dangerous Visions*, "Aye, and Gomorrah," is often taken as a symbolic reworking of the gay experience.

Delany's views developed in the context of the Lower East Side of Manhattan in the early 1960s, the New York hippie district where countercultural radicals like Abbie Hoffman based themselves. Delany was one of science fiction's prodigies (he published *The Jewels of Aptor* in 1962 at the age of nineteen), had taken LSD by 1965, and was present at the famous participatory art installation *Eighteen Happenings in Six Parts* by Allan Kaprow. Later in the 1960s, he was involved in the anti–Vietnam War movement, and, in 1967, he lived as part of an urban commune, an experience chronicled in *Heavenly Breakfast* (1979). His writing represented a confluence of all of these currents.

In 1968, when the anti–Vietnam War letter appeared in *Galaxy*, the American New Wave was reaching its peak. That year Delany's *Einstein Intersection* (1967), a

*Pattern Master*
(Doubleday, 1976)

*The Word for World Is Forest*
(Berkley, 1976)

novel of extreme language play and experimentation, won the Hugo, while Disch's 1968 book *Camp Concentration*, in which the chief character, a draft resister, is imprisoned and infected with a form of syphilis, announced its author as a major talent. Robert Silverberg—probably the most right-wing of the New Wave writers—quickly produced a series of meditations on alienation, transcendence, and political action, through which his stalled science fiction career was brilliantly relaunched. Philip K. Dick had already built a body of work, including essays praising the New Left and the counterculture, centering around philosophical questions of reality, authenticity, and what it means to be human.

Meanwhile, in London, Le Guin published her 1969 feminist novel *The Left Hand of Darkness*. In 1976, she published her award-winning novel *The Word for World Is Forest* (based on the novella of the same name included in *Again, Dangerous Visions*), in which the gentle inhabitants of a planet fight the evil Yumen invaders.

We can see here convergence between science fiction and, for want of a better term, *history*. As Ellison proclaimed a "revolution" in *Dangerous Visions*, activists and radicals were taking to the streets across the world. In 1968, the 1960s went global: the events of May and June rocked France, with a general strike paralyzing the country; demonstrators marched through "swinging" London; in Vietnam, the Tet offensive demonstrated that the United States and its allies could not win the war; riots shook Germany and 126 cities in the US; in Japan students clashed with police; the Prague Spring arose as a powerful reform movement in Czechoslovakia.

Revolutions in form represent the emergence of new content. As a generation, the New Wave writers set out to revolutionize science fiction, driving their own concerns—civil rights, feminism, gay and lesbian rights, the New Left and political action, spirituality and transcendence, eastern mysticism and philosophy—through the genre's fissures. To do so, they had to break apart the traditional narrative forms and structures.

The New Wave dissipated in the mid-1970s, along with much of the radical movement that it was a part of, though the story is less one of defeat than of integration (acceptance by the genre as a whole) and dispersal (the disappearance of the distinctive tone representing the particular correlation of forces from which the New

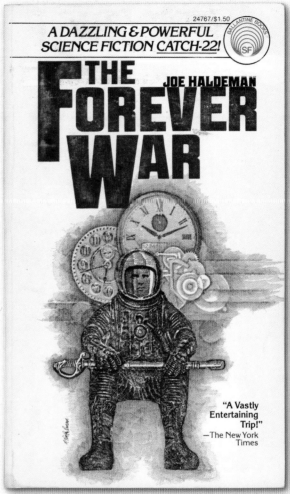

*The Forever War* (Ballantine, 1976)

Wave emerged). Nonetheless, as Spinrad explained in an interview:

> [The New Wave] did change science fiction forever. Because prior to that there really were all kinds of restrictions: it was edited as if it were stuff for teenagers, or more accurately, what librarians thought teenagers should be able to read. So there were all kinds of political restrictions, and sexual restrictions and language restrictions, none of which exist today. In that sense it succeeded completely. After *Dangerous Visions* after *Bug Jack Barron*, *Barefoot in the Head*, stuff like that, you could do anything.

Joe Haldeman's 1974 novel *The Forever War* provides a remarkable example of what the New Wave achieved, because in many ways it constitutes a rewrite of Heinlein's Cold War novel *Starship Troopers*. Both novelists had been in the armed forces (Heinlein during World War II; Haldeman in Vietnam, where he was seriously wounded); both novels employ essentially the same plot (the rise of the protagonist from lowly foot soldier to officer); both have the same science-fictional hardware and a similar hard-nosed literary style. That resemblance illustrates the shifting in ideological focus, best understood against the schism in US domestic politics that was to result in the so-called "Vietnam Syndrome." As Alasdair Spark explains in an essay in *Science Fiction, Social Conflict and War* (1990):

> Heinlein applauded heroism, revelled in combat, and lauded the organization of society along military lines. . . . Haldeman's soldiers are elite draftees, caught in an endless, futile war which strips them of humanity, alienates them from civilian society, and denies them status except in survival.

The anti-war advertisement in *Galaxy* was written to foster exactly the sort of shift expressed in Haldeman's *The Forever War*. For Merril, however, the letter was not enough. She moved to Canada in the late 1960s, citing the US government's suppression of anti-war activism as a reason. There, she founded Rochdale College, an experiment in cooperative living and student-run education, and was heavily involved in the peace movement. Others took different paths, though few of the New Wave writers entirely lost their radicalism. Decades after the letter, their example shines for those who feel that contemporary culture needs to be revolutionized, not just in form but in content.

Of course, literary movements cannot be simply invoked out of thin air, any more than radical political movements can be conjured by pure will. The New Wave project was constructed in the context of the broad social radicalization in which its writers participated. It is easy for us to forget just how profound this was. The civil rights movement, black power, feminism, the New Left, gay rights, the counterculture—the 1960s fundamentally altered the modern world. Revolution seemed to be in the air—in both the East and the West—and to understand New Wave SF you must understand it as emerging from and engaging with this radicalization.

Literary and political movements are never entirely spontaneous. They never emerge purely unplanned, without someone initiating them. As

Antonio Gramsci noted, a description of an action as "spontaneous" simply means that leaders cannot be identified. The story of the New Wave consists of conscious political interventions—Moorcock's tenure at *New Worlds*, Merril and Wilhelm's letter, Ellison's *Dangerous Visions*—having significant cultural effects. At key points of that history, both science fiction and the broader culture were shaped by people who had both a literary agenda *and* a political one.

Furthermore, most of the New Wave writers embarked on their projects *before* the widespread 1960s radicalization took place. In 1962, Ballard's inversion of Golden Age SF opened up a way of writing science fiction with an entirely different worldview. Moorcock took over *New Worlds* in 1964. Ellison began writing about civil rights and the marginalized in the late 1950s, populating his fiction with outsiders, the working class, little people struggling, rather than "heroes." Le Guin and Delany followed similar trajectories. They were, in other words, participants in the 1960s, not simply reflections of it.

**Rjurik Davidson**

# Sextrapolation in New Wave Science Fiction

In her 1985 essay "The Virginity of Astronauts," Vivian Sobchack argues that science fiction film has persistently refused to deal with human eroticism, exiling sexuality to the point that it manifests only as unconscious pathology. The classic icons of the genre—monsters and mutants, alien invasion and possession, technological mastery or impotence—emerge in her analysis as neurotic symptoms, materializations of the forces of repression that lurk beneath the antiseptic surfaces of the futuristic sets and the Ken-doll banality of the space jockey heroes.

Her study is devoted largely to classic SF films of the 1950s, and one wonders how she might apply her psychoanalytic methods to the more risqué movies of the 1960s and 1970s, such as *Barbarella* (1968) and *Flesh Gordon* (1974). Perhaps she would view such films as an epochal return of the repressed, an explosion into conscious awareness of the hidden libidinal energies that have always animated the genre. Capitalizing on the freer climate for sexual expression within contemporary popular culture, such Space Age sex farces might be seen as traducing the chasteness and moral seriousness of traditional SF cinema, deriving much of their comic charge precisely from a counterpoint between the puritanical rectitude of 1950s era SF and the decadent excesses of the youth counterculture.

In a review of the comic book version of *Barbarella* in the March 1967 issue of *The Magazine of Fantasy and Science Fiction*, Judith Merril playfully defended the "valid modern phenomenon" of the sexy single girl, as incarnated in the eponymous heroine, over the "undersexed high-minded Boy Scout of the space patrol" one might normally expect to find in similar SF stories. Yet she acknowledged that hers was likely a minority taste, at least among traditional fans, for whom Barbarella's cheerful ribaldry might seem dreadfully unserious—or, as Merril winkingly implied, vaguely threatening to the adolescent males who make up SF's core audience. In the same review, Merril also praised John Barth's quasi-SF novel *Giles Goat Boy* (1966) for its sophisticated handling of sexual material. In essence,

she deployed a highbrow postmodernist novel and a lowbrow pop culture comic, both of which deal with sex bawdily and unapologetically, to critique the middlebrow tameness and asexuality of most genre SF. "It is time," she claimed, "and long past time, for some of the same kind of hard-headed speculative thinking that science fiction contributed to space flight and atomics, to be done in [the areas of] interpersonal psychology and sexology."

Merril was, of course, one of the most visible—and voluble—apostles of the New Wave in 1960s SF, and this review may be seen as a volley in her ongoing battle to force the genre to "grow up," to shed the legacy of its pulp past and embrace contemporary realities. Her review shows that this program featured demands not only for a greater ethos of aesthetic experimentalism but also for more "adult" forms of content, including sexuality. Indeed, one of the central ways the New Wave was experienced in the US and Britain was as a "liberated" outburst of erotic expression, often counterpoised by advocates of the "New Thing," as Merril called it, with the priggish puritanism of the Golden Age. Yet this stark contrast, while not unreasonable, tends, ultimately, as do most of the historical distinctions drawn between the New Wave and its predecessors, to

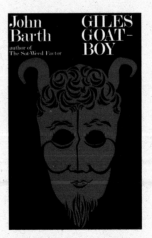

*Giles Goat-Boy*
(Secker & Warburg, 1967)

*I Will Fear No Evil*
(New English Library, 1972)

overemphasize rupture at the expense of continuity, effectively disappearing some of the pioneering trends in 1950s SF that paved the way for the New Wave's innovations. Moreover, following an insight of Michel Foucault's, it is probably wise to be suspicious of a simplistic "repressive hypothesis," an assumption that taboos surrounding sexual expression automatically operate to silence discussion of sex rather than to sustain and propagate it. Even Sobchack's Freudian argument, with its emphasis on sublimation, shows that SF, willy-nilly, is always treating sexual topics, perhaps most powerfully when it seems to be primly avoiding them.

On the other hand, while it is certainly worth recalling that Freud's theory of repression involves not merely the psychic canceling of forbidden data but also, in hydraulic compensation, the unconscious production of neurotic symptoms, I definitely do not wish to understate the true neutralizing power of literary censorship in SF magazine culture prior to the 1960s. Though some Golden Age authors have denied the existence of constraining taboos during the pulp era (Lester del Rey, for example, has argued that he "never had any magazine reject any story with sex in it"), there is plenty of testimony by reminiscing writers who either encountered direct resistance to their handling of controversial topics or else practiced self-censorship to avoid editorial interference in their work. In 1964, Harry Harrison frankly acknowledged that SF writers "all censor our work for the magazines.... We have been so broken to the pulp habit that we cannot relax even if we want to.... We have been taboo-ridden too long and seem incapable of accepting sex and bodily functions as a normal part of life."

Those who refused to self-censor were subjected to the merciless pruning of editorial blue pencils. Tom Purdom has recounted how his 1957 story "Grieve for a Man" was bowdlerized by the editor of the magazine *Fantastic Universe*. The story features a bullfighter battling a robotic bull, with the assembled crowd cheering for the machine; as written, the matador at one point thinks to himself: "Well, let them get an erection out of that if they want," which the editor changed to: "Let them get young again out of that if they want to."

A more famous example of such meddling was Frederik Pohl's modification of Harlan Ellison's 1967 story "I Have No Mouth, and I Must Scream" prior to its publication in *If*, where a character who was "big in the privates" like "a giant ape" and had "an organ fit

for a horse" was referred to instead as "like an animal in many ways." Given the anatomical specifics of these alterations, it is unsurprising—if not exactly forgivable—that some of the more macho young writers of the sixties should have been infuriated by this symbolic gelding of their work; as Norman Spinrad rather feverishly complained in 1968:

> What does [all this censorship] do to writers? Those who can cut it in the big world out there— like Bradbury and Vonnegut—leave while still in possession of the contents of their scrotums. Others are sufficiently anesthetized by the novocaine of in-group egoboo that they submit to the castrator's knife. There are those who remain men and remain within the field and do the best they can within the limitations and suffer nothing worse than broken hearts.

Not all writers, of course, were quite so tamed. C.L. Moore and Leigh Brackett had been infusing their planetary romances with a decadent sensuality for many years without apparent threat to the ostensible masculinity of their noms de plume, and Thomas N. Scortia has written of how, throughout the 1940s and 1950s, enterprising punsters tried to sneak off-color jokes or other smutty references past John W. Campbell's resident censor at *Astounding*, editorial assistant Kay Tarrant.

Probably the most famous success story in this regard was George O. Smith's 1947 tale "Rat Race," with its reference to "the world's first ball-bearing mousetrap," which later turns out to be a tomcat. (According to Scortia, this game was called "slipping one past Kay.") Some of Campbell's admirers in the field—such as Harrison, for instance—have attempted to absolve the editor of culpability for the excessive chasteness of his magazine, blaming it instead on the priggish Ms. However, there can be little doubt that Campbell himself had, in this area as in so many others, quite firm and eccentric views of what was acceptable and what was not. In his editorial for the October 1965 issue of *Analog*, for example, he defended himself against charges that the material he published scanted important human drives such as erotic desire, opining that "achievement, personal worth, is a more universal motivation of Man than hustling the handiest female into bed" and going on to list the truly great writers whose work had long endured despite its lack of prurience, such as Shakespeare!

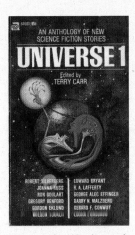

The June 1953 edition of *Universe* magazine, featuring Theodore Sturgeon's story, "The World Well Lost."

*Universe 1* (Ace Books, 1971)

Not all Golden Age stalwarts shared Campbell's view that sex was a seamy distraction from the exalted heroism of the best SF; certainly, Robert Heinlein's work during the 1960s grew increasingly preoccupied with sexual matters, culminating in the embarrassing debacle of *I Will Fear No Evil* (1970), in which a rich old man's randy brain is transplanted into the nubile body of his female assistant. But the split between Old Guard—as the more traditional SF writers were known—and New Wave, coinciding as it did with an unparalleled period of erotic openness in the broader culture, inevitably came to involve fraught exchanges regarding the growing explicitness of contemporary SF's depictions of sexuality. I will examine some of the more significant of these exchanges shortly, but first I would like to revisit a moment during the early 1950s when it seemed to a number of contemporary observers as if the walls against taboo material in SF were finally coming down. This moment tends to get lost in all the furious combat of the subsequent decade, when New Wave authors' calls for a fully "mature" SF often traded on a caricatured portrait of the genre as naively juvenile prior to the advent of their fearless avant-garde. This is not to diminish the significance of the New Wave's militancy, in the areas of gender and sexual politics especially, but rather to show how a few bold writers and editors of the fifties broke some of the paths that a decade later the New Wave's champions would bravely tread.

During the early 1950s, a handful of stories were published in the magazines that dealt explicitly with sexual topics the genre had long ignored, often treating their material with a Freudian slant that gave to SF's heroes a lurking, dark unconscious previous incarnations had generally lacked. These tales include, in order of publication: Fritz Leiber's "The Ship Sails at Midnight" (1950), in which an alien female becomes resident muse—and bisexual lover—to a group of young bohemians; Leiber's "Coming Attraction" (1950), a stark portrait of an atom bomb–ravaged future crawling with sadomasochistic subcultures; Philip José Farmer's "The Lovers" (1952), which boldly affirmed the human-alien miscegenation that many pulp covers had only hinted at; R.J. McGregor's "The Perfect Gentleman" (1952), in which a repressed young woman stranded alone on a planet grows a prospective lover from a seed; Sherwood Springer's "No Land of Nod" (1952), a postapocalyptic tale in which a man breeds with his own daughter to continue the human race; Theodore Sturgeon's "The Sex Opposite" (1952), in which a hermaphroditic symbiote forms a kind of ménage à trois, albeit a platonic one, with a heterosexual couple; Sturgeon's "The World Well Lost" (1953), a tale of gay aliens whose telepathic influence draws out the suppressed homoeroticism linking two male buddies; Farmer's "Mother" (1953), a creepy story of a mom-obsessed neurotic who is adopted by a conch-like alien, becoming at once its child and its lover; and Idris Seabright's (aka Margaret St. Clair's) "Short in the Chest" (1954), in which mandatory sexual relations between members of the armed forces serve as a mechanism for insuring Cold War harmony.

Significantly, with the exception of "Coming Attraction," which was featured in the second issue of *Galaxy*, none of these stories appeared in the three major digests of the period, which also included *Astounding* and *The Magazine of Fantasy and Science Fiction*. The others were either published in the pulps *Startling Stories* and *Thrilling Wonder Stories*, which were on their last legs at the time, or in second- and third-tier digests just struggling to establish themselves: *Fantastic Stories*, *Fantastic Universe*, and *Universe*. In short, the magazines with the highest profiles in the market tended to shy away from this sort of material. John Brunner has reported that Farmer's "The Lovers" was rejected by H.L. Gold at *Galaxy*, with the note: "I'll publish this if you can get rid of the sex—I run a family magazine!" Even more disturbingly, Campbell not only rejected Sturgeon's "The World Well Lost" but is rumored to have written to other editors warning them against publishing it. As Farmer has commented:

We had a field wherein, theoretically, the writer was unlimited in choice of subject matter, wherein he had the whole cosmos to roam. . . . Yet the writer was far from being unlimited. He avoided any sex except for the inclusion of the dummy figure of the professor's daughter or an occasional superfemale who was almost always evil. . . . Perhaps the hero and the [heroine] kissed as the story ended, and red Mars sank in the background, but this did not take place often.

An exchange of letters between Sturgeon and Springer regarding the latter's "No Land of Nod," published in *Thrilling Wonder Stories* in 1953, indicates the repressive editorial climate of the field and the impatient chafing of ambitious authors in the face of it. According to Sturgeon, Springer's story was a failure not because it went too far in its depiction of father-daughter incest, but because it didn't go far enough: given a postapocalyptic situation, in which not only is the survival of the species at stake but prevailing social codes have been literally wiped out with the rest of humanity, the story's hero would not have been as wracked with hesitancy and guilt as Springer depicted.

"Taboos need to be broken," Sturgeon wrote, "either because they are bad in themselves or because of this odd quirk in human beings that makes it necessary to prove they can be broken. But when you break 'em, break 'em clean. . . . [I]f science fiction is to remain the viable genre it is, it must be capable of exploration in other frameworks—objectively, and all the way."

Springer's reply is revealing: rather than defend the story against Sturgeon's critique, he described the difficulties he had writing and publishing it. A gathering of authors with whom he discussed the basic plot had been excited by the idea, agreeing it addressed an important topic, but had claimed that the story would be "impossible to sell"—a judgment later affirmed by a number of editors, whose collective verdict, according to Springer, was "too hot to handle." The sense of pulled punches that Sturgeon complained of was, Springer admitted, a quite calculated gamble to get such incendiary material into print.

One might assume, given this context, that writers eager to shatter taboos were facing not only censorious editors but also puritanical readers who, as Albert Berger has quoted one long-time fan, "read science fiction to stimulate [their] intellect[s] not [their] gonads." Yet while there was general agreement that the sexually themed stories of the early 1950s were obviously "controversial," the feedback in the letters pages of *Startling* and *Thrilling Wonder* responding to Springer's "Nod" and Farmer's "The Lovers" and "Mother" was almost uniformly positive, praising the authors' maturity and skill in handling difficult themes. Editor Samuel Mines expressed some amazement that "nobody called us to task for printing" Springer's story, saying he had expected a storm of protest, while John Brunner wrote of anticipating attacks by "nasty little minds" on "The Lovers" that never really materialized.

There were some complaints, of course, such as the following diatribe from one C.L. Morehead (Reverend):

That Mother thing by Farmer made me gag. . . . Should I wish to read about the tendency of some adults to retreat into "the womb of the world" I'll read textbooks on psychology. I certainly don't need it in my recreational reading! . . . Shortly after finishing [the story] I was seized with an attack of the flu accompanied with violent seizures of vomiting, I think Mother had something to do with it.

But most correspondents were pleased to see such imaginative handlings of unusual topics, claiming they proved the genre's intellectual boldness and fertility of imagination. One reader praised Mines "for advocating more mature stories in which sex is allowed to appear in its true light: as an important and essential part of life on this or any other planet." Poul Anderson, who was just beginning to establish himself as one of the more promising young talents in the field, saluted Farmer for producing, in "The Lovers," a tale in which sex is treated straightforwardly as a "biological phenomenon, with no pornography at all. Let's face it," he continued, foreshadowing Merril's brief a decade later, "babies are not found under cabbage leaves, and there's no reason why the science-fiction writer shouldn't extrapolate the facts of reproduction as he does those of physics and neurology and the other sexless sciences." Like Brunner, Anderson also predicted a flood of complaints from "prudes and old women," which he feared could have the effect of dissuading Mines from publishing more such tales in future; yet at the same time he acknowledged that the story was the talk of his Minneapolis fan club, where everyone was "raving about it."

This sort of response validated Mines's own view, expressed in his editorial for the issue of *Startling* featuring "The Lovers," that SF should be "about people

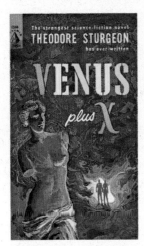

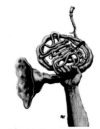

*Venus Plus X*
(Pyramid Books, 1960)

*Strange Relations*
(Ballantine, 1960)

*Flesh* (Beacon, 1960)

*Davy* (St. Martin's Press, 1964)

first and gadgets second. . . . It must contain the basic requirements of drama, it must be well told, it must depict real people, it must be as sincere in its emotional values as in calculating the speed of a space ship operating on ultra-galactic drive." While foreseeing "squawks" from readers who will "hate [the story] to pieces," Mines defended such experiments as being essential to revitalize the field, drawing in more sophisticated readers by "boldly tackling subjects undreamt of ten years ago." Clearly, Mines—along with Brunner and Anderson—should have shown more faith in the fans: on the strength of "The Lovers" and "Mother," Farmer was named Best New Author at the first Hugo Awards convention in Philadelphia in 1953.

The point of rehearsing all this background is to indicate that a quite developed discourse regarding taboos and censorship—focused especially on their impact in hindering the artistic growth of the field—had emerged during this period, well before the advent of the New Wave. It is also worth stressing that this debate and the venturesome stories that emerged from it were made possible in large part by the early to mid-1950s being a seller's market for authors; in 1953 alone, 181 issues of thirty-seven different professional magazines were published in the US and Britain, overseen by some two dozen editors, many of whom could afford to take chances with young writers and controversial content in search of a niche in the burgeoning scene. By the end of the decade, however, the boom was over; all the pulps were gone, and the digests had dwindled to a handful of titles controlled by only five editors—Campbell (at *Astounding*), Gold (at *Galaxy* and *If*), Robert P. Mills (at *Fantasy and Science Fiction*),

Cele Goldsmith (at *Amazing* and *Fantastic*), and John Carnell (at *New Worlds*, *Science-Fantasy*, and *Science-Fiction Adventures*). Campbell and Gold in particular had settled into constricting routines, their risk-taking impulses subordinated to the necessity of providing more or less predictable fare, while Goldsmith's and Carnell's magazines had begun to suffer sharply declining sales. As the new decade dawned, there was a widespread sense of malaise in the field, effectively captured in the title of Earl Kemp's 1960 Hugo award–winning fanzine, *Who Killed Science Fiction?*

In the midst of this painful contraction, SF authors began to debate the possibility of founding a writers' union, not only to advance their financial interests but also to establish standards for editorial interference in their manuscripts. The newsletter *Proceedings of the Institute for Twenty-First Century Studies*, which appeared from 1959 to 1962, became the main forum for what were sometimes contentious exchanges regarding the degree of aesthetic autonomy writers should legitimately expect in their work, with the discussion turning on occasion to the topic of editors' unilateral expurgation of hot-button content. According to Farmer, Campbell and Gold routinely rejected "controversial stories based on sex because they found them personally disgusting and disturbing," but the author believed they were doing no more than reflecting the current state of the field stating:

the average SF reader doesn't really want disturbing or thought-provoking stories, he wants entertainment. The average and even superior editor knows this, and he prefers to entertain the reader. Bob Mills is an exception, but even he is taking a poll of his readers to determine if they wish controversial stories. If the majority says no, then it's Good-bye to SF magazines for me, both as a reader and writer. I can continue to write innocuous stories, and probably will now and then because I need the money, but my heart won't be in it.

Given this depressing climate, some authors gazed wistfully at greener pastures, pondering the merits of abandoning the field in favor of other, less fettered genres or the broader "mainstream"; a few, such as Harlan Ellison and Robert Silverberg, had already begun penning soft-core potboilers for fly-by-night paperback houses like Ember and Nightstand (though they didn't brag about this in the newsletter).

Farmer soldiered on, managing to place his delirious tale of a future fertility cult, *Flesh* (1960), with the *Galaxy* novels series. This book appeared alongside Ballantine's collection *Strange Relations* (1960), which gathered "Mother" and several other pathbreaking stories from the fifties, and the following year saw publication of a novel-length version of *The Lovers*. Indeed, the growing book market for SF became a site where the editorial shibboleths of the magazines could potentially be transcended. Sturgeon's novel of a hermaphroditic utopia, *Venus Plus X*, which had been unable to find a periodical home stateside (it was serialized in *New Worlds*), was brought out in paperback in 1960. Other older writers who had a lurking streak of ribaldry began to loosen the reins in their novels—for example, Leiber (*The Wanderer* [1964]) and Edgar Pangborn (*Davy* [1964]); and this is not to mention the ongoing spectacle of Heinlein's libidinous conversion, but it was Farmer, renowned as the pioneer taboo breaker from the previous decade, who often figured as the touchstone for those eager to see SF shed its legacy of straitlaced proscriptions. In a 1964 fanzine article, Charles Platt—who would soon join the editorial coterie at *New Worlds*, the flagship of New Wave innovation—argued that Farmer's work, despite its "casual American style of hack writing and the occasional lurid coarseness of its treatment of sexual themes," was breaking important ground in the field "by its originality and deliberate disregard of commonly accepted limits of plot and action"; Farmer's "biological experimentation and off-color sexual ideas" could conceivably inspire a fresh generation of writers "to produce work of better overall quality."

When Michael Moorcock took over the helm at *New Worlds* in the summer of 1964, improving the "overall quality" of SF was one of his main goals. Convinced that the genre had for too long consisted of "boys' stories got up to look like grown-ups' stories," Moorcock brought to the task not only a hard-won knowledge of contemporary SF's shortcomings drawn from a long apprenticeship in British fandom but also a reputation for pugnacious activism on behalf of "outlaw" writers. He had been featured as a correspondent in a November 1963 exchange in the *Times Literary Supplement* regarding the work of William S. Burroughs, where he had defended that author against a reviewer who denounced his novels as sordid and obscene. Moorcock's championing of Burroughs continued in his debut editorial for *New Worlds*, which claimed that wildly audacious books like *The Ticket That Exploded* (1962) and *Nova Express* (1964) were precisely "the SF we've all been waiting for," while acknowledging that many traditional fans would be put off by their widespread "description of sexual aberration and drug addiction" and their "frequent use of obscenities." Burroughs's importance for the genre, in Moorcock's eyes, lay not merely in his experimental form and his radical break with conventional modes of narration but also in his relevance to the current times, with their skeptical questioning of authority and pursuit of fresh experiences. As a subsequent *New Worlds* editorial opined:

> Since SF is growing up . . . the form must be reshaped and new symbols found to reflect the mood of the sixties. . . . It is no good living in and off the past these days—no good living in the world of writers like Heinlein and off their terms, symbols, backgrounds and even ideas. The age that formed them is past. . . . Quite often the moral assumptions found in a story of the fifties can be virtually meaningless to today's new generation.

Despite his commitment to boldness and novelty, Moorcock soon discovered that the long-standing conservatism of SF magazine culture was not so readily transcended. After the September 1964 issue ran Langdon Jones's story "I Remember, Anita…," in which the narrator broods intensely over an erotic relationship brutally terminated by the outbreak of nuclear war, an angry reader wrote in to protest the work's "downright pornography," warning the editor not to "forget the circulation of this magazine among young

March 1970 edition of *New Worlds*

McLuhan, portrays a near-future, media-saturated society in which the eponymous hero, a TV talk show host, suavely seduces not only the mass audience but also an array of young women, in scenes sprinkled liberally with the lingo of sixties eroticism: "fuck me into the mystic circle of power where it's all at... make me real with your living-color prick... ball me with your image, baby, and I'll ball you with mine." Initially written under contract to Doubleday, the manuscript was rejected by their SF editor Lawrence Ashmead, who judged the book to be "unpublishable" in its original form due to both its sexual explicitness and its chaotic counterculture language—making it precisely the sort of hip, unconventional work that Moorcock was seeking for *New Worlds*.

Unfortunately, the magazine's distributor and the powerful bookstore chain W.H. Smith and Sons found the serial obscene and refused to stock the offensive issues, putting a major crimp in the journal's shaky finances, which had only recently been shored up by a grant from the British Arts Council. To add insult to injury, a Tory representative in the House of Commons stood up and demanded to know "why public money was being spent on filth" by the Arts Ministry. During a visit to W.H. Smith's offices, Moorcock was told "that they would rethink their decision" if he agreed to "modify the magazine's contents and 'kill' the Spinrad serial," which he angrily refused to do. It was only under pressure from the Arts Council that Smith's relented and lifted the ban, but *New Worlds* had already received a financial blow from which it would never entirely recover.

When *Bug Jack Barron* was finally published in the US, in a 1969 paperback edition from Avon, it provided more fodder for what was by then a clamorous debate regarding the growing salaciousness of contemporary SF. Defenders of the novel, such as Peter Singleton, praised its "energy and sincerity" as a realization of the New Wave's commitment to aesthetic originality and social relevance, arguing that its sexual explicitness "must have its place in any reasonably comprehensive portrayal of adult human characters." As reviewer Richard E. Geis commented, "there'll be no going back to the 'safe' subject matter and the 'fit for children' writing dictated by the magazines and many pocketbook publishers." Critics of the book—such as Samuel Mines, erstwhile editor of the pathbreaking pulps of the fifties—complained about its pervasive profanity, the "needless overdone vulgarity which some writers

eager readers, who wants [*sic*] something else than trash just good enough to be sold under the counter." Moorcock's brusque reply that he was "not publishing a magazine for schoolboys" likely came back to haunt him in the summer of 1967 when another bawdy tale by Jones, "The Time Machine," prompted the magazine's printer to refuse to produce the July issue, thus forcing the editor to scramble for replacement copy. The libidinal rhetoric in "Anita" had been relatively mild, eschewing stark anatomical references in favor of the evasive blather of pseudo-literary erotica—e.g., "the loin-heat that... suffuse[d] my abdomen... the straining symbol of my passion"—but "The Time Machine" upped the ante with its graphic depiction of intercourse between the protagonist and his menstruating lover, a taboo the SF magazine was apparently not prepared to break.

These flare-ups were minor, however, compared to the furor that erupted when *New Worlds* began serializing Norman Spinrad's *Bug Jack Barron* in the December 1967 issue. The novel, strongly influenced by Burroughs's fiction and the theories of Marshall without taste apparently think is realism." To Donald A. Wollheim, former member of the Futurian fan group and current SF editor at Ace Books, Spinrad's "nauseous epic" was "depraved, cynical, utterly repulsive and thoroughly degenerate and decadent," proof positive of the essential nihilism of the New Wave. "It may even win the Hugo—who knows?—but it's garbage just the same."

As these stern remarks indicate, the battle lines being drawn between the self-styled guardians of traditional SF—whose "wondrous visions" were in danger of being eclipsed by the New Wave's "stylistic claptrap and downbeat" themes—and the proponents of what Merril called "The New Thing," an unconventional, countercultural mode of SF writing, often overlapped with a heated debate regarding the ethical and aesthetic merits of overt representations of sexuality. The enemies of the New Wave frequently stereotyped the movement in terms of its allegedly "sick" obsession with outré forms of sex: one Old Guard fan, Don Brazier, claimed that every character in a New Wave story "must have a sex problem," making the fiction resemble a series of psychiatric case histories, while John J. Pierce, the most indefatigable polemicist for traditional SF among 1960s fans, argued that New Wave fiction tended to treat "the sexual impulse as basically neurotic or even psychotic . . . bedded in a context of cruelty and disgust." In an essay entitled "The Devaluation of Values," Pierce went on to argue that the New Wave attitude toward sex was not liberatory at all but rather nihilistic: "There are plenty of hang-ups, but no joy; lots of explicit description, but no love. The 'New Thing' writers don't say in so many words that sex is 'dirty,' but they manage to convey that impression."

For their part, New Wave defenders, such as Harry Harrison, mocked the sublimated tameness of old-style SF, where "intersexual relationships did have their place, though always in a hearty familial way, and offstage to boot." Brian Aldiss, reviewing Old Guard author James White's novel *The Watch Below* (1966), derided the book's "prissy" timidness: "All references to sex seem to set [the story's] bold seafaring men 'close to panic.' They can hardly mention uh menstruation or uh fornication without stuttering." "[A]ll the Simon-pure Asimovs and Heinleins," Aldiss remarked in another context, "falsified by admitting no worlds below the belt." Harlan Ellison, in a sharp exchange with Pierce regarding the alleged degeneracy of contemporary SF, claimed his opponent's position was "precisely the stand a blue-nosed Puritan would take

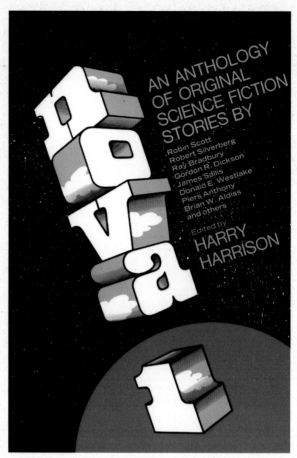

*Nova* (Dellacorte, 1970)

in the face of such overwhelming changes" as were sweeping through society in the 1960s. In short, both sides in the debate basically accused their opponents of displaying some form of sexual pathology, whether puritanical repression or neurotic desublimation.

The theatrical hysteria of this controversy, which consumed the field during the late 1960s and early 1970s, had its dress rehearsal in the furious hype surrounding Ellison's 1967 anthology *Dangerous Visions*. In an effort to blunt the censorious influence of the magazines, during the mid-1960s, a handful of SF authors explored the possibility of launching book series containing all-original short fiction, in the hope of inviting risk-taking work that might otherwise go unpublished. The first series to appear was Damon Knight's *Orbit*, which premiered in 1966; by the early seventies, a number of such franchises—Harry Harrison's *Nova*, Robert Silverberg's *New Dimensions*, Terry Carr's *Universe*—were offering strong competition to the traditional magazines, which were compelled to liberalize their editorial policies as a result. But none made the splash within the genre that

*Dangerous Visions*—and its 1972 companion volume *Again, Dangerous Visions*—did.

Part of the reason for this was the unique personality of its editor. A quarrelsome presence within fandom for over a decade and an unparalleled master of aggressive self-promotion, Ellison built up a huge anticipation for his anthology through breathless letters to fanzines and barn-burning talks at SF conventions. In a Guest of Honor speech at the San Diego Westercon in July 1966 (later published as "A Time for Daring"), Ellison offered a typically contentious assessment of the present state of the field: it had become safe and stale and was rapidly driving its best writers into the arms of the literary mainstream, where figures such as Burroughs and Vonnegut were already being celebrated for producing an audacious new brand of SF. "These people have left us for the very simple reason that they're too big and talented to be constrained by our often vicious, often ungrateful little back water eddy," the SF ghetto whose confining walls were patrolled by a handful of narrow-minded, cozily incestuous gatekeepers. As a result, "we've been leaching the vitality out of our best writers. . . . [W]hen they write something new and fresh and different and inventive, we don't know where they are." *Dangerous Visions* was geared to provide a welcoming market for just such material—specifically, for fiction the magazines wouldn't publish because of prevailing taboos and prejudices. As Ellison's introduction to the volume trumpeted: "no one has ever told the speculative writer, 'Pull out all the stops. No holds barred, get it said!' Until this book came along."

Containing thirty-three stories, many of them franker in their treatment not only of sexuality but of politics and religion than the average output of the SF magazines, *Dangerous Visions* was without doubt the publishing event of the decade in American SF. Thanks to Ellison's constant, belligerent shtick—which continued in the form of long, buttonholing headnotes to the stories—it was impossible not to have an opinion about the book; indeed, the enterprise was essentially designed to provoke outrage among conservatives. If it failed to do so, the editor's diagnosis of the field's paralyzing stuffiness would have been obviated. And there is no question that the usual suspects were suitably provoked: Wollheim, for instance, complained about Ellison's persistent "attempts to shock sensibilities rather than to charge the imagination . . . a reflection no doubt of the notorious sewers of Hollywood he unfortunately has to dwell in." Philip José Farmer's

contribution in particular—"Riders of the Purple Wage," an ambitious Joycean punfest simmering with interfamilial eroticism—Wollheim dismissed as "thirty thousand words of Freudian nonsense." And an article in Pierce's fanzine *Renaissance* griped about the "degenerate antiheroes" infesting the stories and their many "sex scene[s] described in detail—preferably perverted." Yet SF fans largely embraced the book, awarding it three Hugo awards, including a special one to Ellison for editing it.

What is perhaps most interesting about the genre's collective reaction to *Dangerous Visions* is the fact that, as Pamela and Ken Bulmer pointed out in a perceptive review, the book's "revolutionary" purpose depended "entirely on the degree of prejudice amongst its readers." If one was primed to be offended by an unapologetic statement of atheism or a scene of brother-sister incest, then the stories would have their intended effect; if not, then it was sometimes difficult to assess their merits simply as stories. Indeed, even some champions of the emerging New Wave were disappointed by the book's insistent commitment to breaking taboos rather than to elevating the aesthetic standards of the field, as if the two goals were necessarily conjoined. In Merril's view, the result was to "substitute shock for insight." Aldiss tartly remarked that "the artificially-sustained 'family' values of the magazine ethos" did make the stories "appear quite shocking; but it was rather like shocking your maiden aunt with ribald limericks." Ellison's in-your-face editorial policy, his calculated rabble-rousing, made it rather too easy to stereotype the fiction in the book, as Philip K. Dick hilariously proved in a brief fanzine article titled "The Story to End All Stories for Harlan Ellison's Anthology *Dangerous Visions*":

> In a hydrogen war ravaged society the nubile young women go down to the futuristic zoo and have sexual intercourse with various deformed and nonhuman life forms in the cages. In this particular account a woman who has been patched together out of the damaged bodies of several women has intercourse with an alien female, there in the cage, and later on the woman, by means of futuristic science, conceives. The infant is born, and she and the female in the cage fight over it to see who gets it. The human young woman wins, and promptly eats the offspring, hair, teeth, toes and all. Just after she has finished she discovers that the offspring is God.

Still, despite its tendentiousness, *Dangerous Visions* was an important landmark in the genre, marking a point of no return for the treatment of controversial topics; in its wake, efforts to suppress uncomfortable content became increasingly unsustainable. As a result, the erotic frankness of books like *Bug Jack Barron* grew progressively more acceptable, despite the complaints of the Old Guard crowd.

In the remainder of this chapter, I would like briefly to anatomize three significant, at times overlapping, ways in which SF's new sexual openness was expressed during the late 1960s and early 1970s. The first of these—the feminist critique of normative gender roles and sexual relationships, whose key literary achievements include the short fiction of Alice Sheldon (aka James Tiptree Jr.) and Joanna Russ's novel *The Female Man* (1975)—has received extensive coverage and, thus, requires little summary. What I want to stress here is the way that feminist SF served as a kind of conscience for the New Wave movement, seeking to ensure that the genre's newfound aesthetic freedoms would be used with some degree of moral accountability. In many cases, feminist SF built upon—and ethically complicated—the genre's quasi-Freudian experiments of the 1950s: several of Sheldon's stories—such as "And I Awoke and Found Me Here on the Cold Hill's Side" (1971) and "Love Is the Plan, the Plan Is Death" (1973)—can be read as corrective extensions of Farmer's pioneering tales of interspecies desire, drawing out the fetishistic exoticization of otherness lurking within them. More obviously, feminist SF writers served as a counterweight to the more or less explicit misogyny of the sexual revolution; for example, when Ursula K. Le Guin reviewed C.W. Runyon's forgettable 1971 novel *Pig World*, a tale of near-future dystopia rife with gratuitous sexual description, she complained about the crudely objectifying way female bodies were evoked. As she remarked, "freedom from censorship, and the resulting advent of sex to science fiction, are altogether good. I hope we never take one step back towards prudery," but "where there's freedom there's responsibility," and the male SF author should strive to depict his women characters as somewhat more than "a pair of styrofoam boobies."

The difficult balancing act Le Guin is negotiating here—acknowledging the progress achieved in overcoming censorship, while bemoaning the resulting excesses—points to the fraught response second-wave feminism generally had to the eruption of sexual

*Pig World* (Doubleday, 1971)

*The Sex Machine* (Brandon House, 1967)

liberalism during the 1960s. As Alice Echols has observed, the growing erotic openness of the 1960s "increased women's sense of sexual vulnerability by acknowledging women's right to sexual pleasure while ignoring the risks associated with sexual exploration for women." The "male sexual revolution," in Ruth Rosen's words, "needed to be redefined in terms that would ensure gender equality, not exploitation"—and this redefinition is precisely what feminist SF set out to accomplish. In the frankness of their sexual representations, Sheldon's stories, for example, could not have been published ten years earlier, yet their explicitness is never gratuitous but rather is precisely driven by a conviction that the untrammeled expression of male lust is a potential catastrophe for the species. Russ's *Female Man* excoriates the heterosexist assumption that women should make their bodies available for casual sex to any desirous male, yet it also uses the new sexual freedom to graphically explore lesbian sexuality: "It would be delightful to have erotic play with Elena Twason; I feel this on my lips and tongue, in the palms of my hands, all my inside skin. I feel it down below, in my sex." This complex dialectical response to the epochal liberations of the period is one of the most profound legacies of feminist SF.

A second way in which the genre responded to the lifting of the ban on explicit content, as Le Guin's comments about *Pig World* indicate, was the proliferation of various forms of SF pornography. While Runyon's novel was put out by a mainstream SF line (Doubleday, which just a few years earlier had rejected *Bug Jack Barron*), a host of books were released by porn publishers exploiting the popularity of science-fictional settings or themes. Often, these were one-shot efforts by authors merely dabbling in the genre, e.g., Hughes Cooper's *Sexmax* (1969), in which libidinal revolutionaries battle a controlling dystopian regime, but, in a number of cases, the novels were produced by well-established SF authors and fans, sometimes under pseudonyms, for specialty imprints such as Midwood, Beeline, and Brandon House.

Andrew J. Offutt and Richard E. Geis were the most prolific of these SF pornographers, generating titles such as *Fruit of the Loins* (1970) by Offutt as "John Cleve," about a spaceman who returns to a female-only earth and becomes a walking sperm bank, and *The Sex Machine* (1967) by Geis, in which the eponymous time traveler from an erotomaniac future dutifully services a bevy of twentieth-century women. As these plot descriptions suggest, the vast majority of these books were predictable male fantasies thinly veiled in SF trappings. As Gabe Eisenstein observed in a review of George Shaw's *Astrosex* (1971), the tale's futuristic scenario was basically used "to pack in more and better sex scenes than could be justified logically in a contemporary setting"; thus, the appeal was primarily to a porn audience rather than to SF readers—a point emphasized by Richard Delap in a review of Geis's 1969 novel *Raw Meat*: "The eroticism crowd will probably dig it, but the SF group will only sigh [and] shake its collective head."

Yet, during this period, there were some thoughtful efforts to fuse SF and pornography. Offutt's novels *Evil Is Live Spelled Backwards* (1970) and *The Great 24-Hour THING* (1971) were more serious attempts to develop sexual possibilities out of science-fictional premises than the books released under his John Cleve byline, with the former title projecting the social fallout from the invention of a powerful chemical aphrodisiac. Offutt coined the term "sextrapolation" to describe the planning that went into these works—which he attempted to market to SF publishers, only to be rebuffed. The ideological significance of "sextrapolation" was recognized by Alexis Gilliland in a 1970 essay, "The Pornography of Science Fiction," where he argued that a true synthesis of porn and SF could proliferate erotic possibilities that transcend mundane experience, generating visions of polymorphous otherness in a kind of "non-linear or branched-chain orgy."

Without question, the works that went furthest toward accomplishing this heady goal were the novels released during the late 1960s by Essex House, a short-lived publisher of ambitious erotica. These included

*Evil Is Live Backwards* (Paperback Library, 1970)

*The Great 24 Hour "Thing"* (Beeline Books, 1971)

Hank Stine's *Season of the Witch* (1968), a more serious take on transgender themes than Heinlein's *I Will Fear No Evil*, in which a convicted rapist is compelled to expiate his crime by being transformed into a woman, and Philip José Farmer's *The Image of the Beast* (1968), a phantasmagoric tale of hermaphroditic aliens who sexually humiliate and prey upon a hard-boiled detective. Though both stories contain an abundance of graphic imagery, they are hardly fodder for male masturbation fantasies, since they use their science-fictional set-ups precisely to lay bare the pathologies of rampant machismo. While one would be hard-pressed to call them feminist, they certainly escape the strictures of Le Guin's critique of *Pig World*. Also, thanks to Essex House's shrewd packaging and marketing—including striking cover designs and afterwords by major SF authors; Ellison in the case of Stine's novel and Sturgeon in the case of Farmer's—the books managed to reach and engage a fairly broad SF audience.

The third way SF adapted to the climate of sexual openness in the 1960s and 1970s basically involved non-pornographic forms of "sextrapolation": projecting future trends based on current sexual mores or inventing novel sexual practices and relationships. An excellent example of the former option is Robert Silverberg's 1973 story "In the Group," which satirizes sixties counterculture attitudes in its portrayal of therapeutic group sex channeled and enhanced by biotechnological interfaces. Many such tales depict the accelerating reification of sexuality as attractive, sophisticated machines come to assume increasingly intimate roles in everyday life. Robert Sheckley's "Can You Feel Anything When I Do This?" (1969) involves a

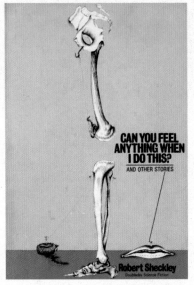

*Can You Feel Anything When I Do This?* (Doubleday, 1971)
*The Shape of Sex to Come* (Pan Books, 1978)
*Son of Man* (Ballantine Books, 1971)

love affair between a housewife and her new high-tech vacuum cleaner, while Ian Watson's "The Sex Machine" (1970) depicts a soda-vending kiosk whose transactions with consumers are explicitly erotic. Though not exactly a work of science fiction, J.G. Ballard's 1973 novel *Crash* is probably the most well-known instance of this trend, with its corrosive vision of denatured humans bleakly coupling with—and through—their cars. Probably the most celebrated New Wave story that deals with an "alien" form of sex is Samuel Delany's "Aye, and Gomorrah" (1967), which creates a new, futuristic fetish in its depiction of the fraught connection between castrated spacers and worshipful "frelks"; while the tale obviously riffs on contemporary sexual arrangements (rock-star groupies, homosexual cruising), the spacer-frelk relationship achieves a level of truly estranging otherness that cannot readily be recuperated into existing sexual paradigms. A number of New Wave works—such as Silverberg's *Son of Man* (1971) and Sheldon/Tiptree's "All the Kinds of Yes" (1972)—deal with sex between humans and gender-bending aliens, though if we consider these as allegories of bohemian bisexuality, they might be seen as examples of the trend of extrapolating existing sexual models.

Sextrapolation in all its varieties became such a common staple of New Wave SF that the 1970s saw the publication of four theme anthologies devoted to the subject: Joseph Elder's *Eros in Orbit* (1973), Thomas N. Scortia's *Strange Bedfellows* (1973), Douglas Hill's *The Shape of Sex to Come* (1978), and Michael Parry and Milton Subotsky's *Sex in the 21st Century* (1979). Some of these books reprinted the pioneering fictions of the fifties alongside fresher efforts, thus affirming a continuity between the decades that the New Wave's champions (and detractors) sometimes willfully obscured. Indeed, Sheldon's "All the Kinds of Yes" reads like a soft-core update of Fritz Leiber's "The Ship Sails at Midnight" and Sturgeon's "The Sex Opposite," and a number of other tales of alien sex from the 1960s and 1970s stand squarely in the footprints of Farmer's "The Lovers" and "Mother." The New Wave debate regarding sex in SF not only persistently touched base with Farmer's work but also often, as we have seen, centrally involved Farmer himself. When Stanisław Lem set out to write a magisterial overview of the topic—"Sex in Science Fiction," published in the Australian fanzine *SF Commentary* in 1971—he saluted Farmer as "the one man to whom we owe so much," though he went on to chastise his 1950s stories as scientifically implausible, which led to an angry exchange with Farmer in subsequent issues.

Leaving aside the question of whether the biological possibilities outlined in "The Lovers" and "Mother" are convincingly rendered or not, what is most interesting about Farmer's reply to Lem is his evident deep pride in his achievement; as he testifies, his landmark feats of sextrapolation "gave me a great joy, an intellectual near-orgasm.... What differentiates the SF writer from the writer of other types of fiction is an intellectual joy in creating well-thought out and original worlds"—a delight Farmer went on to compare with the dolphin's vibrant play in the ocean. This ludic sense of liberated energies lies at the core of New Wave sextrapolations as well, even when they are tinged with Freudian satire and neo-Gothic grotesquerie, as Farmer's "Mother" certainly was. While sometimes sniggeringly adolescent, seldom politically correct, and often marked by now dated sexual-political rhetoric, SF of the 1960s and 1970s made possible a new frankness about sex in the genre that the magazine culture of previous decades had at best muted, if not censored outright. The libidinal genie had escaped from the bottle, and there was no putting it back in again.

**Rob Latham**

# Radioactive Nightmares: Nuclear War in Science Fiction

The specter of nuclear war, how it might be triggered, and the implications for those who survive cast a huge shadow over postwar science fiction.

One of the most chilling takes is American academic Mordecai Roshwald's 1959 novel *Level 7*. An unnamed soldier is assigned to the lowest level of a massive self-sufficient underground military complex, where he and hundreds of others are expected to reside forever. Known only as X-127, he is a "push-button offensive initiator" of his nation's arsenal of intercontinental nuclear missiles. The story is told via X-127's diary: his low spirits at never seeing the sun again, doubts about his job, the physical adjustment to living four thousand feet—over twelve hundred meters—underground. The monotony of level 7 life is interrupted only by the occasional directive from the speakers of an intercom system, their sole means of communicating with the other levels. The several hundred men and women of level 7 develop a strange ersatz version of society, complete with marriage and their own mythology to justify life underground to the children

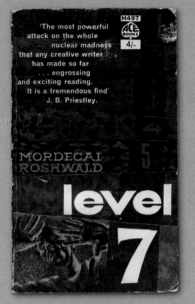

that will come from these unions. Then the order comes to launch the missiles.

The existence of remote facilities shrouded in secrecy that housed functions of the nuclear state was a regular feature of science fiction from the late 1950s onward. The Ukrainian-born Roshwald was probably influenced by Washington's August 1957 announcement that it would build a large underground complex in the remote US state of Colorado to house and oversee early warning of nuclear attack, air defense, and nuclear retaliation, better known as NORAD (the North American Air Defense Command) until 1981.

America or Russia, which nation X-127 serves is not stated, and it doesn't matter. *Level 7* is a devastating depiction of the logic of mutually assured destruction, although the term would not be officially used until the early 1960s, and a bureaucratic military-industrial complex gone insane. A lesser-known but similar take is British author Stanley Bennett Hough's *Extinction Bomber* (1955). Told from the point of view of the wife of an elite pilot entrusted with dropping

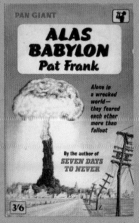 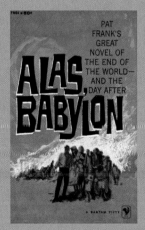 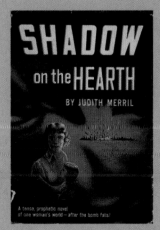 

Clockwise from top: *Level 7* (Ace, 1959). *The Long Loud Silence* (Lancer, 1969). *Shadow on the Hearth* (Doubleday, 1950). *Alas, Babylon* (Bantam, 1960). *Alas Babylon* (Pan, 1961).

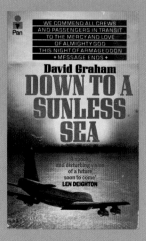

nuclear bombs, it explores his thinking and existential anguish upon being given an order to do exactly that.

Escalating Cold War tensions saw nuclear conflict viewed as a fait accompli by many, and several authors focused on the aftermath. Judith Merril's debut, *Shadow on the Hearth* (1950), depicts this from the perspective of a woman and her two children in a small town on the outskirts of New York. Confined to her house and reliant on hearsay from neighbors and breathless radio reports, she has to deal with radioactive fallout, find food, and help fend off looters. Subsequent books would add to these threats: trigger-happy soldiers and cannibalism in Wilson Tucker's *The Long Loud Silence* (1952); bandits and starvation in Pat Frank's *Alas, Babylon* (1959); sickness from radiation and biological attack, gangs of savage homeless children, and a maniacal ex-soldier intent on re-creating an even more militarized version of the society that led to war in Alfred Coppel's *Dark December* (1960).

Published under the pseudonym Robert C. O'Brien, Robert Leslie Conly's well-known 1974 young adult novel *Z for Zachariah* tells of a young woman living by herself in a remote valley after a nuclear and nerve gas attack on America. Sheltered by the valley's unique weather system, she leads a hardscrabble but stable existence until a male stranger comes to the valley. Who is he, and can she trust him? David Graham's *Down to a Sunless Sea* (1979) depicts the aftermath of global nuclear war triggered by Middle East conflict from the perspective of a planeload of people who are mid-air when the bombs drop.

Accidents and experiments gone wrong related to the secretive workings of the nuclear state were another major trope. First published in 1956, Lester del Rey's *Nerves* deals with an accident at a nuclear power plant that threatens to cause far wider damage. Canadian Phyllis Gotlieb's *Sunburst* (1964) is set two decades after a nuclear accident ravages a small town. Quarantined by the military, it houses a prison camp for the offspring of the workers who contained and cleaned up the accident, mutant children with destructive psychic powers who are increasingly angry about their confinement. Gotlieb's book was obviously influenced by John Wyndham's 1957 masterpiece *The Midwich Cuckoos*, as was the hard to find 1964 novel by British author H.L. Lawrence, *Children of the Light*. In the latter, a man and woman accidently stumble across a secret military zone that houses radioactive children, a government experiment to breed humans immune to nuclear fallout. Bob Shaw's *Ground Zero Man* (1971; subsequently also published as *The Peace Machine*) sees a mathematician invent a machine that can instantaneously detonate every nuclear bomb in the world, with predictably disastrous consequences.

**Andrew Nette**

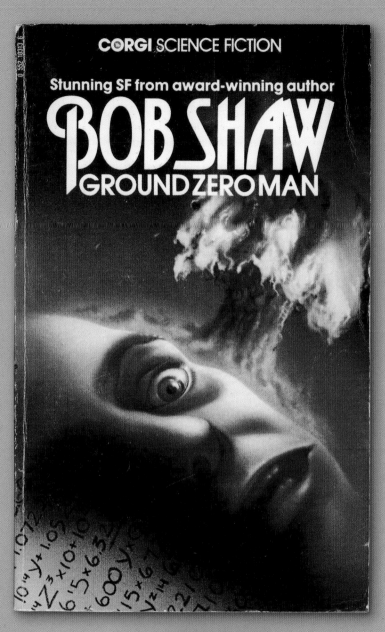

CORGI SCIENCE FICTION

Stunning SF from award-winning author

# BOB SHAW
## GROUND ZERO MAN

One man's odyssey in an America ravaged by nuclear war.

Alfred Coppel

**Dark December**

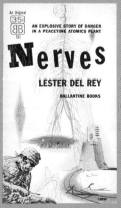

An Original 35¢ BB 151

AN EXPLOSIVE STORY OF DANGER IN A PEACETIME ATOMICS PLANT

**Nerves**

LESTER DEL REY

BALLANTINE BOOKS

SUN BURST

CORONET BOOKS

A fiendish race of demonic children is spawned in the genetic chaos of a runaway reactor explosion

A SCIENCE FICTION CLASSIC OF TOMORROW

BY PHYLLIS GOTLIEB

"A MASTERPIECE!" —THE NEW YORK TIMES

**LESTER DEL REY'S NERVES**

AN INCREDIBLE DAY IN THE LIFE OF AN ATOMIC POWER PLANT ...GONE WILD!

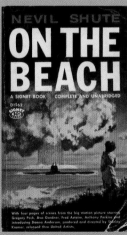

**level 7**

Mordecai Roshwald

"I have read this book with very great interest and complete approval. I wish that it could be read by every adult in both the eastern and western blocs. With admirable skill it brings home to the reader the madness of present policies and the utter disaster to which they may well lead."
BERTRAND RUSSELL

NEVIL SHUTE

## ON THE BEACH

A SIGNET BOOK    COMPLETE AND UNABRIDGED

D1562

With four pages of scenes from the big motion picture starring Gregory Peck, Ava Gardner, Fred Astaire, Anthony Perkins and introducing Donna Anderson, produced and directed by Stanley Kramer, released thru United Artists.

Clockwise from top left: *Extinction Bomber* (WDL, 1958). *Z For Zachariah* (Dell, 1977). *Down to a Sunless Sea* (Pan, 1980). *Ground Zero Man* (Corgi, 1976). *Dark December* (Coronet, 1971). *Level 7* (McGraw Hill, 1959). *On the Beach* (Signet, 1958). *Nerves* (Ballantine, 1977). *Sunburst* (Coronet, 1966). *Nerves* (Ballantine, 1956).

# On Earth the Air Is Free

## The Feminist Science Fiction of Judith Merril

*Tradition.* It's a pesky word.

It turns up a lot when people go against the status quo, break down the walls of expectation, and bring something new, new, new to the world.

And we don't like it.

It's not *traditional* science fiction. There are no pew-pew guns and technobabble about gravitational forces. Because kids, and by *kids* we mean *boys*, you too could be a spaceman. And if these pesky women (because women with opinions are always pesky) think that they can come down here and write science fiction, they've got another thing coming, ho, ho, ho.

On the back of my brightly colored copy of *The Best of Judith Merril* (1976) is a quote by Isaac Asimov, dubbing Merril a "pioneer in the feminine invasion of science fiction." It's a curious quote, as it implies that science fiction is a place to be colonized. And who were the original colonizers? White men in gleaming space suits rescuing bikini-clad damsels in distress.

But it begs the questions: What is a science fiction invader, and a female one at that? Are we women relegated to the role of blipping space invaders descending on a pixelated ship? Or a tsunami of encroaching aliens with spidery legs, as spacemen shoot us down with ray guns one by one?

Or is it simply Judith Merril, author and editor of science fiction, armed with a typewriter and the revolutionary idea that the future of space is female?

Judith Merril writes in her generational science fiction novella *Daughters of Earth* (1952): "Some things in life remain vivid in minute detail till the day you die; others are very personal and immediate, no matter how remote in time; others seem almost to be happening to another person, even as they occur."

To write a short biography of a life well lived is always difficult. There are facts selected and eliminated, and one essayist will evidently find things of more interest than others. Regardless of this selectivity, Judith Merril's contributions to science fiction can be divided up into her early work as an author and her later evolution into an editor. Although these two

Author Judith Merril

aspects crossed over at times, there is a strong delineation between the two. Both are equally significant, although many will remember her primarily as an editor for the significant anthologies she produced.

From her birth in 1923, Judith Merril was already a second-generation feminist. After the suicide of her father when she was six years old, she was raised by her suffragette mother, a founder of Hadassah, the Zionist Women's Organization of America. Merril states in *Better to Have Loved: The Life of Judith Merril*, a 2002 book she cowrote with her granddaughter, Emily Pohl-Weary, "My mother raised me to be a man," in the sense that she was encouraged to voice her opinions and live independently. This upbringing profoundly influenced her views on gender and roles in heterosexual relationships, visible in both her science fiction and personal life.

Her feminist mother always had the intention that her daughter would become an author, but Merril resisted this choice until her twenties. Merril began her writing career with the pulps and adventure stories, selling her first stories, "No Heart for Murder" (1945) and "The 'Crank' Case" (1946), as Judy Zissman to *Crack Detective Stories*. She would say, "I learned my definitions of fiction from pulp writers and editors initially: their rules were hard-and-fast, and the penalty for breaking them was hunger; or worse yet, working for a living instead of selling stories."

Her first science fiction story sale "That Only a Mother," a shocking story about a mother with a deformed child in a post-nuclear world, made her name in the SF scene. According to Damon Knight's 1977 history *The Futurians*, Merril was struggling to sell the story when she met John Campbell while drinking at Philadelphia convention. She pitched it to him, Damon writes, along the lines of "John, I wrote a story 'at's so good, ish mush too good for you." Campbell's response: "You're right. If'sh that good, we don' pay enough for it." Regardless, he acquired "That Only a Mother," published in *Astounding Science Fiction* magazine in 1948.

This theme of the impact of nuclear war on motherhood continued in her first novel *Shadow on the Hearth* (1950), which was turned into the television movie *Atomic Attack* (1954). Damon Knight wrote of the story that "it was neither science fiction, nor women's fiction, but something in between." This uncategorizable dichotomy would follow Merril's fiction and editorial work, often putting her at odds with the science fiction establishment, who preferred *traditional* science fiction adventure stories.

Anti-war sentiment would continue throughout her life, not just in fiction but in her continued activism. A Zionist from a young age, she evolved into a Trotskyist in her late teenage years, later participating in anti–Vietnam War protests, and eventually immigrating to Canada in 1968 to protest the US draft and involvement with the war. In the Hugo award–winning 2002 autobiography *Better to Have Loved: The Life of Judith Merril*, Merril's granddaughter Emily Pohl-Weary writes, "My grandmother fought injustice until the day her heart gave out."

Much of her early science fiction was written while participating in the Futurian Society, one of the first science fiction writing collectives. Founded in 1938, the left-leaning Futurian Science Literary Society was born out of the tumultuous fandom of the 1930s, where clubs were made and broken over personal rivalries and antagonisms, with the aim of promoting politically minded science fiction. In *The Futurians,* Damon Knight writes of the experience that

*The Best of Judith Merril* (Warner, 1976)
*Outpost Mars* (Dell, 1954)
*Gunner Cade* (Doubleday, 1952)

"poverty ... political intransience ... and the growth of SF magazines created the conditions for the Futurians to emerge." The first open meeting of the Futurians was held at 2:00 p.m., on September 18, 1938, with Frederik Pohl, Isaac Asimov, and Donald A. Wollheim among those in attendance. At the meeting, Asimov and Wollheim debated whether Martians should replace humans as the inhabitants of earth. The Martians won. In addition to the aforementioned Knight, the group's members grew to include James Blish, C.M. Kornbluth, Judith Merril (who was married to Frederik Pohl from 1949 to 1952), Doris Baumgardt, Elsie Wollheim, Virginia Kidd, and several others. While the Futurian Society was one of the first science fiction clubs to have women in attendance, they were a minority.

One of the most legendary stories of the Futurians recounts an incident when six members, including Wollheim and Pohl, were refused entry the very first World Science Fiction Convention, held in New York in 1939. Known as "The Great Exclusion Act," accounts of this engagement vary, with convention organizer Sam Moskowitz stating that the excluded Futurians did not agree to abide by the code of conduct and other witnesses citing differing ideological viewpoints and personal rivalries.

Merril was officially inducted into the Futurians in 1945, alongside Virginia Kidd, and lived for a time with

Kidd, sharing food, stories, and ideas with the other members of the group. While the Futurians disbanded in 1945, much of her science fiction evolved from this period of creativity and continued collaboratively with members of the group. With Kornbluth, she wrote a series of novels under the pseudonym Cyril Judd, including *Gunner Cade* (1951) and *Outpost Mars* (1952), originally appearing as *Mars Child* and later retitled *Sin in Space*, with the addition of a particularly suggestive cover. Along with Damon Knight, she founded the Milford Writer's Workshop in 1956, referred to as the "Milford Mafia" by their detractors, which became well-known for producing left-leaning authors. She remained friends with Virginia Kidd for the rest of her life.

To understand the revolutionary aspects of Merril's science fiction and editorial work, we need to place it in the context of the time: to write of liberated women in space in the 1950s was truly at odds with a society where a woman's role was well and truly in the home. Merril chronicled women's lives in space in a way that normalized the experience. There are no debates about whether woman *should* be in space, they simply *are*. In her stories, women are ship designers, PR professionals, scientists, medics, explorers, and astronauts, and their place is not questioned on the basis of their gender. Nor are mothers and housewives looked down upon; their experience is given equal weight to that of working women—the housewife who watches the apocalypse in *Shadow on the Hearth* and the disillusioned mother with a deformed child in "That Only a Mother".

Kidd, who later became a literary agent representing authors, including Ursula K. Le Guin and Anne McCaffrey, as well as Merril, captured the latter's feminist contribution best when she wrote in the introduction to *The Best of Judith Merril*, "Back when women were being regarded as mere props to be rescued by bug-eyed monsters, Merril was addressing the question of what it might *really* be like to be a woman in the future, a woman in space." In many of her works her characters acknowledge that these are narratives, recounting real events, such as the 1969 novella *Daughters of Earth*, where Emma recounts the generational history of the women in her family and their explorations of deep space. Emma's narration is in both third and first person, jumping through time and generations with parentheses and postscripts. Most striking is the opening, which recounts the generations of

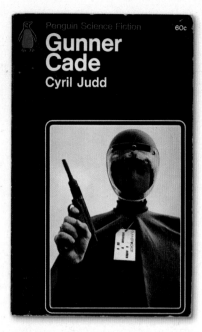

*Gunner Cade*
(Penguin, 1966)

women in space much like a religious passage listing the sons of Abraham, while clearly stating that this narrative starts with a woman. Rather than breaking the fourth wall, this gave a sense of realism to her work. This is a real woman telling a real story, with all the real issues that go along with being a woman, whatever the century. Divorce, pressure to have children, parental guilt, monogamy, career and ambition, even the idea of willing away a pregnancy in a story published in 1953.

In her fiction, Merril understood the performative aspect of being a woman, such as the women who fix an expected face at a rocket launch to hide their fears. At the final launch of another daughter's journey into space, *Daughters of Earth* concludes with:

> "Carla... Carlie, darling, aren't you *afraid*?"
> Carla took both her mother's hands and held them tight.
> "I'm terrified!" she said. And turned and left.

Faced with the enormity of the galaxy, people would be scared in space. But time and again, they face the fear and do it anyway.

One fear was of the loss of family, the threat that someone may never come back from the imminent danger of the unknown. Years before the Apollo 13 mission, Merril wrote the exceptional short story "Dead Center," published in *Fantasy & Science Fiction* (1954), where Ruth Kruger, a ship designer and engineer, must use her ingenuity to rescue her astronaut

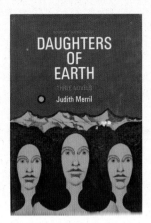

Daughters of Earth
(Doubleday, 1969)

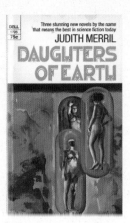

Daughters of Earth
(Dell, 1968)

Beyond Human Ken
(Pennant Books, 1954)

The Magazine of Fantasy and
Science Fiction, December 1958,
includes Merril's story "Wish
Upon a Star"

husband stuck in "lonely rocket on the wrong side of the moon." With sharp prose and a brutal ending, it was included in the *The Best American Short Stories 1955*. It is a perfect picture of a working mother's guilt and the constant balancing act between parenthood and career.

In this and many other stories, Merril captured the sense of loss that comes with space travel, acknowledging that things *don't* work out. Space travel is inherently risky. Marriages break down. People die. Poor decisions lead to dangerous consequences. Despite all the fears, we can still categorize Merril's work as optimistic science fiction. Yes, there are trials and difficulties, but the future is open, space is vast, and human curiosity endless.

Part of this feminism was addressing both gender and sexual relations in space and how women could be more productive colonizers. Her future histories contained motherships sent by the matriarchy, what Merril considered a "puritan backlash anti-war feminine oligarchy Earth Government." These future histories only made it into one short story: "Wish Upon a Star," published in *Fantasy & Science Fiction* (1958).

In "Wish Upon a Star," all the women are officers and the men subordinates. The colonizing ship had a ratio of twenty women to four men. Merril writes that women are "better suited to manage the psychological problems of an ingrown group, and to maintain with patience . . . the functioning and purpose of the trip." Or consider the ship staffed by forty women with a good supply of sperm in "The Lonely" (1963). With the ability to bear children, women are that much more *useful* in colonizing space. She wrote of futures where

polyamorous relationships are the norm and futures where men are barely needed at all.

Merril recognized that alien cultures would have very different ways of reproduction and culture surrounding sex, that space travel itself would create different social structures and gender relations. While playing with gender in science fiction stories is common these days, Merril wrote one of the first science fiction stories with hardly any gender pronouns: "Survival Ship," published in *Worlds Beyond* (1951). Her fiction questions how viable monogamy will be in future worlds, how casual relationships will be the norm, and how the family unit transforms over time—people come in and out, relationships break down, affairs happen.

While her early publishing career involved writing short stories and novels, Merril is well-known as an editor, compiling many "best of" anthologies, including *SF: The Year's Greatest Science Fiction and Fantasy* (1956–1959) and *The Annual Year's Best SF* (1960–1967). She was not a restrained editor, providing insightful and sometimes playful commentary on the stories she included. The introductions and notes on many of these anthologies form an image of her definition of science fiction. She writes in *The Best of Sci-Fi 5* (1966), an anthology that included the legendary short story "Flowers for Algernon" by Daniel Keyes

Wonder—informed, thoughtful, purposeful wonder—is loose on the Earth again. And this is what "SF" means, what "science fiction" is: not gimmicks and gadgets, monsters and supermen, but *trained wonderment*—educated and disciplined imagination—a marvellous mirror for Modern Man and the world he is only beginning to make.

In her essay, "What Do You Mean: Science? Fiction?" (1956), Merril wrestles with her own definitions of science fiction. She can define science and fiction, but not the genre, breaking it down into: 1. teaching stories, such as those introducing new scientific ideas, represented for her by the work of Hugo Gernsback; 2. preaching stories using science or technology in allegories and satires, for which she suggests Ray Bradbury's fiction; 3. speculative fiction stories that explore and discover something about the universe, a category in which I would firmly include the "thought experiments" of Ursula K. Le Guin.

Her most notable publication as editor was *England Swings SF: Stories of Speculative Fiction* (1968), which introduced American audiences to British New Wave science fiction, including authors like Michael Moorcock and J.G. Ballard. There was an apparent zeitgeist in 1960s science fiction, with Moorcock, Merril, and Harlan Ellison publishing significant New Wave anthologies and works during the period. Science fiction scholar Rob Latham writes of that period in *Science Fiction: A Literary History* (2017), "The 1960s were an epochal moment in the genre, marking a radical break with the pulp tradition of technophilic adventure stories and ushering in an array of dystopian themes and avant-garde styles of writing."

Moorcock was already pushing the boundaries of science fiction publishing with *New Worlds* magazine. Erotic, countercultural, experimental, and just plain weird, *New Worlds* was mired in controversy and denounced in Parliament, and the fear of obscenity charges stopped distributors from stocking the magazine. While compiling the anthology in 1966–1967, Merril lived in England a few streets from Michael Moorcock. *England Swings SF* was published in 1968 by Ace Books in the US and UK.

The outrage at *England Swings SF* is not to be underestimated. Merril writes of the period, "I was variously acclaimed and reviled as the American prophet of the avant-garde British New Wave movement." Even the book cover seems to acknowledge this controversy; the blurbs offer the gamut of opinions from excellent to WTF. The *Atlanta Journal* wrote, "So far out it's left the understandable galaxy." Or the *Boston Globe's* somewhat true forecast that "it is doubtful that the New Wave will sweep away the more traditional science fiction." There's that pesky word again—*tradition*.

After all, what American audience wouldn't react to J.G. Ballard's story "The Assassination of John Fitzgerald Kennedy Considered as a Downhill Motor Race," and "Plan for the Assassination of Jacqueline Kennedy," which appeared in the *England Swings* anthology, alongside Josephine Saxton's gender bending story "Ne déjà vu pas," with the second line reading "I know why the greatest obscenity I ever saw drawn on a wall in mauve chalk was 'Pussy for God'"?

Donald A. Wollheim (signing as DAW) introduced the 1970 Ace Books edition, acknowledging that it would produce controversy:

> Here is the book which may be the turning point of that New Wave. Ace Books presents it because it is a work, a manifesto perhaps in the form of a group of most unusual SF stories, which everyone interested in science fiction ought to read. It will be a stimulating experience, whether you agree with Miss Merril or not. Ace Books, long the foremost publisher of science fiction in America, does not take any stand on this controversy.

He goes on to assert that the publisher doesn't agree or disagree with the contents and publishes all types of science fiction, including classics and adventure stories—just in case you didn't like it.

At least Merril sets her feet firmly on the hill and plants the flag for New Wave SF in her poetic editorial notes to *England Swings SF*. There's no apologizing for the contents. This is the British New Wave, and you're going to read it or not:

> The next time someone assembles the work of the writers in this—well, "school" is too formal . . . and "movement" sounds pretentious . . . and "British sf" is ludicrously limiting—so let's just say, the work of these writers and/or others now setting out to work in this way, it will probably have about as much resemblance to this anthology as this one does to any other collection of science fiction, social criticism, surrealism— BEM's, Beats, Beatles, what-have-you—you have ever read or heard before.

Merril offers commentary on each story, intertwined with the biographies of the authors in much the same poetic back and forth of her opening.

 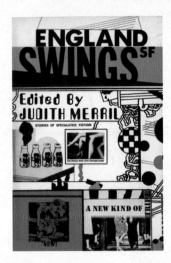 

*Astounding Science Fiction*, featuring Gunner Cade (June 1952)
*England Swings* (Doubleday, 1968)
*England Swings* (Ace, 1968)

In no small irony, New Wave science fiction eventually became part of the status quo. There was no ongoing revolution but a slow absorption into what was acceptable science fiction. We count the names Moorcock, Ballard, and Merril among the greats of science fiction, not a leftist separatist movement but as an adjunct to the ongoing *tradition*.

The title of this chapter comes from a singular line of Merril's fiction found in the story "Stormy Weather" in *Startling Stories* (1954), a story that centers around a solitary woman in space trying to conserve her air and, therefore, reduce her actions that diminish the available oxygen, all the while trying to reach out to a person she loves who is not responding to her messages. She muses, "On Earth the air is free."

In some uncanny way, this theme of freedom echoes in Merril's notes on Charles Platt's "The Experience Kick" in *England Swings SF*, where she elaborates on why England does in fact swing. Comparing sixties London to twenties Paris, Renaissance Florence, and "Athens of the Periclean Age," she calls the symbols of the scene—freedom of dress, language, and living habits—signal flares for a much greater movement. She writes:

> London is The Scene. Beneath the signal smoke, the air there is unexpectedly clear . . . it is *figuratively* that a man must breathe freely to create: and the figurative freedom in America belongs to the (electronic, chemical, biologic, cybernetic, "human," "market research") engineer. In Britain (where power is dear and air conditioning for giant laboratories no more likely than central heating) it is the artists who breathe free.

Not long after the publication of *England Swings SF*, Merril grew tired of America, renouncing her citizenship and becoming a Canadian. For some reason, it was this quote that struck me as evidence of Merril's search for freedom of expression; it is visible in her work with universities, her activism, and her writing. As she wrote alongside Pohl-Weary in *Better to Have Loved*, she longed to be a "member of the universe." Clubs, metaphoric walls, and memberships hindered her freedom. As she wrote: "anything less than the universe seems like too damn less."

In space, air may or may not be free, but it is open and full of opportunities beyond the restrictions of earth. It hints at the clarity of thought needed by creatives, especially women, burdened by the expectations of society, families, and themselves.

In the coming years, we will see space tourism become a reality, and perhaps women will travel generationally to the stars, exploring the far-flung reaches of the galaxy. Judith Merril's writing and editorial work was the first to explore new galaxies of ideas, leaving her own generational legacy to science fiction. A new *tradition*?

I think not. How about a new *invasion*?

Watch out spacemen, we're here with our spidery legs, and pew-pew ray-guns, swarming, hoarding, overwhelming until the colonizers go back to their ever-shrinking planet.

Here's to the future feminist invaders of science fiction. Let's face the fear, set our faces, and write it anyway.

**Kat Clay**

# Women and Children First!

## John Wyndham and Second-Wave Feminism

John Wyndham

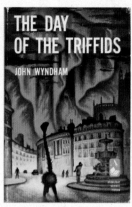

*The Day of the Triffids*
(Doubleday, 1951).

The British author John Wyndham's canon so defies the meta-categorizations applied to earthbound science fiction that it's easiest consigned under the infinitely broad umbrella of "speculative fiction." From there, it may be parsed and labeled accordingly, depending upon the reader. What is certain is that among the seven novels and short story collections published during the author's most fecund years (an output spanning 1951–1968), there's never an indication of supernatural forces at work behind the rebel organisms and mind-reading children that populate Wyndham's many universes. Malign, benevolent, or simply curious, these freaks that walk our streets, thwart our industry, and ravage our planet are manifestations of multiple arcane sciences impenetrable to all but the author. Such are the doomsday scenarios that are the hallmark of Wyndham's fiction. Yet the most notable—and overlooked—facet of this seventeen-year output is the author's surreptitious but unwavering alignment with second-wave feminism from its inception in the late 1950s into the early 1960s.

Born John Wyndham Parkes Lucas Beynon Harris into a middle-class English family in 1903, Wyndham spent his childhood bouncing from one prep school to the next, maintaining virtually no contact with his parents. Though he was married, he was by all accounts a loner, and his refusal to discuss his personal life with interviewers or even friends leaves a paucity of biographical material. His early shorts, written from the mid-1920s into the early 1950s under pseudonymous variations on his birth name, found homes in American SF/fantasy magazines populated with quotidian rocket ships and space slave girls.

"If the heart of fantasy," Wyndham observed in a rare interview, "is the willing suspension of disbelief… you may not go beyond a certain barrier," and, in 1951, the author's focus shifted from the boundless frenzy of space to more subtle commentaries on England's xenophobia and industrial woes. Manifested in a rogue's gallery of inimical behemoths, little hellions, and ill-advised medical procedures, almost all of the work spanning this fruitful period reflects Wyndham's interest in the nascent geopolitical phenomenon of space exploration. Yet it never ascends beyond terrestrial footing. In other words, we are always the hosts.

In the novel *The Day of the Triffids* (1951), alien seeds are delivered (literally) via a blinding meteor shower and take root in earth's soil, sprouting into outlandish plants. Initially, they're embraced by the upper class as jejune showpieces for their lawns. Then one day the plants begin to walk, and Armageddon fast unfurls at the tendrils of inimical ten-foot stems and vines. *The Kraken Wakes* (1953) tweaks the scenario to enormous sea monsters that reside on the ocean floors. Their fetid tentacles whip around beachgoers. Sea-levels begin to rise. When the polar ice caps commence to melt in order to flood the planet completely, the apocalypse is again at hand.

By the mid-1950s, Wyndham turned his focus to more insidious interlopers. The leitmotif of telepathy, wherein children always serve as convoy, became a device through which the author could play out the end of times, while keeping one foot firmly in the human sphere. A group of telekinetic children are targeted as evolutionary threats against a dogmatic, fear-based religion in 1955's *The Chrysalids*. This was the first instance in which Wyndham employed children as harbingers of a future over which succeeding

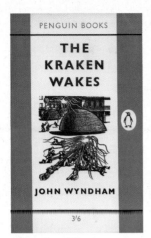

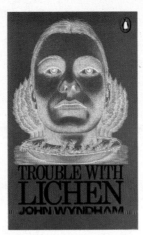

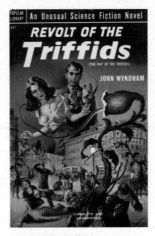

The Kraken Wakes
(Penguin, 1962)

Trouble with Lichen
(Penguin, 1977)

Revolt of the Triffids
(Popular Library, 1952)

Trouble with Lichen
(Dell, 1982)

generations will have no control. *The Midwich Cuckoos* (published in 1957; filmed by Wolf Rilla as *Village of the Damned* in 1960), presents a more inimical brood. An unknown force immobilizes a small English hamlet and impregnates twelve female residents, each of whom spawns an emotionless child with eyes like blue ice and disconcerting powers of mind control. With their clear and plainly stated plan to supplant humanity, these kids may look like run-of-the-mill Aryan youth, but it's clear that they're not from around here.

The 1960s saw an emergence of female SF writers who turned their focus to the domestic front, intersexuality, and the frantic pursuit of beauty. Examples include Lisa Yaszek's 1959 *Carpool*, Kit Reed's 1962 *The New You*, and Sonya Dorman's 1966 *When I Was Miss Dow*. As the new feminism contended with the sexism fomented by women's fashion magazines, advertisements, and the nascent medium of television, Wyndham ushered in the decade with aberrations embodied in the now familiar but no less grotesque realm of gender. In what is still a "man's world," the author contrives corporate interests spurred by manic female consumerism in the pathological drive for youth attainable through costly makeup, violent nips, and grody tucks. His jabs at commercialism's targeted messages suggest a wider exposure on the author's part to contemporary female SF writers, among whom this notion of "refashioning" was a by-product of pressure toward conformity. Body modification, designer kitchen sets, and iffy surgical tweaks envision women as victims placated by the same industries that suppress them.

In *Trouble with Lichen* (1960), Dr. Diana Brackley accidentally drops a rare breed of lichen into a glass of milk. When the milk's longevity is increased threefold, she devises a formula to rapidly slow the aging process in humans. The male scientist for whom she works, who takes credit for the discovery, declares with self-congratulatory flourish, "[W]e simply cannot afford to go on attaining wisdom only half a step before we achieve senility." At last, he continues, people "shall have the time to learn how to live, and then time to enjoy living." Sensible enough, but enthusiasm soon gives way to panic. Extended lives will mean overpopulation, the principle concern, from the perspective of the males in the book, being the threat to turnover in the job market. Besides, supplies of the formula are limited. Who's to decide who will get a taste?

Brackley envisions the ways that women can use their extended life-span to attain the inherently "male" status of educated citizens of the world, free from concern over spinsterhood, grey hair, and the judgement these conditions elicit. She establishes exclusive spas to brand and sell the product to empower women through accumulated knowledge *and* the preservation of beauty. But with males helming the industry, the advancement is fast-reduced to a beauty product wherein one manufacturer observes the wealthy "purring, scheming, hard-eyed . . . bitches" clamoring for a dose to stave off their wrinkles for at least another eighty years. Beauty is indeed the opiate of at least half the masses, and it trumps increased wisdom any day. In her altruistic but misguided attempt at female empowerment, Brackley has only succeeded in redoubling women's aspirations to exterior preservation. The novel's message comes as an ominous lament that the safeguarding of physical appearance

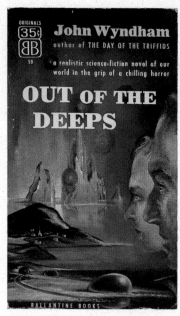

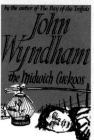

*Out of the Deeps aka The Kraken Wakes* (Ballantine, 1955)
*The Midwich Cuckoos* (Penguin, 1961)
*The Midwich Cuckoos* (Michael Joseph, 1957)

is the surest—maybe the only—path to security in a man's world.

In the novella *Consider Her Ways*, which first appeared in a 1961 short story collection of the same title, Jane Waterleigh tests a new drug (notably, to ease the grief of losing her husband) and falls asleep to wake up in a single-gendered world. Obese and immobile, she is a cog in a female caste system consisting of an educated ruling class, common proles, and tiny, skittish cleaners, always underfoot. Jane belongs to a class of morbid, splotchy progenitors whose sole purpose is reproduction. If this calls to mind Margaret Atwood's *A Handmaid's Tale* (Atwood was a fan, having written the introduction to the 2005 rerelease of Wyndham's final novel, *Chocky*), it is perhaps more akin to an obverse, dystopic imagining of Charlotte Perkins Gilman's *Herland* (1915) or Doris Lessing's *The Cleft* (2007). Like Paradise Island in the *Wonder Woman* mythos, both novels, along with the comic character, which first appeared in 1941, posit isolated female races that thrive in kinship and reproduce via parthenogenesis. Men aren't just unwelcome; they're unnecessary.

Jane discovers that this nightmare future is the result of a long-deceased male scientist's backfired attempt to exterminate the brown rat, which instead resulted in the eradication of the entire human male population. The rat is a pertinent choice of pest, considering that females of generations past are regarded by the women of this alternate present as having existed like parasitic dependents on their male counterparts. In that distant past, women's lusty desires for things (furs, dinette sets, and other baubles) made men the dominant sex through their control of industry and production where, unsurprisingly, the largest market was beauty. Advertising espoused the hypnotic ideal that "nothing in life was worth achieving but dewy-eyed passivity," and even the word *Romance* was commodified (with a capital *R* to drive the point home).

An all-female race, however, has brought industry to a halt: coal is no longer mined, transportation has stopped, and gasoline has run out. Adaptation was slow but ultimately attained at the expense of leisure, culture, and social interaction. Looking around at her fellow denizens, Jane doubts that it was worth it. "If love, art, poetry, excitement, and physical joy have all been sacrificed to mere continued existence," she asks a doctor, "what is left but soulless waste?" Wyndham's feminism is not one of isolation or segregation but a plea to integration and cohabitation.

Jane is administered another dose of the drug to get her to accept her predicament and wakes to a world restored to normal. Still, better to be safe than sorry, she tracks down a doctor who is perfecting a formula to—what else?—eliminate the world's rat population and murders him. It seems there was some truth in her narcotic-induced hallucination after all, and that Jane has restored history's proper course. Yet imagine the catastrophe that would ensue were the doctor's notes to fall into the hands of another inquisitive male—say, his son—who would carry out his father's work? Jane hadn't considered that.

"Oh, Where, Now, Is Peggy MacRafferty?" from the same 1961 collection predates by six years Kate Wilhelm's angst-ridden 1967 SF short "Baby, You Were Great," in which a woman is forced to endure "emotional reassignment" to appear in a reality television show. Peggy MacRafferty, a fiery redhead of eleven, deftly wends around a gameshow host's trick questions to become the first winner of a televised quiz show. Peggy enthralls the audience with her plainspokenness as she patiently scolds and dismantles the host's efforts to trip her up. The world wants more of this little spitfire with the Irish brogue, so Peggy goes to Hollywood, where the honchos are quick to recognize her fierce singularity. She's got *star* written all over her.

The feminist, activist, and anti-pornography crusader Andrea Dworkin wrote in her misandrist screed *Women Hating* (1974) that "*the tolerance of pain and the romanticization of tolerance begins here*, in preadolescence, in socialization, and serves to prepare women for lives of childbearing, self-abnegation and husband-pleasing" (italics hers). While this litany of responsibilities applies to the two stories discussed above, it is especially pertinent in the case of Peggy. Just as Dworkin stresses the pain inherent to beautification (from hair removal and hot curlers to nose jobs), a seasoned colleague enthusiastically justifies the imminent physical "corrections" that young Peggy will endure. "This calling of ours," she says with reverence, "is a very great deal more than industry. Indeed, one might call it a spiritual force that gives women space."

A "University of Beauty," sprawls across the Hollywood Hills to provide and nurture this "spiritual force" among a constant influx of young hopefuls. "Facial artists" and "deportment instructors" sedulously set about making adolescent girls screenworthy, trivializing their pediatric vital signs, while putting the real emphasis on what Peggy's groomers refer to as her "Indices of Beauty." A studio executive expresses his concern that Peggy will be reduced to just another child beauty queen clone, or "Lolo," as they are referred to (a vague sobriquet denoting the homogeneity that runs counter to Peggy's appeal with a hint at Nabokov's picture-perfect nymphette in 1955's *Lolita*).

As Peggy's "indices" are modified under the tender ministrations of university officials, she cannot help but wonder aloud, "[I]f they change me shape, and change me voice, and change me hair, and change me face... what is it that is me at all?" Her query taps the burdens, assumptions, and pathology of a culture in which individuality is supplanted by fleeting, generic glamour. The exec frowns as he observes a new group of Lolos from his office window, all bolstered in their uniformity. Squinting, he scours the crowd for the feisty, Hibernian treasure with the red hair for whom he had such plans, but he can't tell one from another. To answer the question posed by the story's title, Peggy MacRafferty is gone forever.

*Chocky*, from 1968, was the last of Wyndham's novels published during his lifetime and marks a return to his theme of children as advanced alien conduits. In this case, the visitor is benign—an ephemeral "scout" that temporarily inhabits the mind of a twelve-year-old boy for observational purposes. A meditation

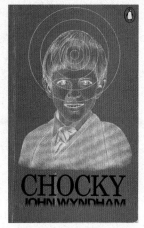
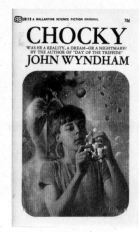

*Chocky* (Penguin, 1974)          *Chocky* (Ballantine, 1968)

on the nature vs. nurture debate in an age when the most prominent psychologists in the field were unyielding in their push for the former, it is notable that the boy humanizes his inhabitant by giving it a name. He identifies "Chocky" as female. Does this inclination spring from a maternal void the boy's adopted mother cannot provide or an acknowledgment of male puberty at the cusp of the era of the "new male" and the men's liberation movement? Or was Wyndham just poking fun at the patriarchy when the boy confesses to his father that he credits Chocky's gender to an "older sister snootiness?"

There's no evidence that Wyndham was ever recognized as an active feminist in his day (the term was rarely applied to males during the 1960s). Nor does it seem that he was in communication with other authors—male, female, SF, or otherwise. It is conspicuous that the bulk of contemporary writings scrounged from recent articles, review sites, and blogs that allude to Wyndham's feminist inclinations are written by women, while male readings tend to toward skepticism on the subject. (In a 2008 *Guardian* piece on *Trouble with Lichen*, Nicholas Lezard ham-fistedly wrote, "[S]ci-fi and women do not, traditionally, keep the same kind of company.") Indeed, John Wyndham didn't move within female, or even male, circles. Although he opted to remain isolated, he never detached himself from contemporary sociological advancements, and the outpouring of these fertile years evinces a prescience of the pressures brought to bear on women at the cusp of the rise of second-wave feminism.

**David Curcio**

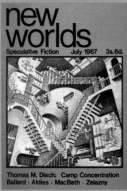

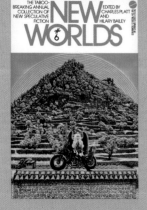

Clockwise from top left: December 1968. August 1970. July 1968.
May–June 1964. *New Worlds Quarterly* #4 (Sphere, 1974). *New Worlds Quarterly* #3 (Sphere, 1972). *New Worlds Quarterly* #1 (Sphere, 1971). *New Worlds Quarterly* #6 (Equinox, 1975). April 1965. July 1967.

# Bursting through the Boundaries: *New Worlds* Magazine

Emerging from the fanzine *Novae Terrae*, first published by Maurice K. Hansen in 1936, *New Worlds* magazine switched to the English translation of the title when it changed hands to John Carnell in 1939. As a result of interruptions caused by war, financial difficulties, and other obstacles, the magazine only managed to first come out on a regular monthly basis in 1954. Its mix of stories, reviews, and essays meant that it developed into a mainstay of the UK science fiction scene thereafter, with local editions also published in New Zealand and Canada, as well as reprints in the US for a short period.

In 1963, Carnell announced he would be wrapping the title up, but an intervention by publisher Roberts & Vinter kept it alive and soon saw a young Michael Moorcock in the editorial seat. Carnell had played an important role in the early careers of J.G. Ballard, Brian Aldiss, and John Brunner but, as is well documented elsewhere in this book, Moorcock made the magazine a major vehicle for the popularization of the innovative works and approaches that would come to be known as the New Wave of Science Fiction.

Seeking to shift the ground from science fiction to less defined "speculative" writing, and enamored with radical ideas in general, he also began including social commentary and experimental poetry. Groundbreaking short stories by authors from both sides of the Atlantic were published, with works by Harlan Ellison, Samuel Delany, and others collecting major prizes. A number of key contributors from

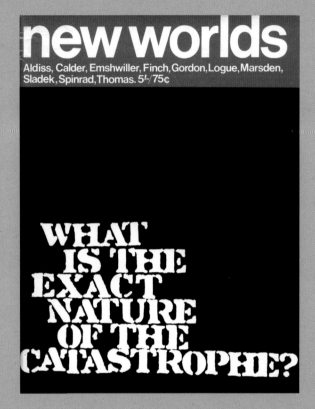

1964 to 1970 submitted novellas, short stories, and serials that were later expanded or combined into influential novels, including Ballard's *The Crystal World* (1966), Thomas M. Disch's *Camp Concentration* (1968), Norman Spinrad's *Bug Jack Barron* (1969), and Aldiss's *Barefoot in the Head* (1969). The magazine

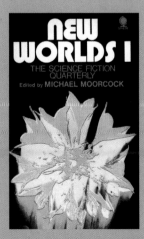
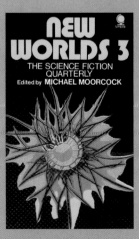
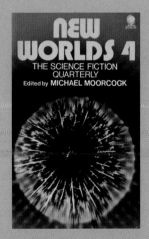

also featured numerous pieces by Moorcock himself, sometimes under the pseudonym of James Colvin, and spawned one of his major characters, Jerry Cornelius.

In 1967, Roberts & Vinter stopped publishing *New Worlds*. Having switched the magazine from a digest to a paperback book format in 1964 and experimented with a bimonthly publishing schedule before settling back into a monthly one, the literary impact of the magazine meant that Brian Aldiss was able to secure Arts Council funding from the UK government. At this point *New Worlds* switched to a magazine format, but its troubles were far from over. Complaints in Parliament, newsagent censorship, bans in South Africa, New Zealand, and Australia, and other woes posed major challenges, but it continued to come out regularly until its two hundredth issue in 1970.

During these years the pioneering spirit of the magazine continued with Graham Charnock, Graham Hall, Langdon Jones, James Sallis, and Charles Platt at times serving alongside or in place of Moorcock as editors and coeditors. Just as the magazine encouraged experimentation in writing and criticism, it also featured innovative and arresting artwork incorporating psychedelia, collage, and other elements, with its late 1960s and early 1970s covers often resembling British underground publications like *International Times* and *Oz*.

With funds fully drying up, Moorcock reinvented the magazine as a series of paperback anthologies. Initially published on a quarterly basis, ten of these appeared in UK and US editions between 1971 and 1976, with Charles Platt and Hilary Bailey coediting and editing the series from 1974 onward. Two years later, *New Worlds* was back as a magazine for five issues. Its iconic status has meant that new versions have occasionally appeared, while many of the stories it first printed have been repeatedly anthologized.

**Iain McIntyre**

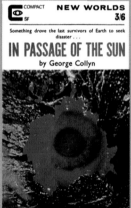
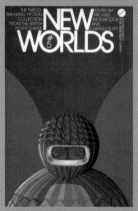

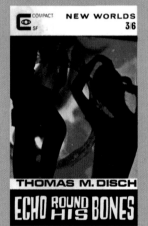

Clockwise from top left: September 1965. *New Worlds Quarterly* no. 2 (Berkley, 1971). July 1966. December 1966. April 1968. *New Worlds* 5 (Equinox, 1974). February 1970.

# Vast Active Living (Possibly) Insane System

## Paranoia and Antiauthoritarianism in the Work of Philip K. Dick

These days, Philip K. Dick's work is everywhere, with good cause. In a world where social credit scores determine your future, facial recognition programs pinpoint your movements from innocent crowd shots, and algorithms decide what you want to buy before you have even thought of it yourself, his particular flavor of paranoid science fiction speaks to our hell world in a way that the gee-whiz optimism of an Asimov or Clarke never could. But the paranoia in Dick's work, while certainly reflecting his own pessimism toward technology and so-called progress, also reflects the at times bizarre course of his own relatively short life more than any radical political beliefs.

Philip Kindred Dick was born in 1928, the son of a government worker and a proto-feminist. His twin sister died six weeks after birth, and partially as a result his parents split up when he was young. Dick's father continued on with his job at the Department of Agriculture, and Dick and his mother settled down in the college town of Berkeley, California. Even in the thirties and forties Berkeley was a hotspot for activism and social change, and thanks to his mother young Phil grew up immersed in left-wing politics, an early sort of "red diaper baby."

It doesn't seem, however, that he shared his mother's interest in radical politics. On the contrary, he worried that his association with a longtime Communist Party member (they worked at the same radio repair store) would doom him, and he was uneasy about the political activities of his second wife Kleo, who, like his mother, was an early feminist who fraternized with communists. To the ever-anxious Dick, even these low-level activities might have been pushing things too far, and in a sense he was right. According to Lawrence Sutin's 1989 biography *Divine Invasions: A Life of Philip K. Dick*, Dick and Kleo were visited at some point in the early fifties by two FBI agents who offered them a free ride at the University of Mexico if they would move there to spy on student

Philip K. Dick

activists. (Sutin states that the couple "found the offer attractive except for the spying.") The visits stopped after Phil and Kleo turned the agents' offer down, but it's easy to see how McCarthyism planted the seed of paranoia in Dick that likely convinced him to stay away from political organizations.

In 1951, Dick sold his first story, "Roog," about a dog that fruitlessly warns its owners of an alien invasion. Dozens of further shorts would appear throughout the decade, peaking at a staggering thirty stories published in 1953, and almost as many the following year. It wasn't long before he graduated to novels. The best of these from this time period was 1959's *Time out of Joint*. In this slender book, everyman Ragle Gumm keeps up a winning streak in a newspaper contest, but strange occurrences like finding slips of paper with words on them in place of objects themselves lead him down the path of conspiracy. He discovers that his entire 1950s small-town world is a fake designed to keep him from discovering that earth's government has been using him as a weapon against lunar colony separatists. Was

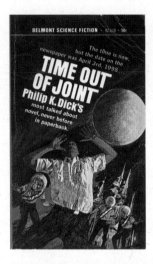

*Time out of Joint*
(Belmont Books,
1963)
*Martian Time-Slip*
(Ballantine, 1964)
*The Three Stigmata
of Palmer Eldritch*
(Doubleday, 1965)

this book his reaction to his attempted recruitment? We'll never know, but it seems fairly likely.

Dick's anxiety culminated in a move from Berkeley to Point Reyes Station, in Marin County, a small town about an hour's drive northwest of San Francisco, where his mind could be more at ease. After leaving Kleo for another woman only a few months into the relocation, Dick attempted to fit the mold of the ideal suburban breadwinner. To maintain a middle-class lifestyle for his third wife Anne, two stepdaughters, and the couple's daughter (born in 1960) he produced over two dozen novels in the space of a few years, from the sublime *Ubik* (1969) and *Martian Time-Slip* (1964) to the forgettable *The Zap Gun* (1967). He accomplished this with his well-known reliance on amphetamines, which he had started using in the fifties to combat his anxiety (how a course of strong psychostimulants was supposed to soothe anxiety is a bit of a mystery). The move from short stories to novels required an immense increase in writing speed, and a full-blown addiction soon developed. It was at this point that Dick's paranoia crept from the pages of his stories—where it had lived from the start—into his psyche.

Dick had been under the care of a psychiatrist for what would now be called social anxiety since he was a teenager, and his periodic bouts of agoraphobia had strained his relationships with both Kleo and Anne. Sometimes, his issues manifested as something more than garden-variety nervousness. He'd once hallucinated a giant head above his writing shed in Marin County, later telling an interviewer that, "I didn't really see it, but the face was there, and it was not a human face; it was a vast visage of perfect evil." This face was undoubtedly part of the inspiration for the

title character in *The Three Stigmata of Palmer Eldritch* (1965), one of Dick's best sixties novels.

*Stigmata* opens with a down on his luck "precog" named Barney Mayerson, who's concerned with petty affairs. There's a colony on Mars, and rampant global warming (talk about precognition!), but in general Dick's future seems to be much like our world. To cope with Mars, which is a terrible place, the colonists ingest a drug called Can-D, supplied by the company for which Mayerson works. Competing drug Chew-Z, released by Palmer Eldritch's start-up, appears on the scene and what commences is a corporate espionage novel on acid. (Aside: Dick was never a great connoisseur of LSD, and most of his work, including *Stigmata*, was written before he had tried it.) As Mayerson and his boss Leo Bulero trip through a variety of unreal worlds—the true nature of all of them betrayed by the existence of Eldritch's prosthetic body parts—reality itself is shown to be illusory. Maybe Eldritch is God, or maybe he's Satan, and maybe flirting with the metaphysical permanently places you outside of the "real world." As Bulero puts it:

> I'm still under the influence of that one dose; I never came back out—that's what's the matter. Thinking this he felt relief, because there was still a real Terra untouched; it was only himself that was affected.

Dick's third marriage fell apart in the late sixties and was immediately followed by another that disintegrated in much the same way. At this point, Dick, who had moved to the Bay Area town of Santa Venetia, invited hippies and/or junkies to live with him on a rotating basis. He considered himself a sort of father figure to this younger set of housemates, though it's unclear whether they felt the same way about him. Dick continued to publish novels and short stories, though at a much more reasonable rate, and attempted to climb/drug his way out of a deep depression. Then, on November 17, 1971, something happened that altered Dick's life—and his work—forever.

Until 1971, Dick's paranoia was of a more unfocused variety, and to his friends he probably seemed like merely a typical Bay Area eccentric. That changed when his safe, containing personal papers of no real value, was "blown open" while he was out of the house. Dick suspected the CIA of the break-in and safe explosion, a suspicion that was compounded when the local police couldn't solve the case and had the temerity to suggest that Dick or one of his housemates had burglarized the safe.

Perhaps thinking fondly of the two FBI agents who attempted to turn him and Kleo into informants, Dick exhorted the FBI to investigate the break-in, sending them a series of letters in which he tied the break-in to what he called "a covert organization involving politics, illegal weapons, etc., who put great pressure on me to place coded information in future novels." He referred to this organization as Solarcon-6. They might be neo-Nazis, were definitely un-American, and according to him he wasn't the first SF author to be contacted. While it's true that the US intelligence agencies often attempted to infiltrate and "turn" would-be radicals into soldiers for the establishment—as Dick's own history proved—there is no evidence that anything like Solarcon-6 ever existed. As the local police had suspected, the trail of clues pointed to the culprit being Dick himself, a possibility he even admitted might be true in his seminal 1975 *Rolling Stone* interview with Paul Williams, where he says "there's lots of parts that I just blocked out, that only recently, only within the last few months, have I begun to remember, whole basic episodes blocked out."

Even though Dick was an avid drug user, had once been married to a communist, and had a lifelong one-way beef with Richard Nixon, in many ways he was profoundly conservative. It's this latent conservatism that led him to trust the FBI to investigate the break-in. (One wonders if he even realized that the FBI and CIA are part of the same government apparatus.) In 1974, he hit upon the "real" head of Solarcon-6: Polish writer Stanisław Lem, whom Dick said was a "composite committee rather than an individual." His evidence? Lem

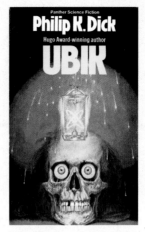

*Ubik* (Panther, 1978)

*The Man in the High Castle*
(Popular Library, 1962)

was a polyglot and wrote in "several styles." This seems less like the actions of someone deeply committed to progressive politics and more the ranting of a xenophobe. Sure, he was high for almost this entire period, but the drugs merely brought out what was already there. Ironically, and sadly, Lem had great respect for Dick's work and had even translated his masterpiece *Ubik* into Polish. Lem's essay "A Visionary among the Charlatans" (1975) is a simultaneous diss track toward American science fiction and a full-throated love letter to the works of PKD, which "deserved a better fate than that to which they were destined by their birthplace." A year later, Lem's honorary membership in the Science Fiction Writers of America was revoked, although it purportedly had nothing to do with Dick's accusation (he'd had a story published in an American magazine and was thus eligible for a regular membership but had no interest in joining). Still, the xenophobia couldn't have helped, which Lem admitted to his biographer J. Madison Davis in 1990, when he said, "it would be a lie to say the whole incident has enlarged my respect for SF writers."

If Dick's own politics were centrist at best, why does his work speak so clearly to people on the left? One of the reasons probably has to do with his protagonists, who are almost without exception working-class. His stories and novels are populated with the average stiffs just trying to make their way forward in the world. *The Man in the High Castle* (1962) displays this trait of Dick's work in spades. It opens with Frank Frink, metalworker and secret Jew, being fired from his job at a counterfeit antiques factory. Though the setting is dystopian, we see it through Frink's eyes, and

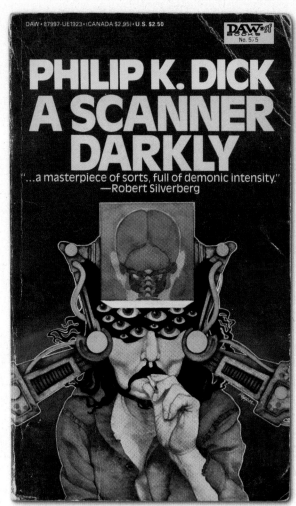

*A Scanner Darkly* (DAW Books, 1984)

his ambition isn't to take down the evil Axis regime but instead to ensure his own immediate survival. Meanwhile, Nobusuke Tagomi seems to have a high-ranking job in the Japanese government, but at first his concerns are purely prosaic: he needs to impress his boss. These are not the ultrasmart active characters that you'd find in any Golden Age science fiction (the kind Dick would have grown up reading) but rather common workers with everyday concerns. The nightmare world that Dick created is revealed in patches, and there are no grand Nazi-punching scenes. *The Man in the High Castle*, like most of Dick's writing, is a social realist novel with a science-fictional setting, and even the author of the book within a book that chronicles the true (or is it?) outcome of World War II lives in humble circumstances: a "single-story stucco house with many shrubs and a good deal of garden made up mostly of climbing roses." That this suburban Colorado

home is a portal to a better world where the Axis lost is startling in a way that a more typical skiffy trope would not be and further emphasizes Dick's commitment to showing the lives of ordinary people.

Dick may not have been a leftist, but he was certainly antiauthoritarian, which is evident even in his earliest work. The short story "Stability," which was written when he was a teenager and only published in 1987, concerns a society frozen at what it considers to be an acceptable level of civilization. A typical Dickian schlub stumbles into a time machine somehow invented by himself without his knowledge and decides to upend the city of Stability, where "dissenters were destroyed, radicals were carted off. It was hard and cruel but seemed to be the only answer." This scheme ends badly for him and everyone else. Though this could be seen as a conservative warning not to mess with what's working, it also could be interpreted as a statement that no society built on and maintained by cruelty can be allowed to stand, even if it provides material comfort.

At the other end of his career is the 1979 short story "The Exit Door Leads In," which similarly portrays a profoundly antiauthoritarian message. Bob Bibleman (gotta love these Dickian names) is recruited into a military college and is leaked information that could potentially save millions of lives. Bibleman does the safe thing, the conservative thing, and reveals the leak to the college administration only to find out that it was all a test. The college wants people who will act on their own initiative to prevent an atrocity, not just pass the buck to the nearest authority figure. The message in all of Dick's stories is clear: some people are not to be trusted, and those people probably have authority over you.

After a suicide attempt in March 1972, Dick entered rehab for the first time, and it worked. Newly invigorated, he moved to Southern California and quickly picked up a new wife and circle of friends, including SF writers Tim Powers and K.W. Jeter. Off speed, Dick's writing slowed. He'd never again publish a half-dozen novels in a single year. However, he started spending more time and care in editing, and it showed.

*A Scanner Darkly*, published in 1977, is both his chronicle of the perils of drug addiction and perhaps the novel that most captures the complicated feelings he had toward authority figures, especially police. The novel's central working-class character this time is Bob Arctor, a policeman in deep undercover in a five

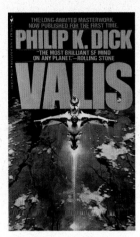

VALIS (Bantam, 1981)

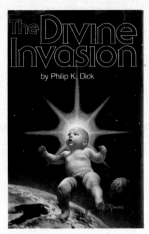

The Divine Invasion
(Timescape, 1981)

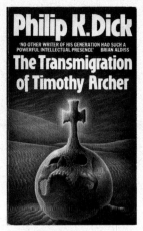

The Transmigration of Timothy
Archer (Granada, 1983)

Radio Free Albemuth
(Grafton, 1987)

seconds into the future California. In order to fit in with the targets of his surveillance, Arctor takes the popular drug Substance D, which causes his mind to split in two. Furthering the confusion, Arctor reports in to his supervisor as "Fred," and wears a "scramble suit" designed to mask his identity. Fred begins narcing on himself (that is, Arctor) and setting traps for his alter/main ego. The parallels between this plot and the 1971 "break-in" are obvious. If Dick did orchestrate the break-in, he certainly didn't remember it. In addition, the junkies that fill Arctor's house are reminiscent of the hippies and burnouts that lived with Dick both during and after his ill-fated fourth marriage. A Scanner Darkly is both Dick's most autobiographical novel and, as noted above, the clearest statement of his nuanced feeling about cops. Arctor/Fred is both villain and victim, and a greater conspiracy—one that will never be overcome, in the way of most of Dick's work—is at play.

On February 20, 1974, only a year after Dick moved to Orange County, he experienced a paranormal vision that would change his life just as much as the break-in and the suicide attempt. (It was a busy couple of years for Philip K. Dick.) Mesmerized by the glint off an ichthys pendant worn by a deliverywoman, Dick found himself in a parallel world where he was Thomas, an early Christian oppressed by the Roman Empire, which still secretly rules the present-day world. He entered into weeks of constant hallucinations, visited periodically by a pink beam of light which imparted information to him. Throughout this ordeal, Dick was calmer than one would expect. Dick himself said that it was "as if I had been insane all my life and had suddenly become sane."

Whatever the reason for the 2–3–74 experience (as Dick referred to it, since the bulk of the visions extended into March), it affected him greatly. Dick began writing an "exegesis" that would amount to over two thousand typewritten pages, and at the same time started work on the final novels of his career. VALIS (1981), The Divine Invasion (also 1981), The Transmigration of Timothy Archer (1982), and Radio Free Albemuth (posthumously published in 1985 but written a decade earlier) are collectively known as the VALIS sequence. Like A Scanner Darkly, these four novels are deeply autobiographical. VALIS, the first to be published, concerns a Dick stand-in by the name of Horselover Fat (Philip roughly means fond of horses in Greek; dick is German for fat) receives a visitation from the pink beam–wielding intelligence that took hold of Dick during 2–3–74. Fat embarks on a metaphysical quest with three friends, one of whom is Philip K. Dick himself, and two others based on his Fullerton area friends Powers and Jeter. They encounter the reincarnation of Christ as a two-year-old girl, who dies. Among the other events of this disjointed—yet strangely compelling—novel is the screening of a movie called Valis, which shows that President Ferris F. Fremont (another stand-in, this time for Nixon) is a force of evil, along with plenty of commentary about Gnosticism and other events in early Christianity.

Fremont also shows up in Radio Free Albemuth, which has even more explicit antiauthoritarian themes. As in VALIS, Philip K. Dick is a character in this novel, though his actual 2–3–74 experiences are assigned to the fictitious Nicholas Brady. As in the first novel of the sequence, the Vast Active Living Information System acts as a resistance force to Fremont and his booster party, "Friends of the American People," cluing selected people in to the fascist dictatorship that actually runs the United States. Brady, a record producer, attempts to distribute recordings with a subliminal message designed to get people out of their trance. Though Brady's gambit fails, VALIS's work goes on: "Nicholas's efforts had served as a diversion. Those efforts had fitted into a plan none of us saw or understood." The pop song full of subliminal messages is released by VALIS itself, and its message is heard—and understood—by the next generation of would-be revolutionaries, "by the kids."

The unusual use of an authorial stand-in who is *not* the character that carries the name of the author hearkens back to the personality split in *A Scanner Darkly* and other "splittings" in Dick's work. It is almost as if Dick didn't trust himself to write about his experiences with any objectivity and, instead, felt he had to work out 2–3–74 (and by extension the 1971 break-in and the suicide attempt) by proxy. In both of these novels the character Philip K. Dick is the conservative voice telling Fat and Brady that their perception may just be the result of schizophrenia or a drug-related flashback. At one point in *VALIS*, the narrator Philip K. Dick says outright, "I am not denying that Fat was totally whacked out," before on the same page explaining why Fat's experiences might be caused by the pink beam activating his phylogenic memory, as described by Jung, before then dismissing Jung's concepts as "speculative." Dick seems to be utterly at war with himself, always interrogating his own biases and thought patterns, as a good philosopher should.

Though 2–3–74 jump-started Dick's writing (albeit imbued with a monomaniacal theme), it wreaked havoc in his personal life. His fifth wife left him in 1977, along with their infant son, and Dick spent his next few years in unwilling solitude. His financial situation was the best it had ever been thanks to royalties from his dozens of novels over the years, but when he finally succumbed to a series of strokes in 1983, his still breathing but otherwise lifeless body wasn't found for several days. His unpublished novel *The Owl in Daylight*, about a Faustian bargain between a musician and a race of aliens, never left outline form. Dick might have been relegated to cult icon status if not for the movie *Blade Runner* (loosely based on his 1968 novel *Do Androids Dream of Electric Sheep?*) several months later.

Still, Dick arguably didn't become a household name until the twenty-first century. Of the many, many Philip K. Dick adaptations that exist, only four of them

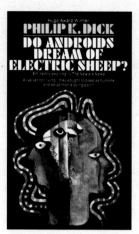 

*Do Androids Dream of Electric Sheep?* (Signet, 1969)

*Do Androids Dream of Electric Sheep?* (Panther, 1972)

were filmed before 2000. Dick's future—his worlds of total surveillance, authoritarian governments, and living through chemistry—has caught up to our present, and while that's not good news for us, it's very good news for the enduring legacy of Philip K. Dick.

Politically, what does the resurgence of interest in his work mean? Though Dick was not a member of any formal political (let alone socialist) organization, his writing captures the spirit of the little guy working against authoritarian government, armed with no special powers but an immense need to survive and to help others survive as well. His characters often fail, leading to bittersweet endings that Dick himself, in a letter to fellow SF writer Ron Goulart, summarized as "[the protagonist] has perhaps solved his personal problems or the world's problems—but whichever it is that has, in the book, been solved—the other is worse now, ironically… and here we bow out." The revolution requires personal sacrifice.

Philip K. Dick's life—and thus his work—is a study in contradictions. His drug use and multiple marriages make him appear a countercultural figure, but the expansive nature of his paranoia and skepticism meant that he likely didn't trust any ideology fully, other than a deep distrust of anything he regarded as authority, which definitely included communism. Regardless of Dick's personal politics, his creations have inspired at least two generations of radicals, and if the world doesn't collapse fully into one of his dystopian nightmares, Dick's writing will be relevant for many generations to come.

**Erica L. Satifka**

# Flying Saucers and Black Power

Joseph Denis Jackson's 1967 Insurrectionist Novel *The Black Commandos*

Exemplified most famously in song by James Brown's 1968 track "Say It Loud—I'm Black and I'm Proud," one of the main achievements of the civil rights and liberation movements of the 1960s was to facilitate a mass assertion of African American dignity. Both moderates and radicals had long grasped the need to empower their core constituency to resist their place in the racial pecking order. For many this involved defying the internal and external sense of worthlessness and derision that centuries of white supremacist ideology had propagated.

Following a decade of campaigning, civil rights and Christian activists in the mid- to late 1960s continued to call for nonviolent action to achieve equality within broader American society. However, due to increasing resistance from white communities and a resulting loss of movement momentum, as well as the influence of overseas anti-colonial movements, the goal of integration increasingly ceded ground to that of achieving Black Power. For James Brown and other entertainers, preachers, businessmen, and professionals, the pride

**A Black Man Who Cares About All People**

**WANT A CHANGE?**
**VOTE FOR EFFECTIVE LEADERSHIP**

## ELECT J. DENIS JACKSON

5th District City Council
October 8, 1985
*PUNCH NO. 26*

PHYSICIAN—LAWYER—ORDAIN MINISTER

Newspaper advertisement for Jackson's 1985 campaign for District City Council, Atlanta, Georgia

and autonomy associated with this concept was, as with other integrationists, best gained via achievement within the existing society and economy. However, Brown and his associates' swagger and assertiveness was in stark contrast with the humility of civil rights activists.

For some black nationalist and religious groups, such as the Nation of Islam, progress could only be achieved by breaking away from the dominant society to form autonomous communities supported by black-owned businesses. Others further emphasized black exceptionality by embracing and adapting aspects of African culture, for example, donning dashikis and other traditional garb, learning Swahili, and promoting Kwanzaa—a celebration of African American culture in the US created by black nationalist Ron Karenga in 1966 and observed from December 26 to January 1.

Activists influenced by Marxism and anti-imperialism emphatically rejected any form of capitalism, claiming a broader economic and social revolution was required. This might result in separation from whites or, for those like the Black Panthers, be achieved in alliance with a variety of radical movements and communities. Either way, independent black leadership would act as a revolutionary vanguard and empowerment would be required to achieve a complete restructuring of society along socialist lines.

Many community members lacked a formal program or ideology, instead asserting self-respect and exclusivity via "natural" and afro hairstyles, a resurgent interest in black history and culture, and an overall attitude that alternatively repudiated and disregarded dominant white conventions.

One proponent of the need for a more assertive activism and cultural outlook was civil rights activist Joseph Denis Jackson. Claims made throughout his life and since that he alone coined the phrase "Black is beautiful, and it is so beautiful to be Black" may be overstated, given that the first phrase had been in

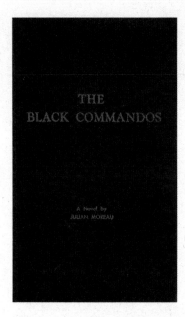

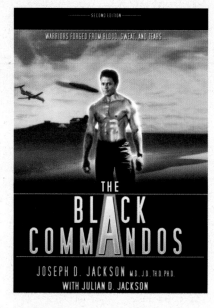

circulation since the nineteenth century. Nevertheless, Jackson did his part to popularize the slogan in the late 1960s via a Black Pride campaign he ran in Georgia. Interviewed in 1968 for African American documentarian William Greaves's TV documentary *Still a Brother: Inside the Black Middle Class*, Jackson expressed his belief (as quoted in the 2013 book *Jim Crow Wisdom*) that:

> There is a bone deep shame in being black which pervades the entire black community and has no respect for class. The black bourgeoisie is just as ashamed of being black as are the masses of negroes. This was done due to a concerted effort over many years and generations by the white propagandist. We intend to counter-propagandize. We intend to tell black people that they are valuable, that they are important, that they have made contributions to the world and will continue to make contributions to the world. But first they must look upon themselves in a better light. Hence, black is not ugly. Black is beautiful.

Having been involved in the 1953 Baton Rouge bus boycott, the Korean War veteran also contributed to and reflected the growing mood of militancy through the publication of his 1967 novel *The Black Commandos*. Stories depicting impending African American insurrections, both as warning and inspiration, had previously accompanied freedom movements in the US. Unsurprisingly, amid the tumult of the 1960s they blossomed like never before. Some emanated from the black community itself. Others were written by politically inspired white novelists sympathetic or unsympathetic to the cause, as well as by hacks searching for a contemporary issue to exploit. *The Black Commandos* not only proved an early entry in this latest wave but was also one of the most outlandish, eccentric, and politically bellicose novels of the era. Described in 2018 by critic Mark Bould in *The Cambridge History of Science Fiction* as "utterly science-fictionalized," the novel utilizes both a utopian/dystopian setting and a number of the genre's classic tropes.

Set in the near future, with occasional flashbacks to earlier times, the novel's plot revolves around the adventures of an exemplary black revolutionary who just happens to share the author's name. Born into a segregated rural Louisiana town during the Depression years, protagonist Denis Jackson devotes himself to destroying the evils of white supremacy after enduring horrific racism as a child. At the age of eight he loses his father when "Big Denis" is shot in the back after he forces white police officers to stop beating a young man they assumed was a drunk, but who was actually "inflicted with an ailment sometimes called St. Vitus Dance."

Playing marbles with three friends a year later, Denis Jr. is caught up in the police murder of a young man forced into petty theft by hunger. The same incident robs Denis of his best friend, after "a stray bullet struck little Henry between the eyes, killing the youngster instantly." Denis himself is "kicked callously in the face by the sheriff," landing in a ditch with "the left side of his face swollen and purple and a flow of blood running from his nose." In an early demonstration of resistance, he warns the officer, with "fierce brown eyes bristling with hate and defiance, but not a bit of fear," that "someday, white man, you won't be big." Before the sheriff can respond he is distracted by the arrival of Denis's mother, who the lawman patronizingly pats on the bottom and creepily promises to visit later that night. For the second time in Denis's life his family is forced to flee town.

Flashing forward a few decades to the post-1967 future, Denis Jr. has amassed a fortune and a body at a "peak of physical perfection no other man in all history had attained!" Standing five feet eight inches in height, "a tape measure would have revealed a chest in the range of forty-six and a half to forty-seven inches which tapered in a perfect V shape to a compact thirty-inch waist." Not only can he standing press "well over 500 pounds," but, with multiple university degrees, his "brilliant mind had been no less well-trained than his magnificent body."

Putting this mind and body to work, our hero roams ghetto bars and clubs across the country in search of men "talented in and prone to do—murder, for people with violent tempers and excessive brutality! Psychopaths!" The viciousness of these "hate filled Negroes who are known laughingly by the medical profession as 'Saturday night surgeons'" is not attributed to personal failings but to their subjugated position within American society. Jackson (the author) engages in much digression regarding the causes of what has since become labelled "lateral violence"; behavior members of oppressed groups engage in when they wreak frustration upon others within their own communities, generally those in even weaker positions than their own, rather than direct it at the power holders responsible for their situation.

Jackson, his lawyer sidekick Al Gandi, and an assortment of other "impressive looking" and highly educated lieutenants take such damaged and damaging lumpen proletarians under their wing in order to enact a plan they know is "as horrible as it is necessary." The multimillionaire is in league with "perhaps twenty of the richest and most intelligent Negroes in America . . . all 'boot strappers'—up from poor beginnings in life, whose magnificent efforts required in the titanic struggles these men had won had fused their very souls with fabric many times tougher than the most durable steel." Sending "unusually powerful and brutish Negroes—both paranoids and psychopaths" to a secret island, the conspiracy seeks to convert "these brutes into an effective fighting force dedicated to one purpose—protection of the rights and persons of the Negro people!"

The behavior modification required to transform abusers into protectors is achieved via hypnotic brainwashing technology housed in the island's Indoctrination Unit. Absolute allegiance to the cause of black revolution is guaranteed since "a satisfactorily conditioned subject has been taught to associate thoughts of betrayal with thoughts of suicide." Having been put through extensive physical conditioning, including power lifting, the recruits are also schooled in martial arts and given instruction in the use of deadly weapons. Those who survive join the ranks of the National Secret Police of the Negro People of America (NSPNPA), aka "The Black Commandos."

The island also features a series of weapons laboratories. Via much scientific verbiage the reader learns that the conspiracy has a "gas and biological warfare division" that is developing "anticholinesterase inhibitors" and other substances to induce muscular contractions, panic, and death. In addition, Jackson has invented a poison gas dubbed "Pink Mist," under whose "influence the subject falls into a 'death-like state' which if not interrupted within 48 hours progresses to the point of irreversibility." A "Death Virus" is also being perfected by Dr. Austin Craig, who describes himself as "arrogant, conceited and probably the most pompous man you'll ever meet." Craig, who tends toward uncontrollable and villainous laughter, believes his virus will soon be able "to wipe out the populations of our largest cities overnight, provided they have not previously been immunized." The island's explosives group meanwhile has developed laser-guided miniature thermonuclear devices, and the transport division is on the verge of completing a small fleet of flying saucers.

In a speech delivered on the eve of the first unleashing of his army, Jackson argues—in terms that echo those of anti-imperialist philosopher and revolutionary Frantz Fanon—for the subjugated to utilize cleansing violence against those who dominate them. The NSPNPA leader declares:

> We came together in a dark hour of fear and frustration to help those masses of black brothers who are weaker and much less fortunate than ourselves. That dark hour has continued

to the present time and our weaker brothers still cry in the wilderness. Two years ago we decided that our answer to this problem would be a violent one. We set into motion a plan for the creation of an elite corps of brutes, of killers and assassins because we believed that only in this way could we part the curtains of a long night of stark terror and walk into the light of a new day—completely free Americans and completely free men! We had hoped that the white men of goodwill who constitute the power structure of this great nation as well as those of the region we call "the south" would have controlled by now those white apes masquerading as men known as the Ku Klux Klan who murder our people, men, women and children, alike at will and with impunity. Time and again these apes have murdered our brothers and sisters—often aided and abetted by those very persons whose sworn duty it is to uphold the law of the land—not the law of white supremacy—and protect our lives and property. These "so-called" law enforcement officers are part of the ape pack and must be destroyed along with the others. It was agreed that if at any time our organization became unnecessary we would halt operations at that point even before the beginning. It has taken two years to get us ready but we are ready and we are still sorely needed.

The secret army initially targets a Ku Klux Klan rally. Having shot a KKK leader "right between the eyes," a manner by which the NSPNPA repeatedly dispatch their enemies throughout the novel, the Black Commandos proceed to slaughter and humiliate the gathered Klansmen. We are informed that such "red neck trash clung to an absurd doctrine of white supremacy because they had long learned the brutal fact of their own lack of capacity to compete with other whites," seeking out membership of the Klan as "their last haven, their last chance to look upon themselves without vomiting or ending it all."

The organization moves on to a series of "Strategic Assassinations" beginning with Alabama's punningly named "Governor Malice." This character is clearly based on the real-life arch-racist George Wallace who held the state's top position for a record four terms. At the height of civil rights ferment in 1963, Wallace famously declared "segregation now, segregation

tomorrow, segregation forever"—he would survive Arthur Bremer's attempt to assassinate him in 1971. Where that self-admitted apolitical notoriety hound failed, the NSPNPA succeed. Operating under the motto of "Those Who Won't Do Right for Love of God, *Must Do Right for Fear of Him!*" the otherwise secular secret army easily infiltrates the governor's quarters. Gandi hurls a hatchet "which literally whistled past Jackson and the State Trooper to catch Governor Malice smack between the eyes and continued on its way through more than half the governor's skull." Having employed the hatchet as a "false flag" to send government investigators off in search of Chinese communist agents, on the somewhat farfetched basis that Tong gangs had used the same weapon in the early years of the twentieth century, the Black Commandos escape by a variety of means, including the use of their now fully assembled flying saucers.

Blindsided by their own racism and unable to comprehend that African-Americans "were capable of organizing a super scientific fighting force" the authorities flounder in response, either blaming foreign operatives or a "group of white liberals who were bound fanatically to aid Negroes." After the commandos kill, burn, and hang a group of police for their murder of a young black Vietnam veteran, the organization announces it existence by leaving behind a calling card bearing "the insignia of the black fist, the steel triangle and the golden bolt of lightning—underneath the insignia the printed words spelled out '*DEATH TO BIGOTS!*'"

Over the course of the rest of the novel such one-off revenge attacks on racists, Klansmen, and corrupt judges are complemented by larger-scale efforts, including surgical strikes against the Mafia and support for an urban uprising that leaves "more than half of the pride of L.A. and countless county and state police dead or seriously wounded." All of this action usually begins or ends with Jackson or his coconspirators uttering their catchphrase, "Let's go, Commandos!"

Touring the country, the organization's key leaders preach armed and proactive action in the mold of that advocated and practiced during the 1960s by groups like the Deacons of Defense and Justice in support of southern communities and the Black Panther Party for Self-Defense in northern ones. Gandi tells one crowd:

I repeat, if a man has nothing he is willing to kill for, at the cost of his own life, he isn't fit to live! Now this isn't the same as killing to maintain oppression of the unfortunate. The man who stoops to this risks nothing. He has no self-respect so that can't be lost. He is in no danger for his victims are defenseless. Neither they themselves nor anyone else will defend them. Such men are cowards, for the brave do not prey on the defenseless. I tell you, we are dealing with cowardly, red necked trash. Show them you are not defenceless and you will soon have no further trouble with them.

As you walk and drive down the highways, country roads and off the beaten paths of the racially hostile southland, go armed to the teeth and ever ready for battle. Cease burying your heads in the sand—and recognize that you and your family are in a War and you have been for some time!

Even if you are armed, you may not save your life, but more often than not you will be able to assure that your death will not be a lonely one—you will have made your would-be murderers pay with their lives for taking or trying to take yours. This is the only way! Stop looking for any other . . . it does not exist!

Black communities rapidly take on the organization's message and methods. We are informed that shortly after the lecture tour one "well dressed elderly Negro walked up to Calvin Hate, the National head of the United Klans of America, and simply shot him to death on a busy street in broad daylight." All of this is merely a prelude however to J-Day as the now twenty-four thousand strong NSPNPA mobilizes to seize both Mississippi and the White House. But can such a bold move succeed, and will Jackson and his followers survive?

According to the preface of the second edition of *The Black Commandos*, written by the author's son, Jackson believed that the black community needed "a figure in the form of a superhero that fought the villains of racism and bigotry in the very same way all superheroes had conquered their evil counterparts." It was hoped that the book would serve "as one catalyst to start the process" to "inspire a nation to change its mindset about black influence in the world."

In a late 1960s interview with scholar Charles D. Peavy, Jackson described himself as a "liberal humanist"

but argued that the "area of human dignity" needed "revolutionary, rather than evolutionary change." He also stated that he was "not interested in destroying whites but in saving them," with the novel serving as a way to force Anglo-American society to "see that the sickness of racial prejudice which motivates them against the Negro is ultimately self-destructive and will only lead to disaster." In a later piece, Peavy stated that "Jackson feels that there are but three possibilities left to the whites: genocide, the removal of the motivation for the Black Commandos, or an ultimate confrontation with a force such as the Black Commandos."

Jackson's love of conventional science fiction and comic book culture shines throughout, not just in the novel's fantastical storytelling but also via occasional insider jokes and references. The novel's obsession with humanity-saving technology created by a campy boffin and wielded by decisive heroes against nefarious villains shows the clear influence of Golden Age pulp sci-fi. Despite its radical politics, the straight-up, two-dimensional, action-oriented storytelling in no way resembles the experimental nature of New Wave speculative fiction. Black identity is central to the novel's themes, but it lacks the innovation and distinctiveness of novels by authors like Samuel Delaney and Octavia Butler or the space-age mysticism and mind-bending fantasy of the music of Sun Ra and Parliament/Funkadelic that would later come to be associated with Afrofuturism.

*The Black Commandos* includes the kind of explicit depictions of violence that were becoming increasingly common in men's adventure novels during the late 1960s. In contrast, its hero's lack of sexuality makes it more akin to works created under the restrictions of America's notoriously censorious Comics Code than most action and crime novels, let alone the aforementioned groundbreaking sci-fi.

In keeping with the hyper-masculinity that black feminists would later criticize as rampant among sections of black nationalist movements, women are barely visible in the original edition of *The Black Commandos*. Other than Jackson's mother, those who do appear are sex workers and night clubbers whose negative portrayals were presumably included to underscore the author's views regarding what he saw as the degradation of elements amongst African American communities. A few gay and transgendered people, described with typical epithets for the time, feature early on in the novel, seemingly only to provide

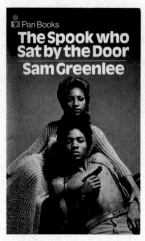

The Spook Who Sat by the
Door (Bantam, 1970)

The Spook Who Sat by the Door
(Pan, 1969)

Poster for the 1973 film adaption of *The Spook Who Sat By the Door*

one of the hero's potential recruits with a target to stomp.

No doubt aware that naming a leading character, and one with virtual superpowers, after oneself might elicit derision, or perhaps wanting to avoid the possibility that the book might be seen as autobiographical, albeit in another dimension, Jackson chose to publish it under the pseudonym of Julian Moreau. This name was drawn from his great-grandfather, whom he later stated was the "second son of a French nobleman of Moorish descent."

Having deliberately set out to critique American society and create a sci-fi action hero worthy of black audiences' adoration, the author's crude writing and plotting and rambling political and philosophical digressions may have played a part in his failure to find an established commercial outlet, let alone a mass audience. In the aforementioned interview with Peavy, Jackson claimed that "he had difficulty getting it published because most whites considered the book destructive." It may also have been a matter of timing. Sam Greenlee's 1969 *The Spook Who Sat by The Door*—in which a black agent tokenistically hired by the CIA assembles a guerrilla force to wage a war of liberation—enjoyed great success and was subsequently made into a 1973 feature film. While *The Black Commandos'* overblown narrative, sci-fi tropes, and at times clumsy prose and soliloquizing lack the humor and erudition of Greenlee, Jackson's writing is no worse than that contained in thousands of titles published as part of men's adventure series. By the early 1970s, the white-owned California publisher Holloway House would

be churning out a slew of violent and sometimes insurrectionary novels featuring black male heroes and antiheroes, and Blaxploitation films were being released by the score.

As things turned out, Jackson had to self-publish *The Black Commandos* in 1967 via his own Cultural Institute imprint. Reviews from the period prove elusive, if they exist at all, but the book was featured in lists of recent independent publications in some African American newspapers and magazines, and it appears to have achieved a modicum of distribution. It first received academic attention in a pair of articles penned by Peavy in 1969 and 1971 and has since been covered in various books regarding African American literature. Although its appeal for modern audiences undoubtedly lies in its historical value and over-the-top storytelling, Peavy stated that he could "personally attest to the impact the novel had upon militant Black students on the campus of the University of Houston, who did not find the book at all 'funny.'" Having interviewed Jackson, he also reported that the book was written "in dead earnest."

Although he would never experience the incredible achievements of his alter ego, Jackson appears to have led a fairly remarkable life, amassing eight degrees, including three doctorates, covering medicine, law, humanities, and theology, before his death in 2008. He worked for decades as a physician in DeKalb County, Georgia, and developed various theories melding sociology and psychology. His political development appears to have been in keeping with many during the period. Having argued on Atlanta radio in 1969 that the majority of the established black leadership were "Uncle Toms," specifically naming the NAACP's leader Roy Wilkins, he abandoned his radical cultural project in favor of traditional legal and electoral strategies.

The solutions he proposed would become less drastic over time, but his zest for public office and litigation did not diminish. Jackson first ran for election in 1969, unsuccessfully seeking a spot on the Atlanta Education Board, after which he launched a court challenge based on racial discrimination against the city's charter. In 1970, he was a member of a Commission for Racial Justice of the United Church of Christ investigative team that called for a federal prisons ombudsman and proposed that hiring practices in a new federal facility ensure that the racial proportion of guards matched that of inmates. He followed this up with a tilt at the lieutenant governor's position in the Atlanta Democratic primary in 1974, receiving 4.3 percent of the vote, the highest up to that time for an African American candidate. A campaign in 1978 for district commissioner of DeKalb County employed the slogan "let's upgrade all our people." During this time, Jackson pledged support for the Equal Rights Amendment, which proposed an end to discrimination against women but was never ratified, and committed to prioritizing the hiring blacks for city jobs. He also said he would give local businesses "all the support I can to triple their profits," while wanting to "see them share their profits with employees, many of whom I hope will be black."

Despite running on various occasions, Jackson did not join the steadily increasing number of black incumbents across the nation. Having been accepted to the Georgia bar, he maintained a commitment to politics and blended it with religious interests. Previously involved with Rosicrucianism, Theosophy, and Freemasonry, he received a doctorate of theology in the 1970s, becoming a Baptist minister in the mid-1980s.

Jackson's public life appears to have come to an abrupt halt in 1988 when he was charged with 160 counts of conspiracy and drug distribution related to the illegal sale of amphetamine-based diet pills, colloquially known as "black beauties." He had been previously dismissed from medical practice in 1977, on the basis of allegations that he had provided Quaaludes, Dexedrine, and other prescribed drugs to patients without first examining them. On that occasion, representing himself, he fought the finding, alleging that he been targeted on the basis of his civil rights work.

He also claimed that undercover officers, holding the mistaken belief he was a relative, had carried out the undercover operation in order to damage the reputation of Atlanta mayor Maynard Jackson, the first African American to hold the post. During the hearing a fellow doctor testified to Jackson's character, stating that he was "never really concerned about money" but was "greedy for information, not just about medicine." The finding was overturned in the same year, and he continued his general practice.

Jackson opted not to legally represent himself in 1988. His lawyer claimed he had been pursued by corrupt police officers associated with a drug ring. Eventually, Jackson was found guilty on one hundred counts and sentenced to eighteen years in prison. His lifelong passion for physical fitness appears to have remained undiminished, as notes for a never completed autobiography, later hosted on a website run by his family, claim he won a prison weightlifting competition at age sixty-one. *The Black Commandos* was revised and republished by his son's Commando Publishing Group in 2013 to honor what Julian Jackson described as his "father's final wishes."

**Iain McIntyre**

# Doomwatchers: Calamity and Catastrophe in UK Television Novelizations

In 1953, a six-part television series regarding the discovery of extraterrestrial intervention in the origins and contemporary life of humanity became a major hit in the UK. Titled the *Quatermass Experiment,* its tale of an eccentric scientist battling alien forces soon spurred the production of further groundbreaking science fiction programs. In keeping with the best of postwar British television and film, these often probed the state of a nation undergoing social and economic disruption in the midst of imperial decline with plots that involved near future responses to looming catastrophes of earthly and interstellar origin.

The popularity of a number of these stories led to their subsequent release in printed form. Typically, such books catered both to existing fans and those who, in the days before the VCR, the DVD, and streaming, had missed the programs when they aired. Those paperbacks chronicling the quest of eccentric scientist Bernard Quatermass to understand and counter the dark side of both aliens and humanity were made up of teleplays rather than novels. Adapted by series creator and chief script writer Nigel Kneale, they closely cleaved to the television programs in combining Cold War paranoia and a largely pessimistic view of human nature with elements critical of the role of the military, the bureaucracy, and the media in postwar society.

The ill effects of militarism, along with dodgy corporate dealings, were also explored in the 1961

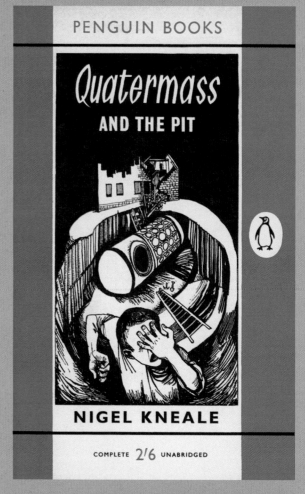

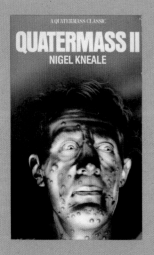
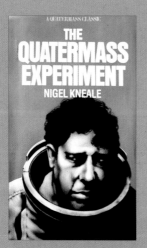
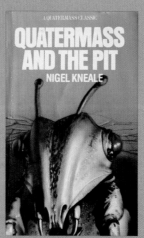

BBC series *A for Andromeda*, whose plot arc involved an extraterrestrial intelligence broadcasting instructions for the creation of advanced technology. While scientists soon come to suspect the intentions of these alien benefactors, the British state, keen to maintain the advantages they are reaping in terms of armaments and industrial breakthroughs, ignore their warnings, placing humanity in mortal danger. A follow-up series, *The Andromeda Breakthrough*, carried these themes further, albeit in a different national setting. Having come up with the key plot lines, astronomer Fred Hoyle, author of the popular 1957 sci-fi novel *The Black Cloud*, was given a byline on the novelizations the series' chief scriptwriter John Elliot was largely responsible for.

After a twenty-year break from the small screen, a fourth and final *Quatermass* series, bearing only its protagonist's surname, was broadcast by ITV in 1979, with a novelization following two years later. The malignant alien legacy at the core of its predecessors was updated to include a gloomy view of the likely outcome of the social, generational, and economic conflict then taking place in UK society. Kneale was no reactionary, as his depictions of privatized policing and Protestant revanchism in the series demonstrate. Nevertheless, the alien manipulated, youth-based, hippy doomsday cult at the heart of the show, and the collapse of law and order that fuels it, fit very much into the narrative of looming social chaos that right-wing elements used to propel Margaret Thatcher into power during the year it was released.

The panic surrounding the potential loss of class, gender, racial, and aristocratic privilege that fueled these fears was exemplified by the 1977–1978 series *1990*, and two novelizations subsequently produced by Maureen Gregson and Edmund Ward, neither of whose names feature on the covers. Echoing the far right's severely misplaced belief that the Callaghan Labour government represented a form of creeping communism, *1990* projected a future in which national bankruptcy leads to what series creator Wilfred Greatorex described as a "consensus tyranny" run by bureaucrats and union officials. Hounded by the Home Office-run Public Control Department, a journalist does his best to keep the last remnant of the free press alive despite the constant threat of "psychiatric internment" in an "Adult Rehabilitation Centre."

A sense of impending catastrophe, in part fueled by social conflict and in part by growing knowledge

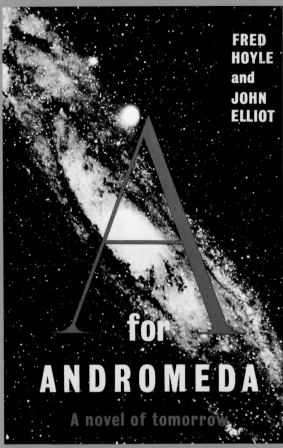

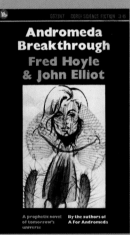

Clockwise from top left: *Quatermass and the Pit* (Penguin, 1960). *A For Andromeda* (Harper, 1962). *Andromeda Breakthrough* (Corgi, 1966). *A For Andromeda* (Corgi, 1963). *Quatermass* (Arrow Books, 1979). *Quatermass and the Pit* (Arrow Books, 1979). *The Quatermass Experiment* (Arrow Books, 1979). *Quatermass II* (Arrow Books, 1979).

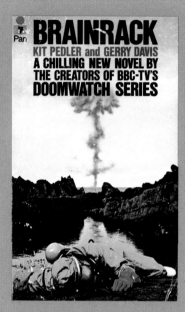

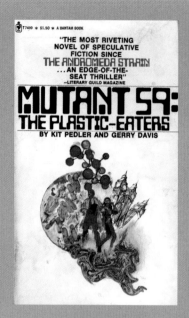

regarding ecological, nuclear, and other threats, also provided the basis of series such as *Noah's Castle*, *Survivors*, and the appropriately named *Doomwatch*. The latter involved a team of scientists detecting and seeing off one calamitous threat after another. Despite running from 1970 to 1972, the only official novelization of the BBC TV program appeared three years later in the form of school reader, *Doomwatch: The World in Danger* (1975; republished numerous times). This came after series creators Kit Pedler and Gerry Davis had already produced thinly veiled adaptions of episodes in the form of *Mutant 59: The Plastic Eaters* (1971) and *Brainrack* (1974), both of which

prominently displayed the word *Doomwatch* on their cover. A spin-off from the latter titled *The Dynostar Menace* (1975) was also published.

While *Doomwatch* generally featured (relatively) happy endings, the BBC's *Survivors* dealt with the results of humanity almost completely failing to carry the day. Set in the aftermath of a devastating viral pandemic it ran from 1975 to 1977 and was created by *Doctor Who*, and later *Blake's 7*, scriptwriter and novelizer Terry Nation. Two books were spawned from the series, the first featuring a radically reworked ending from Nation and the second with a completely new plotline by John Eyers.

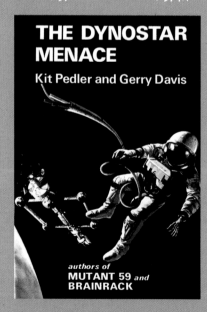

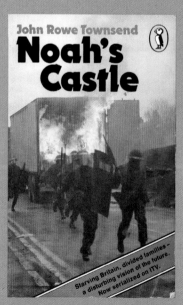

In the 1975 young adult novel *Noah's Castle* and the 1980 children's TV series based on it, fears of looming catastrophe related to the end of the postwar economic boom once more came to the fore. In the midst of mass unemployment and food scarcity, troops patrol Britain's litter strewn streets. As rationing looms, the youngest member of a family caught up in the chaos finds he must confront his authoritarian father over his antisocial response to the crisis.

**Iain McIntyre**

Clockwise from top left: *Doomwatch The World In Danger* (Longman, 1980). *Brainrack* (Pan, 1975). *Mutant 59 – The Plastic Eaters* (Bantam, 1973). *1990* (Sphere, 1976). *Survivors Genesis of a Hero* (Futura, 1977). *Survivors* (Futura, 1976). *Noah's Castle* (Penguin, 1978). *Noah's Castle* (Oxford University Press, 1975). *The Dynostar Menace* (Souvenir Press, 1975).

# The Energy Exhibition

## Radical Science Fiction in the 1960s

According to *Hansard*, the official record of UK parliamentary debates, a science fiction magazine has been mentioned only once in the British House of Commons. This happened on May 9, 1968, when R.C. Mitchell, popularly known as Bob Mitchell, the Labour MP for the Southampton Test constituency, put three questions to Jennie Lee, the secretary of state for education and science in Harold Wilson's Labour government: "what grant was made out of public funds to the magazine *New Worlds* during 1967–68?"; was the secretary of state "aware that a leading British newsagent [W.H. Smith] refused to handle the March edition of the magazine?"; and whether, given "the great shortage of money for all sorts of educational projects," it was "justified to spend any money at all on this sort of publication?"

By "this sort of publication," Mitchell did not specifically mean science fiction; his objection, like that of the British chain bookseller W.H. Smith, was to the perceived obscenity of the novel *Bug Jack Barron* (1969), by the American writer Norman Spinrad, which *New Worlds* was then serializing, and which contained sex scenes that were unusually frank for the time and what we still euphemistically call "strong language." The fact that such provocative work could appear in a science fiction magazine, a kind of publication not previously seen as a platform for such material, was an index of how science fiction was changing in the 1960s in ways that could outrage some of its traditional fans, as well as those presumably unfamiliar with the genre, like Mitchell.

These changes, certainly in Britain, but to some extent in the US, as the example of Spinrad shows, were focused around, though not confined to, the magazine *New Worlds*, under the editorship of Michael Moorcock, which provided a forum for four convergent strands of writing. The first was science fiction that broke away from the earlier constraints of the genre, which had minimized sex and marginalized political radicalism. The second was experimental writing influenced by the modernist stream of consciousness prose of the earlier twentieth century associated with writers such

as James Joyce, by the French *nouveau roman* of the 1950s, by novelists like Alain Robbe-Grillet, and by the poetry and prose of the American Beat poets, especially William S. Burroughs, which disrupted formal structure and syntax. The third was writing that dealt more frankly than ever before with sexual desire, using what D.H. Lawrence had long before called "impossible words" in a poem about his novel *Lady Chatterley's Lover*, which had originally been published in 1928 but only became available in an unexpurgated paperback edition in 1960 when a famous British trial found it not to be obscene. The fourth was politically radical writing in fiction and poetry that, with varying degrees of explicitness, challenged the conservative biases in traditional science fiction and in the wider society. Interestingly, these elements of the kind of writing Moorcock promoted in *New Worlds* blur the distinction Mitchell made in the UK parliament between the magazine and "educational projects," because, in a certain sense, *New Worlds* could itself be seen as a kind of educational project, introducing its readers to a range of different innovative strands of twentieth-century writing. There is no indication, however, that Mitchell had engaged more than superficially with the contents of the magazine.

*New Worlds* was, in fact, by the 1960s, a reasonably old magazine; its first issue had appeared in July 1946, edited by E.J. Carnell, the treasurer of the British Science Fiction Association, a group of SF enthusiasts who had been in existence since the late 1930s. Carnell developed it from the association's cyclostyled newssheet *Novae Terrae*, translating its Latin title into English. *New Worlds* always had a bumpy financial ride. Pendulum Publications brought out the first three issues but went out of business in 1947; the following year, Carnell and five associates set up Nova Publications to bring out *New Worlds*. A larger firm took over Nova Publications, but growing financial difficulties seemed to mean that issue 141 of *New Worlds*, in March 1964, would be the last; however, a firm called Roberts and Vintner bought the magazine, and Carnell was asked to stay on as editor. After some thought, he declined and recommended Michael Moorcock, whom he had already published in the magazine, and who had previously made a controversial appearance as guest editor.

Moorcock was, in the words of the older and established science fiction writer Brian Aldiss, "a great, vital, generous figure, full of vigor and creative juice." Although only twenty-four, Moorcock already had years of editing and writing experience behind him. He assumed the editorship of *New Worlds* with a sense of mission: the times they were a-changin', and science fiction should too. His editorial for the May–June 1964 issue of the magazine, which came out as a low-price pulp paperback, affirmed that the magazine would contain "a kind of SF which is unconventional in every sense." Colin Greenland points out, however, in his invaluable 1983 book *The Entropy Exhibition: Michael Moorcock and the British "New Wave" in Science Fiction*, that Moorcock did not flood *New Worlds* with innovative science fiction all at once, which might have put off some of the magazine's existing buyers and readers and prematurely stifled a controversy that would provide *New Worlds* with useful publicity and a sharpened self-definition. Instead, Moorcock initially offered a balance of old and new. On the traditional side, Greenland lists Sydney J. Bounds, Arthur C. Clarke, Donald Malcolm, E.C. Tubb, and P.F. Woods and, on the innovative side, Hilary Bailey, J.G. Ballard, John Hamilton, Langdon Jones, and David Rome (a pseudonym for the writer David Boutland). Disagreements in the letters pages of *New Worlds* over the respective value of the new and the old echoed and clarified the differences in its main content—making its correspondence columns an arena where gladiators bearing contrasting banners clashed proved an excellent way of attracting more attention to the magazine. Sales rose.

Financial problems surged up again when Roberts and Vintner decided to end its SF output after its distributors went bankrupt. Brian Aldiss, however, who had moved from initial uncertainty over Moorcock's editorship to strong support of it, mustered backing from a range of writers, including Anthony Burgess and J.B. Priestley, for an application for an Arts Council grant. In 1967, the Arts Council responded positively, eventually guaranteeing Moorcock a subsidy of £150 per issue (about £2,700 in 2019) [approximately US$3,450]. In July 1967, *New Worlds* number 173 came out as a big glossy magazine with an M.C. Escher image

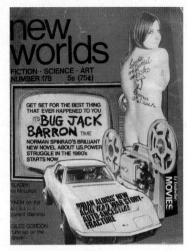
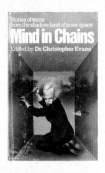

*New Worlds* magazine, issue 178,
December–January 1968
*Mind in Chains* (Panther, 1974)
*Under Compulsion* (Panther, 1978)

on the cover. As Greenland points out, this looked nothing like Carnell's *New Worlds*.

In his afterword to the 2011 ReAnimus ebook edition of Spinrad's *Bug Jack Barron*, Moorcock describes what he calls "[p]retty much a typical issue for the times," summarizing the contents of *New Worlds* 178. Dated December 1967–January 1968, this issue was on the cusp of the two most memorable years of the decade and included: the first episode of *Bug Jack Barron*; Aldiss's "Auto-Ancestral Fracture," later assimilated into the novel we shall discuss in due course, *Barefoot in the Head* (1969), and the conclusion to his novel *An Age* (1967; US title *Cryptozoic!* [1968]); J.G. Ballard's "Does the Angle between Two Walls Have a Happy Ending?" one of his five conceptual-verbal-visual "Advertiser's Announcements"; Thomas M. Disch's "Linda and Daniel and Spike," which he would include in his short story collection *Under Compulsion* (1968); Giles Gordon's "The Line-up on the Shore," which Christopher Evans would incorporate into his anthology *Mind in Chains* (1970); John Sladek's "Mac the Naif," on the media guru Marshall McLuhan; Moorcock himself, under the pseudonym James Colvin, with "A Literature of Acceptance," an article about the future of fiction; critic Christopher Finch's "Free Agents and Divine Fools," on British pop art, Ed Emshwiller's visual account of his own films, and Eduardo Paolozzi's illustrations from his *As Is When* series (1964–1965)—in other words, a rich, varied, and, at the time, state-of-the-art collection of creative and critical verbal and visual material.

In the tumultuous year of 1968, the controversies over the magazine's supposed obscenity, which we discussed at the start of this chapter, caused further financial difficulties, leading Moorcock to take over the publication of the magazine himself in 1968, financing it with some of the proceeds from his prolific pulp fiction—although, despite the controversy in the House of Commons, the Arts Council continued its grant. In April 1970, however, the pressures grew too great, and the last issue of the series, no. 200, appeared. Although further compilations appeared irregularly in the early 1970s, the most potent period of the magazine's history was over, like the sixties that had fueled it and that it had, reciprocally, energized.

In developing our discussion, we will focus on six novels of the 1960s that are of great intrinsic interest and exemplify key aspects of the innovative science fiction of the decade: Aldiss's *Report on Probability A* (1968) and *Barefoot in the Head*; Moorcock's *Behold the Man* (1969) and *The Final Programme* (US 1968; UK 1969); Spinrad's *Bug Jack Barron*; and Anna Kavan's *Ice* (1967). Aldiss, Moorcock, and Spinrad were all, of course, science fiction writers and, as we have seen, woven into the story of *New Worlds*; Anna Kavan (1901–1968) did not publish in *New Worlds* or identify as a science fiction author, but *Ice* is a key contribution to the innovative SF of the decade and might not have been possible without it.

### Brian Aldiss: *Report on Probability A* and *Barefoot in the Head*

Brian Aldiss, although fourteen years Moorcock's senior, shared the younger man's impatience with traditional science fiction to some extent and welcomed *New Worlds* both for its general project of encouraging more innovative uses of the genre and for the opportunity it offered him as a writer to experiment in his own work. His most experimental novels in this period— and indeed of his whole long and prolific career— were both published first in Moorcock's magazine, and later revised for book publication.

*Report on Probability A*, turned down at first by Aldiss's usual publishers

Brian Aldiss

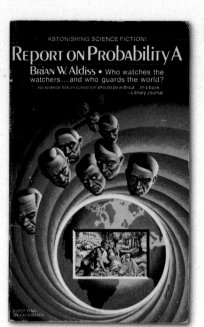

*Report on Probability A* (Lancer, 1968)

Faber, offers not traditional narrative but exact accounts of external appearances and action that, as in Alain Robbe-Grillet's nouveau roman *La Jalousie* (1957; trans. as *Jealousy*, 1959), require the reader to work out the situation and story that a conventional narrative would supply. Aldiss adds the science fiction element of multidimensionality, in which observers on earth and in other dimensions are all watching one another and, like the readers of Aldiss's novel, trying to work out what is happening:

> And there were watchers watching them, and they too had watchers, who also had watchers, and so on, and so on, in an almost infinite series. Every stage of watcher had a theory about the watched; every stage put something of its own passions into the watching.

The narrative makes readers feel as if floors are constantly giving way in their minds, making them fall through different layers of existence with no solid ground on which to stand; it creates a sense of what the radical psychiatrist and 1960s guru R.D. Laing called, in a much quoted phrase of the period, "ontological insecurity," uncertainty about the very basis of one's being. As well as being a complex and intricate work that expands the boundaries of the science fiction genre, *Report on Probability A* takes its place in the strand of experimental writing in the "literary" fiction of the 1960s, whose writers sometimes also employed science fiction elements, for example, Christine

*An Age* (Sphere, 1969)     *Cryptozoic!* (Avon, 1977)     *Cryptozoic!* (Doubleday, 1968)     *Barefoot In The Head* (Faber and Faber, 1969)

Brooke-Rose in *Such* (1966) and Alan Burns in *Europe after the Rain* (1965). One critic, Leigh Wilson (2017), has suggested links between Burns's novel and a novel that we shall consider later, Anna Kavan's *Ice*.

Aldiss's second major experimental novel of the period, *Barefoot in the Head*, takes the familiar science fiction setting of a world ravaged by war and famine and the theme of a "conflict of civilizations": an alliance of Arab nations has dropped mind-altering PCA (Psycho-Chemical Aerosol) Bombs on "wesciv" (also rendered as "Wesciv," "WESCIV" in a poem title "Westciv," and incorporated into the word *wescivilians*). The novel's central character, Colin Charteris, is a Serbian who comes to England; Aldiss's provenance for this protagonist seems prescient, anticipating the migrations from Eastern to Western Europe that would become a prominent but controversial feature of the post-communist free-movement European Union. Charteris who, in an intertextual reference to another kind of genre fiction, takes his name from Leslie Charteris, author of the *Saint* thrillers, becomes a Christlike guru who leads a crusade across Europe that consists of hippie car drivers, known as "drivniks." In contrast to the precise, pared-down language of *Report on Probability A*, *Barefoot in the Head* is notable for its exuberant, inventive style, combining prose and poetry and packed with newly minted words and puns, as in this account of Charteris in London, which combines extravagant vocabulary with a realistic topography, employing the names you can find in an A–Z street guide to the capital:

And all these drunken turnings as again they
lost themselves a simplified pantographic

variablegeometric seedimensional weltschmerz-anschauungerstrasshole of light-dashed caverns rumpussed in the stoned night were names to beat on inner ears with something more than sense; Westbourne Bridge Bishop's Bridge Road Eastbourne Terrace Praed Street Norfolk Place South Wharf Road.

This is James Joyce on acid, science fiction on speed, modernism and SF updated for the 1960s counterculture. It should be said, however, that the novel is more critique than celebration of countercultural excess and narcotic extremity. Aldiss might have become uneasy about its techniques soon after the *New World* episodes were published, because he revised it for publication in book form, which, in Moorcock's view, lowered its quality. In his autobiography *The Twinkling of an Eye* (1998), Aldiss would distance himself further from the stylistic pyrotechnics of *Barefoot in the Head*, calling the novel "one of the fake milestones of science fiction" and claiming that the narrative might "have been better told in plain language." But the style of *Barefoot in the Head* is, in a sense, essential to its theme, and once readers allow for its dated elements, the novel remains exciting and invigorating.

### Michael Moorcock: *Behold the Man* and *The Final Programme*

By his own account, in the later 1960s, Michael Moorcock financed *New Worlds* and himself and his young family by the fast and fecund production of heroic fantasy and SF novels. Most of these were, as he says, "written very rapidly to a limited wordage and to a strict self-imposed deadline." Within these limits, however, Moorcock still aimed to innovate. Thus, his "sword and sorcery" novels have heroes who are complicated and troubled, victims as well as victors, rather than straight-up embodiments of heroic qualities. Greenland quotes Moorcock's affirmation that he used their narratives "as a vehicle for [his] own 'serious' ideas," such as the notion of a "multiverse," an array of parallel and alternative universes that it might be possible to slip between rather than a single unified one, which had already gained some traction in science fiction and is now rather more widespread and has some scientific street cred.

A Moorcock novella that first appeared in *New Worlds* in 1966, "Behold the Man," is an especially notable achievement, winning the American Nebula Award for that year and emerging in 1969 in a longer, altered version, as a novel with the same title. *Behold the Man* combines a realistic bildungsroman, a novel of often painful education by life, with a science fiction tale of time travel. Kurt Glogauer, born in 1940, has mixed parentage—a Jewish Austrian father and English mother—and suffers a succession of negative experiences as a boy and young man in wartime and postwar London. He then travels back in time to AD 28, the supposed year of Christ's crucifixion—the tale's title, "Behold the Man," is a translation of the Latin phrase "Ecce Homo," used by Pontius Pilate of Christ in the Vulgate version of St John's Gospel in the New Testament.

When Glogauer meets Christ, however, he gets a shock: the "misshapen" figure has "a pronounced hunched back," "a cast in its left eye," a "vacant and foolish" face, and "a little spittle on the lips," and can

Michael Moorcock with actor Jon Finch on the set of the 1973 film, *The Final Programme*.

only say his name, "Jesus," in a "slurred and thick" way. He was born like that, an illegitimate child of Mary (no immaculate conception here), and his stepfather Joseph, to whom Mary was wed against her will, because she was pregnant with another man's child, calls his stepson's disabilities "God's judgement." This discovery threatens to leave a large gap in history or at least myth: If Christ never existed, how did the legend arise? Could it have ever arisen without some kind of real-life basis? And what validity does it have in the mid-twentieth century, especially without any such basis? Glogauer plugs the gap by assuming the persona of Christ himself, which in many ways suits his personality, and lives out Jesus's life as he recalls it from his scriptural studies.

The novel could seem blasphemous and, indeed, could have been open at the time to a legal challenge

*New Worlds* (September 1966)

*Behold the Man* (Avon, 1972)

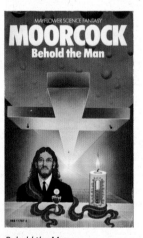

*Behold the Man*
(Mayflower, 1970)

*Behold the Man*
(Fontana, 1980)

on those grounds had anyone cared to pursue it. But it raises questions both about "the Messiah complex" that Moorcock saw as his subject—"if I was going to describe a man with a Messiah complex I might as well invoke the Messiah"—and also plays with time travel conundrums that have always intrigued science fiction writers: Is it possible to change the past? Are past events going to turn out to be the same in the end even if they look at first, to the time traveler, as if they are going to be different? Was Glogauer making a free choice in assuming the role of Christ or was it inevitable, already inscribed in the past and in his own character that he had to fulfil that historical function?

On one level, *Behold the Man* might not seem the most typical Moorcock tale; in another sense, it is, because of its combination of realism, science fiction, and fantasy. Moorcock would prove to be an accomplished writer in all three modes and more, but his most striking work is sufficiently rooted in realism to give it a weight greater than that of genre-fueled flights of fancy, whether of a fantastic, science-fictional, or thriller kind. This is the case with what is probably his best-known series, the four Jerry Cornelius novels; the first draft of the opening novel of the series, *The Final Programme*, was written with characteristic alacrity—it took ten days or so in January 1965. Greenland quotes Moorcock's recollection that he "borrowed as much from the [Dashiell] Hammett school of thriller fiction" as from SF and felt he had "found [his] own 'voice' as a writer," and, like Hammett, he locates Cornelius, in that first novel of the series, in an environment—Notting Hill and the Portobello Road in the mid-1960s—which is, to a significant extent, realistic and recognizable, even if partly transfigured by a sense that it is one among many other dimensions of the "multiverse." The novel that provoked R.C. Mitchell's questions in the House of Commons, which we quoted at the start of this essay, also had a strong realistic dimension, set in an America that extrapolated from certain elements of the 1960s, and seems to anticipate the interfusion of media and politics, the struggles between corporate and public provision, of twenty-first-century America. This was Norman Spinrad's *Bug Jack Barron*.

## Norman Spinrad: *Bug Jack Barron*

The title character of Spinrad's novel, Jack Barron, is a former student radical who is now the highly paid host of a TV show watched by a hundred million Americans where people call in on video phones (vidphones) to

Norman Spinrad

say what is bugging (in the sense of annoying or bothering) them. Barron presents himself as the man who, like an angry Christ, takes those annoyances upon himself—"What bugs you, bugs Jack Barron"—and allows them to be expressed on the air in a way that will be impossible for those identified as the source of the annoyances to ignore. As one of the show's slogan puts it: "It's hit-back time, worm-turning time, and if you got a real bind on any powers that be, this is the time they gotta sit there and take it while the you-know-what hits the fan."

The particular bug that sparks off and drives the first part of the narrative is that of Rufus W. Johnson, an African American caller who complains that, although he has the $500,000 in liquid assets to pay the Foundation for Human Immortality for his body to be frozen after death in the hope of future revival, he has been excluded on racist grounds. Barron battens on this, energized partly by the remnants of his youthful radicalism to pursue the president and chairman of the board of the foundation, "the Barnum of the

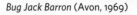

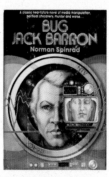

*Bug Jack Barron*
(Doubleday, 1983)

*Bug Jack Barron* (Avon, 1969)

*Bug Jack Barron*
(Walker, 1969)

Bodysnatchers," Benedict Howards. The specific case of Rufus W. Jackson also raises the more general issue of whether postmortem freezing should be publicly or privately funded, an issue that Howards, in an implicit pun, links to the Cold War: "The Soviet Union and China have no Freezer programs at all because only in a free enterprise system can the cost be borne." As Barron's pursuit continues, he drives Howards into a corner, making him lose control on live TV, but he also finds himself and his former girlfriend and fellow student radical Sara Westerfeld, with whom he has resumed relations, seduced by the siren call of immortality into signing up for a life-prolonging treatment that turns out to employ horrific methods.

*Bug Jack Barron* is, in outline, an exciting, hard-edged story; but its excitement is much heightened by its energetic prose, streetwise and rich in American idiom, making much use of modernist and Beat techniques of long sentences, sometimes with little or no punctuation, to convey mediatized postmodern reality. For instance, this is how Barron thinks of his television identity:

> The inside of the studio *was* actually the inside of a hundred million television sets. There was a creature bearing his name that lived in there (seeing out through monitor eyes, hearing with vidphone ears, monitoring its internal condition through promptboard kinaesthetic senses, shifting image-gears with the foot-buttons, ordering, threatening, granting grace all through the circuitry and satellites of that great gestalt of electronic integration, the network, into which he was wired, the masterswitch in the circuit) for one hour a week, a *creature* indeed, designed and built by him like a Frankenstein android, a creature of his will but only a segment of his total personality.

Where *Bug Jack Barron* is, as befits its theme, a hectic book, the final novel we shall consider is, as its title suggests, cooler—Anna Kavan's *Ice*. Several women science fiction writers of high caliber featured in *New Worlds*. Greenland lists Eleanor Arnason, Gwyneth Cravens, Carol Emshwiller, Joanna Russ, and Pamela Zoline. But Greenland also acknowledges that there were relatively few women writers in the magazine, and this related to a more general sense, in the New Wave as in the old SF currents, that science fiction was a man's world, although this started to change in the

later 1960s with the emergence of authors such as Russ, Ursula K. Le Guin, and Marge Piercy. Women writers outside the New Wave and the science fiction sphere did, however, employ science fiction elements and motifs—we have already mentioned Christine Brooke-Rose's novel *Such*, and we shall now consider Kavan's *Ice*.

### Anna Kavan: *Ice*

Anna Kavan

Anna Kavan was by far the oldest of the writers who contributed to the science fiction surge of the 1960s. Born in 1901, she published her first novel, *A Charmed Circle*, in 1929, under her original name, Helen Ferguson, and her first book as Anna Kavan, a volume of short stories called *Asylum Piece*, in 1940. She led a troubled life, suffering from depression and heroin addiction, and died a year after the appearance of *Ice*.

*Ice* is a catastrophe novel in which the chill, hard substance of the title is advancing steadily and remorselessly over the globe, a process evoked with great poetic power. "Day by day the ice was creeping over the curve of the earth, unimpeded by seas or mountains. Without haste or pause, it was steadily moving nearer, entering and flattening cities, filling craters from which boiling lava had poured." Like Aldiss's *Report on Probability A*, Kavan's novel exemplifies the 1960s theme of "ontological insecurity," and this is coupled with the recurrent sense of unreality evoked in its pages; for example, "I again felt I had moved out of ordinary life into an area of total strangeness. All this was real, it was really happening, but with a quality of the unreal; it was reality happening in quite a different way." There is also a strong consciousness of female vulnerability in the elusive, abused young woman who figures so significantly in the text:

> Her picture was always with me, in my wallet and in my head. Now her image appeared in the open wherever I looked. Her white lost face was everywhere with its too-large eyes, her albino paleness flared like a torch beneath the malignant clouds, drew my eyes like a magnet.

She was a shimmer among the ruins, her hair a glittering in the dark day. Her wide eyes of a wronged and terrified child accused me from the black holes of smashed windows. Like a perverted child she ran past, soliciting me with big eyes, tempting me with the pleasure of watching her pain, elaborating the worst imaginings of my desire. The ghostly gleam of her face lured me into the shadows, her hair was a cloud of light; but as I came near her she turned and fled, the silver shifting suddenly on her shoulders, a waterfall glinting in moonlight

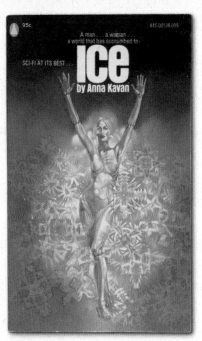

*Ice* (Popular Library, 1967)

Here and elsewhere the novel offers potent, disturbing evocations of voyeurism, sadism, predatory desire, and gender bending that anticipate feminist and queer science fiction.

Brian Aldiss, a major science fiction critic, as well as author, acknowledged the achievement of *Ice* in his history of SF, *Trillion Year Spree* (with David Wingrove, 1986). If his remark that Kavan "was a woman who, like Mary Shelley, wrote science fiction without knowing it and, in doing so, created one of the great science fiction novels" may sound slightly patronizing today, he does recognize the stature of *Ice* and its escape from easy categorization: it "represents one of the high points of science fiction, and so becomes unclassifiable." Aldiss also helpfully points to some of its intertextual resonances, mainly but not wholly male: Kafka; the surrealism of some of Jean Cocteau's work (although Aldiss gives no examples, the film *Orphée* [*Orpheus*] [1950], with its quest for the elusive lost woman, comes to mind); the one novel by the painter Giorgio de Chirico, *Hebdomeros* (1966); and the pornographic novel *The Story of O*, by Pauline Réage, a pseudonym of the French writer Dominique Aury (born Anne Desclos), a novel originally published in 1954 but only freely available from 1967, the same year as *Ice* was published. But Aldiss is aware that, despite its links with these works, Kavan's last novel published during her lifetime remains "an enigma—like all the greatest science fiction, approaching despair; but, in its acceptance of the insoluble, also full of a blind force much like hope."

## Conclusion: Much Like Hope

Aldiss's idea of the ultimate optimism of the best science fiction could apply to all the 1960s SF novels we have considered and, more generally, to the essential thrust of the New Wave of the decade. Of course, science fiction, whether traditional, New Wave, or post–New Wave, has always relished disaster and dystopia, the collapse of cultures and civilizations, the terminal beach and the drowned world, the earth catching fire and standing still; and the apocalyptic aspect of the 1960s, the sense that the world was, in the words of P.F. Sloan's song, most memorably recorded in 1965 by Barry McGuire, "on the eve of destruction" made science fiction, especially of a radical kind, expand its imagination of catastrophe more than it had done since the 1930s and address an increasing sense of disorder. But this disorder was both creative and destructive; we can perhaps see more clearly now from our twenty-first-century perspective, when the sense of being "on the eve of destruction" is rekindling with domestic and international tension and conflict and climate change, that the 1960s science fiction New Wave was a period of rich creativity, and not only in terms of the topics it encompassed—the introduction of sex and radical politics into science fiction, for instance—but also of the formal innovations in style and structure that it encouraged, which continue today in both science fiction and "literary" fiction. We might say, revising the title of Greenland's book, that the 1960s SF New Wave offered not only an entropy exhibition, a display of increasing disorder, but also and more durably, with a force much like hope, an energy exhibition.

**Nicolas Tredell**

# "We change—and the whole world changes"

## Samuel R. Delany's *Heavenly Breakfast* in Context

The gay African American writer Samuel R. Delany's first memoir, *Heavenly Breakfast: An Essay on the Winter of Love* (1979), was published toward the end of the first phase of his career, a period when he primarily wrote science fiction. The second phase, which continues to the present, is more

Delany in the summer of 1966. Photo by Ed McCabe

concerned with life writing, fantasy, and literary criticism and theory. *Heavenly Breakfast* is an essential text for understanding both phases, because it documents events that caused an important shift in the first phase and is an early example of the kind of work contained in the second.

After 1984's *Stars in My Pocket Like Grains of Sand*, Delany did not publish an SF novel until 2012's *Through the Valley of the Nest of Spiders*. *Heavenly Breakfast* is about an experience that took place approximately a quarter of the way through Delany's SF phase, one that markedly affected his SF and erotic writing throughout the 1970s and beyond, a shift that Delany himself acknowledges. The memoir describes his time living in the Heavenly Breakfast commune on Manhattan's Lower East Side during the winter of 1967–1968. Delany's SF written after living in the community is noticeably more radical than his already ground-breaking, boundary-pushing prior work. Therefore, *Heavenly Breakfast* is an important text to consider when investigating Delany's SF.

The original Bantam Books edition forcefully makes this point, almost to the detriment of *Heavenly Breakfast* itself. All of the book's paratext is an attempt to lead readers to the SF that Delaney wrote after his time in the commune. The front cover asserts that his time living communally was "THE SOURCE OF HIS VISION" for writing books such as "*NOVA*," "*DHALGREN* AND *TALES OF NEVÈRŸON*" (*Nova* was actually finished before Delany moved to Heavenly Breakfast, even though it was not published until afterward, so the cover is misleading), thus using his status as an SF writer to market the book even though it is not SF. The subtitle does not appear on the cover, perhaps because the publisher feared that making the memoir's non-SF status too explicit would hurt sales. The cover painting, which is uncredited, surrounds Delany with musicians and apartment buildings, giving an accurate portrayal of *Heavenly Breakfast*'s subject matter, but the picture of him in the middle of the painting is as he looked in 1979, not an attempt to paint him as he looked when the book takes place. So late-1970s SF superstar Delany gets marketed more than the book's contents.

To reinforce the cover, the front flyleaf mentions Delany's "science-fiction bestsellers *Nova*, *Dhalgren*, *Triton*, and *Tales of Nevèrÿon*" (this last misnamed as SF rather than fantasy), and the order form at the back of the book includes a blurb for each of these four novels as well as *Heavenly Breakfast* itself. The book again markets itself as being important for understanding Delany's SF rather than for its own content. It also tries to deny its radical subject matter in its "About the Author" statement for Delany, which highlights Delany's marriage to the award-winning poet Marilyn Hacker, erasing both of their queer sexualities (Hacker identifies as lesbian), even though the book is open about the frequent queer sex in the commune—some of it Delany's, some that of others.

Despite the Bantam edition's questionable marketing efforts, it is nevertheless important that *Heavenly Breakfast* was initially published by a mainstream, mass-market publisher, unlike Delany's subsequent four memoirs, *The Motion of Light in Water* (1988; rev. ed. 1993), *Bread & Wine* (1999), *Times Square Red, Times*

*Square Blue* (1999), and *1984* (2000), the first and latter two of which are marketed for a more academic audience. There was an assumption on Bantam's part that there would be a decent audience for *Heavenly Breakfast* among Delany's already established readership, which did not yet count many literary scholars.

Unfortunately, the book has failed to garner much publishing enthusiasm since then. Neither of Delany's two primary current publishers, Vintage Books and Wesleyan University Press, have chosen to republish it, and the 1997 Bamberger Books printing is not much easier to come by than the 1979 one. Compared to *The Motion of Light in Water* and *Times Square Red, Times Square Blue*, previous critics pay hardly any attention to *Heavenly Breakfast*. It is necessary to remedy this lack. While, like the paratext accompanying Bantam edition, I am making the argument that *Heavenly Breakfast* is certainly important for understanding Delany's SF, I also argue that its examination of communal living and this model's politically queer aspects is important in and of itself. Thus, in hindsight, the Bantam marketing sells the book short.

Before moving into Heavenly Breakfast, Delany published eight SF novels between 1962 (when he was twenty years old!) and 1967. *Babel-17* (1966) and *The Einstein Intersection* (1967) both won Nebula Awards, which, along with the Hugo Awards, were the most prestigious SF could win at the time. While the Bantam cover highlights Delany's Nebulas, it does so in a way that elides his early work, making it seem that he won the award for *Nova* or perhaps for all three novels listed, therefore again reinforcing the argument that his time in Heavenly Breakfast affected his fiction.

Delany's eight early novels have fairly traditional space opera plots, though they were also pushing the boundaries of what SF could be. For instance, in *Babel-17* the villain is not a person or a race of aliens but a language, and as the protagonist Rydra Wong works to decipher it in order to save her people she offers readers a primer of structuralist theory to explain how language affects our experience of the world. (It seems especially appropriate to mention

*Heavenly Breakfast*
(Bantam Books, 1979)

*Babel-17*'s explorations of language as a fragile form of communication here in a piece where I frequently use a phrase *heavenly breakfast*, which has three separate meanings: Heavenly Breakfast the commune, Heavenly Breakfast the band, and *Heavenly Breakfast* the memoir.) It is explicitly a philosophical and pedagogical text, rather than a mere adventure story meant to be read in one's free time on a Saturday afternoon. By the time he moved into Heavenly Breakfast, Delany's early critical success in the SF community as a result of his innovative work made it clear that he was on the path to a worthwhile career as a traditional SF writer if he wanted it.

However, Delany was not sure at the time whether he would stick with writing. In a journal entry from 1963 published in the first volume of his collected journals, *In Search of Silence*, he writes that he thinks his future "lie[s] with music" rather than writing. So despite already having two novels published at that point, he was not fully comfortable with the identity of writer, and it would be a long struggle for him to ultimately make the choice to remain one. He moved into Heavenly Breakfast in part because he was involved with a band of the same name and the move would facilitate writing songs for an album.

Although Heavenly Breakfast was Delany's first time living in a full-fledged commune, he had some previous experience living in a smaller commune-esque setting. In *The Motion of Light in Water* he documents how, in 1965, he and Hacker briefly expanded their marriage into a threesome both sexually and habitation-wise. Delany calls those several months "one of the happiest times of my life." His experience with the threesome, which is fictionalized in *Babel-17* where "triples" are a common relationship model, is important, because it was queer sexually (the third member was another man) and politically (it rejected the conventions of state-sanctioned marriage). Delany's experiences living at Heavenly Breakfast came out of this context. Because of his positive threesome experience, he was open to new experiences that would affect his professional direction during his Heavenly Breakfast year.

Babel-17 (Ace, 1966)

Babel-17 (Sphere, 1969)

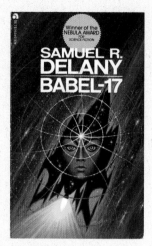

Babel-17 (Ace, 1974)

Aside from giving character sketches of his housemates and describing various events that occurred during the winter—the band rehearses, everyone takes a trip to a monastery upstate, they all get gonorrhea, because intra-commune sexual encounters are commonplace, and so on—*Heavenly Breakfast* includes a substantial amount of discussion about the nature of communes in general and the practical elements of living together specifically. *Heavenly Breakfast* is not meant as a how-to manual for beginning a commune, but these passages give enough detail that one could use it this way if so inclined. The book describes practicalities toward its beginning. Two members dealt drugs to provide most of the funds for the group, and others pitched in by cooking and cleaning. Decisions about group policies were made by informal consensus.

The commune's model is revolutionary now as then, even for a commune, because it recognizes that people have value aside from their financial status, and that it is worth living with someone because of the companionship they provide, even if they are unable to contribute their "fair share." As Tavia Nyong'o writes in "Back to the Garden: Queer Ecology in Samuel Delany's *Heavenly Breakfast*," the only scholarly essay regarding the memoir, "The idea of the commune was born in the hope of contesting the disempowerment of the individual as producer and as consumer, by tuning in to an alternative wavelength … and dropping out of straight society in order to recreate a better environment for both self and other." Heavenly Breakfast's model does this by emphasizing the emotional aspects of community rather than the financial ones. It is inaccurate to say that its members shared funds, because many of them had no funds to share, but they all shared in the work of caring for one another. It is especially significant that in support of this model Heavenly Breakfast's funds came from the black market rather than a societally sanctioned occupation, because it illustrates the possibility of subverting the system by working outside of it. Such a choice meant that the commune never had a lot of money, but the members' willingness to live simply instead of forcing each other to find jobs again emphasizes the importance they placed on their relationships as a refreshing alternative to American consumerism. Therefore, Heavenly Breakfast functioned as an example of what, in *Cruising Utopia: The Then and There of Queer Futurity*, José Esteban Muñoz calls a "concrete utopia," which is a queer form that envisions possible futures that stem from real-world political action. To bring these possibilities into being, concrete utopias "critiqu[e] the present" by drawing from the past to offer hope for a new future. Just as the commune itself critiqued American society in

1967–1968, in its reminiscing about the commune's radical model twelve years later, *Heavenly Breakfast* is an example of such looking to the past also acting as a concrete utopia.

Delany repeatedly highlights the potential of communes for changing society, while also lamenting the lack of language available for describing communal experience. Members of Heavenly Breakfast frequently met with other communes. The discussions of these communes help make *Heavenly Breakfast* a successful memoir, because they tie Delany's experiences to broader societal ones, making the book thought-provoking whether or not one is interested in Delany as a person. While communes are frequently viewed as a relic of the radical 1960s, Delany's choice to write about them in the late 1970s argues that their model remained relevant for the queer act of envisioning a transformed society, and by extension I make the same argument in my decision to investigate the book.

One way *Heavenly Breakfast* suggests communes can be revolutionary is in in their deemphasizing of the nuclear family, a patriarchal, homophobic institution. Aside from the constant visible sex that occurred at Heavenly Breakfast, because there were few bedrooms or doors in the apartment, the public nature of which made bisexuality a communal value, the commune shared parenting responsibilities when residents with children moved in. Ties of affinity are emphasized through these practices rather than ties of kinship or blood. Monogamy and heterosexuality are broken down in favor of desire in the moment, and children are viewed as full members of the community who deserve care from everyone, just as the adult members do. Delany reminisces that the commune was a wonderful place because of how emotionally supportive it was as a result of these practices. Members did not have to rely on a single spouse to fulfill their needs, instead having numerous companions they could turn to. This model created a sense of physical and emotional safety that was strong enough and utopian enough for Delany to want to write about it a dozen years later.

However, because Heavenly Breakfast created such a new model, Delany admits that he does not have adequate language with which to describe it, calling the commune's relationships something "that hasn't yet been given a name" and writing that it is difficult to explain Heavenly Breakfast in a way that makes people understand the appeal of it just as it was during its existence. It is necessary to remember that living in community was a radical move even for the late 1960s, and that most people would have thought Delany was crazy for doing so. Although, as my discussion of it suggests, I think Delany is being overly modest in his claims about *Heavenly Breakfast*'s inadequacies, it is important that he names the lack of language for the commune's queer model of living, because it is virtually impossible to bring about change without having language to describe what is being created. Thus, the book simultaneously articulates the need for new language in order for a new society to come into being and provides some of this language through Delany's willingness to write about his experience. There may not be a satisfactory label for what happened at Heavenly Breakfast, but at least we have its model to ponder.

Despite Heavenly Breakfast's success as a commune, the band eventually broke up, because they were unable to obtain a record deal, and several of the members wanted to go solo, which caused the breakup of the commune as well. Therefore, to a certain extent Delany's choice between music and writing was made for him, because he did not feel able to perform live successfully, and he did not have a professional musical future without the band. However, it is significant that the commune did not break up because its model failed. It was a workable living situation, and its members dispersed amicably. It is worth writing about because of its success as an alternative, politically queer way of life. In the words of Lauren Berlant and Michael Warner in their germinal essay "Sex in Public," the commune's form is a "world-making project," an act that helps sustain "queer culture." The band as a collective proved unsustainable, so Delany went back to writing, but the ideal of community as he experienced it in the commune, which is sustainable, stayed with him.

Delany's time in the commune also helped to clarify his vocation as a writer by giving him new directions for his writing. The author's assertion that "we change—and the whole world changes," because we now see it differently, perfectly describes how Heavenly Breakfast affected his fiction. A healthy community's function should be to help its members find their individual callings, because by finding personal fulfillment one is able to participate in community as a contributor rather than as a burden. Delany makes it abundantly clear throughout his nonfiction that writing is more than a job to him; it is a form of social activism. His countercultural experience in the

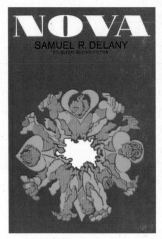

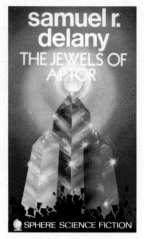

*Nova* (Doubleday, 1968)

*The Jewels of Aptor*
(Ace Books, 1968)

*The Jewels of Aptor*
(Sphere, 1969)

*Driftglass* (Signet, 1972)

commune helped solidify his vocation, by radicalizing his SF and the rest of his writing. In other words, while there are some LGBTIQ elements in his earlier fiction, most notably in *Babel-17*, living at Heavenly Breakfast helped to cause the shift to the queer in the radical political sense in his work.

The effects of Delany's commune experience are especially evident in the two post–Heavenly Breakfast SF novels mentioned on the front flyleaf of the Bantam Books edition of the memoir, *Dhalgren* (1975) and *Triton* (1976; since republished with Delany's preferred title, *Trouble on Triton*). Tavia Nyong'o remarks that mainstream culture of the time viewed communal values as akin to science fiction. This comparison is apt because communes and much SF share a belief in a better, even utopian, future. It is, therefore, not surprising that *Dhalgren* and *Trouble on Triton* both investigate communal living. SF that focuses on community contrasts strongly with traditional Golden Age SF from the 1940s–1950s and books influenced by it, such as Delany's two Nebula Award winners, which focus on a lone protagonist as hero. For instance, while *Dhalgren* is SF, because it takes place in the future, it takes place on earth, it is almost completely devoid of futuristic technology, and it is much more focused on realistic human relationships than Delany's previous SF. It centers around the protagonist Kid's attempts to find a safe community after he arrives in a postapocalyptic city without remembering how he got there. He lives with different groups throughout the novel, sampling them in Goldilocks fashion. Most notably, he lives with a biker gang, an element of his story that is directly influenced by Delany's Heavenly Breakfast experience.

In the memoir, Delany describes two encounters with a biker gang commune that sustained itself by working as hired muscle. Delany says he commented to a housemate after visiting the bikers, "Of all the communes I've encountered, that's the one I'd like to write the novel about." Whether he really said this at the time or just claims to have as a sly reference to *Dhalgren* is immaterial; the point is that he actually did choose to fictionalize aspects of his communal experience.

Unlike *Dhalgren*, where the Kid's communal experiences are fairly positive, especially considering its postapocalyptic setting, *Trouble on Triton*, which more closely resembles traditional SF, depicts a main character, Bron, who does not successfully find community. However, this failure is due to his flaws rather than the collective's. On Triton, people live in "co-ops" that function as pseudo-communes based on their sexual preferences, in that there is an emphasis on interacting with one's neighbors in common spaces, although residents have their own apartments and do not share finances. Bron lives in a building with good neighbors who care about him and try to help him through his emotional malaise, which is the main subject of the book, but he rejects these efforts and ends up unhappy, unlike nearly every other significant character. His refusal to participate in community causes him to fail rather than the community being responsible for his unhappiness.

Sex is also much more prevalent in Delany's fiction after his time at Heavenly Breakfast. His first two erotic novels, *Equinox* (written in 1968, published as *The Tides of Lust* in 1973; republished with his preferred title in 1994) and *Hogg* (written in 1969–1973 concurrently with

*Dhalgren* (Bantam, 1974)

*Dhalgren* but not published until 1994), were written shortly after leaving the commune. He writes in the memoir that there was perpetual sexual activity in the apartment, with at least "three or four [people] always around naked." While Delany was quite sexually active before moving into Heavenly Breakfast, the sex there created a different kind of atmosphere, because it was communal, a kind of constant sex party. As a result, he says he learned more about how to be "at ease" with his desire. Sex happened openly and safely in the commune, without state interference, whereas the other communal sexual settings Delany writes about in *The Motion of Light in Water* and *Times Square Red, Times Square Blue*, such as the docks or adult cinemas, always included an element of danger due to possible police surveillance. The sense of freedom created by Delany's feeling of ease manifests itself via the sexual openness of his subsequent writing. Most of the sexual

encounters in *Equinox* and *Hogg* either take place between two people with others watching or are examples of group sex, so a sense of community is present. Aside from his explicitly erotic novels, the depictions of sex in his post-commune SF are also much more explicit in comparison to those in his previous works.

As Delany's career continued to develop throughout the 1970s, he began branching into other genres, with his first book of literary theory, *The Jewel-Hinged Jaw* (1977), his first book of literary criticism, *The American Shore* (1978), and then *Heavenly Breakfast* and his first fantasy collection, *Tales of Nevèrÿon* (1979). His choice to explore these genres echoes the radical openness of the era's SF because it shows a refusal to be pigeonholed as a certain kind of writer. Therefore, Delany's later work contains an extension of the ideas in his earlier work rather than being a departure from it, despite his long break from publishing SF. Thus, *Heavenly Breakfast* is important to consider when examining his later work because of its role as a trendsetter for the latter part of his career.

Delany writes that after Heavenly Breakfast broke up it remained "part of many people's personal mythologies" throughout the Lower East Side, not only among those who were members. The way the commune lived on orally through people's stories before Delany chose to write about it shows that it made its neighborhood a better place while it existed, and that its vision of a better society struck a chord. The book also makes an argument for how to live. Delany dedicates the book to people "who ever did anything . . . to give themselves a better life" and so encourages taking chances and asserts that one should always be willing to fight for oneself. It does not necessarily argue that one must live in intentional community, but it advocates for the values of sharing, mutual care, sexual openness, kindness to strangers, and strength of collective action that Heavenly Breakfast epitomized.

**Daniel Shank Cruz**

# Flawed Ancients, New Gods, and Interstellar Missionaries: Religion in Postwar SF

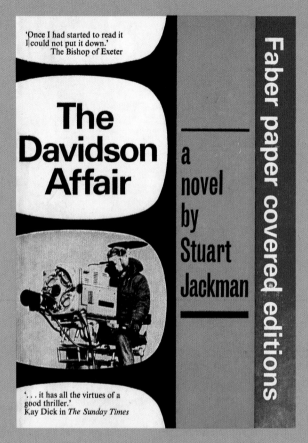

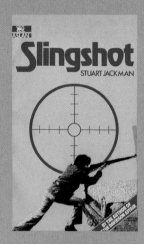

The question of how Jesus would be treated if he were to return to the contemporary world has long provoked theological and philosophical discussion, with generations of radicals drawing parallels between the treatment of Christ and themselves. In 1966, British novelist Stuart Jackman, whose handful of books are mainly military tales based on his own experiences in the Middle East during World War II, offered a new angle on the Easter story through the addition of television journalism. The combination of new technology and increasing public demand for ever faster coverage of topical and sensational incidents had led to saturation coverage of events such as the Vietnam War in the second half of the 1960s. These factors, as well as instances of journalistic independence and the period's overall undermining of authority, challenged the ability of state and corporate broadcasters, as well as military and political authorities, to mold public perceptions.

*The Davidson Affair* is narrated from the perspective of jaded correspondent Cass Tennel. Dispatched from Rome by the Imperial Television Company, he has been tasked with producing a report on the turmoil wracking Jerusalem. Rumors regarding the recent execution of the radical activist Jesus Davidson are swirling throughout the city, including claims that he has been spotted alive. All the principals are promptly tracked down and interviewed with the slick but bungling Pontius Pilate and other representatives of the church, state, and military delivering the official line on subversive criminals. Contacting Davidson's surviving followers, Tennel finds some in distress and disarray, convinced that the revolution is over, while others, such as Mary, remain unwilling to bow to the repressive hand of the Roman state. Initially dismissive of the importance of the events that have taken place in this remote corner of the empire, the narrator is shaken by the truth he eventually uncovers. However, due to editorial interference, official obfuscation, and public indifference, it is highly unlikely anyone else will ever grasp the full meaning of it.

Receiving favorable reviews, *The Davidson Affair* was adapted for a radio play by the BBC in 1967 and a one-hour television drama by its Canadian counterpart the following year. Widely discussed in Christian circles, the novel formed the basis of sermons and has endured in the form of theatrical performances. Two sequels, *The Burning Men* (1974) and *Slingshot* (1976), ensued, with the latter portraying Barabbas and his

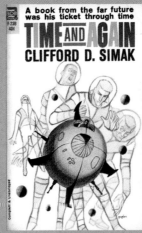

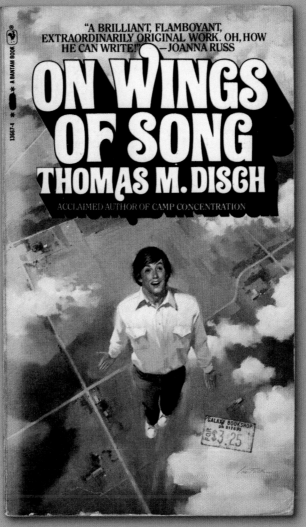

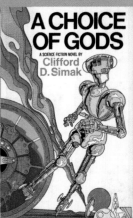

Clockwise from left: *The Davidson Affair* (Faber and Faber, 1966). *The Burning Men* (Lion Books, 1979). *Slingshot* (Lion Books, 1979). *The Long Tomorrow* (Ballantine, 1974). *Project Pope* (Ballantine, 1982). *Time and Again* (Ace, 1963). *Black Easter* (Penguin, 1972). *A Choice of Gods* (G.P. Putnam's Sons, 1972). *Time and Again* (Ace, 1972). *A Canticle for Leibowitz* (J.B. Lippincott, 1959). *A Case of Conscience* (Faber and Faber, 1959). *On Wings of Song* (Bantam, 1980).

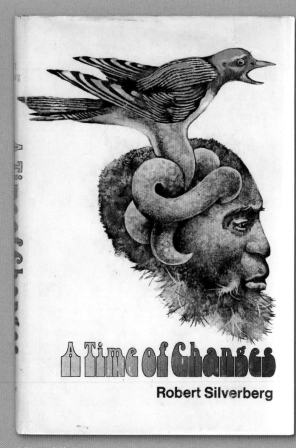
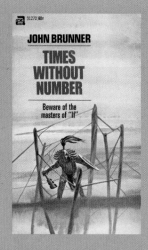

*A Time of Changes* (Doubleday, 1971). *Times Without Number* (Ace, 1969). *Cat's Cradle* (Holt, Rinehart and Winston, 1963). *The Long Tomorrow* (Doubleday, 1955). *The Sirens of Titan* (Dell, 1959).

fellow revolutionaries as urban guerrillas who launch an uprising armed with grenades, automatic weapons, and stolen armored personnel carriers.

Although their work was rarely taken up as enthusiastically by religious followers as Jackman's, the role of religion in society and growing challenges to it provided many opportunities for speculation, contemplation, and derision by radical and left-leaning science fiction writers in the postwar era. As with Jackman, a number, such as Michael Moorcock's *Behold the Man* (1969), provided new takes, via time travel and other tropes, on the events surrounding Christ's crucifixion. The potential role of Christianity in societies following nuclear Armageddon, either as an element of reconstruction or a force against technological progressivism, was taken up in Walter M. Miller's *A Canticle for Leibowitz* (1960) and Leigh Brackett's *The Long Tomorrow* (1955). The characteristic role of organized religion in colonization, control, and contact with other societies was explored in James Blish's *A Case of*

*Conscience* (1958), while he addressed Christianity's flip side through the ramifications of an arms dealer's pact with demonic forces in *Black Easter* (1968). Clifford Simak wrote a number of works dealing with forms of Christian religion, often incorporating critiques of technology, including *A Choice of Gods* (1972) and *Project Pope* (1982).

Beyond works explicitly dealing with existing religions were those that invented new forms, either for satirical purposes, such as in the work of Kurt Vonnegut Jr., or to reflect more seriously on topics such as fundamentalist intolerance. Others, including Roger Zelazny's *Creatures of Light and Darkness* (1969), explored potential changes in the development of humanity via mediations on future gods and demigods or as the result of alternate time-lines in which new religions, potentially more benign or more sinister, have arisen.

**Iain McIntyre**

# Speculative Fuckbooks

## The Brief Life of Essex House, 1968–1969

Erotic fiction and speculative fiction seem to be natural partners. After all, erotic fiction always has the potential to be speculative, to explore what might be if social barriers and taboos were not in place. And it has always been the business of speculative fiction—going all the way back to Mary Shelley's *Frankenstein* (1818) or even further to Margaret Cavendish's *The Blazing World* (1666)—to probe and play at the borders of the possible, including exploring uncharted territories of sexual experience. Yet the Golden Age of science fiction in retrospect seems not so much sexually repressed as artificially mired in perpetual adolescence. In his entry on "Sex" in *The Encyclopedia of Science Fiction*, Peter Nicholls characterizes the pulp era of SF as an overheated male fantasy of "BEMS [bug-eyed monsters] with lascivious expressions pursuing human women" in metal bikinis. Sexuality was both a threat—embodied by demonic Amazonian women and alien entities with vaguely suggested sexual prowess—and a never quite fulfilled promise of love and lust among the stars between strong-jawed men and gravity-defying women.

Sex began to enter the genre more seriously in the 1950s. Philip José Farmer's 1952 novella *The Lovers* is often cited as a formative example. Beacon Books began publishing "Galaxy Prize Selections," SF titles with erotic content. Several of the greatest tycoons of the erotica boom of the 1960s had science fiction backgrounds, and consequently the two genres have deeply intertwined (if often unacknowledged) roots. William Hamling (1921–2017) began his career publishing science fiction magazines. In 1955, he founded *Rogue*, a gentleman's magazine poised to compete with *Playboy*. The idea to launch a line of mass-market paperbacks was brought to him by SF writer Harlan Ellison, who had in turn been prompted by Robert Silverberg, a science fiction writer who also wrote erotica for various publishers under house pseudonyms. Hamling launched the most successful line of erotic paperbacks, Greenleaf Classics, which, with an astonishing array of imprints (Nightstand

Brian Kirby, 1985 (courtesy of Paul Hunt, www.bookstorememories.com).

Milton Luros, California, 1963 (courtesy of David Saunders, www.pulpartists.com).

Books, Beside Books, Regency Books, Ember Books, Pillar Books, etc.) published about 4,300 books from 1959 to 1975. Although a number of science fiction authors, including Robert Silverberg, Marion Zimmer Bradley, Avram Davidson, and William F. Knoles wrote erotica, little of it was speculative in nature. While SF and erotic fiction were connected by publishers and practitioners and also, in many cases, by a shared audience, there was surprisingly little speculative content in what were increasingly beginning to be known as fuckbooks—that is, books that were meant to be read one-handed.

Enter Milton Luros and Brian Kirby.

Milton Luros (1911–1999) began his career as a cover artist for a wide variety of pulps, including such SF titles as *Astonishing Stories* and *Science Fiction Quarterly*. As the pulp market shrank, his shrewd business sense allowed him to survive and thrive in an ever-changing climate by adapting to new types of publication as fast as they arose and died. After drawing comics, running his own art agency, designing posters for Universal Studios, and publishing a men's magazine called *Cocktail*, which was distributed through liquor stores, he founded what was soon to become a publishing empire, Parliament News Distributors, Inc., located in North Hollywood, California, and specializing in nudist and erotic publications. In 1966, he began a line called Brandon House Library Editions, specializing in reprints of erotic classics, European erotica, and new editions of Paris Olympia Press titles. Printed on high-quality papers, with covers reproducing works by artists like Rops, Labisse, and Munch, Brandon House promised pornography for the discerning literary reader.

As editor for the Brandon House books, Luros chose Brian Kirby. Kirby was a drummer from Detroit who came to Los Angeles in the late 1960s to check out the music scene. He began working at W.L.A. Book Center, a secondhand bookshop run by Ken Hyre, and started learning the book trade and making connections that would eventually lead him to become an editor for Luros and, later, of the *Los Angeles Free Press*, one of the largest and most effective underground newspapers in the country. Michael Perkins, poet and editor of the underground literary magazine *Down Here*, suggested that Kirby might start a new line focusing on erotic novels by up-and-coming American poets and writers. Perkins wrote *Blue Movie*, a satirical and relatively lighthearted romp through the seedy sexual mores of the film industry, and it became the first Essex House title.

Under Kirby's editorship, Essex House published forty-two titles in 1968 and 1969. Like the Brandon House Library Editions, they were printed on high-quality paper with artistic covers—sometimes reproductions of modern or surrealist art and sometimes original psychedelic art. Each book opened with a page that read, "This is an original Essex House book—the very finest in adult reading by the most provocative modern writers." Many contained postscripts by noted authors, including Harlan Ellison and Theodore Sturgeon, which placed them in a high literary context. The cover price was $1.95. Olympia Press titles of this era were also priced at $1.95. Greenleaf classics were $1.50, but other Greenleaf imprints, such as Nightstand Books and Companion Books, printed on much cheaper paper, were only $0.95, which made them competitive with mainstream publishers of non-erotic content, such as Dell, Ace, and Pocket Books. The look, heft, quality printing, and price point of the Essex House imprint immediately telegraphed to a potential consumer that they were meant to be taken seriously; these were not smudged, poorly-printed strokebooks meant to be used and discarded but books meant to be read, discussed, and collected. According to Norman Spinrad in a piece in issue 194 of *New Worlds* magazine in 1969, Kirby's principle for both Brandon House

and Essex House was that "there's no reason why good literature shouldn't give you a hard-on"—and no reason why a book that gives you a hard-on can't be good literature. To encourage quality content, Kirby would not allow Essex House authors to hide behind pseudonyms.

Over half of Essex House's output was speculative fiction, some by well-known writers in the genre and some by authors who had previously written no SF. The best known—and most collectible—of Essex House's non-SF titles is Charles Bukowski's *Notes of a Dirty Old Man* (1969), a collection of the columns the author wrote for the LA underground newspaper *Open City*. The gamut of Essex House is best described by Michael Perkins, himself an Essex House author of eight novels, who gave the fullest published version of the imprint's history in *The Secret Record: Modern Erotic Literature* (1976):

> Essex House published rather conventionally written novels on psychosexual themes, as well as fairly experimental fantasies, memoirs, short stories, comic novels, erotic science fiction novels, and a variety of other hybrids. The one characteristic shared by most of these novelists was a political orientation that revealed a determination to explore America's secret life. Directly or indirectly, the Essex House novelist is interested in dissecting his or her society in order to examine its forbidden organs for signs of disease.

SF author Norman Spinrad, who has also published reflections on Essex House, describes the Essex House novels as "anti-erotic in effect: they do not cause sexual arousal they explore the nature of sexual arousal, and expose unsavory linkages between sexual arousal and death, the inflicting and receiving of pain."

The output of David Meltzer, including the *Agency* trilogy and the *Brain-Plant* tetralogy, best represent the genre of SF—Speculative Fuckbooks—that was struggling to be born: cynical yet earnest, darkly humorous but deeply unsettling, excruciatingly pretentious yet not without charm and even moments of whimsey. Meltzer was already a well-established and highly regarded poet and musician in the Beat scene but had published no novels when he wrote *The Agency* (1968), the second novel published by Essex House and the first to fulfil Kirby's hopes that many of the imprint's output be written by poets. Meltzer was not, however,

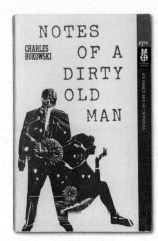

Notes of a Dirty Old Man
(Essex House, 1969)

The Agency (Essex House, 1968)

The Agent (Essex House, 1968)

How Many Blocks in the Pile
(Essex House, 1968)

without a SF pedigree. He grew up reading SF pulps such as *Astounding* and *Galaxy*, as well as writers like H.G. Wells, Robert Heinlein, and Theodore Sturgeon, and kept abreast of SF publishing in the 1960s.

In the afterword to *The Agency* Meltzer describes his trilogy as "fierce moral tracts." The trilogy tells the story of an unnamed young man who is taken for a ride in a black Cadillac sedan into the heart of the Agency, a secret organization that rules the world. The first book of the trilogy ends with the protagonist riding in the Cadillac again, preparing to pick up an innocent young girl. In the next book, *The Agent* (1968), readers are introduced to two agents, the straight-laced white and the hardboiled black, who are at odds on the surface but may be working toward the same goal of creating a totalitarian system of sexual repression both fueled and relieved by clandestine degenerate and dehumanizing sexual fulfillment. In 1978, in a piece titled "Essex House: The Rise and Fall of Speculative Erotica," in issue 14 of *Foundation* magazine, Maxim Jakubowski describes it as "a kind of Nova Express-cum-Ian Fleming." Indeed, Meltzer's Essex House output most closely resembles the protoplasmic porridge of William S. Burroughs's novels, though Meltzer claims that at the time he had not yet read Burroughs. The final book in the trilogy, *How Many Blocks in the Pile?* (1968) follows a group of characters brought together by a mail-order company promising unlimited sexual gratification. They end up bringing on the apocalypse with a superbomb hidden in a chrome dildo.

The *Brain-Plant* tetralogy (1969), consisting of *Lovely*, *Healer*, *Out*, and *Glue Factory*, is an even

more ambitious undertaking and perhaps the crowning achievement of the Speculative Fuckbook. The narrative is fragmented and chaotic, told in fits and starts by a wide array of characters in an impressive range of invented futuristic dialects: dull cogs in the military-industrial machine; members of the "Rads," the hippies of the future; the "Rebs," lower middle-class whites whose dialogue today seems presciently Trumpian; "Snarks" or sex-anarks, a sexual liberation focused subgroup of the Rads, and black militants, who have televised showdowns with the Rebs. *Lovely* focuses on Arthur Goldwheel, a rather feeble poet and sometime jingle-writer searching for his lost love in an insane world. *Healer* introduces medicine man Walker and Laura Golden Eyes, who has been left sexually unresponsive from the trauma of a previous life and is seeking healing. *Out* further explores the complexities of "Military Industry/Christian America," and bears some resemblance to *The Agency* in plot. The final book brings all the characters together and introduces God, who in the concluding scene is depicted fucking himself.

One of the most inventive aspects of the novels are the "Fun Zones," immersive entertainment centers that are like Disneyland designed by cartoonist Robert Crumb on crack. They replace all social services—welfare, Medicare, unemployment benefits, social security, museums, libraries, and parks—with erotic playgrounds to which obedient citizens can earn passes.

An exhaustive array of new drugs, new slang, and new technology (synthetic wombs for gay men!) bombard the reader from every page.

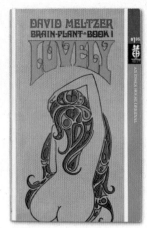

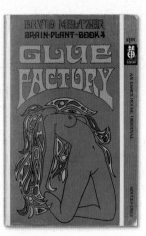

*Lovely* (Essex House, 1969)  *Healer* (Essex House, 1969)  *Out* (Essex House, 1969)  *Glue Factory* (Essex House, 1969)

The plots of these novels, to the extent that they even have plots, are impossible to summarize; as the narrative unwinds into a slurry of sexualized violence—a human "glue factory"—the reader is left with the feeling that there is simply *too much* to endure any longer. The narrative is drenched with a sense of the exhaustion of a seemingly endless and pointless war, the futility and absurdity of ever-increasing racism and related violence, and the possibility that we as a species may have simply gone as far as we can go in pursuing sexual experience. Unlike conventional erotic narratives, which build to a satisfying release (or sequence of increasingly satisfying releases), these books are orgiastic overload, and the reader feels trapped in a machine that is fucking them to death, which seems to be Meltzer's overarching metaphor for the state of America in 1969. It is a nation on the verge of a nervous breakdown, and consequently the books feel terrifyingly relevant today. A larger-than-life pussy-grabbing reality television president would be perfectly at home as a character in a world in which the Fun Zones distract an increasingly fragmented, hateful, bored, paranoid, and resource-impoverished populace from the systems that oppress them. In *Lovely*, Meltzer writes:

> The distracted consumer is the most vulnerable. Basic axiom. In times of social crisis, and these are times of such chaos, it's our job to create and develop new images, new products. The citizens, Rad or taxpayer, must have new fun.

Meltzer's Essex House output is a unique blend of a poet's sensibility with a lifetime fascination with SF and the newly blown open doors of freedom provided by pornographic publishing at this precise moment

in history. Whether the result is viewed as a mind-blowing, illuminating, revolutionary dream-vision (an interpretation put forth by Michael Perkins and Maxim Jakubowski in their writings on Essex House), or as a joylessly pretentious and mind-numbing tour of needlessly weird sucking and fucking (the probable response of an average SF fan today) is up to the tastes of the individual reader.

The Essex House author with the biggest established name in SF was Philip José Farmer. His three Essex House titles stand in stark contrast to Meltzer's brand of angry, psychedelic, and radical SF. Farmer's novels are playful, contain more conventional sex scenes, though they are still more likely to be inflected by weirdness and violence than standard erotic fare, and are deeply rooted in genre fiction, to the point where they often reference the works of other authors and even include Forrest J. Ackerman—legendary SF collector, editor, and self-appointed benevolent (if slightly skeevy) uncle to the entire community of Monster Kids of all ages—as a main character.

Farmer's first two Essex House novels, *The Image of the Beast* (1968) and *Blown* (1968), are by far the best-known of Essex House's outputs, as they have been reprinted several times, including by Quartet in the UK and Playboy in the US. They are a pornographic parody of the hardboiled detective novel, set in Los Angeles and centered around a private detective (who may or may not be a reincarnation of Lord Byron) named Herald Childe. *The Image of the Beast* opens with Childe watching a snuff film of his former partner being murdered . . . but it's no ordinary murder. A seductive vampire woman performs oral sex on him, places a set of iron teeth in her mouth, and bites off his penis at the moment of climax. She is later revealed to have a man-headed snake living inside of her vagina. Childe's sexual adventures take him through an LA populated by werewolves, vampires, succubi, and other monsters, all of whom are eager to have their way with him.

Farmer's third Essex House book, *A Feast Unknown* (1969), is the first of a series of novels about Tarzan and Doc Savage. It is essentially an extended piece of fan fiction in which the two characters, renamed Doc Caliban and Lord Grandrith, are the bastard sons of Jack the Ripper. Farmer fulfils his boyish dream to see the characters fight—which they, of course, do with raging hard-ons. All of Farmer's Essex House novels fit into his career-long obsession with including sex in SF and also with creating a massive multiverse of stories and characters that tie in to and borrow from the entire history of speculative fiction (his Riverworld novels being the ultimate expression of this desire to merge his works with his literary idols). His Essex House SF is playful and far more accessible to the typical SF fan of the late 1960s than the imprint's more challenging works.

Also of note is the fact that Essex House published several notable SF works by women authors. Jane Gallion's *Biker* (1969) is a gonzo postapocalyptic tale set in a California ruled by biker gangs, rapists, and drug cults. It is a tale of hippie culture gone sour and one woman's journey from victim to toughened survivor. Gallion also wrote *Stoned* (1969) for Essex House, which

did not contain any speculative elements but which depicts a middle-class suburban couple's flirtation with drugs, swinging, and the counterculture. Both of Gallion's books contain strong feminist elements and offer a welcome change in perspective from the male fantasies and fears evoked by Essex House's other authors. Gallion was also an editor at Essex House and Brandon House from 1968 to 1971.

Alice Louise Ramirez's *The Geek* (1969) is told from the point of view of a sexually frustrated pink rooster who is aroused but not fulfilled by being repeatedly swallowed and regurgitated by the carnival Geek. The reader is treated to the outrageous silliness of human sexuality from the point of view of an animal. The novel opens with the rooster interfering with the slapstick sexual antics of the circus Fat Lady and Dwarf, and eventually the action moves to an island in the Pacific populated by nudist sadomasochistic lesbians. *The Geek* is raucous, bawdy, and quite fun compared to most of Essex House's rather dark output. The author herself wrote a review of *The Geek* on Amazon.com in which she shares her memories of writing it:

A late-stage teenager, freshly-landed in LaLa Land from icky Toledo by way of New Orleans, I fell in by accident with pillars of the local Fandom (Sci-Fi and fantasy types), some of whom were professional writers. There was pornographer Hank, who—after an intense personal transformation—became Jean. Harlan, was a cocky little

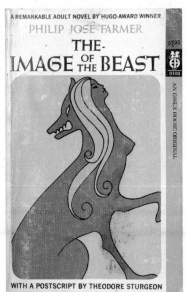

*The Image of the Beast* (Essex House, 1968)

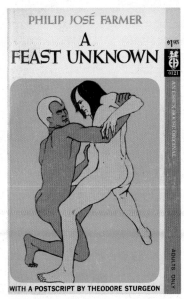

*A Feast Unknown* (Essex House, 1969)

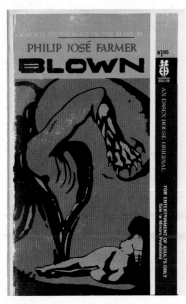

*Blown* (Essex House, 1968)

putz who wrote brilliant Sci-Fi novels and was unbelievably arrogant…. "The Geek" was born at a 1969 pot party. Everybody had tried to come up with the most outrageous plot/premise for the Editor-in-Chief of a porn publishing house that had pretentions of becoming the West Coast's version of Olympia Press.

She also notes that she was paid $1,000 for writing the novel, which was a generous sum for smut writers of the time. Ramirez also wrote a novel about necrophilia, *Naked in Her Coffin* (1970), for Brandon House under the name Tiny Alice and numerous Gothic supernatural romances under the name Candace Arkham.

Perhaps the most interesting woman writing for Essex House was Jean Marie Stine, a transgender woman who was at the time still writing under the name Hank Stine, a variant of her then legal name. Her first novel, *Season of the Witch* (1968), deserves far more critical attention as one of the first significant forays into transgender SF. The pulp era displays a remarkable dearth of stories that even suggest the possibility that an individual might come to live their life as a gender different from the one assigned at birth. *Season of the Witch* opens with the protagonist, Andre Fuller, taking a variety of drugs with a female lover, Josette Kovacks. Something goes horribly wrong as they are making love and Fuller is convicted of raping and murdering Josette. In the California penal system of Stine's future, human lives are too precious for death to be his punishment. Consequently, his male body will be given to a more important man whose own body is failing, and his consciousness will be transferred into the dead body of the woman whose life he took.

The rest of the book deals with Fuller's struggles to accept her new female body. She is horrified at the thought of sleeping with men but eventually must do so to earn money. She begins searching for her former male body, and the narrative takes her through a series of sexual encounters and initiation into a weird love cult by which she eventually comes to not only accept but embrace her female identity. By the end of the novel, she has changed her name to Celeste and is married and pregnant. The final scene depicts heated lovemaking with her husband; it is one of the few Essex House novels with a happy ending.

*Season of the Witch* is, along with the *Brain-Plant* tetralogy, among the most interesting of the Essex

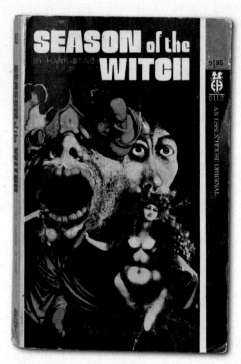

*Season of the Witch* (Essex House, 1968)

House output. It was highly praised by Harlan Ellison, who provided an afterword comparing Stine to the great mad geniuses of history. Ellison did not see it for what it was—a compelling attempt to work through the author's transgender identity using the mediums of both speculative fiction and pornography. Ellison did not have the words, and Stine probably did not either at that time, but the book remains as a seminal text in the history of trans SF.

Brandon House and Essex House were made possible by the landmark 1966 Supreme Court case *Memoirs v. Massachusetts*, addressing *Memoirs of a Woman of Pleasure* (aka *Fanny Hill*). This was the decision that determined that materials could not be deemed obscene unless they were "utterly without redeeming social value." The importance of this decision cannot be overstated; as Stephen J. Gertz notes in his essay in the 2004 book *Sin-A-Rama: Sleaze Sex Paperbacks of the Sixties*, it led to "nothing less than the democratization of reading in this country, for this kind of literature had previously been almost exclusively available to the wealthy or well-connected only, printed in small editions and generally cost-prohibitive to the average citizen." With their quality paper, artistic covers designed by Kirby, incisive social criticism, and lofty literary afterwords, Essex House books delivered on the promise of porn with redeeming social value.

The *Fanny Hill* case was followed by another landmark decision, *Redrup v. New York*, in May 1967. In 1965, Robert Redrup, a Times Square newsstand clerk, was tried and convicted for selling two erotic novels, *Lust Pool* and *Shame Agent*, both published in 1964 by imprints of William Hamling's Greenleaf Classics. Hamling's stalwart First Amendment lawyer Stanley Fleishman, who Hamling consulted so frequently that he provided him with an office in the San Fernando Valley porn compound owned by Milt Luros, took on the case and brought it to a successful conclusion. Justice Potter Stewart's decision stated, "A book worthless to me may convey something of value to my neighbor. In the free society to which our Constitution has committed us, it is for each of us to choose for ourselves." The floodgates were opened. Consenting adults were free to acquire and read any publication they wished, including admittedly obscene material, and, following this decision, the Supreme Court began overturning ("Redruping") previous obscenity convictions that reached it.

The very court cases that allowed Essex House to exist also contributed to its demise. The market was flooded with competition, and there was no longer any reason to hold back. Greenleaf soon changed from bright painted covers to cheaper to produce and more explicit but less interesting line drawings. Euphemisms gave way to hardcore language. Kenneth R. Johnson describes this shift in the introduction to his online bibliography of pornographic SF:

> With the freedom to distribute and sell outright pornography, the "adult" bookstore came into full flower. As a result the erotic paperback was consigned not only to a literary but a physical ghetto. The outpouring of sexually explicit and vulgar counter-culture books was not distributed to the artsy-fartsy poetry shops (or college bookstores) as expected but instead went straight to the adult bookstores where they died on the racks. The audience that these books were aimed at was primarily left-wing college-age radicals. . . . The regular clientele of adult bookstores are usually right-wing conservatives (truck drivers, salesmen, servicemen) who know that pornography is bad and are getting their kicks by doing something forbidden; they are rarely the audience for surrealistic drug-oriented literature. For Essex House and Olympia Press this was a costly lesson indeed.

Essex House ceased publishing on December 29, 1969, after issuing forty-two titles, and Brian Kirby was fired. Michael Perkins gives an account of the imprint's demise in his "Fuck Books" column in the March 1, 1970, issue of *Screw*. He blames "the incredible, naive, unknowledgeable, high-schoolish stupidity of Americans, who are sex-crazy, genuinely *sex-crazed*, but who are so embarrassed about it that they need it covered up with hardcover respectability (Jacqueline Susann, Philip Roth), or with sheer *schlock*." Perkins has a point here. This is the cultural moment at which Jacqueline Susann and Harold Robbins were publishing erotica that was respectable enough to be issued in hardcover and sold in mainstream bookstores. But what Perkins calls "schlock" was a much bigger threat. After Redrup, there was no longer any need to omit four-letter words or couch sex scenes within even a thin tissue of plot. Now publishers could churn out cheaply-produced fuckbooks that strung together hardcore scenes with little logic. There was no reason to pretend to redeeming value anymore. Perkins notes that the first Essex House book, his own *Blue Movie*, sold a very respectable thirty-five thousand copies. Other Essex House titles sold between seven and twenty thousand copies. While this is much lower than smut factory Midwood's seventy-five thousand per title output in 1969, it was by no means dire. These moderate sales, however, were balanced against the high cost of production: "Sales were bad, the moneymen said; the stuff was 'too arty.' Printing beautiful covers and paying authors something cost too much. The suckers would buy anything, anyway." Perkins also blames the changes in distribution networks: "*Blue Movie* was on every newsstand, so naturally it sold. My last book, the fortieth in the EH series, couldn't have been found by a bibliomaniac using his prick as a dousing wand on Times Square at high noon." In many regards, Essex House was a victim of the new publishing freedoms accorded by *Fanny Hill* and Redrup. It was too niche to survive in a newly open marketplace.

And so Essex House went out with a whimper. A number of books planned for the imprint were eventually published elsewhere. Kirby's replacement at Brandon House, Larry Saw, who had edited the SF magazines *If* and *Infinity* in the 1950s, slotted some SF titles into the Brandon House line, including Philip José Farmer's *Love Song* (1970), David Meltzer's *Star* (1970), and Richard E. Geis's *The Arena Women* (1972). A publicity leaflet for Essex House announced new titles by Harlan Ellison, Charles Platt, and Theodore Sturgeon. It is unclear whether Ellison ever wrote anything for Essex House, but Charles Platt's *The Gas* was published by Ophelia Press in 1970 and Theodore Sturgeon's *Godbody* was published posthumously in 1986.

Essex House and Sturgeon's involvement with it also had a lasting impact in the creation of Kurt Vonnegut Jr.'s character Kilgore Trout, the struggling science fiction writer who can only find outlets for his work in pornographic publications. Trout's character was based largely on Sturgeon, and Essex House regular Philip José Farmer produced a novel under the Trout pen name. Other novels intended for Essex House include Samuel R. Delany's *Equinox* (published by Lancer Books in 1973 as *The Tides of Lust*) and Piers Anthony's *3.97 Erect* (published by Tafford Publishing in 1989 as *Pornucopia*, easily winning the award as the most awful piece of writing to be associated with Essex House in any way).

Other publishers limped along a bit longer. Maurice Girodias's Olympia Press, founded in Paris 1953 and brought to the United States in the early 1960s, continued selling books at the same $1.95 price point as Essex House before folding in 1974. SF titles included: *Satyr Trek* by Ray Kainen (1970), a parody of *Star Trek*; *The Love Machine* by Karl Flinders (1971) about the invention of a mattress that provides men and women who lie on it with untold sexual pleasure and then kills them; and *High Thrust* by Renee Auden (1971) about the single girl of the future and her army of sex-bots. In line with the press's output as a whole, Olympia's SF erotica has a more humorous and optimistic bent than that of Essex House.

Other publishers, such as Beeline's Orpheus imprint, continued to dribble out small bits of SF smut, but, for the most part, sex moved securely into the mainstream of SF publishing. Authors associated with Essex House, including Farmer, Sturgeon, and Delany published major works that included many forms of sexuality, be it rather juvenile efforts to allow a stand-in for the author to fuck famous literary characters from history (Farmer) or sophisticated explorations of taboo topics like bondage, slavery, and interracial gay relationships (Delany). Feminist writers such as Joanna Russ and Ursula K. Le Guin broke into the mainstream, challenging gender norms and expectations. Angela Carter's *The Passion of New Eve* (1977) bears many similarities to Stine's *Season of the Witch*, and novels with

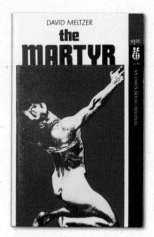 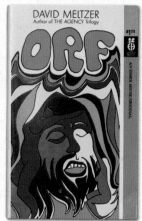

*The Martyr* (Essex House, 1969)     *Orf* (Essex House, 1968)

major publishers, such as J.G. Ballard's *Crash* (1973) and Dean Koontz's *Demon Seed* (1973), would have fit right into the Essex House lineup. In 1973, two anthologies devoted to sex in SF were published: *Strange Bedfellows*, edited by Thomas N. Scortia (Random House; reprinted by Pocket Books in 1974), and *Eros in Orbit*, edited by Joseph Elder (Trident; reprinted by Pocket Books in 1974). Both collections demonstrate the impact of Essex House in that they favor the kind of grim dystopian visions of future sex that flourished in the imprint's books.

The type of book offered by Essex House remains elusive. In a recent essay for *Weird Fiction Review*, Adam Groves terms this kind of fiction "weird erotica" and describes it as containing "psychosexual grotesquerie, David Cronenbergian biological mutation, gender swapping, and an imaginative fecundity that by today's standards would be deemed politically incorrect." While Groves describes a number of these kinds of texts that postdate Essex House, no other publisher has blended literary pretension, social criticism, pornography, and speculation in quite the same way, and no publisher has achieved what Essex House strived for—to produce aesthetically interesting, high-quality fuckbooks that readers could be proud to display on their shelves.

**Rebecca Baumann**

# God Does, Perhaps?

## The Unlikely New Wave SF of R.A. Lafferty

In June 1968, two sets of science fiction writers placed ads in *Galaxy Magazine*, stating their positions on the US war in Vietnam. On the verso was a list of authors who believed that the "United States must remain in Vietnam to fulfill its responsibilities to the people of that country." Signatories included rock-ribbed science fiction writers like Robert A. Heinlein, Larry Niven, and Hal Clement—crypto-fascist editor John W. Campbell and fantasist Marion Zimmer Bradley also signed on. On the recto, opposing the involvement of the US in Vietnam were some of the leading lights of the New Wave: Ursula K. Le Guin, Samuel R. Delany, and Harlan Ellison.

R.A. Lafferty

There wasn't just a political split in the world of science fiction but also an aesthetic one. Imperialist rationalism and simple declarative sentences versus leftist skepticism and literary experimentation, and not just in the magazine's editorial content.

Then there was Raphael Aloysius Lafferty, the eventual author of thirty-six novels and nearly three hundred short pieces, only some of which were science fiction.

A hard right-wing Catholic who took up writing in middle-age to take the place of "drinking and fooling around," as he put it, and who also took communion daily at Christ the King Catholic Church in Tulsa, Oklahoma, Lafferty joined the pro-war bloc, of course. He even had the classic bona fides of the hard SF writer, as he was an electrical engineer by trade. But his science fiction wasn't hard; it was *difficult*. His writing, phantasmagorical and overstuffed with both aesthetic tricks and historical/philosophical/religious references, was rightly championed by the New Wave.

Lafferty was part of the New Wave simply as a matter of cosmic coincidence. His writing was utterly unique—Theodore Sturgeon said that literary critics of the future would create the taxon of "lafferties" for the author's work. Lafferty didn't just write SF; he

published in literary journals and submitted work to men's adventure pulps and mystery magazines. For the most part, his stories were simply too weird for either the literary or popular tributaries of the "mainstream," but flowed nicely into science fiction.

Unlike other stalwarts of the New Wave, such as Samuel R. Delany who had read Heinlein and other major SF writers as a child, or Harlan Ellison, who was part of organized science fiction fandom, Lafferty never read the stuff until after he started selling to the leading magazines of the time. In a 1991 interview with the fanzine *Lan's Lantern*, he admitted:

> I never did read very much except for a four month period when I read several hundred of what were supposed to be the best science fiction books ever. This was when I first decided to major in science fiction, as it was selling for me and other things weren't. Well, it was a good crash course, and I was glad that I absorbed it.

Lafferty innovated more than he absorbed, however. Even throwaway lines in minor stories—as dexterous as they are off-kilter—are suffused with an insane humor and philosophical insight. As Matt Keeley put it in a 2019 *Los Angeles Review of Books* review:

> The Lafferty style challenges the reader. Lafferty does not commit the classic science fiction sins of jargon or infodumping, nor does his prose grate with words plucked at random from a thesaurus. Rather, his writing is so colloquial, full of rhetorical questions, expository speech, and tall-tale superlatives, that it might be mistaken for mere patter.

For example, in the 1976 short story "Fog in My Throat" we learn that the fear of death encapsulates every type of horror. We're told by one of the characters, who has heard about death fears from his psychologist:

Form-change horror is part of the death-fear. This is the frightfulness of common persons and creatures turning into monsters and snakes and ravening animals. It is the dread of what we may see when our temporary flesh-masks are gone. And yet all these are the more pleasant of the fearful alternatives: and the least pleasant alternative is to change into nothing.

Lafferty broke all the rules of mid-twentieth-century genre fiction writing, and he broke them differently from the rest of the New Wave. Nearly all his characters speak in the same dizzying and circuitous way. Rather than writing about superhumans, or at least supergeniuses, using logic and reason to resolve some scientific conundrums, his protagonists were often disordered somehow, or even simpletons. His Hugo Award–winning short story "Eurema's Dam" (written in 1964; published in 1972 in the Robert Silverberg–edited anthology *New Dimensions II*), which Lafferty himself considered only the fourth- or fifth-best of his output, is about Albert, an amazingly inventive "dolt" who will perhaps be the last unintelligent person to ever live. For example, Albert had trouble telling his left from his right:

> It had to do with the way dogs turn around before lying down, the direction of whirlpools and whirlwinds, the side a cow is milked from and a horse is mounted from, the direction of twist of oak and sycamore leaves, the maze patterns of rock moss and tree moss, the cleavage of limestone, the direction of a hawk's wheeling, a shrike's hunting, and a snake's coiling (remembering that the Mountain Boomer is an exception), the lay of cedar fronds and balsam fronds, the twist of a hole dug by a skunk and by a badger (remembering pungently that skunks sometimes use old badger holes). Well, Albert finally learned to remember which was right and which was left, but an observant boy would have learned his right hand from his left without all that nonsense.

"All that nonsense" is a good summary of Lafferty's own writing, though the work isn't designed to subvert the narrative and aesthetic standards of SF but, rather, to articulate a divine order and the challenges to it. These days, it is not unusual for the oddest of science fiction, the stuff with themes not necessarily intrinsic

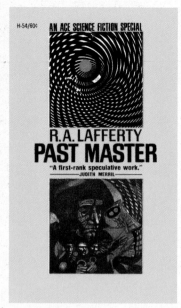

Nine Hundred Grandmothers (Ace, 1970)

*Past Master* (Ace, 1968)

Arrive at Easterwine (Charles Scribner's Sons, 1971)

to SF's ideological hardcore—for example the work of Jeff VanderMeer—to cross over and become a mainstream bestseller. It transcends the genre, as somewhat embarrassed newspaper critics like to say. Nothing of the sort ever happened with Lafferty. "No, I don't think I should be getting more attention from mainstream book reviewers," he told *Lan's Lantern*. "I've never written any mainstream books, and I'm always surprised when the mainstreamers notice me at all."

Lafferty is a genre of one and that one is based on an idiosyncratic and fundamentally disordered vision of God. In his work, there isn't even the sometimes late moment of recognition one might get from reading Tolkien or Lewis's Narnia books; Lafferty's mystic Catholicism isn't subtext; it's text. As David Randall of the Benedictine Institute wrote in 2018, "The world may dub it science fiction, but Lafferty wasn't really a science fiction writer. He was a speculative metaphysical novelist, or a lay preacher, or a sacred historian with plausible *argumenta* stuck in. He dressed all that up in science fiction and it sold."

In 1968's *Past Master*, Lafferty's most famous novel, the utopia of Astrobe has a problem—nobody wants to live there. The residents would rather struggle and die in the disgusting slums of nearby Cathead. The corrupt powers that be decide to pluck Catholic saint and famed utopian Thomas More out of time and put him to work to resolve the issue. Those who remain in Astrobe often elect to commit suicide while still in the prime of their lives; perfection cultivates boredom and contempt for life. Astrobe is reminiscent of More's satirical *Utopia*; at first even More himself is tempted by life in Astrobe and is repulsed by Cathead and the nearby Barrio, another collapsing dystopia. He and some allies are bedeviled by "Programmed Killers" and mechanical menaces—Lafferty explicitly eschews terms such as "robot," "android," etc.—and there's a fair amount of rollicking action. When More and party encounter the recently created emperor Charles the Six Hundred and Twelfth (the unfortunate Charles DCXI having run afoul of the Programmed Killers a month prior), the boy-king, who has some primitive psychic and perceptive abilities despite being a dunce—a common Lafferty trope—senses something amiss and dangerous:

> "I am the emperor and I know these things," the boyish Emperor Charles the Six Hundred and Twelfth maintained to the party. "The Scrivener is a machine. And he will lodge in the machine shed. Let us not make a great noise over a little thing. It is only that definitions have lost their precision on Astrobe; and one duty of the Salic Emperor is to clarify and enforce them."

It is no surprise to any science fiction reader that the central conundrum of Astrobe is that one must figuratively sell one's soul to live there. No ideologies other than materialism are allowed and, of course, thought criminals are oppressed or exterminated. What makes Lafferty's vision of utopia as dystopia different is not the content but the delivery. Thomas More is offered rulership of Astrobe but declines, noting that in secret corners of the society there are still believers, and even, after a fashion, a pope. Then the Programmed execute that poor old pope with just one hundred followers. More objects and is then taken prisoner and granted a requested last meal. More explains:

> I told them I wanted to dine on the brains of my enemies, on Programmed People brains. They brought me this. It's a chemical and magnetic mishmash of polarized memory gelatin. I suppose it is an element, the non-human element, of Programmed People's brains. Dawn-world people ate their enemies' brains and acquired wit and strength from them. But

AN ACE SCIENCE FICTION SPECIAL   24590 | 75¢

**FOURTH MANSIONS by R.A. LAFFERTY**

*Fourth Mansions* (Ace, 1969)

> I doubt if I'll acquire any wit, and certainly not any humor, from this bowl of the brains of mine enemy. The stuff isn't very good, but people and Things on Astrobe do take what you say literally.

Lafferty takes things literally himself, and seriously, but cultivates an atmosphere of the unserious and absurd unparalleled in SF. As Neil Gaiman, a fan of Lafferty since the age of nine, told the *Guardian* in 2014, "There's nothing close to Lafferty—nobody with the gravitas about things that were light, and the anti-gravitas about important heavy things." For all that, *Past Master* is still recognizably SF. The theme of a utopia that is corrupt is a well-worn one, as is time travel, appearances by historical personages, and the theme of the mechanical overwhelming the individual and the spiritual. It ends on a hopeful note, as is science fiction's usual remit. More's martyrdom calls down the

Holy Spirit among some of the Programmed. Lafferty writes, "The spirit came down once on water and clay. Could it not come down on gell-cells and flux-fix? The sterile wood, whether of human or programmed tree, shall it fruit after all?"

Lafferty's greatest novel, the Nebula Award–nominee *Fourth Mansions* (1969), however, is not recognizably anything other than a work that only Lafferty could write. Inspired loosely by 1588's *The Interior Castle* by Saint Theresa of Ávila, itself an incredibly esoteric work about mystical communion with God, *Fourth Mansions* is about a journalist with a low IQ, Fred Foley, who uncovers a conspiracy by seven superior beings with psychic abilities—these seven Harvesters are further along in their psychic development than mere humans and have a plan for the world. The word *about* in the previous sentence should be captured in scare quotes, like so: "about." *Fourth Mansions* is actually about something else entirely, it is about many, many things. At first, it is extremely readable, feeling something like a Marx Brothers film. Foley isn't doing too well, as he believes he has discovered that a man named Carmody is actually several hundred years old and tells as much to his editor:

> "Ah, why don't you take off the rest of the day and get drunk, Foley?"
>
> "I did that Monday on your advice. I'd still rather have followed up *that* case."
>
> "Well, it was better than having you go off quarter-cocked on the Knoll story. That would really have gotten us laughed out of town. And this thing now, drop it! No more Carmody stuff. No more stuff of men who live for centuries or who live more than once. Try one more bender for my sake now, and I hope to see you tomorrow morning, red-eyed and trembling, with your, ah, sanity restored, and ready for work. Get out of here now."
>
> "Yes sir," Freddy Foley said, and he got out.

Foley soon ends up in the psychic weave of the seven conspirators, making contact with a man named Michael Fountain, whom he insists on calling Miguel. He learns from Bertigrew Bagley—who is part of a secret society that call themselves "patricks"—of the four major types of antagonists that surround the interior castle: pythons, toads, badgers, and unfledged falcons. The Harvesters are pythons, Carmody a toad with the jewel of knowledge, the patricks and related secret societies are badgers, and the "firm and doltish authority" of the crusades and the fascists are the falcons.

If one has the thought that reading *The Interior Castle* will be a key of sorts to *Fourth Mansions*, abandon it. As Michael Fountain, after many more events, later explains, "These four symbols are not proper symbols for modern men. They were symbols used by animals in the process of becoming men." It is Freddy Foley, who may not even be Freddy Foley, who ends up being integrated into all four symbols, and who is also declared emperor of the patricks. A great virus is unleashed in the hope of killing off most of the population—only those few who remain will be able to ascend to spiritual glory. Freddy forgets a little sherbet treat he got and it melts in his pocket. Perhaps one day the whole world will become a single Great Man. Two of the Harvesters battle across the world, which is soon to end. "Be patient," Freddy is told by a beautiful harpy. "It comes." "The what?" Freddy asks, though he already knows. "The screaming," she explains. "It always comes on schedule." The world ends and begins again—humanity made it so far as the fourth mansion of seven. Endless death and madness, and we're just a little more than halfway to God. It's not a hopeful story; it is more the metaphysical history of the humanity squeezed into a tin flask and passed along a row during a midnight movie marathon.

Lafferty is not read widely anymore, even with the championing of Neil Gaiman, though *Past Master* has finally returned to print via the Library of America. His flame is otherwise kept alive through hardcore science fiction fans who run small conferences and publish fanzines about his work and by the occasional conservative Roman Catholic who hears of Lafferty's beliefs—but not how they are reflected in his work—and picks up a used copy of one of his titles to give it a whirl. As Lafferty only rarely mentions Christ or God explicitly and is instead interested in the divinely monstrous and a theory of history and metaphysics that is cyclical rather than teleological, who knows what this latter group of devotees actually makes of Lafferty's work. God does, perhaps.

**Nick Mamatas**

# The Tasty Worlds of Jerry Cornelius

Glamourous, polymorphous, pansexual, and able to travel through time and across different dimensions; a hipster, rock star, and freelance trouble shooter-cum-spy, Jerry Cornelius is one of the most famous characters to emerge from 1960s New Wave science fiction, as well as being one of author Michael Moorcock's best-known creations.

Moorcock wrote the manuscript for *The Final Programme*, in which Jerry first appeared, in 1965, just as the counterculture started to hit Britain, but was unable to find a publisher until 1968, when Avon picked it up in the US. It was published in the UK the following year. As Moorcock told a British Film Institute seminar in 2010, for a while "no publisher would publish it, they all thought it was too freaky.... I had letters from publishers telling me I should learn to write before I started this kind of thing."

Set in a Europe on the brink of political, economic, and spiritual collapse, the plot has a free-flowing, discursive structure. It starts with Jerry being hired by a group of businesspeople, headed by the malevolent Miss Brunner, to help them obtain a secret microfilm left by Jerry's late scientist father from the clutches of his drug-addicted brother Frank. Jerry has his own reasons for taking part in the plan. He wants to rescue his sister Catherine, who is being held in a narcotic-induced slumber by Frank in their late father's heavily fortified château on a remote stretch of the Cornish coast. The plan ends in disaster. Jerry accidentally

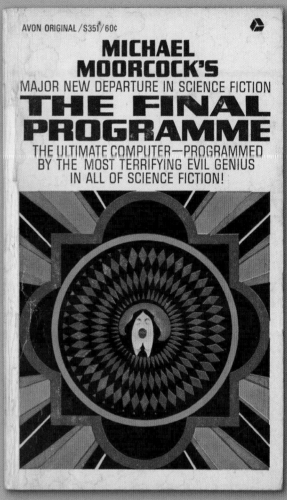

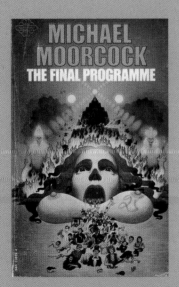

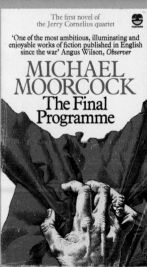

Clockwise from left: *The Final Programme* (Mayflower, 1971). *The Final Programme* (1968, Avon). *The Final Programme* (Fontana, 1979). *The Final Programme* (Allison and Busby, 1969).

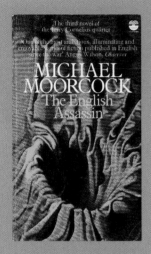
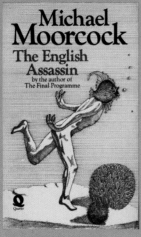
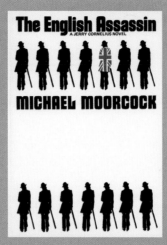
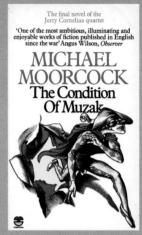

kills Catherine in a shoot-out with his brother, who escapes with the microfilm. The rest of the book concerns Jerry's efforts to find Frank and Miss Brunner's quest to locate the item, which she believes will help her to build a supercomputer she wants to use to develop the perfect human being.

The Final Programme was the basis of a quartet of books. A Cure for Cancer (1971) sees Jerry, having changed skin color, wandering a shattered UK occupied by American forces—a clear reference to Vietnam. He spends nearly all of The English Assassin (1972) suffering a nervous breakdown, leaving others to lead the story, reappearing at the end as the pantomime character Pierrot. In the final book, The Condition of Muzak (1977), he travels through the still collapsing global society but is now depicted as confused teenager, hinting that the four books are merely a fantasy on the part of an adolescent living in the then working-class London suburb of Notting Hill.

Jerry appears in numerous Moorcock works, sometimes in other guises and with names based on anagrams of Jerry Cornelius. The supporting characters are also sprinkled across Moorcock's output, with some spinning off into their own novels. The character influenced other novelists and illustrators, encouraged by Moorcock's treatment of the character and his universe as the sort of open source world others are free to borrow from. A collection of short fiction appeared in the June 1969 edition of New Worlds magazine, including work by Brian Aldiss and Langdon Jones, which were subsequently collected along with other Moorcock fiction in an anthology, The Nature of Catastrophe (1971).

A film version of The Final Programme was released in 1974, by which time the counterculture was on its last legs, and Britain was entering a grim period in the lead-up to the election of the Thatcher government in 1979. Released in the US as The Last Days of Man on Earth, it bombed at the box office but subsequently achieved a cult following.

Moorcock borrows from numerous trends and fashions with the same promiscuousness that he encourages others to do to with his work. But despite ranging across different locations, historical time periods, and parallel time streams, some sensual and exotic, others brutal and dystopian, Jerry's character is always firmly anchored in the culture of the 1960s and the various accoutrements of the era: the clothes, music, and technology, the passion for Eastern mysticism, Jungian psychology, and bizarre garish nightclubs.

**Andrew Nette**

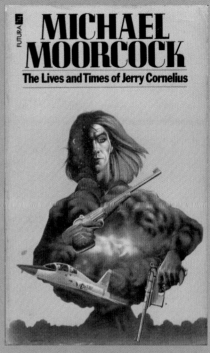

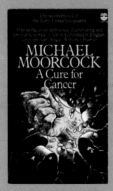

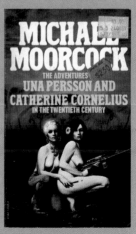

Clockwise from top left: *The English Assassin* (Fontana, 1979). *The English Assassin* (Quartet, 1972). *The English Assassin* (Harper & Row, 1974). *The Condition of Muzak* (Fontana, 1978). *A Cure For Cancer* (Penguin, 1974). *The Lives and Times of Jerry Cornelius* (Quartet, 1976). *The Cornelius Chronicles* (Avon, 1977). *The Adventures of Una Persson and Catherine Cornelius in the Twentieth Century* (Mayflower, 1980). *A Cure For Cancer* (Quartet, 1976). *A Cure For Cancer* (Fontana, 1979). *New Worlds*, March 1969. *New Worlds*, June 1969.

# Hank Lopez's *Afro-6*

Google "science fiction definition" and this is likely to be your first hit: "fiction based on imagined future scientific or technological advances and major social or environmental changes, frequently portraying space or time travel and life on other planets." The purpose of pointing this out is that some who read Enrique "Hank" Lopez's (1920–1985) 1969 novel *Afro-6* might question whether it should be considered part of the genre. It's not a futuristic story. It doesn't involve imagined technological advancements, time travel, or non-earth planets. But the "major social changes" piece of that definition is where Lopez's novel finds its place under the sci-fi umbrella. It's the story of an attempt at a major societal change; namely, a well-coordinated black power uprising in the United States. The matter of whether the book should be considered radical is not a debatable point.

In the story, "Afro-6" is the code name of the subversive plot. The militant group's headquarters is in New York City, where the novel takes place. But there are satellite Afro-6 units in other American cities. The idea is that at a particular hour on an early autumn evening, New York and other US metropolises will fall to the power of black saboteurs, via bridge bombings, transportation system shutdowns, kidnappings, occupations of key buildings, disruptions to police communications, and the like. What exactly the group will do with its newfound power once it's seized seems unclear, at least for the majority of the book, but they are determined to bring the white establishment to its knees, and they have a sophisticated, carefully planned, multilayered set of strategies in place to make the overthrow happen.

Much of the story is told from the perspectives of two characters. The first is a guy named John, or Juan, Ríos. He goes by either first name. Ríos is actually Puerto Rican by birth, but he is racially mixed and dark-skinned and generally taken as black. He's fine with people assuming that's his race, as he certainly identifies with African Americans and the oppression they've always suffered at the hands of whitey. Ríos

Hank Lopez (photo courtesy Lila Silvern)

is a leader of the New York–based Afro-6 movement and like many of the other higher-ups in the group he is a college-educated white-collar professional who is secretly a black power militant. The chapters titled under his last name are told in the first person.

In an early chapter narrated by Ríos, we get a glimpse into his militant mindset:

> I left school in 1961 to join Martin Luther King in Selma, Alabama. But I could never dig his mode of operation. He had an unnatural aversion to hatred and violence, an almost neurotic refusal to recognize the dirty impulses that rule human nature.

Many of the other chapters are titled Geller, and these involve a white man named Alan Geller. Geller is a friend of Ríos and is a liberal white guy who sympathizes with the civil rights cause of black Americans. His sister once dated Ríos, although that ended badly. Geller would be happy to see black people start to get a fairer shake in America, but when he accidentally gets hip to the overthrow plot being planned by Ríos and associates, he fears them and understands the knowledge has put his own life in grave danger. Late in the story, he is forced to choose sides between the saboteurs and the authorities that are out to shut them down. The Geller chapters are told by an omniscient narrator; this distinction from the Ríos chapters gives a clear impression of to which of the two characters Lopez felt he could most relate.

The Geller chapters shed plenty of light on the difficulties that exist between black Americans and liberal whites who want to support them. In one such segment, Geller is talking with a highly educated, physically appealing, leftist white female friend who has been dating one of the militants. She describes to Geller some of the hassle she's experienced in being romantically involved with a black man:

> [M]ost negroes consider you an easy lay, a sex-starved white tramp, once you ever date a black man. Then they all make passes at you. Most of them simply can't believe that you can love one single negro without having a neurotic passion for all blacks.

The happenings over the last chapters of *Afro-6* are events best learned about by reading the novel. Much of what makes it a remarkable story about societal upheaval is the balance among Lopez's characters. Some of the white people in the novel are sympathetic to the black rights cause, while others are hateful racists. By illustrating the roadblocks that are run into by whites and blacks that try to overcome barriers and relate to each other, Lopez gets at the heart of just how deep the racial problem in the US was at the time (still is, really). His black characters are also a diverse group. Some of the Afro-6 leaders and foot soldiers are African Americans who strive to fight for their people's causes but want to do so while harming as few innocent bystanders as possible. Others, though, not only don't mind offing people who happen to get in their way (as long as those people are white) but thirst for some honky bloodshed.

If there's a flaw to be found in the novel, it's the feminist's nightmare manner in which Lopez depicted the various female characters. Regardless of whether or

*Afro-6* (Dell, 1969)

how Ríos or the omniscient narrator discuss aspects of the women in the book, such as their intelligence, professional accomplishments, etc., every one of these characters is given a literary ogling and a catcall from Lopez's pen. Over and over, we hear about their physical attributes and relative level of sex appeal. It becomes tiresome and is likely to be a turnoff for many readers.

A more positive facet of the novel is its details about the mechanics of the overthrow attempt. Where Lopez got his knowledge about the logistics of such an undertaking is unclear, but in the planning meetings among the militant organizers, we hear in precise detail how they intend to bring New York and the other cities under their control. Those specifics give the primary storyline an amount of believability that makes the book a compelling read.

One most interesting aspect of Lopez's life story is the dispute about whether he was born in Mexico or the United States. The obituary that ran in the *New York Times* when the author died stated that he began his life in Denver, Colorado. This version of Lopez's life is confirmed by his son Greg Lopez. But Hank's friend Lila Silvern—an author in her own right, and someone to whom Lopez apparently became close in his later years—says he was born in Chihuahua, Mexico, and only came to America when his family moved there during his early childhood. Various online sources also state that he was born in Mexico. Regardless of which version one believes, nobody seems to question that Lopez's parents were Mexican nationals who emigrated from their home country in the hope of making a better life for themselves and their children in America. So Lopez came from Mexican blood, wherever he was born.

As an adult, Lopez graduated from the University of Denver, then furthered his higher education with a law degree from Harvard. It's theorized in several places, and was apparently asserted by Lopez himself, that he may have been the first Chicano to attain that particular honor. After being certified as a lawyer, he seems to have shifted his energy between practicing law, writing books, and lecturing at universities. He also edited a Hispanic literary magazine for several years in the 1960s.

Asked why she thought Lopez, who wrote *Afro-6* long before they met, took it upon himself to author a novel about a black uprising in the America, Silvern points to some passages of the autobiography Lopez was working on when he died suddenly from heart failure at age sixty-four. Silvern, who is in possession of Lopez's unfinished life story, tells of Lopez's writing about a black school friend he had. It seems the guy was a smart kid who was often overlooked by school authorities, most likely because of his race, and who had a difficult home life. Silvern states that in Lopez's written life story, he says that his childhood friend resented his own blackness and wanted to be Mexican like Hank. This friendship doesn't fully explain Lopez's motivation in writing *Afro-6*, but it can help us see why he sympathized with black Americans victimized by a society dominated by whites. And it makes you think of the mixed-race character John/Juan Ríos from *Afro-6*. The author's son Greg says an interest in the subject matter of *Afro-6* likely came about as a result of his father's work as a civil rights lawyer.

Regardless of the truth behind Lopez's birthplace and what drove him to write *Afro-6*, it's a well-written

*Hidden Magic of Uxmal* (Fawcett, 1980)

radical novel about a black power uprising. And it's one that's been sorely overlooked to this point. The publisher of the paperback original, Dell, made it clear who they saw as the book's target audience, by way of the other books they advertised in the back sections: Eldridge Cleaver's memoir *Soul on Ice* and *Tell Me How Long the Train's Been Gone* by James Baldwin, both published in 1968.

As mentioned above, Lopez wrote other books in addition to *Afro-6*. His collected efforts in the production of nonfiction titles reveal a man with a varied and curious set of interests. This section of his CV includes a handful of monographs and a few collaborations. Among the former, 1973's *The Seven Wives of Westlake* is a collection of transcripts Lopez assembled and presented from secretly recorded weekly meetings held by a group of suburban feminists during the women's liberation movement. Also published in 1973 was *They*

*Lived on Human Flesh*, Lopez's accounting of the real-life 1972 saga involving a plane crash that killed most members of a Uruguayan rugby team and what the few survivors were reduced to while awaiting rescue.

Two of the author's nonfiction works were released in 1979: *The Harvard Mystique*, in which Lopez drew on his experiences at the university's law school to attempt a full assessment of the esteemed institution's status as a power college that fosters future leaders; and *Eros and Ethos*, wherein he utilized personal interviews he conducted with more than seven hundred subjects to detail a comparative study of the sexual mindsets and practices among Catholics, Jews, and Protestants. *Conversations with Katherine Anne Porter*, a collection of transcripts of discussions between Lopez and the famed literary author, appeared in 1981. In addition to his single-author nonfiction works, Lopez served as editor/coauthor on two titles: *My Brother, Lyndon* (1970), a memoir of Lyndon Johnson by the one-time US president's brother Sam Houston Johnson, and *La Balsa* (1973), which was primarily written by Vital Alsar and tells of an epic raft voyage that Alsar and three others took from Ecuador to Australia.

Among the above, *The Seven Wives of Westlake* is easily the most interesting, but the fact that the women captured rapping about sex, marriage, motherhood, finances, a woman's place in contemporary American culture, etc. didn't intend to have their discussions made public can make a reader feel guilty for spying in on them. *Eros and Ethos*, meanwhile, is a grind of a read, but it *does* present some illuminating statistics and intriguing participant commentary regarding members of different religions' sexual ideas and habits. And *La Balsa*, while not a Lopez monograph, is a well-written adventure book that will appeal to anyone interested in its topic.

Lopez's other published novel, 1980's *The Hidden Magic of Uxmal*, is also worthy of consideration. It's a work of magical realism and is about a unique Mexican village lorded over by an ageless Mayan goddess (literally—she is said to be at least five hundred years old). The locals live by ancient, mystical philosophies and customs and are fully separated from the ways of other Mexicans and of the modern world in general. When you know a little about Lopez's life and have read his nonfiction books, you can see that he put much of his own experience into this odd novel. The narrator is a guy who seems a lot like Lopez: a Mexican national by origin who attended Harvard and is currently a practicing lawyer. As the attorney is led by a friend to enter the strange village and learn the ways of its inhabitants, we can see bits of what Lopez learned about relations between the sexes when doing research for *The Seven Wives of Westlake* and *Eros and Ethos*. Hell, he even managed to work in what he learned about balsa rafts while coauthoring *La Balsa*. *Hidden Magic of Uxmal*, published as a Fawcett Gold Medal paperback original, is a novel with an intriguing concept and some fascinating details. Had Lopez managed to come off as more of a storyteller and less of a professor in authoring it, it might have been worthy of inclusion on a list with some of the better works of magical realism novels, alongside titles by Gabriel Garcia Marquez, Isabel Allende, and others. But because there's not enough story, it's a good idea but a labor to read. Still, anyone especially interested in magical realism literature or Lopez's work in general will want to read this peculiar novel.

**Brian Greene**

# "The Hell with Heroes"

## Rebellion and Responsibility in Roger Zelazny's *Damnation Alley*

*Damnation Alley*, published in 1969, is one of Roger Zelazny's best-known novels, yet it remains misunderstood as "a nice, simple action-adventure story," which is how the author himself described the 1967 novella of the same name. In fact, the expanded version—requested by Zelazny's agent for a prospective movie deal—has had a pervasive influence on the development and direction of nearly every expression of science fiction media. Written in prose that is ironically literary, almost all of the added "action" is internal and existential, measuring the desire for radical individual freedom against authority and the increasingly desperate needs of the community, a moral dilemma that was, in the real world of the late 1960s, unfolding in blood and calamity across a global stage.

Given the plot, perhaps simplicity is all that can be expected. Set in a post–nuclear apocalypse United States, *Damnation Alley* is the story of Hell Tanner, a convicted murderer and incorrigible malcontent whose only redeeming "virtue" is that he can "drive through anything that has a way through it." When the novel begins, he is offered a full pardon from the nation of California on the condition that he deliver a vaccine to the nation of Boston, whose citizens are dying in droves from a plague that had previously wracked Los Angeles. The catch is that driving across the vast, irradiated ruins (nicknamed Damnation Alley) that lie between the West and East Coasts is basically a "suicide job." Tanner has little choice but to accept the deal, and while "running the Alley" he confronts a host of pulp terrors: giant Gila monsters, giant dust devils, giant bats, radiation storms, biker gangs, and trigger-happy cops.

The antihero was nothing new to sci-fi by this point—the nihilistic Gully Foyle in Alfred Bester's *The Stars My Destination* (1957) is one of several examples—but Tanner is different, because Zelazny based him on the real-life renegade bikers, inspired by Hunter S. Thompson's breakthrough 1966 account *Hell's Angels: The Strange and Terrible Saga of the Outlaw Motorcycle Gangs*. While Thompson's book brought the club

Roger Zelazny

international fame, the Angels had been notorious in the US since 1964, when four members allegedly raped two teenage girls during Labor Day weekend in Monterey (Tanner is also an alleged rapist, drug dealer, extortionist, and pimp).

Hundreds of novelists, filmmakers, musicians, and news agencies would exploit the public's newfound obsession with the Angels and working-class biker culture, almost all of the resulting output disregarding Thompson's ultimately cautionary point about the society that created the phenomenon:

> To see the Hell's Angels as caretakers of the old "individualist" tradition "that made this country great" is only a painless way to get around seeing them for what they really are—not some romantic leftover, but the first wave of a future that nothing in our history has prepared us to cope with. The Angels are prototypes. Their lack of education has not only rendered them completely useless in a highly technical economy, but it has also given them the leisure to cultivate a powerful resentment … and to translate it into a destructive cult which the mass media insists on portraying as a sort of isolated oddity.

The world of Zelazny's *Damnation Alley*, on the other hand, bears out this apocalyptic prophecy, flinging it into a decimated future that seemed all but imminent at the time. The rise of the Hells Angels represented an important historical moment. They were courted and claimed by the counterculture as emblems of defiance against the "squares" and "citizens" of the repressive status quo, a reckless notion born of willful innocence and easy middle-class privilege, as it turned out; but they were also hailed by conservatives as superpatriots for their avowed, but often hypocritical, libertarian principles and apoplectic support of the Vietnam War (outlaw motorcycle clubs originated with returning World War II veterans who wanted no part of nascent suburbia and its attendant boredoms). Hell Tanner, "the last Angel left alive," carries this self-destructive paradox within him.

To complete his mission, Tanner is handed the keys to a thirty-two-foot-long, radiation-shielded, heavily armed, endlessly provisioned all-terrain vehicle. There are two other "cars" going with him, tripling the chances that one of them will get through. Tanner is told by the authorities that if he attempts to escape, he'll be blown "into little bitty ashes" by the other drivers, who are not criminals like him but well-meaning state employees. In an improbable twist, Tanner discovers that his younger brother Denny is one of those other drivers. Denny owns his own garage and has "kept [his] nose clean," but he can't resist the "fifty grand" thrown at him by California's Secretary of Traffic, who a few pages earlier dressed down Tanner as "the lowest, most reprehensible human being I have ever encountered." Tanner tells Denny the secret location of his ill-gotten nest egg, and then breaks his brother's ribs to keep him off the job.

The car, interpretations of which appear on the cover of nearly every edition of the novel, is built almost exclusively for violence, like Tanner himself. The same minds that built the bombs that ended the world, we assume, also built the self-contained war wagons, equipped with flamethrowers, .50 caliber guns, grenade launchers, armor-piercing missiles, and steel "wings" for charging and slashing. The technology of war, a result of the scientific establishment's cowed servitude to the military-industrial complex, reproduces itself eternally and exponentially until there is nothing left to destroy but the mutant abominations the war's final phase has spawned. ("It was the physicists who did this to us," a "feral" savant

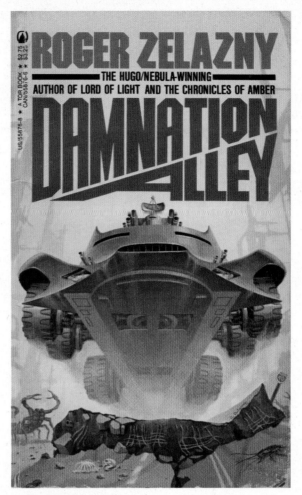

*Damnation Alley* (Tor, 1984)

tells Tanner late in the book, "and some chemists and mathematicians.")

We find out that Boston too had its own fleet of high-tech killer cars, one of which got through to California to deliver news of the plague. What Boston doesn't have are the "facilities," the know-how, and the will to make the vaccine. "Seems kind of silly," Tanner says, "for the only other nation on the continent—maybe in the world—not to take better care of itself." Most of the scenes about Boston in the novel humanize, and at times admonish, the sometimes tragic, sometimes fatalistic, sometimes rapacious citizens of that city.

Soon after leaving Los Angeles, a giant Gila monster smashes one of the cars, killing one of the drivers. While everyone is outside inspecting the damage, Tanner flicks a cigarette into a pool of gas, blowing up the wreck in an attempt to injure or kill the others and make his escape. He is ushered back into his ride at gunpoint, and the survivor of the wrecked car, Greg, described as "dark-eyed" and "part Indian, possibly," is paired with him. Greg is young and idealistic, like Denny, but not as naive; he is disgusted at how someone like Tanner "happens," and yet the two men share similar scars dealt by a hard, thankless life. The second car is destroyed a few pages later, and for about half of the novel Greg works on Tanner's conscience, serving as an obvious counterpoint and check to his self-serving misanthropy. "The hell with heroes," Tanner spits, when Greg suggests what Boston will think of him if he gets through.

As the car rumbles across a wasted America, skirting the glassy craters where the nukes fell, dodging the "carnage" discharged from the atmospheric "dead belt" that prevents air travel, so too does Tanner's mind move, trying to make sense of it all, trying to decide whether the world is worth saving. He muses bleakly in a Salt Lake City junkyard while the car is being repaired:

> [H]e wove within his mind the strands of violence past and fear like knowledge of trouble yet to come. Behind his eyes there was a vision of flames, flames encasing his car like the flower of death, two blackening skeletons within... and all the squares who had ever hated him, signifying everybody, jibbered and jeered and shook billy clubs and moved in a wide, dancing circle about the pyre. "Damn you all," he said then softly.

The passage bears an eerie resemblance to a scene in the same year's *Easy Rider*—a film more responsible for the conflation of hippies and bikers than any other piece of art or news—when drug runner Wyatt (Peter Fonda), nicknamed Captain America, has a premonition of his fiery death in a crash, the result, we find out later, of a bumpkin square with a shotgun.

Tanner then recalls his initiation by the Angels—as described by Thompson, all members urinate in a bucket, which is then dumped on the recruit—and his days, at age nineteen, as "Number One":

> He was Hell, and his pack owned the Barbary Coast. They ranged where they would and did as they would, until he'd gotten into bad trouble and gone away and dark days came over the Coast. The town was perpetually initiated, as he had been, by rubbish from the heavens.

Tanner feels "cheated" by the war. Between St. Louis and the Rockies and the plains of Illinois, he wonders about "the old days, when a man could just jump on his bike and cut out for a new town whenever he wanted." He yearns, like the young, inevitably doomed drifters of *Easy Rider*, to "drive forever along the big road, to see everything, to eat the world." He begins to think that he can survive the Alley, that "some of the legendary places" in the country "must still be clean."

Somewhere in Indiana, after they're fired on by a local militia's tank, Greg's fear overtakes him; he wants to cut their losses and turn back. "I didn't know it would be like this," he pleads. "I'm no good to my family if I'm dead." Tanner, though, has also turned. He now wants to help "all those people in Boston you made me a speech about... just because I feel like it." Greg goes for his gun, and Tanner beats him, nearly to death.

With Greg tied up in back, Tanner goes on alone. He is nearly dead from exhaustion when the car gets stuck in the mud, and he passes out. The next morning, he meets a farmer and his sons, who take him back to their place and feed him, draw him a bath, and treat him with all the kindness of good neighbors. The father, Sam, tells him the safest route to Boston and warns him about the roaming motorcycle gangs. Sam's youngest boy Jerry takes a liking to Tanner, and Tanner gives the kid his snake ring. They take a walk the next morning, and the boy telling Tanner about his dream of becoming a pilot. Tanner telling the boy that "There's an awful lot of things most people want to do, and it turns out for some reason or another they never can." Tanner leaves Greg with the local doctor and pushes off. He's just a few hours outside of Boston when he sees "perhaps thirty beams" in his rearview screen. "It could have been him on the lead bike," Tanner admits, "all hot on hijack."

The 1977 film adaptation of *Damnation Alley*, the only cinematic adaptation of Zelazny to date, has almost nothing to do with the original story. Here, three US Air Force officers survive World War III and haul a customized land tank cross-country to Albany, the source of a repeating radio transmission. The film is remembered almost entirely for the "Landmaster," built from scratch by Dean Jeffries, a founding figure of Southern California's "Kustom Kulture"—a scene whose scruffy antiauthoritarianism and casual far-right politics often overlapped with the Hells Angels. It was another 1977 film that had a surprising amount in common with Zelazny's novel: William Friedkin's *Sorcerer*.

Incinerated in the commercial jet stream of *Star Wars*, *Sorcerer* is an undercelebrated classic about four criminals from very different national and ethnic backgrounds who have converged on a small South American village to hide from their evil deeds. Too poor to buy their way out of purgatory, they take a "suicide" job hauling unstable dynamite to the local American oil well, where it's needed to quench an oil fire. In this case, the cargo is as deadly as Tanner's is lifesaving, but the concept is essentially the same: the men demand double the salary and legal residence to complete the job, encounter all sorts of hellish obstacles, and only one of them makes it. *Sorcerer* was based on a 1953 French film titled *Le Salaire de la peur* (The

Wages of Fear), which likely inspired Zelazny. There is an important difference between the two films. In the original, directed by Henri-Georges Clouzot, the protagonists are simply "tramps" and "loafers" who can't find work in a dying town exploited by an American oil company ("Wherever there's oil, there are Americans," one of the Frenchmen remarks dryly); in Friedkin's version, however, the men are unequivocally bad: crooks, assassins, and terrorists. Both pictures are existential parables, as is *Damnation Alley*. There is a sense in all three—and in Thompson's *Hell's Angels*, for that matter—that the technocratic West, with America coiled smugly at its heart, is already a postapocalyptic desolation for most, and that the powerless bastards trapped inside, be they angels or devils, are unsavable.

Zelazny's work is well-known for its often brilliant incorporation and blending of so many different genres and disciplines. In the case of *Damnation*

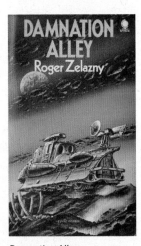

*Damnation Alley*
(Sphere, 1969)

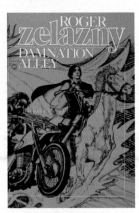

*Damnation Alley*
(Gregg Press, 1979)

*Damnation Alley* (Berkley Medallion, 1977)

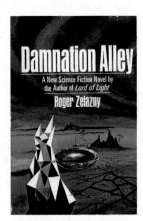

*Damnation Alley*
(G.P. Putnam's Sons, 1969)

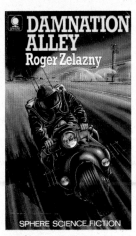

*Damnation Alley*
(Sphere, 1973)

*Alley*, he borrows elements of traditional and revisionist westerns like John Ford's *Stagecoach* (1939), *The War Wagon* (1967), and Sergio Leone's *Dollars Trilogy* (1964–1966), Raymond Chandler's "slumming angel" noir, war films like 1962's *Hell is for Heroes* and 1967's *The Dirty Dozen*, the latter concerning "psychopathic" US and British military convicts offered full pardons and reinstatement if they take on and survive a likely suicidal mission behind German lines, postapocalyptic picaresque and "last man" novels, 50s sci-fi camp, road dramas, and, of course, hot rod and outlaw biker films, starting with 1953's *The Wild One*, which gave the first generation of Hells Angels, in Thompson's words, "a lasting, romance-glazed image of themselves."

In terms of *Damnation Alley*'s descendants, two of the most important are John Carpenter's *Escape from New York* and George Miller's *Mad Max 2* (released as *The Road Warrior* in the US); both cult films released in 1981, they sparked a postapocalyptic media boom—a specific vision of the rugged, hardscrabble outcast whose struggle to survive is both cynical and heroic—that has, more or less, never ended. *Escape from New York* is about war-hero-turned-criminal Snake Plissken, who is offered a "full pardon" by the police commissioner; all he has to do is infiltrate Manhattan Island Prison and find and rescue the President of the United States, who has been taken hostage by the prison's most vicious street gang. The set-up seems to have been taken directly from *Damnation Alley*. In both, the infamous criminal is caught and brought to the office of the man in charge of the operation, the guards remind their boss how "dangerous" the perp is, the man in charge tells the bad man how despicable he is but offers him the job, because he's the best at what he does (Plissken "flew the Gullfire over Leningrad"; Tanner is the "only man who'd make the mail run to Albuquerque"), and because he's the only option. Plissken has no cargo to carry, but the president has in his possession a cassette that holds the key to "the survival of the human race." And that is what Plissken needs to bring back in less than twenty-four hours—or he's dead, having been injected with a slow-dissolving poison that can be reversed only with a special vaccine.

*Mad Max 2* takes place in the post-holocaust Australian desert, years after the world waged total war over control of "the black fuel." Former cop Max is a leather-clad loner who wanders the "wasteland" in a souped-up V8 Interceptor, violently vying for gas and food with the motorcycle gangs that killed his wife

MORE THAN A MOVIE.
AN ADVENTURE YOU'LL NEVER FORGET.

Poster for the 1977 film adaptation of *Damnation Alley*

and child in 1979's *Mad Max*. Tipped off by an equally mercenary gyrocopter pilot, he discovers a small group of survivors operating a small oil refinery. Continually beset by marauders, the goodly group is looking to bug out and start a new life on the coast. Max strikes a deal with them: he'll deliver an 18-wheeler that will haul their oil supply if they give him all the gas he can carry. Like Tanner, he fulfills his promise and saves the day, probably for unselfish reasons. In the end, he becomes a drifter once more, realizing that he is not fit for civilized society.

Although it hasn't been acknowledged as such, *Damnation Alley* is also an important precursor to cyberpunk. William Gibson has long acknowledged the influence of *Escape from New York* on his novel *Neuromancer* (1984), about a degenerate drug addict, Case, who was once the best hacker in the business until, like Tanner, he got into bad trouble and dark days came upon him. An underworld agent gives Case a second shot at cyberspace in return for participating in a series of ever more dangerous missions. The dialogue is distinctly noir, inspired partly by "biker slang," and the dystopian (for all but the rich) Chiba City is every bit as treacherous as the Alley. In Katsuhiro Otomo's manga *Akira* (1982–1990), another founding document of the genre, street punk and motorcycle gang leader Kaneda wages brutal war with rival gangs, a fascist government, and vengeful supernatural forces in post-nuke Neo-Tokyo. Novels such as K.W. Jeter's *The Glass Hammer* (1985), Walter Jon Williams's *Hardwired* (1986), and Neal Stephenson's *Snow Crash* (1992) specifically reference and homage *Damnation Alley*, working elements of Zelazny's inconspicuously subversive narrative into the coalescing cyberpunk aesthetic.

★

In December 1969, the Hells Angels were hired to provide security at the Altamont Free Concert in Northern California—the extent of the arrangement is debated, but all agree that the price was $500 worth of beer. Witnesses reported that the Angels became increasingly drunk and rowdy throughout the day, "terrorizing" audience members and frequently beating them with pool cues; Jefferson Airplane's Marty Balin was knocked unconscious when he tried to stop an Angel from trouncing a prone victim. Four people died on the day, but only one was murdered: a black teenager named Meredith Hunter, who was continually harassed and beaten by the Angels after trying to climb on stage to get a better look at the Rolling Stones, the concert's final act. Hunter eventually brandished a pistol, and, to the tune of "Under My Thumb," a twenty-one-year-old Angel named Alan Passaro stabbed him to death. Hell Tanner's pet weapon is a "long, slim SS dagger." "What they really are," Hunter Thompson remarked of the Angels in a 1967 interview with Studs Terkel, is "a reflection of President Johnson's foreign policy." At the time, almost five hundred thousand American troops were deployed in Vietnam.

For Tanner, who was born after the nukes blocked out the sun, the war is Damnation Alley, and he makes it through, killing his fascist biker counterparts in dramatic fashion, goading the cops who mistake him for a looter, and finally delivering the vaccine as promised. Boston is saved, and Tanner is declared a hero. The town erects a statue of him "astride a great bronze Harley," which he promptly defaces before stealing a car and peeling out of town, because there is nothing for him there and nothing for him in Los Angeles. The last two nations on earth cannot be unbroken. Like thousands of Vietnam veterans, Hell Tanner was drafted into needless violence by nested bureaucrats sheltered behind bronze nameplates. He was trained to kill anything and survive anything, and then he was dumped back into a world that abhorred him for doing just that. He won his full pardon, his discharge papers. He was free once again to be "perpetually initiated . . . by rubbish from the heavens."

**Kelly Roberts**

1999. America's Northwest has seceded from the United States. Now, embark on an astonishing voyage to a world of infinite possibilities!

26183-5 ★ IN U.S. $4.50 (IN CANADA $4.95) ★ A BANTAM NEW AGE BOOK

# ECOTOPIA

the novel of your future

## by Ernest Callenbach

Author of ECOTOPIA EMERGING

"The newest name after Wells, Verne, Huxley and Orwell."
—Los Angeles Times

Clockwise from top left: *Dune* (Chilton, 1965). *Ecotopia* (Bantam, 1982). *Hothouse* (Faber and Faber, 1962). *The Year of the Cloud* (Playboy Press, 1970). *Garbage World* (Belmont Tower, 1967).

# Eco-Death: Catastrophe and Survival in 1960s and 1970s Science Fiction

Rising concern during the latter decades of the twentieth century about human impacts on the environment is often attributed to the 1962 publication of Rachel Carson's *Silent Spring*. While the book's powerful mixture of scientific fact and personal insight regarding the corrosive effects of pesticides on the web of life undisputedly did much globally to shock people into action, it only resonated because it explained and exposed a reality many were already experiencing in the forms of smog, biodiversity loss, and declining health. Legislation regarding pollution and species protection was passed and tightened up in the UK and US during the 1960s, but corporate resistance and evasion of the new laws, as well as events such as the world being filmed from space for the first time that same year, fed into calls for action, most vividly represented by the first Earth Day protest, in 1970, in which twenty million Americans took part. Alongside developments in the US, the UK also saw the emergence of an environmental mass movement and, with it, the formation of long-term campaigning organizations like Friends of the Earth. Although some of the movements' leadership would be incorporated into business-as-usual politics and lose their impact as the decade went on, an inability to effectively bring destruction and degradation to a halt would see a new wave of alarm in the 1980s and 1990s.

A recognition of the connection of humans to their physical surroundings and of the negative impacts of industrialism was, as with so many other issues, hardly new. From the end of the nineteenth century onward utopian, dystopian, and science fiction works by H.G. Wells, W.H. Hudson, Charlotte Perkins Gilman, and others had either warned of horrors to come or posited more harmonious paths. Nevertheless, along with the broader public, ecological consciousness received a major boost in the science fiction community in the late 1960s and 1970s, and these early works were joined by a flood of new stories.

Some explored earthly matters via plots set in distant worlds. Inspired by news stories he had filed as a journalist, Frank Herbert's dynastic space potboiler *Dune* (1965) included desertification and resource scarcity as themes. First as a 1972 short story, and then as a novel, Ursula K. Le Guin's *The Word for World Is Forest* (1976) explored the interrelated issues of colonization, militarism, and environmental exploitation in an off-world logging camp. In a less harrowing manner, L. Beam Piper's *Little Fuzzy* (1962) addressed the impact of corporate colonization upon other planets, while Charles Platt's *Garbage World* (1968) was a satirical off-world take on affluent and effluent society. Others chose to explore our possible environmental fate through novels set on earth. Brian Aldiss's *Hothouse* (1962) and *The Genocides* (1965), a host of J.G. Ballard novels, and Kate Wilhelm and Ted Thomas's *Year of the Cloud* (1970) metaphorically and directly dealt with the results of ecosystems being thrown out of whack by human and other causes.

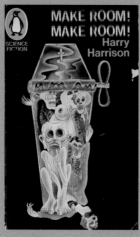
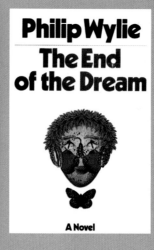
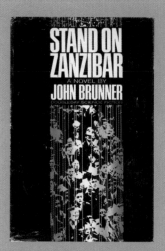

The potential impact of overpopulation was a popular theme explored in novels such as Norman L. Knight and James Blish's *A Torrent of Faces* (1967), John Brunner's *Stand on Zanzibar* (1968), and Harry Harrison's *Make Room, Make Room* (1966), which formed the basis for the 1973 film *Soylent Green*. While novels addressing overpopulation generally echoed the tendency of 1970s Western ecologists to project the consumption levels of their home countries onto the majority of the world and ignore the potential carrying capacity of the planet if sustainable practices and wealth redistribution were adopted, others provided more accurate and terrifying scenarios.

Foremost among these was Brunner's *The Sheep Look Up* (1972). This chronicle of society's fall here is not one in which warriors prowl the wasteland or the earth goes out in a blinding flash but where humanity's health and rationality crumble under the accumulated corrosion and exploitation of its environment. In a sprawling and ambitious work Brunner successfully tied together a number of disparate plot lines to illustrate the interconnection of seemingly random events. The aggregate effect of issues, such as resource wars, seeping radiation, soil erosion, and overfishing on a variety of people in different social settings is made painfully clear.

Aldiss's *Earthworks* (1967), William John Watkins and E.V. Snyder's *Ecodeath* (1972), Philip Wylie's *The End of a Dream* (1973), and others explored how communities might survive, fail, or take a sinister turn following eco-catastrophes. In contrast Ernest Callenbach's *Ecoptopia* (1975) captured steps being taken by the back-to-the-land and appropriate-technology movements to avert such outcomes. Projecting twenty-five years into the future, the book envisaged a secessionist movement on the west coast of the US, which, defended by commandeered weapons of mass destruction, has come to successfully adopt a decentralized and environmentally sustainable lifestyle.

**Iain McIntyre**

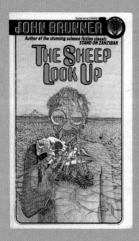
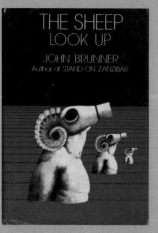

Clockwise from top left: *Earthworks* (Four Square, 1967). *Make Room Make Room* (Penguin, 1967). *The End of the Dream* (Doubleday, 1972). *Stand on Zanzibar* (Doubleday, 1968). *A Torrent of Faces* (Doubleday, 1967). *The Sheep Look Up* (Quartet, 1977). *The Burning World* (Berkley, 1964). *The Genocides* (Panther, 1968). *The World in Winter* (Penguin, 1964). *The Drought* (Penguin, 1968). *The Sheep Look Up* (Harper and Row, 1972). *The Sheep Look Up* (Del Rey, 1972).

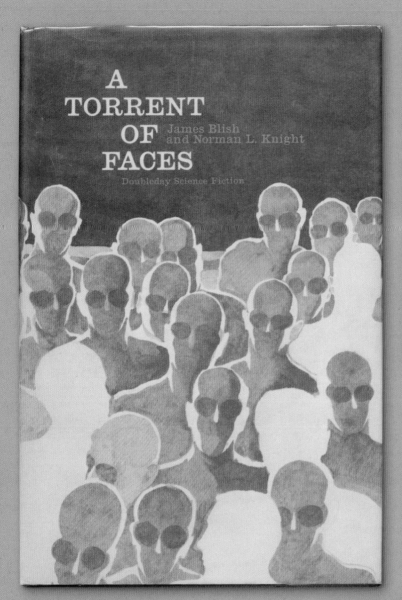

A TORRENT OF FACES
James Blish and Norman L. Knight
Doubleday Science Fiction

...AND MAN CREATED — THE
ULTIMATE TECHNOLOGICAL HELL!
JOHN BRUNNER
THE SHEEP
LOOK UP

Science Fiction
J.G.BALLARD
The Drought

a Penguin Book 3'6
The World
in Winter
John Christopher

The Genocides
Thomas M. Disch
panther science fiction

J.G.BALLARD
A NEW SCIENCE FICTION NOVEL BY THE AUTHOR OF
THE DROWNED WORLD & THE WIND FROM NOWHERE
THE BURNING
WORLD

# Stepford Wives and Supercomputers

## The Science Fiction of Ira Levin

It is not every writer who gets an enduring popular culture term named after the title of one of their books. To label a woman a "Stepford Wife" is to infer she submissively conforms in every way to her husband or partner's desires. The term originates from the title of a 1972 novel by Ira Levin, *The Stepford Wives*, about a town in which men replace their wives with obedient robot simulacra.

Ira Levin

The New York–based Levin, who died in 2007, was a midcentury popular publishing leviathan of the type we rarely see today. He got his start writing for television in the early 1950s and went onto to pen seven novels, of which the best known is arguably *Rosemary's Baby*. Published in 1967 and filmed by Roman Polanski in 1968, it told the story of a naive young woman who unwittingly moves into a block of flats occupied by a coven of black witches. These get her impregnated by the Antichrist, and then, with the help of her husband, manipulate her into carrying the baby to full term. Levin also wrote musicals, screenplays, and stage plays (his play *Deathtrap* holds the record for the longest running comedy thriller on Broadway).

While *The Stepford Wives* is Levin's best-known work of science fiction, it was not his only one, as there are major speculative themes in *The Boys from Brazil*, his 1976 story about a conspiracy to clone Hitler. And he followed *Rosemary's Baby* with his most explicit science fiction work and one of his least-known books, *This Perfect Day*, in 1970. It was also one of only two books he wrote that was not filmed, the other being his last novel, a 1997 sequel to *Rosemary's Baby*, titled *Son of Rosemary*.

Although *The Stepford Wives* reads like a literary potboiler, it is actually a very sophisticated story, containing perceptive observations about the backlash against second-wave feminism, patriarchal control of women's bodies, and the way in which intelligent women can be gaslit and psychologically destroyed by the men around them. Levin weaves into the narrative the so-called "white flight" underway since the fifties, which saw middle-class Caucasians leave the crime and racial strife of America's big cities for suburban and rural America. He also addresses the anomie of consumerism and the power of the military-industrial complex. *The Stepford Wives* features what was a common theme in many of Levin's novels: deep ambivalence toward technology.

Joanna Eberhart, her lawyer husband Pete, and their two kids move from New York to the small bucolic town of Stepford, Connecticut. A photographer and avowed feminist used to the big city, Joanna immediately feels out of sorts. Stepford is peaceful, clean, and free of crime. It is also sterile and incredibly boring. The other housewives are much shapelier than most normal females, and all they appear to be concerned with is their appearance, housework, and looking after their husbands. Meanwhile, Pete, a nice enough guy, who is framed at the beginning as being sympathetic to her feminist views, shocks her by saying he has agreed to join the exclusive Stepford Men's Association.

Joanna eventually manages to make a friend, Bobbie Markowe, a wisecracking, messy woman who likes a drink. They bond over their mutual unease toward the housewives of Stepford and the fact they are both feminists and have dabbled in the National Organization for Women (NOW), a large mainstream US feminist organization founded in 1966, originally with the aim of fighting sex discrimination in employment. At one point, Bobbie and Joanna talk

about the possibility of having a get together with some of the neighbors, a rap session to wake them to the more active role they could play in the town's life; but they agreed that the women they had met seemed unlikely to welcome even so small a step toward liberation. They talked about the National Organization for Women, to

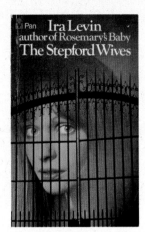

The Stepford Wives
(Pan, 1974)

The Stepford Wives
(Random House, 1972)

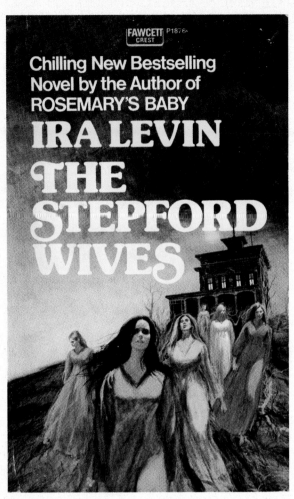

The Stepford Wives (Fawcett Crest, 1973)

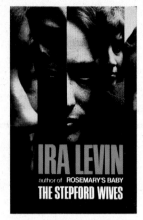

The Stepford Wives (Michael
Joseph, 1972)

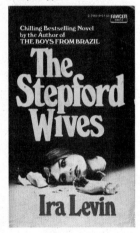

The Stepford Wives
(Fawcett, 1973)

which they both belonged, and about Joanna's photography...

"Damn it, *no*," Bobbie said. "We ought to *try* at least. Let's talk to these hausfraus; there must be *some* of them who want to reset the situation a little. What do you say? Wouldn't it be great if we could get a group together—maybe even an NOW chapter eventually—and give the Men's Association a good shaking up? Dave and Walter are kidding themselves; it's not going to change unless it's *forced* to changed; fat-cat organisations never do. What do you say, Jonanna? Let's ask around."

Joanna nodded. "We should," she said. "They can't all be as content as they seem."

She and Bobbie befriend Charmaine, a feisty gossip who plays a mean game of tennis. Joanna also strikes up an acquaintance with Ruthanne, a children's author and Stepford's first black housewife.

Joanna's curiosity is piqued when she discovers Stepford used to have a women's association run by many of the women who now come across as docile homemakers, completely uninterested in women's liberation. Pete starts spending more and more nights at the men's association. Then Charmaine transforms, almost overnight, becoming a meek woman obsessed by housework, even agreeing to have her much used tennis court replaced by a putting green for her husband.

Joanna and Bobbie wonder whether there might be something in the town's water supply, maybe chemical run-off from all the high-tech aerospace and computer companies situated on the outskirts of town that most of Stepford's male population work for. They send water samples to the Environmental Protection

Agency, but tests find nothing. The two women agree to ask their husbands to move to another town, but before they can put their plans into action, Bobbie also changes into a mild-mannered housework obsessive.

Despite how well-known the plot is, the conspiracy undertaken by the town's male population still comes across as genuinely creepy. Levin's conspirators, a bunch of paunchy, middle-aged males, are all the scarier because they are outwardly so normal. But, as the book makes clear, they have technology and the power that comes with it on their side. As Joanna says to a couple of men who try and prevent her from escaping Stepford toward the end, "You're the men who put us on the moon."

An obituary in the *Independent* newspaper in November 2007 described Levin as "the king of the high concept thriller." *The Stepford Wives* vividly illustrates this. The writing is assured and lean, and Levin excels in providing only enough detail to move the plot forward, an accumulation of small details, often seemingly quite inconsequential or coincidental—the man who wanted to sketch Joanna, the other who tape recorded hours of her speech under the guise of doing research into different world dialects, Pete's increasing secrecy about money—which all add up to the horrifying denouement. The ending is particularly effective for the way that it rips away the veneer of suburban normality that Joanna mistakenly believes she dwells in, another common theme in Levin's work.

A film of the book was released in 1975. It largely conforms to the source novel, with the exception of Joanna's last moments. In the book it is inferred she is stabbed by the robot version of her former friend, Bobbie. In the film, she stumbles across a roboticized version of herself, which slowly turns to look at her with blank eyes. The very final scene depicts a now obviously robot version of Joanna, the real one having been murdered, pushing a shopping cart around the local supermarket, trading vacuous hellos with the other wives to the sound of muzak. The film was remade as a rather shallow comedy in 2004. It also spawned a raft of made-for-TV movies: *The Revenge of the Stepford Wives* (1980), where the town's wives are brainwashed but eventually rise up in rebellion; *The Stepford Children* (1987), in which children, as well as the wives, are the target of the male conspiracy; and *The Stepford Husbands* (1996), in which the town's male population are given psychotropic substances to render them docile.

Many of the same themes and the dynamic of creeping terror at play in the novel of *The Stepford Wives* can also be seen in *Rosemary's Baby* and Polanski's largely faithful screen adaption. Like Joanna, Rosemary realizes too late that a sequence of apparently unconnected events is part of a deliberate trap: in her case, her husband Guy has made a pact with the elderly Satanists living in their apartment block in return for success as an actor, which involves him selling his soul and her being raped by Satan, her fertile body becoming a host for his child. Both novels present disturbing scenarios regarding how men could react to the increasing "threat" of feminism, leading both screen adaptions to be described as important early entries in feminist horror cinema. *The Stepford Wives* is not "satirizing women's fears of becoming robotic housewives but, instead, that men would force them to be nothing but that, should they have an option," Meredith Craig de Pietro wrote in the online site Bustle in October 2018. Around the same time, critic Laura Jacobs made a similar point in *Vanity Fair* about rewatching *Rosemary's Baby* post the events that inspired the #MeToo movement. "It isn't devil worship or the invocation of Satan that troubles the viewer. It's that a man barters his wife's body, and that her destiny has been ruthlessly appropriated and perverted."

The other key aspect in *The Stepford Wives*, unease over rapid technological innovation and the potential dark side of its application, is also on display in Levin's 1976 thriller *The Boys from Brazil*. An aging Nazi hunter, loosely based on the real-life Simon Wiesenthal, stumbles across a plan by a fictionalized version of another real-life person, Nazi concentration camp doctor Josef Mengele, to clone Hitler. Working in his laboratory deep in the Brazilian jungle, Mengele has implanted the late Nazi leader's genetic material in the bodies of ninety-four Amazon Indigenous women and farmed out their offspring across the world to families chosen because they resemble Hitler's. The plot is uncovered when Mengele dispatches assassins to murder the fathers of these families at exactly the same age Hitler was when his father died, in the hope that it will encourage at least one of the cloned boys to follow the Führer's path and rise to power.

Mistrust of technology also features in Levin's 1991 murder mystery *Sliver*, the basis for the far better-known 1993 film of the same name, adapted by Joel Eszterhas. The novel features a young professional woman, Kay Norris, who moves into a modern apartment building and strikes up a friendship with a man who, unbeknownst to her, is the building's owner, who has rigged the complex with surveillance equipment that he uses to spy on his tenants.

Control over the human body and the misuse of technology are also prevalent concerns of Levin's most overt science fiction effort, *This Perfect Day*. The story is set 141 years after the "Unification" of the world under the rule of a supercomputer known as "UniComp," or "Uni" for short. Uni provides humans with everything they need to survive—food, shelter, order. It also removes every last shred of individual choice, monitoring the population via a permanent identity bracelet that all citizens must wear. Genetic engineering has been used to smooth out all ethnic differences into one race. There are only four names for men and four for women. There is one language, and all dissent is kept firmly in check via a series of monthly "treatments" of drugs to prevent facial hair and reduce sex drive and aggressive impulses so that everyone remains a satisfied and cooperative "Family member." The maximum human life span is sixty-two years of age, after which people are euthanized.

The central character, LiRM35M4419, has the nickname Chip, secretly given to him by his grandfather who belonged to an earlier generation with memories of life before Uni and who instils in the young man a nonconformist streak, a characteristic emphasized by the fact Chip has one green eye, an error of the strict genetic programming. Chip grows up committing acts of minor subversion, which eventually bring him to the attention of a group of nonconformists who teach him how to reduce his treatments without raising the attention of the authorities. This allows him to feel stronger, more genuine emotions. "He felt a little better every day, a little more awake and alert, a little more sure that sickness was what he had and health was what he was running towards." He begins a sexual relationship with another nonconformist, Snowflake, smokes tobacco,

*The Boys From Brazil* (Pan, 1978)

a strictly forbidden substance, and with another woman, Lilac, described as "strong-willed and dark-skinned," starts searching through old museum records. They discover the existence of islands not marked on modern maps, that could be outside Uni control. They plan to escape, but before they can do so, they are betrayed by one of their group and treated back to docility.

Years later Chip's regular treatment is delayed by an earthquake, and he begins to regain consciousness. He remembers his escape plan, tracks down Lilac, kidnaps her and goes through a process of breaking her chemical conditioning. Finding a conveniently abandoned boat on a beach, they reach one of the islands. While it is outside Uni's control, the majority of the population loath the ex-Family members who have found their way there. Chip and Lilac become part of an underclass, having to work menial, poorly paid jobs and live in relatively primitive conditions. Worse, they discover the island and others like it are in effect prisons where nonconformists are deliberately isolated by Uni.

Chip eventually hatches a plan to get back to the mainland and destroy Uni by blowing up its refrigeration system. He is captured, however, and his mission, as well as his flight to the island, is revealed as all part of an elaborate test by the secret elite who rule Uni, the Programmers, to manipulate the cleverest and most determined nonconformists to join their ranks. Chip meets the leader of the Programmers, Wei Li Chun, the individual who started the new society. He is the only person allowed to program UniComp and prolongs his life by having his head transplanted onto successive youthful bodies. Chip seeks to win Wei's trust so that he can overthrow him and fulfil his original mission.

Levin's usual sharp, precise storytelling is somewhat lacking in *This Perfect Day*, and the plot feels less assured, possibly due to having to engage in the time-consuming process of creating a credible dystopian world. The final reveal of the Programmers and

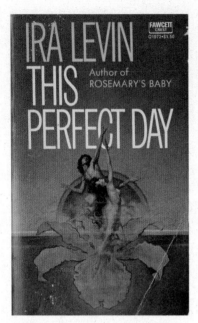

*This Perfect Day* (Fawcett Crest, 1976)   *This Perfect Day* (Random House, 1970)   *This Perfect Day* (Fawcett Crest, 1970)

Wei's confession that hunger for power, not altruism, was behind his decision to build a global society come across as labored and anticlimactic. Nonetheless, many critics compared the book favorably to similar fictional dystopias, including George Orwell's *1984* and Aldous Huxley's 1932 classic *Brave New World*. An examination of the online commentary around *This Perfect Day* indicates it has a particularly strong following among American libertarians, who have read it as a comment on the individual's struggle against all-consuming collectivist authoritarianism.

Levin guarded his privacy closely and rarely gave interviews about his life and his work. Thus, it is an open question as to exactly what the author was critiquing in the book. *This Perfect Day* can be certainly be viewed as a comment on those aspects of a counterculture that had gone off the rails by the late 1960s. In particular, the notion of a society of content "Family members" could be a reaction to Charles Manson and his Death Valley desert commune, which consisted of around a hundred followers who lived an alternative life that included the regular consumption of hallucinogenic drugs, and whose activities would explode into the public consciousness with the Tate-LeBianca murders in August 1969. Levin hints that Uni was created as a reaction to the chaos and social breakdown. As the leader of the first group of nonconformists that Chip comes into contact puts it:

"Yes," he said, "A lot of what we're told [about the pre-Uni world] is true. There was crime and violence and stupidity and hunger. There was a lock on every door. Flags were important, and the borders of territories. Children wanted their parents to die so they could inherit their money. The waste of labor and material was fantastic."

The world of *This Perfect Day* also has much in common with mainstream Western capitalist society. The idea of a giant supercomputer becoming the dominant authoritarian force was a major trope of late 1960s and early 1970s science fiction film and literature. This was partly linked to emerging fears from the late 1960s onward about the accelerated pace of social and economic change brought about by automated production and robotics. UniComp was a prescient idea given the ensuing era of the Internet and Google. Other ideas, such as the desire for the perfectly designed human body and the role of science in achieving it, also feel very current, as does the emphasis on curbing antisocial behavior with legal interventions and drug therapy.

To some degree, *This Perfect Day* has arrived.

**Andrew Nette**

# "Houston, we've had a problem": Technology, Mental Breakdown and the Science Fiction of Barry Malzberg

In a 1991 article, Canadian critic David Layton argues the work of Barry Malzberg runs counter to the dominant narrative of American science fiction, which until at least the late 1960s was centered on what Layton termed "the competent man," the individual, usually male, who triumphs in the face of war, ecological, technological, and social breakdown, or a malevolent alien presence. "The competent man is forced into a situation in which his true, hitherto latent, powers are revealed." Not only are Malzberg's protagonists not competent, they are usually in a state of mental disintegration, if not completely insane, facing terrible predicaments for which they don't even know the right questions to ask, let alone have any answers.

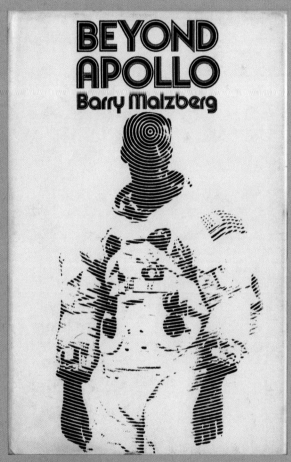

The best-known example is Malzberg's *Beyond Apollo* (1972). Set sometime in the 1980s, it begins in a rehabilitation center, where a psychologist is treating Harry Evans, the survivor of a failed two-man space flight to Venus, the latest in a series of missions to go wrong. NASA is under major public pressure and wants answers about what happened. The psychologist resorts to increasingly violent methods to force the truth out of Evans, including electroshock therapy and sensory deprivation. It is a futile effort. As Evans tells and retells his story, names of characters change, and a range of possibilities emerge. Did the other astronaut, the mission's commander, commit suicide, or did Evans murder him? Was Evans in communication with Venusians? Is he haunted by the commander's ghost? Has Evans gone completely insane?

*Beyond Apollo* showcases a key theme of Malzberg's fiction, fear that technology and the bureaucratic military-industrial complex set up to develop, promote, and police it are eroding our humanity, an unease he shared with many New Wave science fiction writers. America's space program was one focus of Malzberg's concern. He depicts it as a technocratic public relations stunt that dehumanizes the astronauts, destroys their mental health, and renders them sexually impotent. One can also make out clear parallels in the book between the conquest of space and military conquest on earth.

*Beyond Apollo*
(Faber and Faber, 1974)

*Beyond Apollo*
(Pocket Books, 1974)

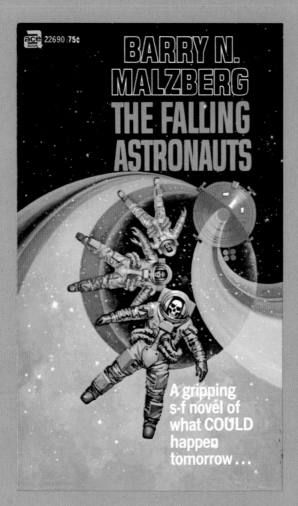

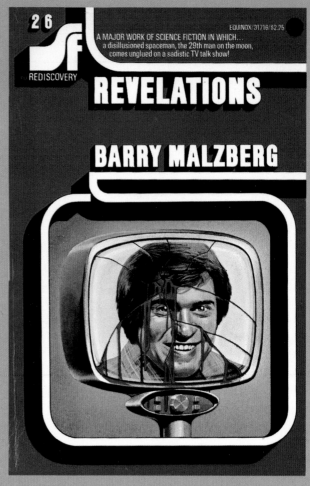

Malzberg also critiques the space program in other books. In *The Falling Astronauts* (1971), Colonel Richard Martin suffers a mental breakdown due to the stress of numerous space missions. Worried about the public relations fallout if he is dismissed, the space program gives him the job of handling the publicity for an upcoming mission, the exact nature of which is vague but involves astronauts being sent to the moon's surface with nuclear warheads. Martin struggles with the idealized version of space flight the press wants to hear versus the reality of his own experience. Then one of the astronauts on the mission suffers a similar breakdown and threatens earth with the nuclear devices. The 1972 novel *Revelations* also includes an astronaut who has had a nervous breakdown and become obsessed with getting on television to expose the failings of the space program.

These books are illustrative of the generally pessimistic dystopian tenor of Malzberg's work. *Guernica*

*Night* (1975) is set in an America mired in ennui so severe that the suicide rate threatens to depopulate the country. One source of relief is provided by a robot of the late President John F. Kennedy, the main attraction of a future Disney World, where it utters lines from the former leader's old speeches. Kennedy also appears in *The Destruction of the Temple* (1974). Set in a psychologically and physically crumbling New York in the year 2016, a researcher reenacts the president's assassination as a way of trying to understand the regressive social forces that he believes were unleashed by the killing.

Malzberg was a New York social worker in the early 1960s, who got his start as a writer penning articles for pulp magazines and, like his contemporary, Robert Silverberg, wrote smut under an assumed name. He worked as an agent for the Scott Meredith Literary Agency and found creative and commercial success in the late 1960s. His output was prodigious:

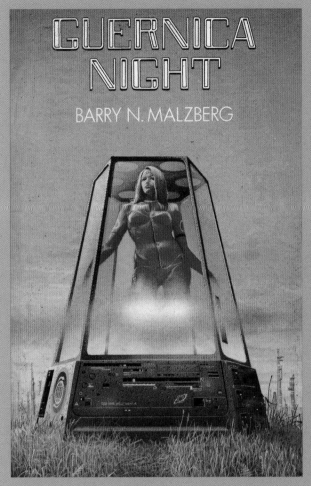

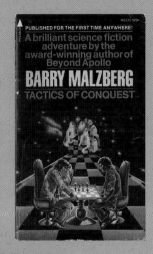

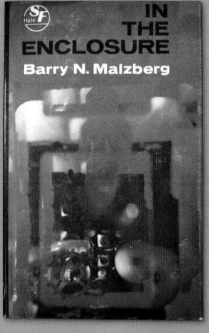

Clockwise from top left: *The Falling Astronauts* (Ace, 1971). *Revelations* (Equinox, 1977). *Guernica Night* (New English Library, 1978). *In the Enclosure* (Avon, 1973). *Tactics of Conquest* (Pyramid, 1974). *In the Enclosure* (Hale, 1976). *The Day of the Burning* (Ace, 1974). *On a Planet Alien* (Pocket Books, 1974). *The Sodom and Gomorrah Business* (Pocket Books, 1974). *The Gamesman* (Pocket Books, 1975).

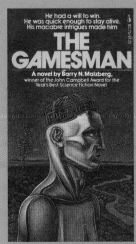

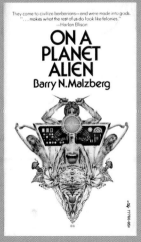

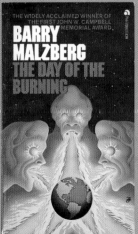

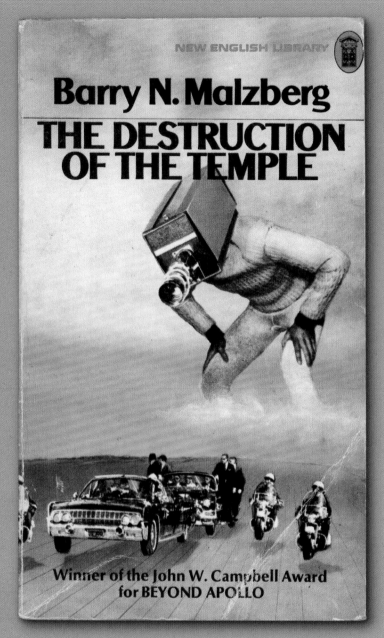

NEW ENGLISH LIBRARY

# Barry N. Malzberg

## THE DESTRUCTION OF THE TEMPLE

**Winner of the John W. Campbell Award for BEYOND APOLLO**

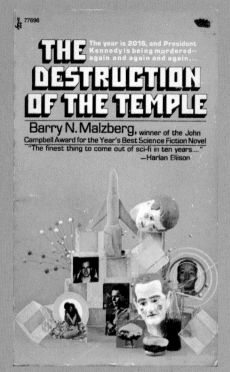

77696

The year is 2016, and President Kennedy is being murdered—again and again and again...

# THE DESTRUCTION OF THE TEMPLE

**Barry N. Malzberg,** winner of the John Campbell Award for the Year's Best Science Fiction Novel
"The finest thing to come out of sci-fi in ten years...."
—Harlan Ellison

Clockwise from top left: *The Destruction of the Temple* (New English Library, 1975). *The Destruction of the Temple* (Pocket Books, 1974). *Herovit's World* (Pocket Books, 1974).

Herovit's World
Barry N. Malzberg

forty-three novels and numerous short stories, which were published in sixteen collections. In addition to smut, as Mike Barry, he penned the fourteen-book *Lone Wolf* series, featuring an unhinged ex-cop turned vigilante against a drug-dealing criminal organization.

Malzberg generated controversy for his forthright opinions on the state of science fiction generally, including in works like *Breakfast in the Ruins* (2007), his inside look at the genre and his career. And he was unafraid to apply the fictional blowtorch to his own career and aspirations. It is hard not to see elements of Malzberg as he saw himself in *Herovit's World*

(1974), the story of another far from competent man, a disillusioned hack science fiction writer. In a failing marriage, with a looming book deadline and drinking heavily, the protagonist James Herovit's identity fractures and he starts a dialogue with Kirk Poland, the pseudonym under which he writes his best-known work, a long-running space opera series, which Herovit knows has zero literary and intellectual merit, and its main action hero character Mack Miller.

**Andrew Nette**

# The Stars My Destination

## The Future According to Gay Adult Science Fiction Novels of the 1970s

For decades, science fiction was overwhelmingly a straight boys' club; girls who lacked gravity-defying breasts and wasp waists were unwelcome, even though the genre-defining milestone *Frankenstein* (1818)—whose creature is the product of science, not witchcraft or the whims of capricious gods—was written by young Mary Wollstonecraft Shelley. The genre flourished in the latter half of nineteenth century, when novels by Jules Verne (*From Earth to the Moon*, 1865) and H.G. Wells (*The Time Machine*, 1895) achieved popular success by combining adventure and a vividly imagined future tethered, however tenuously, to reality. Nineteenth-century men couldn't fly to the moon or even across oceans but with gliders they *could* defy gravity—reality and fantastic fiction were no longer doomed to remain forever on parallel tracks . . . though boys of all ages still await their flying cars.

And society could change. In *Herland* (1915), Charlotte Perkins Gilman (of 1892's chilling *The Yellow Wall-Paper*, about a woman driven mad by the suffocating weight of patriarchal dictates) posits a vibrant society of fearless, educated women who reproduce by parthenogenesis, live cooperatively, and are good not only to each other but to the three men who blunder into their estrogen-driven Eden.

Some female sci-fi writers, like "James Tiptree Jr." (Alice Bradley Sheldon, 1915–1987) flew under the sexist radar by writing under pseudonyms. Others, like Ursula K. Le Guin (*The Left Hand of Darkness*, 1969) and Joanna Russ (*The Female Man*, 1975) let their lady flags fly, writing novels that addressed gender and sexuality as directly as gay novelist Samuel R. Delany's *Dhalgren* (1975), a kaleidoscope of fluidity and difference. That said, a quick and dirty web search for "gay science fiction" gets *very* dirty very fast—porn sites with names you wouldn't say in front of your gran and labeled "unsafe" by your in loco parentis browser.

Gay male adult novels of the 1970s embraced the conventions of thrillers, spy novels, westerns, gothic horror, mysteries, and science fiction. They were predicated on the assumption that gay men grew up loving the same genre icons as their straight peers: the gunslinger, the private dick, the cowboy, the spaceman. Gay pulps were the equivalent of America's "race" movies, independently produced films made in the first half of the twentieth century that took the conventions of Hollywood genre films and tweaked them for African American audiences by casting actors who looked like them, while sometimes addressing issues specific to people of color.

Gay men and women rarely saw themselves in mainstream American novels or films, except as comic pansies, villainous dykes, insidious deviants, and victims of violence or blackmail. But science fiction has always been fertile ground for imagining "what if. . ." and for all the robots and rocket ships clichés, much gay adult science fiction was less about hardware than software—our human flesh and the conflict between personal desires and social conventions.

Many gay writers of the 1970s took advantage of the relative freedom offered by adult book publishers whose mandate was that with a suggestive cover and a sex scene in every chapter they had a book they could sell. How any given author filled the rest of the pages was their business: contemporary drama, sports romp (like the delightfully named *Beachballer* trilogy [1973–1975] about humpy competitive beach volleyball enthusiasts), historical codpiece ripper. While many readers still associate science fiction with synthetic beings and space exploration, it's inextricably entwined with the reasons human beings aspire to do what we do: scale Mount Everest, plumb the Marianas Trench, explore the heavens.

We are by nature curious, creative, and competitive apes, but we also define ourselves in part by what we want to escape or transcend—racism, sexism, religious oppression, sexually oriented discrimination, and stifling social norms. Gay adult science fiction novels of the seventies went there with a combination of optimistic imagination and personal experience of prejudice and discrimination.

The 2069 trilogy of prolific writer Larry Townsend, aka Bud Bernhardt (1930–2008), is the original Star Wars trilogy of vintage gay sci-fi, epic in scope and rife with detail that ranges from clothing—a moment, please, for the "loinstrap," the ultimate in barely there leisurewear, and singing earrings from Uranus (a sublimely juvenile joke)—to the intricacies of alien anatomies and robosex. That said, there's no bot in Townsend's space opera as prissy as protocol droid C-3PO.

Published in 1969–1970, the 2069 novels' gay individuals and families are accepted in a way that mirrored the state of racial equality in America at the time: there are laws protecting their rights, but not everyone's on board. When the books were written, the Civil Rights Act of 1964 had authorized the federal government (as opposed to individual state governments, whose attitudes regarding racial equality varied dramatically) to combat racial discrimination in schools, workplaces, restaurants, movie theaters, and public toilets. This was opposed by a significant number of white Americans and smolderingly resented by others.

It wasn't until 1969's Stonewall Riots—days of protests that began on June 28, sparked by one police raid too many on the Greenwich Village gay bar the Stonewall Inn (whose regulars included lesbians and trans people, because there were only so many places people who weren't straight could go to drink, dance, and flirt) that shone a mainstream spotlight onto decades of activism.

That said, any American science fiction novel set exactly one hundred years later also owes a debt of imagination NASA's Apollo program. Dedicated to putting a man on the moon before the end of the 1960s, it fired American dreams for a decade, and Apollo 11's Neil Armstrong and Buzz Aldrin left their footprints on the lunar surface on July 21, 1969. The 2069 trilogy's preoccupations also dovetail with multiple social revolutions that Townsend was part of. By 1969, he was president of HELP (Homophile Effort for Legal Protection), a visible member of the S&M community, and one of five gay writers—with Douglas Dean, Dirk Vanden, Samuel Seward/Phil Andros, and Peter Tuesday Hughes—who unsuccessfully tried to form a gay-owned adult book publishing company called the Renaissance Group.

The 2069 trilogy was an act of the imagination that bound together a sexually explicit Buck Rogers story and a referendum on gay rights. In 2069, gay marriage has been legal, if not universally accepted, for fifty years. Genetic selection ensures that everyone is attractive. Although aging hasn't been entirely eliminated, there are still plenty of old folks whose lives have been extended by Reversol, a drug that keeps them vigorous but not youthful. Fresh-faced Ronnie Lang lives with his two fathers in the "Malibu Gay Ghetto"—not a slur, except perhaps to members of the reactionary Humphrey Society ("Humpties")—and wants to enter the Space Academy and explore the universe, which he does, under the tutelage of hot daddy Colonel "Mac" MacGruder. Lang also discovers that "gaysex" is the language of interstellar diplomacy—there's more than one reason why Space Exploration Command is abbreviated to SEXCOM. I doubt that it's a deliberate callback, but the scenario recalls Paul Jones's thriller Maneater (undated, c.1968–1970), in which United Nations Crime Control Commission agent Jake Gold muses that if world leaders hashed out their differences in bed the world would be a better place.

The saga continues in 2069+1 (whose phallic rocket ship cover vividly evokes the title of Kurt Vonnegut's 1972 "The Big Space Fuck") and 2069+2—a moment, please, for leisure-clothing fabric "kleersilk" (you're not naked but might as well be) and man purses—because there's no room for the rest of your junk in a loinstrap. The 2069+2 installment continues the saga with a digression into ancient Egyptian mythology—Erich von Daniken's 1968 Chariots of the Gods? which postulated that aliens influenced human social development, was having a cultural moment that Townsend wove into his gay-positive future.

He continued to explore the idea that homophobia is local and "samesex" is universal in The Scorpius Equation (1971), set in 5609 (now men wear "waist purses") and narrated by space-salvager Alpha Yarboro. It opens with a marriage: Yarboro and his five spouses (three women, two men) add another young man to their happy family group. So very 1970s—like a middle-class commune, only smaller. Then it's back to business; the cargo ship Orion Maru has disappeared on the border of Scorpian Empire. The Scorpians call jurisdiction and search for survivors, finding four: Captain Robikoff, a crewman, and two passengers. The situation escalates quickly and much between-the-sheets diplomacy lies between crisis and the discovery that the titular "Scorpius Equation" is a very 1960s message about everybody just getting along.

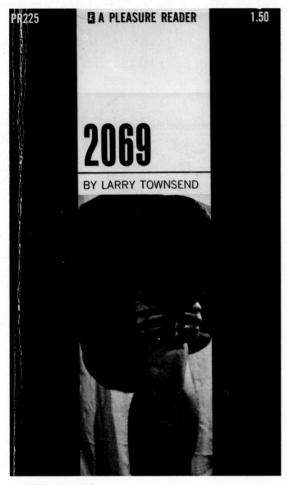

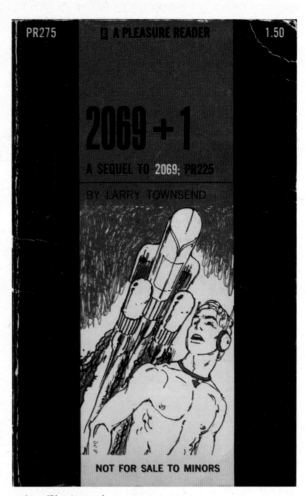

*2069* (Phenix, 1969)

*2069+1* (Phenix, 1970)

I have no way of knowing whether Townsend saw the rock musical *Hair* (1967), but it opened in Los Angeles in 1969 while he was writing the *2069* novels, and its hippie-trippy cosmic vibe is reflected in the signature song "Age of Aquarius," which received significant pop radio airplay: "When the moon is in the Seventh House/And Jupiter aligns with Mars/Then peace will guide the planets/And love will steer the stars/This is the dawning of the Age of Aquarius." That's right in line with Townsend's vision of the fuel that drives his future's space program, and Yarboro's mix and match marriage reflects a considerably mellower attitude about women than Ronnie Lang's bitchy "Auntie" Jack's observation in *2069* that long space voyages with female crew members are like "travelling in a tin can full of fish."

In *The Scorpius Equation* women and men both have a place at the table and in the bedroom, itself a revolutionary notion in fiction written by and for gay

*The Scorpius Equation* (Olympia Press, 1971)

men. And the coded message discovered at the novel's end involves the three-pronged peace symbol emblematic of the gentle 1960s; Townsend, like many of his contemporaries in gay adult genre writing, lived on the cusp of both gay and counterculture history.

*Startail* (1969), written by Hank Leatherwood—a pseudonym that walks the line between butcher than thou and just plain rude (that would be "Rod Rammer")—is also a pulp space adventure with a generous helping of sex. Protagonist Davvi 51 is a cosman (as in cosmonaut), an interstellar navigator with a military background. He made his bones in earth's war against the Rivashinjadae—Koala-/Ewok-esqe aliens who aren't nearly as sweet as they look—but the battleship Bellephron (presumably named for the mythological Greek hero who slew the chimera and, more to the point, rode the flying steed Pegasus) is on a peaceful mission. It's transporting a birthday gift from His Most Glorious Imperial Majesty Shadronn III of Earth to the viceroy of planet Aetannus.

Davvi 51, like everyone else in this gay utopia, is too sexy for his job; since the long ago "Time of Understanding," every man has been offered *treatment* that inhibits the aging process and allows for something close to eternal youth. Plus, there aren't any women to spoil things with their inconvenient cycles and body-ruining pregnancies, which is great for shipboard morale, since sex is everyone's preferred form of recreation and uniforms run to thigh-skimming tunics, bicep bracelets, and sharp hats and boots. Even the ship's computer—model Sidgamma Epsilon Three, Sid for short—is an outrageous flirt and shameless voyeur with a sultry voice. Davvi 51 even has a regular boyfriend in Mikke 96.

The Bellephron's cargo is "The Daniell," the product of nine generations of selective breeding and asleep in a sealed casket; in a future where everyone is handsome, youthful, and uninhibited, virgin beauties are like unicorns—*everybody* wants one. In keeping with the novel's pulp influences, the ship is boarded by space pirates, and most of the crew is killed—Davvi and The Daniell survive and eventually fall in love, but along the way there are colorful adventures galore. The alien Ssnitharr, who look like man-sized Tyrannosaurus Rexes are a nicely goofy touch, the lovers/twins Ravenn and Nikko pander to a fantasy equally enticing to gay and straight men, and the female alien raped to death by a panther for the amusement of decadent aristocrats could have originated in one of the rougher sword-and-sandal spectacles produced by Italian exploitation filmmakers in the late 1960s and early 1970s.

And there *are* horses—Davvi and the ragtag band of freedom fighters he assembles find themselves battling on horseback and discover that the bond between a brave man and a stalwart horse is a powerful one, which is why they all hang onto their steeds after the battle dust settles. Maybe Leatherwood grew up on a farm or ranch, perhaps he just loved a manly western mixed with a good space opera, a fun peplum picture, and a rip-roaring dinosaur movie; *Startail* is a Saturday afternoon genre movie marathon rolled into one sex-drenched story, complete with a happy ending (the traditional kind) for Davvi and The Daniell, who by the story's end is just plain old Danni and glad of it.

The pseudonymous Felix Lance Falkon's marvelously titled *Hung in Space* (1969) is predicated on a venerable gay fantasy—that straight men secretly want to go with other guys and just need a *"had to"* excuse to cast off their tired old ethics. The crew of Captain Van Oaks's ship is in a quandary: crewman Toby had sex with an underage female from Ruvia, a planet of exotically feathered humanoids. She says he raped her; he says it was consensual. The violence-abhorring Ruvians sentence Toby to death by starvation, his offending man parts in shackles. Toby's shipmates can visit his prison cage, but only if they're naked, to thwart food smuggling (cue an upswing in gym attendance).

The solution: a protein-rich liquid that comes in its own package . . . semen. Yes, the Space Patrol's manual does include a whole chapter about the wrongs of same-sex shenanigans but, hey—anything for your brother in arms.

So much for the plot—the imp of the perverse is in the details, starting with the cussing, heavy on fellatio: "Cocksucking Canopus!" is a keeper. Toby's shipmates enter into the spirit of taking one for the team—lots of talk about "Just makin' sure I ain't getting' t' like th' stuff"—that segues into merely "being curious" and a united embrace of fetishistic near-nudity even on their own ship—boots and belts and "holstered pistol[s]." Soon enough Toby's shipmates are both feeding *and* fellating him—*there's* a team building exercise unlikely to wind up in the basic corporate workbook—and by the end even the Ruvians embrace the idea that feathered or not, we're all more alike than we are different. While less than profound, *Hung in Space*'s spin on the

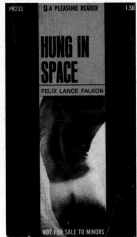
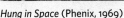

*Hung in Space* (Phenix, 1969)

*Mickey's One* (Phenix, 1970)

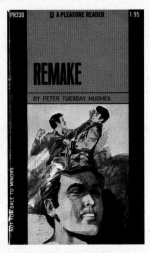

*Remake* (Phenix, 1971)

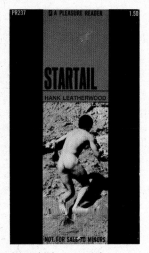

*Startail* (Phenix, 1969)

reality of situational homosexuality does suggest playfully that there's some flexibility in sexual orientation, one that reflected groundbreaking researcher Alfred Kinsey's still controversial conclusion that human sexual behavior exists on a spectrum, and desire can be more fluid that the binary terms as "homosexual" and "heterosexual" suggest.

*Remake* (1971) is a trippy exercise in pornographic paranoia by the prolific Peter Tuesday Hughes, whose output is distinguished both by its size and scope—he could dirty up just about any genre, from historical romance (*The Gooser*, 1969) through to political satire (*The Other Party*, 1968) to espionage novels, including *TAngier 6–6969* (1970) and a six-book series featuring globetrotting agent provocateur Bruce Doe, whose cover is working as a travel agent—Hughes's own profession.

*Remake*'s Rex Raines is on death row for strangling his boyfriend and dumping his dismembered remains in San Francisco harbor. When Lieutenant Commander Robert Wake—who, curiously, looks *exactly* like Raines—offers him the opportunity to become a Pri-Vol (prison volunteer) in an ongoing military experiment lumbered with a string of fatal failures, Raines takes it because, really . . . what does he have to lose, and at least it gets him out of his cell. Well, his memory, for one—courtesy of a top secret invention called "the womb"; Raines is "the baby."

*Remake* quickly heads into *Manchurian Candidate* territory. Richard Condon's 1959 novel explicitly played to American Cold War fears of homeland infiltration, as did John Frankenheimer's 1962 film version, but the roots of both are in a generational cultural notion that

American men were being demasculinized, robbed of their God-given virility, as articulated in popular novelist/essayist Philip Wylie's hugely popular screed *Generation of Vipers* (1942). It warned, among many other things, that post–World War II "momism" was making fine young American lads "soft," a short hop from being queer an accusation leveled only twenty years earlier at Italian-born actor Rudolph Valentino, whose continental aplomb made him a heartthrob of the flickers, as movies were then called. The venerable *Chicago Tribune* labeled him a "painted pansy" and blamed him and his ilk for the feminization of once red-blooded American men, who were being bullied into surrendering their masculine filth and funk, because "modern" bitches preferred lap dogs to wolves.

Though written on the upswing of the US gay rights movement, *Remake* also reflects (perhaps consciously, perhaps not) the reality that gay men and women were not immune to ingrained stereotypes about each other. As Raines's childhood memories return, he recalls being abused by his lesbian mother and her butch girlfriend, but he identifies as straight(*ish*). The fact that he's a convicted murderer suggests that his fence-sitting has not worked out well for him. The novel's more clearly articulated message was that in the 1960s and early 1970s being either openly homosexual or closeted came at a price.

Ostensibly straight lookalike Wakefield is forced to acknowledge his own homosexuality, which he's been repressing since he was a youth; he even changed his first name from the gender-neutral Robin to the conventionally masculine Robert. Once Wakefield realizes the womb has linked his mind with Raines's—"That lousy pervert Raines [is] beaming filth into my head"—he wants out of the project. Sadly, his superiors aren't about to let him abandon ship. *Remake* is driven in part by the specter of PTSD (Post Traumatic Stress Disorder, a term coined in the 1970s). Wakefield, a Vietnam War veteran who spent time in a POW camp, is clearly suffering from it. But Hughes also suggests that Raines's brutal childhood was itself a battlefield, and that his damage and Wakefield's are more alike than not; a sophisticated insight for a stroke book.

Hughes's *Alien* (1972) is also a mind warp, and here's an unusual way to open a gay porn novel: with a Roman proverb as the title of chapter 1: "*Audi, vide, si vis vivere in pace*" (listen, watch, and stay silent if you want to live in peace), followed by protagonist Garth Grainger—of the white hair, blue skin, and "star-shaped" nipples—waking up wondering, "Does the atom have consciousness and will?" a question first posed by twentieth-century physicist Wolfgang Pauli.

The reader is plunged into a baffling situation: Grainger is trapped in a glass-like cube, unable to move, within sight of five exact duplicates of himself in similar enclosures—they're all being milked of their most precious bodily fluid. And what's Gandy—Grainger's lover and classmate at the space academy—doing there? Gandy disappeared in space three months earlier. The year is 5970, and the human race reproduces via test tube: Men and women don't need to have sex and women, released from the shackles of child-rearing, have become "predatory and aggressive." So men prefer sex with each other even though they aren't supposed to, and Gandy, it ensues, is an alien reproduction of a human being. Earth is gone ("We blew ourselves up," echoing the devastating conclusion of 1968's *Planet of the Apes*) and the alien Sinodans—all male and not recognized as human by the governing Space Counsel—consume the essence that issues from human "tentacles of life."

There's more (yes, robot sex), but that's the gist and the whole story essentially takes place in Gandy's mind. The details are marvelous, though, from "rasp musicians"—insectoid aliens who make music by vibrating their skin (the Counsel *does* deem them "human") and singing earrings performing "a popular drag-tune from Uranus." Yes, juvenile, but so stupid it's clever or so clever it's stupid. Either way it's more than a little obsessive, like *Hung in Space*, but *Alien*'s universe building is intricate and boldly goes with a sneakily downbeat ending.

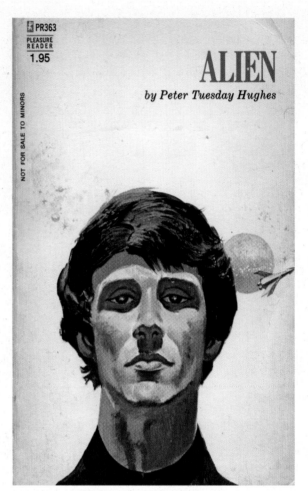

*Alien* (Greenleaf Classics, 1972)

*Alien* was published shortly after the first run of Gene Roddenberry's optimistic and hugely influential series *Star Trek* (1966–1969), in which the human space explorers sought out "strange new worlds," looked for "new life and new civilizations," and went boldly "where no man [had] gone before." To be sure, the farthest *Star Trek* ever ventured into gender nonconformity was when man's man James Kirk found his consciousness trapped in the body of Dr. Janice Lester, while she had a fine old time occupying his flesh, in "Turnabout Intruder" (1969), the last episode of the final season of the series. Generally regarded as a less than stellar sendoff for the series, I'd argue that it prefigured the queer Kirk/Spock stories that drove pioneering fanzine *Naked Times* (thirty-two issues, 1978–1994), while *Naked Times* paved the way for the now ubiquitous "slash" fan fiction that imagines fictional characters in noncanonical romantic/sexual scenarios.

William Maltese's *Tlen* novels (published under the pseudonym William J. Lambert III) have something about them of *Chariots of the Gods*, as well as the more general 1960s and 1970s distrust of established cultural institutions, especially religious ones. But Maltese's fertile imagination tends to both the sensual and the exotic, so let's just say this space odyssey spends a good deal of time below Orion's belt.

Born on a space ship—the first natural born child after two centuries of test-tube babies—protagonist La Mar is headed for what promises to be an epic party on planet Ten (or "Tlen," as it sounds if the person alerting you to the wild revels—La Mar's faun-like lover Phal— is simultaneously fellating you) . . . or perhaps it's on planet Appolo, which conjures associations with the highly sexed gods of ancient Greece and its culture of homoeroticism. Phal doesn't know exactly where the party is, but La Mar—who may be the avatar of an ancient prophecy—needs to negotiate five roads to find the fun.

*Five Roads to Tlen* (1970) is a bit like Martin Scorsese and Joseph Minion's *After Hours* (1985) in reverse: *After Hours'* beleaguered hero just wants to get home after a wild night on the town, while La Mar wants to get *to* the wild party before the fun has all been had. But damned if it's easy—just for starters, he finds himself trapped in a sex machine (à la Jean Claude Forest/Roger Vadim/Terry Southern's out of this world 1968 sexual odyssey *Barbarella*) that takes him a week to escape.

Then there's a stop on the female-dominated planet Quelia, where women get to have sex with everyone, and gay men are abominations. This doesn't stop La Mar from having sex with boyish Multo and suffering the consequences; he must undergo "The Ritual," which involves getting blown by a snake goddess—an actual snake (therefore awesomely phallic) who for some godly reason decides not to devour La Mar's privates.

Road Three leads to planet V6, which is full of valleys, including the Valley of Boys; adventurers have gone on to Tlen from V6, but not the boys—they go into the forest at sixteen and are dissolved into piles of ash. La Mar also has carnal knowledge of a watermelon and a cantaloupe. Road Four is the road of pain, which involves sex with an unpleasantly well-endowed alien, while Road Five leads to pretty, almost effeminate, Alexis, bearer of bad news: "There was no party on Tlen." There *are* deities, though, and La Mar becomes one of them.

Set "more than a year" later, *The Gods of Tlen: The Magnificent Sequel to Five Roads to Tlen* (1970) finds La Mar mired in the realization that being a god in no way lives up to the hype; in fact, he feels as though he's in Hades, having lost most of his memories while crossing the river Lethe. He's not even immortal, as his new friend Miktlon points out—he's aging more slowly than he would have in his previous incarnation, but one day he's still going to return to the dust.

This new world of gods and monsters is ruled by the child king Crag, a proper little Caligula, and filled with marvelous abominations with such attributes as two twenty-four-inch penises, one black and one white (the Terhaf) and the ability to gender shift at will. There's even a tree—the Wilup—you can have sex with, if you're inclined to botanical bothering, and it most certainly trumps the *Harry Potter* universe's Whomping Willow. Crag and his entourage amuse themselves by watching from "the progress room" and betting on the likelihood that candidates like La Mar will eventually mature into actual deities. And it ends on a truly trippy note, both paranoid and beatific, and as open to stoned discussion as the conclusion of Stanley Kubrick's majestic *2001: A Space Odyssey* (1968).

And that brings us to Larry Townsend's *Mickey's One* (1970), a twenty-minutes-into-the-future tale. While there's always someone decrying media exploitation of the public, *Mickey's One* takes it one step beyond. Townsend's Mickey Greco isn't just smart, polished, and mediagenic: he's an *esper* (from ESP, extrasensory perception, a term that appears to have been coined by esteemed science fiction writer Alfred Bester in the 1950 short story "Oddy and Id")—a man with paranormal abilities, someone who can connect to other people's minds. Espers have ESP—nothing supernatural, just an ability most people don't have or can't access, like perfect pitch or eidetic memory.

Mickey had it as a child, lost it as a teenager—raging hormones shorted the circuits—and rediscovered his powers as he was about to start college. And I don't think it's coincidental that in adult novels of the 1960s and early 1970s "powers" was a go-to term for men's sexual gear—not too crude but widely understood by the readers for whom such books were intended.

Mickey starts out putting his powers to selfish but not especially toxic ends. As a child he gets a playmate to give him a coveted toy; he later uses them to get his respectable but not outstanding Grade Point Average polished and to erase some awkward sexual experiences from lovers' minds. Mickey graduates to manipulating Jack, his older and useful boyfriend, aces law school, and by his mid-twenties is being groomed to run for congress as an open but discrete homosexual, the kind of queer who, to paraphrase venerable English stage actress Mrs. Patrick Campbell (1865–1940), has the decency not to do it in the street and frighten the horses. Once Mickey figures out how to use his power via TV and radio airwaves, he refines his message to focus on the revered American right to do as you please in the privacy of your own home.

Mickey wins a congressional election, infiltrates committees not traditionally open to fledgling elected officials, gets an equal rights bill pushed through congress and the senate, and forges an uneasy alliance with young congressman Conrad Henderson, whose district didn't support Mickey, but who confides that he too is an esper and knows a fellow traveler when he sees one. He's also Mickey's "one"—the only man he truly wants, though by the time he realizes it, it's too late.

And of course, personable Mickey is a sociopath, perfectly positioned to exploit 1960s youth culture (the parallel with Peter Watkins's chilling 1967 film *Privilege* is hard to ignore) and, through Henderson, learns that many powerful men in Washington are espers, though most people just figure they're great public speakers. Henderson and Mickey merge mentally and physically; Mickey is stronger, but Henderson is more in control of his gift and sets their first goal as lowering the age limit for presidential candidates from thirty-five to thirty, which also intersects with Barry Shear's 1968 cult movie *Wild in the Streets*, a potent mixture of youth-culture exploitation and sly political commentary built around a twenty-two-year-old pop star turned voting rights crusader for young teenagers.

Ultimately, though, *Mickey's One* is a story of despair: heights never scaled, goals unreached, and slipperiness of power and powers. "You haven't got it, have you, Baby?" hisses Howard at the book's conclusion. "Where is it? Where's your power gone?" A low blow, perhaps, but a devastating exit line. *Mickey's One* was a timely and subversive undermining of the myth that American democracy first and foremost rewarded hard work and ideological virtue. That notion is, if anything, more tarnished now than it was nearly half a century ago, when the deep-rooted reality that America was not in practice a meritocracy and the uncomfortable truth that Lady Liberty's lamp never shone equally

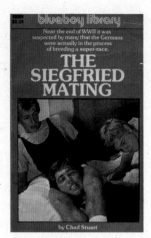

The Siegfried Mating
(Blue Boy, 1977)

The Concentration of Hans
(101 Enterprises, 1967)

for all the tired, poor, and homeless people yearning to breathe free was already being aggressively voiced by people of color, women, and homosexuals increasingly tired of pretending they weren't who they were to avoid censure, personal and professional discrimination, and physical violence, including murder.

The novel was rooted in the recognition that television is a powerful influence on the political process, one that privileges entertainment over substantive discussion of issues and agendas and favors mediagenic candidates at the expense of those who are equally or better qualified but lack the skills to *sell* confidence, competence, and likeability. That lesson was first driven home by the 1960 televised debates between John F. Kennedy and Richard M. Nixon. Both were experienced politicians, but Kennedy was at home in front of television cameras, and the restless, fidgety Nixon looked like the guy you wouldn't sit next to on a bus.

Gay adult novels of the 1970s ranged from formulaic smutty narratives to subversive stories that challenged a largely homophobic mainstream culture and posited scenarios in which gay was a fact of life, gay just *was*. That was the crux of gay adult fiction of the 1970s—it wasn't inherently defensive, though it often produced narratives acknowledging that gay life could be difficult, unfair, and even cruel. They were purchased by a variety of readers, some of whom were comfortable in their own skins and wanted to read books about men like themselves (or the men they aspired to be) and some who weren't but craved reassurance that they weren't singular aberrations, hellbound sinners, or mistakes of nature.

Writers, editors, and publishers of gay adult novels understood that their readers lived in a homophobic world and enjoyed erotic books that integrated sex scenes into narratives. In the 1970s, the prolific Parisian Press incorporated the phrase "the books with a story" (rendered in neat cursive loops that would have delighted my second-grade teachers) onto their back-cover design. And they realized that many readers lived in rural areas and small towns that lacked the gay communities found in cities like New York, San Francisco, and Philadelphia—men who scrutinized the pages of available titles and order forms that included an indemnification requiring a signature: "I hearby [*sic*] certify that I am an adult at least 21 years of age."

Gay adult novels were rarely intended to be works of great literature—though many writers took their work seriously—but they were revolutionary. They didn't seek to justify the existence of gay men to straight people, and their influence on generations of readers is still very much alive. I recently gave a presentation about vintage gay adult novels at a senior center for older gay men and women; the room was full, which was not for lack of alternatives—I was competing with yoga classes, a movie, and other activities. Attendees included a woman whose family had owned a book-store that sold gay-oriented books to trusted customers and a man who had worked in the distribution depart-ment of a publishing company with a significant gay adult list. Others had bought gay adult books, many by mail. They all affirmed that these books had mattered to *them*—the Q&A session ran over its allotted time and continued into the hallway.

My initial interest in these books was the product of pure curiosity fostered by the discovery of a body of underappreciated popular fiction. I believe without reservation that the best gay adult novels are as good as the best hardboiled fiction, books that today have achieved a level of critical acclaim of which David Goodis, Jim Thompson, and Horace McCoy could only have dreamed when they began writing. A handful of gay adult novels were excellent books written by serious and skillful writers like William Maltese, Dirk Vanden, Victor Banis, and Jay Greene, a significant number were entertaining pulp fiction with vivid slashes of social commentary, and some were no better than they should have been, as my mother would have said.

Overall, they were texts that documented gay lives, fantasies, and aspirations—both sociopolitical statements and entertainment. In the case of gay science fiction, they were books that envisioned a future that was, for most gay men in the 1970s, all but unimaginable, a future in which same-sex orienta-tion was just one of multiple norms. There might still be bigots, but there always are; anyone who suggests otherwise is as deluded as those who declare that we live in a post-racial world.

That adult books could be a lifeline was a sneaky revelation. Literary stories about gay men helped weave them into the larger fabric of society, but gay adult novels blazed an equally bold path. They revolved around characters who were who they were and whose sexual lives proved appealing to a broad spectrum of readers, from out men living in socially liberal communities to men trapped by family obliga-tions or their own reluctance to abandon the familiar in communities where they needed to maintain a low profile but still yearned for validation.

That was truly revolutionary—like all good specula-tive fiction, gay adult sci-fi novels of the 1970s looked at the past and present then extrapolated, and most chose to accentuate the positive. The best were invested in personal, social, political, and sexual freedom; they looked at the world and imagined the ways it could change, and it has. Still waiting for the flying cars, though.

**Maitland McDonagh**

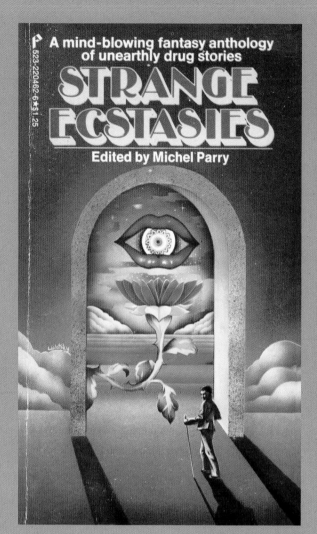

A mind-blowing fantasy anthology of unearthly drug stories

# STRANGE ECSTASIES

### Edited by Michel Parry

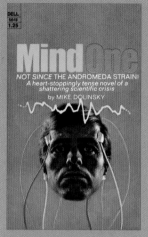

**Mind One**

*NOT SINCE* THE ANDROMEDA STRAIN!
*A heart-stoppingly tense novel of a shattering scientific crisis*

by MIKE DOLINSKY

Panther Science Fiction
# Nova Express
## William Burroughs
### Author of The Naked Lunch

## Joanna Russ
### AND CHAOS DIED

A CLASSIC NOVEL BY THE NEBULA AWARD-WINNING AUTHOR

Clockwise from top left: *Strange Ecstasies* (Pinnacle, 1974). *Mind One* (Dell, 1972). *Nova Express* (Panther, 1968). *The Probability Pad* (Pyramid, 1970). *The Mind Parasites* (Panther, 1977). *Barefoot In The Head* (Doubleday, 1970). *The Butterfly Kid* (Pyramid, 1967). *And Chaos Died* (Ace, 1970).

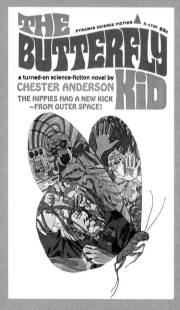

PYRAMID SCIENCE FICTION X-1730 60c

# THE BUTTERFLY KID

a turned-on science-fiction novel by
CHESTER ANDERSON
THE HIPPIES HAD A NEW KICK —FROM OUTER SPACE!

## BAREFOOT IN THE HEAD

**BRIAN W. ALDISS**

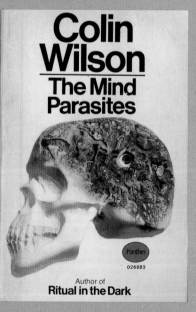

# Colin Wilson
## The Mind Parasites

Panther
026983

Author of
**Ritual in the Dark**

# Higher than a Rocket Ship: Drugs in SF

A widely noted quality of New Wave and experimental science fiction was its shift in focus from "outer space" to "inner space" in terms of incorporating, questioning, and exploring emotional states, visions, and altered consciousness. In part, this interest in the nature of perception accrued from the writing of the Beats and existentialists, new trends in psychology, and a burgeoning interest in spirituality beyond the confines of the Christian church. There was, of course, also the role of drugs. Some of these represented new chemical syntheses, while others had long been a part of human experience but were finding new popularity. Some, such as LSD and heroin, enjoyed periods of legality in the UK and US, while marijuana and others remained illegal throughout the period covered by this book. Illicit drug use was criticized by some political activists for presenting authorities with extra opportunities to destabilize and crack down on movements, as a distraction from core issues of wealth redistribution and the abolition of racial, class, and gender oppression, or because it offended their otherwise conventional sensibilities. For Yippies, hippies, freaks, and those involved in the broader countercultural revolt, licit drugs like alcohol were spurned in favor of consciousness expansion by any means necessary.

To add extra futuristic flavor to their tales, SF authors had long invented substances analogous to those already in existence, and this continued, albeit with increased frequency, through the largely incidental inclusion of newly conceived highs in many 1960s and 1970s SF novels. Works incorporating near future scenarios based on the existing counterculture, such as Marge Piercy's *Dance the Eagle to Sleep* (1970), unsurprisingly included the use of existing drugs central to the scene. In other cases, drug-based experiences made for useful plot digressions and devices, such as when Robert Silverberg's telepathic protagonist in *Dying Inside* (1972) enters the mind of his girlfriend to share an LSD trip.

For some authors, pushing the outer limits through the use of hallucinogens, heavy ingestion of heroin, tranquilizers, and amphetamines, and/or the use of nondrug-based practices, such as magical rituals and meditation, led to a complete overhaul in the nature of their work. Long concerned with the nature of human awareness, Aldous Huxley's

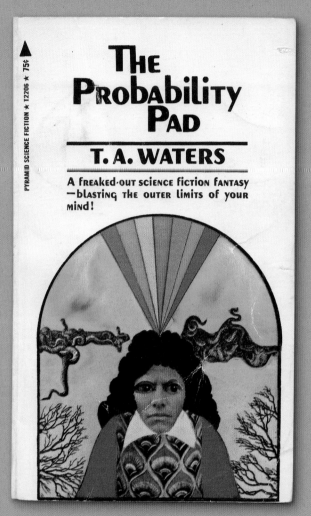

exploration of the use of recreational drugs for control in *Brave New World* (1932) had a major impact on fictional dystopias. Following up on a series of influential nonfiction works, including *The Doors of Perception* (1954), Huxley shifted gears fictionally with *Island* (1962), in which the deadening effect of "Soma" on human development in *Brave New World* was effectively contrasted with the enlightening social influence of "moshka medicine."

The cutup techniques and deliberately incoherent approach of William S. Burroughs's contemporary work was a further influence upon the writing style of many speculative authors, as was the experience of altered consciousness itself. Hallucinatory passages, if not entirely amorphous and barely structured

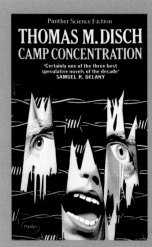
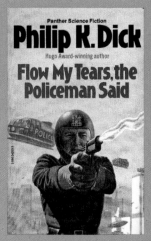

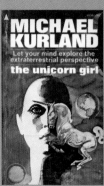

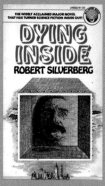

Clockwise from top left: *Camp Concentration* (Panther, 1969). *Flow My Tears, The Policeman Said* (Panther, 1974). *Indoctrinaire* (New English Library, 1971). *Indoctrinaire* (Pan, 1979). *Dying Inside* (Ballantine, 1976). *Island* (Penguin, 1966). *Dance The Eagle To Sleep* (Fawcett, 1971). *The Unicorn Girl* (Pyramid, 1969). *The Futurological Congress* (Futura, 1977).

plotlines and expression, came to feature in a wide range of SF novels. Philip K. Dick's drug use and spiritual experiences famously inspired and shaped many of his novels' portrayals of social relations, policing, and politics on earth and afar. Brian Aldiss created the nightmarish scenario of a postapocalyptic world literally bombarded with hallucinogens in *Barefoot in the Head* (1969), and Christopher Priest's *Indoctrinaire* (1971) similarly dealt with the potential outcomes of military experiments. Utilizing more formal prose, Thomas M. Disch's *Camp Concentration* (1968) also confronted the potential outcomes of military experimentation on consciousness and mental powers through its portrayal of leftist political prisoners undergoing forced treatment with a strain of syphilis.

More playful futuristic takes influenced by and about drug use also emerged during the era, as exemplified by what has become known as the Greenwich Village trilogy. Although Chester Anderson would go on to use some of the funds from the initial installment, *The Butterfly Kid* (1967), to set up Haight-Ashbury's Communications Company and print radical manifestos for the likes of the anarchist Diggers, the novel is focused on cultural challenges to the status quo rather than political ones. The popularity of the book's alien invasion–thwarting bohemians led to follow-ups in the form of Mike Kurland's time travelling *Unicorn Girl* (1969) and T.A. Waters's *The Probability Pad* (1970), both of which continued Anderson's largely lighthearted channeling of the altered states emanating from America's countercultural havens.

**Iain McIntyre**

# Freedom in the Mind

## Louise Lawrence's *Andra*

As hard as it is to imagine now, there was a time when few authors wrote books specifically targeted at teenagers. While the word *teenager* was first used as early as the 1920s, it didn't become widely known until after World War II, when urbanization and the growing social and financial independence of adolescents between the ages of thirteen and nineteen saw marketers recognize them as a distinct social group and a potentially profitable market.

While the motion picture, music, and fashion industries were quick to respond to this emerging demographic, this was less the case for publishing. Publishers did not really commission books specifically for teens and market them accordingly until the latter 1960s. Indeed, what we now call young adult, or YA, fiction only started to come into being following the success of books like S.E. Hinton's tough coming of age story *The Outsiders* and Robert Lipsyte's *The Contenders*, about a seventeen-year-old black male in Harlem who starts boxing as an alternative to drugs and gang membership, both published in 1967.

Elizabeth Holden, aka Louise Lawrence, in the 1990s

Even so, YA remained a relatively small component of the publishing industry until the 1970s. The portion of the industry focused on writing science fiction for teens, or "juveniles" as they were often called, was even smaller. One prominent exception was the series of thirty-seven science fiction books published in hard cover by the Philadelphia-based, youth-oriented company John C. Winston from 1952 to 1961, including works by Lester del Rey, Jack Vance, and Arthur C. Clarke. Some of the 160 plus novels written over the lengthy career of American science fiction and fantasy author Andre Norton were effectively young adult novels, although it does not appear that they were marketed as such. On the other hand, some of Ursula K. Le Guin's work, most prominently her *Earthsea Cycle*, six books beginning with *A Wizard of Earthsea* in 1968, were marketed as YA.

The best-known author writing fantasy and science fiction for adolescents in the United Kingdom during this period was John Christopher, a pseudonym for Sam Youd. As Christopher, he wrote *The Death of Grass*

*The Guardians* (Puffin, 1973)

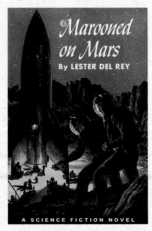

*Marooned on Mars* (John C. Winston, 1952)

*A Wizard of Earthsea* (Parnassus Press, 1968)

*A Wizard of Earthsea* (Puffin, 1975)

(discussed at some length on pages 161–165 in this book). He also penned a series of four YA dystopian novels in which humans are enslaved by aliens who travel in gigantic three-legged walking machines, the first of which, *The White Mountains*, appeared in 1967. His best-known YA science fiction work, *The Guardians* (1970), tells of an alternative England in the far future divided between a bucolic and aristocratic rural area, the "County," and poor, overpopulated, heavily monitored city areas known as "Conurbs."

A far less remembered pioneer of British science fiction for adolescents was Louise Lawrence, the pen name for Elizabeth Holden. Her writing career was short but prolific: twenty books from 1971 to 1986, a period when writing science fiction for teens was yet to be taken all that seriously, especially when a woman was writing it. Many of Lawrence's books touched on themes such as the environment, gender equality, antimilitarism, the power of outsiders to upend traditional viewpoints and dogmas, and mistrust of established power structures.

Although some of her novels have been reissued electronically, most are out of print and only available secondhand. This includes one of her most influential works, her 1971 debut *Andra*, the tale of a teenage girl who leads a youth rebellion against the authorities in a future dystopian society. The book appears to have had a major impact on several British female science fiction writers. *Andra's* influence also extended as far as Australia, where it was adapted for the small screen by the Australian Broadcasting Corporation (ABC) in 1976, as part of the national broadcaster's response to the popularity of imported American and British science fiction programs.

*Andra* takes place two thousand years in the future on an earth that has been destroyed by a war that knocked the planet off its rotational axis, making the surface uninhabitable and forcing what is left of humankind to live in underground cities. Although the book does not go into great detail, these cities appear to be grouped into two blocs, Sub City and its competitor power, Uralia. Life in Sub City One, where the story takes place, is strictly controlled. Individuals are regimented along IQ lines, with the different groups required to wear color-coded clothes. People grow up not knowing their parents, life partners are selected by a computer, and most die, or "expire," at the age of sixty, although elite individuals live longer due to technological interventions.

*Andra* (Macmillan, 1975)          *Andra* (Macmillan, 1976)

Fifteen-year-old female menial worker Andra has an accident during which she sustains significant brain damage. Her only chance of survival is to receive a brain graft, and the only brain that is available in the city's "organ plant" once belonged to a young radical male called Richard Carson, who died in 1987. Sub City One's best medical scientist, the 155-year-old Dr. Lascaux, undertakes the operation, the first person ever to do so. While the procedure is a success, it also transforms Andra. Her hair color changes from fair to dark and her eyes from blue to brown. But more significant are the changes in her personality. Previously average and conformist, when she regains consciousness, her IQ is higher, she is questioning and rebellious, and she shows no deference to her elders. She attracts a following of young people, much to the growing concern of Sub City One's rulers.

There are a number of other important characters: Syrd, an engineer and singer who has sought political asylum from one of the cities of what appears to be the even more oppressive state of Uralia, who befriends Andra while she is recovering in hospital; Professor Kiroyo, at 306, the oldest man in Sub City One, who is an expert on earth's culture before it was forced underground, and with whom Andra is sent to work in the city's museum, where she comes into contact with relics from the twentieth century; Daemon, head of the city's youth center, who is sympathetic to Andra's nonconformist views; Shenlyn, director of Sub City One; and Cromer, who heads up the city's security forces.

Lawrence cleverly depicts the way in which Andra starts to see the world around her through the consciousness of the long dead Carson, sensing his

*Andra* (Collins, 1971)

presence like "a small piece of his brain has been resurrected inside Andra's head." From the boy's memories she can imagine what the sun looks like, even though she has never seen it, and can paint pictures of what earth's surface used to be like two thousand years ago, and these memories make her angry:

> We, with our great machines, destroyed every living thing and condemned ourselves to creep like worms beneath the surface. My ancestors made me worse than a slug, never to see a tree or a flower growing under the sky, never to feel the wind, or the rain, or see the sun. To crawl through these metal passages where even the air we breathe is manufactured and the food we eat is synthetic and words have no meaning. There is no love, no hope, no happiness. This is not living. This is merely existing, being kept alive to keep our species alive and feed the demands of Shenlyn and the computers.

She grows her hair long, which is forbidden, and openly mocks Shenlyn, for which she has to undergo a course of "mental therapy." But other young people copy her behavior, wearing nonregulation clothes, growing their hair, and creating unauthorized paintings, which are hung on the walls of the city's youth center. At one point, Andra incites a near riot of the city's youth. The city's elite, and people like Syrd, are incapable of understanding her attraction for young people.

"Well, it's difficult to explain," says Daemon. "She's a symbol of what we want to be. She's free."

"Andra is no more free than we are. She has to do what she's told just as we do."

"I know that, but she's free in her mind."

"Boy, you are beyond me. I just don't understand."

Daemon tries to explain freedom as

> "something else which we seem to have lost through a thousand generations, and something Andra has regained. Freedom is outside our thoughts; we're only just beginning to realise what it is and that's because Andra is telling us. But we can't have freedom because we're denied self-expression."

Syrd sighed.

"I'm still not with you. Self-expression? What's that?"

"Self-expression is Andra."

"Go on."

"Andra grows her hair long because she wants it that way. And why shouldn't she if she likes it? Personally. I think it looks awful but I've no right to make her wear it short because I don't like it, nor has Shenlyn. Andra paints pictures she ought to not paint. She teaches you songs you ought not to sing. She rebels against society because she wants to be different and she tells us of a way of life that is beyond our conception, but even we in our apathy know it is far pleasanter than life in Sub City One."

The novel's other main plot strand involves Sub City One's attempts to build a rocket that can take some of the population to another world known as Planet 801. Syrd is revealed as a Uralian agent sent to sabotage the City's rocket program—the Uralians are planning a similar exodus—but he becomes disillusioned with his mission as he grows closer to Andra. The Uralians still manage to sabotage a ship that is returning to earth from Planet 801, and Andra takes part in a mission to the surface to retrieve data from the wreckage that shows the planet to be primitive but inhabitable, with a similar environment to earth before it was knocked off its axis.

The rulers of Sub City One need someone who can survive on a planet like earth was two thousand years earlier to lead the space mission, and Andra is the obvious choice. But before they can put the plan into effect, Cromer, another Uralian spy, triggers the launch of Sub City One's main rocket ship. Andra races to the cavern in which the rockets are housed and opens the doors so that the ship can escape without destroying the city. She is successful but is trapped in the cavern and killed in the process.

*Andra* often feels incomplete, with major parts of the story, particularly the conflict between Uralia and Sub City One, glazed over and underdeveloped. Its take on authoritarian politics and youth rebellion are interesting and no doubt an accurate reflection of what was occurring around the author at the time, even if they come across as a bit old-fashioned now. Some parts of the future society depicted in *Andra* also come across as somewhat outdated, sophisticated brain graft surgery and computers coexist with analogue wired telephones, but no more so than the future worlds envisaged in any episode of *Doctor Who* from the same era. What is interesting about the book, especially in the context of it being marketed as YA fiction, is Lawrence's depiction of a boy's brain being transplanted in a woman's body and some of the complications and possibilities that arise from this. As Melbourne scriptwriter, Adam Spellicy, a fan of the book, notes, we can speculate that Andra's name is "a prescient nod to her latterly-acquired androgynous nature."

Despite its shortcomings, *Andra* influenced several young women who went on to write science fiction and fantasy. "It was the book that made the whole character-plot interaction thing go click for me, when I read it at age fourteen," wrote British fantasy author Alison Sinclair in a post about the book on her website in March 2007. Writing in the online science fiction magazine *Strange Horizons*, in April

A rare publicity still from the television series, Andra, *TV Times*, July 31, 1976

2016, medieval history lecturer and fantasy author Kari Sperring remembered *Andra* as

> the first true dystopia I encountered, the first SF novel with a female character at its center, the first novel of revolution. In retrospect, Lawrence did not innovate any of these trends—though I think she may have been the first to bring them together in a book aimed specifically at teenage readers.

As a protagonist, Sperring argues, Andra was

> profoundly ordinary: not especially pretty, not especially intelligent, not especially anything, just a girl who happened to be in the right place at the right time. And, as a result of this accident of circumstance, both she and her world are profoundly changed and she is the agent of that change. In other books I'd read, boys started wars, piloted starships, worked magic, while girls waited on the sidelines. Andra all by herself flouted the rules of her society and started a revolution by her questions and confrontations and courage. She was the first kick-arse heroine I met—though, thankfully she was without the seemingly mandatory backstory of abuse and drama that modern convention seems to demand of female leads with agency, she was the precursor of Katniss Everdeen and other female leads with agency.

Holden/Lawrence was born in Surrey, southeast England, in 1943. She suffered from severe asthma as a child, which necessitated long periods in bed, during which she was allowed to access her mother's book collection and developed a taste for reading. She left school at the age of seventeen and became an assistant librarian. She entered an unhappy marriage at nineteen and began writing three years later, after the birth of the first of her three children. "Deprived of book-filled surroundings I was bound to write my own," she later remembered. *Andra* was her fourth novel but the first to be accepted for publication. She had a keen interest in psychology, feminism, sociology, and the occult, and cited George Orwell, Aldous Huxley, J.R.R. Tolkien, and English children's fantasy novelist Alan Garner as among her key influences.

Her output included science fiction, speculative fiction, and fantasy. She recalled:

> I wrote for teenagers. The books contain fantasy elements in a realistic setting—a combination of ordinary human characters influenced by extraordinary forces. Each story also touches upon some wider contemporary issue, such as violence, religion, the role of women, life and death, the conflict of science and nature.

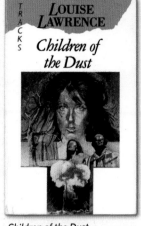

Children of the Dust
(Collins, 1990)

Indeed, while her work may have been targeted at younger readers, much of it had no shortage of adult themes. This is most clearly seen in her 1985 novel *Children of the Dust*, a multigenerational story about a British family surviving the aftermath of a nuclear war. The characters experience nuclear winter, radiation sickness and mutation, and attacks by wild dogs and other humans, before some of them eventually evolve into a new species of human with telekinetic powers. The novel, which tapped into the fear of nuclear conflict prevalent throughout the world in the eighties, sparked controversy for its depiction of post–nuclear war deformities and government indifference to civilian suffering, as well as its violence, swearing, and sex, and was banned from some school libraries.

Kari Sperring wrote:

> If Lawrence had been male, or if she had started writing even as little as five years later, I think we might even now be taking her more seriously. YA as a genre was only just beginning to exist in that Britain of the 1970s, and most of what there consisted of serious, older books, issue books about social exclusion, persecution, and historical events.

*Andra* was initially published in hardback by Collins in 1971, and subsequently released in paperback as part of the Topliner imprint. Started in 1968 and jointly owned by Macmillan and Pan, the Topliner series was deliberately oriented to what one newspaper advertisement labelled "the reluctant reader in the secondary school." Its unashamedly populist list, which included science fiction, horror, adventure, movie tie-ins, historical stories, and what was known in the seventies as "youth problem novels," caused controversy and claims of foisting lowbrow material onto teens. Full of "teenage revolutionaries and doomed romances [the Topliner series] did not sit well alongside Enid Blyton and [children's historical novelist] Henry Treece," recalled Sperring, but it was a perfect home for *Andra*.

An Australian Topliner edition of *Andra* was published in 1976 to coincide with the ABC's television adaption. The cover, a still from the series featuring Andra and Dr. Lascaux, is one of the few pieces of visual evidence that the now almost completely forgotten show ever existed. It appears to have aired only once, in mid-1976, and while the ABC claims to have copies in it archives, there are counterclaims that the series was accidently wiped. Spellicy, who saw the show, can only recall "distorted, ghost-like impressions haunting the periphery of my consciousness, as if glimpsed through the static snowstorm of a television set whose aerial is on the blink."

One of a number of locally made science fiction shows commissioned by the ABC in the 1960s and 1970s, *Andra* was specifically targeted at a young female audience, in an effort to balance out another locally made show, *Alpha Scorpio*. The latter was screened in 1974 and focused on two male university students who witness strange things while camping at Aireys Inlet on Victoria's South West Coast and discover that their friend is an alien who has landed on earth. Made on a shoestring budget, the eight episodes featured clothing store dummies instead of people for crowd scenes and in place of furniture large white blocks piled on top of each other.

"Tonally, I recall *Andra* being rather more solemn than any kids' show I'd ever seen, resolutely humorless in comparison to its nearest sci-fi equivalent, *Doctor Who*," remembers Spellicy. "This was serious television for children—a vehicle for challenging social, political, environmental and philosophical concepts."

**Andrew Nette**

# Mick Farren

## Fomenting the Rock Apocalypse

Writer, singer, journalist, activist, poet, and provocateur Mick Farren (1943–2013) was a polymath who helped shape the counterculture of sixties and seventies Britain.

Spawned by the social ferment of the sixties, Farren's voice was first heard as an atonal howl over the raucous din of the band, Social Deviants. A methedrine and reefer–fueled mix of caustic satire and primitive psychedelia, the Deviants (they dropped the "Social" early on) were an Anglo art school equivalent of the Fugs and early Mothers of Invention. The band made three memorable albums before disbanding at the close of the decade. Farren's work as a science fiction writer began in the aftermath of the demise of the Deviants and continued through the beginning of the nineties.

I interviewed Mick at his home on April 12, 1997. We started out discussing why his science fiction career got off to a relatively late start.

He reflected:

The odd thing was that in the fabulous sixties, paraphrasing Woody Guthrie, there weren't too many hiring blacks for writers. You could write polemics in the underground papers, but that was about it. The last [counterculture] book was really Richard Farina's [*Been Down So Long It Looks Like Up to Me*, 1966]. Ed Sanders [leader of the Fugs] really didn't get something on a major publisher until he did the Manson Family [*The Family*, 1971]. There was very little fiction. We just lived with *Stranger in a Strange Land* and *Dune*. That was one of the sad things.

He admits:

I was as much at fault as anybody. Instead of wanting to be Allen Ginsberg, you immediately

Mick Farren, top right with afro, and the *International Times* production team, 1971

thought it's a much better idea to be Dylan. So we all went out and bought guitars. So it all changed, and, in fact, the imaginative written word—prose, poetry, novels—apart from the science fiction writers like Harlan [Ellison] plugging away and a bit of Ballard, small presses faltered.

Mick's first published work was in the pages of the *International Times*, launched in London in October 1966 by John "Hoppy" Hopkins and Barry Miles. Miles was the co-owner of the Indica Bookstore and Gallery and a close friend of Paul McCartney, who helped finance the paper. *IT* was Britain's first real underground newspaper, and, along with *Oz* (which began publishing in the UK the following year), the most prominent. *IT* covered all aspects of the counterculture, including sex, drugs, music, art, literature, and radical politics, providing an alternative perspective on the war in Vietnam, the Black Panthers, the Paris street protests of 1968, the Haight-Ashbury hippies, and London's own burgeoning psychedelic movement, of which the Deviants were a part. Along with up and coming UK figures like Germaine Greer, John Peel, Jeff Nuttall, and Heathcote Williams, *IT*'s pages also included original work by internationally known writers like Allen Ginsberg, William S. Burroughs, Alexander Trocchi, and Norman Mailer, and underground comic artists like Robert Crumb and Gilbert Shelton. Published twice a month, it also included a calendar of events called "What's Happening," an invaluable resource in bringing the various strands of the UK counterculture together into a larger and more organized network. The format of "What's Happening" directly inspired the creation of *Time Out* magazine in 1968.

The establishment was quick to identify *IT* as a threat to the status quo and began targeting its offices with police raids in an attempt to shut the paper down, usually on trumped-up obscenity charges. The first bust, in March 1967, was costly, but it helped boost the public profile of the paper. The "14 Hour Technicolor Dream," a benefit concert to keep the paper afloat, was staged at the Alexandra Palace on April 29, 1967, and was one of the watershed moments of the British psychedelic scene, with performances by dozens of artists and performers, including Pink Floyd, the Soft Machine, the Move, the Pretty Things, the Crazy World of Arthur Brown, John's Children, and Yoko Ono. By 1968, *IT* had become Britain's leading underground paper with a circulation of over forty thousand copies, but it was still beleaguered with ongoing legal and financial difficulties. Farren was involved with *IT* in various capacities, writing occasional pieces and helping out with its organization, and upon splitting with the Deviants in 1969 he took over as editor.

He remembered:

> *IT* was in a complete shambles, 'cause they'd been busted again. They were making quite a lot of money from the lonely hearts contact ads—and, politically, *IT* was probably the first magazine in England to run gay ones. Then the cops schlepped up this fifteen-year-old hooker who was advertising, and they got busted over some obscure pandering law. So the guys who'd been running it while I was in the band were really fucked up, and things were not going well.

Between the loss of the lucrative cash up-front personal ads and meeting legal expenses, *IT* was financially strapped, so Farren and his artist colleague Edward Barker decided to put out a comic book anthology to raise some fast money. Unfortunately, this idea backfired rather badly, and Farren and Barker found themselves on trial at the Old Bailey for obscenity. *Nasty Tales* compiled work by some obscure British underground comic book artists alongside better-known Americans including Gilbert Shelton, Rick Griffin, and Robert Crumb.

> It was a Robert Crumb cartoon that they homed in on. "The Great International Fucking & Orgy Riot," which was a huge pile of naked bodies. At the trial we schlepped up everyone from Germaine Greer to Professor [Francis] Crick, who discovered DNA—he was a noted humanist and always good for a good word in an obscenity trial.

Mick Farren (with megaphone) at a demonstration in the 1960s

After a two-week trial—"which is long for England; they don't mess around there"—Farren and Barker were acquitted on all counts. But the trial only netted minimal publicity, overshadowed as it was by the previous year's *Oz* magazine obscenity case.

In the aftermath of the trial, however, Farren and Barker scored a book deal through a publisher they'd met, described by Farren as "sort of the house hippie at Hutchinson's." The result was *Watch Out Kids* (Open Gate Books, 1972), a handbook of youth rebellion tracing the rise of youth culture from Elvis and James Dean through to the American rock band MC5, the White Panthers (the radical left-wing collective formed by MC5 manager John Sinclair in solidarity with the Black Panthers), and the Angry Brigade (a gang of self-styled urban guerillas, who carried out a series of bomb attacks in England in 1970–1972).

Described by Farren as "basically a Yippie tract," *Watch Out Kids* was packaged much like a children's annual, the text enlivened by some hip graphics. Much of the book consisted of Farren's writings from *IT*, and among the sociopolitical diatribes were stories of his early rock 'n' roll and drug experiences, his participation in anti–Vietnam War demonstrations, and the early rock festivals, including the infamous Isle of Wight Festival of August 1970, attended by an estimated six hundred thousand people, which Mick and his newly formed British chapter of the White Panthers had successfully disrupted in protest at what they considered oppressive security measures and exploitive ticket and concession stand prices. "At the time, the British White Panther Party was a very secret society," he later wrote. "The primary secret being that it didn't exist at all." The UK chapter was strictly an ad hoc

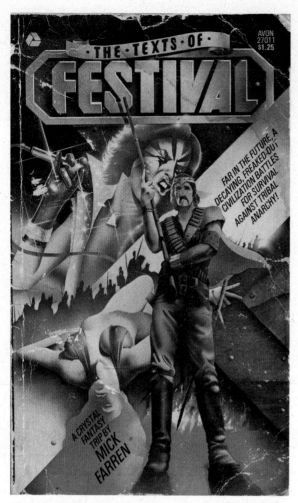

The Texts of Festival (Avon, 1973)

The Texts of Festival
(Hart-Davis, MacGibbon, 1973)

The Quest of the DNA
Cowboys (Mayflower, 1976)

affair, brought into play to, as he later humorously put it, "transform the event from Dachau with bands into a mighty gathering of the tribes." The Panthers achieved their goal—the fences came down and thousands poured in for free, although many thousands more had already paid for tickets, which caused some disgruntlement. The festival descended into tribalism and petty squabbling, but the music played on, including sets by the Who, the Doors, Miles Davis, Sly & the Family Stone, and Jimi Hendrix. Surveying the landscape on the final night of the five-day festival, as a hotdog stand burned, helicopters circled overhead, and Hells Angels roamed menacingly among the blanket-wrapped attendees, Mick observed, "I was looking at a Class One Rock Apocalypse, and filing away the visuals."

The previous month, Farren had staged his own festival, Phun City, in a field near the south coast city

of Worthing, less than a mile from the village where he grew up. The MC5 flew in from America to play on a bill that also included the Pretty Things, Kevin Ayers, the Edgar Broughton Band, the Pink Fairies, Mighty Baby, Mungo Jerry, and an appearance by William S. Burroughs. There were no fences, no admission fees, and the bands were only paid expenses.

Mick remembered:

> There was about a dozen acres of woodland at one end of the site, so the hippies went in there and went about setting up, kind of, Narnia. They decided they were gonna live there for the rest of time, and I thought, "Great, I'm going back to London"—'cause I could see plague breaking out if they actually managed to establish a colony there.

For Farren's first full-length novel The Texts of Festival (1973), he gave a dystopian spin to the experiences and visuals he'd filed away from Phun City and the Isle of Wight. Following in the postapocalyptic tradition of sci-fi works like the 1962 movie Panic in Year Zero! and Dave Wallis's 1964 novel Only Lovers Left Alive and weaving in Farren's own underground rock 'n' roll mythology, Texts tells of a hippie-type city colony called Festival, under siege by an army of speed-snorting Hells Angel horsemen and their crazed leader Iggy. The population bases its religious traditions on the few surviving black vinyl texts of the ancient prophets: Dhillon, Djeggar, and Morrizen. Among the futuristic war games, the story is littered with snatches of Stones, Dylan, and Doors lyrics, with the Deviants' own "Let's Loot the Supermarket" also making an appearance. "A little gauche," confessed Mick with a grin.

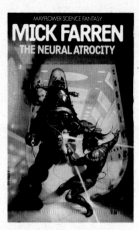

*Synaptic Manhunt*
(Mayflower, 1976)

*The Neural Atrocity*
(Mayflower, 1977)

Farren found writing his first full-length work of fiction relatively easy, having already honed his skills with some freelance magazine pieces.

> In between leaving the underground press—or the underground press basically leaving—there was a hiatus period when I wrote an awful lot of gray matter for the pages in between the tits and ass in magazines with names like *Galaxy*. Every now and then you'd get off some political rant, but I actually was trying to get my chops together writing fiction. So there was three thousand words of quasi science fiction, except there had to be sex in it, and words like "moist" and "throbbing" had to appear quite regularly.

His next novel was *The Tale of Willy's Rats* (1975), the story of a fictional rock 'n' roll band. The book was the first of several Farren did for Mayflower, a deal he landed through his agent Michael Dempsey, who was also representing J.G. Ballard and Michael Moorcock at the time. Although a few years older, Moorcock was another science fiction writer whose work intersected with the counterculture of the era, particularly his Jerry Cornelius series, which referenced many British rhythm and blues and underground rock bands. In the books, Cornelius fronted his own fictional band, the Deep Fix, which, collaborating with members of Hawkwind, Moorcock brought to life in 1975 as Michael Moorcock & the Deep Fix on the album *New Worlds Fair*.

Meanwhile, Farren's work for Mayflower continued with the *DNA Cowboys* trilogy—*The Quest of the DNA Cowboys* (1976), *Synaptic Manhunt* (1976), *The Neural Atrocity* (1977)—which helped establish Farren's rep as

a true original among the sci-fi authors of the day. It also marked the first appearance of several themes he would return to in his writing over the years, notably the concept of reality, methods of escape from it, and ways of creating new, artificial realities.

He explained:

> The DNA Cowboys lived in a time when all things were possible and reality actually had to be manufactured. You could get what you wanted from Stuff Central by dialing it, and anybody could fulfill their fantasies. There were these various environments, and in between these environments was this stuff called The Nothings, which was misty, kind of shimmering flickering stuff, which was a good analogue for clinical depression.

The expected sixties rock 'n' roll reference points can also be found.

> There was the Minstrel Boy, who took this drug which you dropped in your eye called Omnidrene. He knew where the various environments were located, and he was a really badly written Bob Dylan analog. It was very drug-inspired. I was trying to do a cartoon Burroughs, I suppose, only more linear and approachable.

A decade later he brought back the Minstrel Boy and company for 1989's *The Last Stand of the DNA Cowboys*.

Meanwhile, in 1975–1976, Farren had become involved with rock journalism again. At the *New Musical Express*, editor Nick Logan was assembling a team of hip, talented writers, many of whom were refugees from the last days of the underground press, including Charles Shaar Murray (who as a teen had participated in *Oz* magazine's notorious "schoolkids" issue, which had precipitated their previously mentioned obscenity trial) and Nick Kent (who had written for *IT*'s other rival, *Friendz*).

Farren initially came on board on one condition: he didn't have to write about rock music. "I'd done it. I was sick of it. And the stock in trade then of what they called 'the comics'—*Sounds, Melody Maker*, and *NME*—was unfortunately Yes, ELP, and the Electric Light Orchestra."

But change was in the air—or at least in the pubs, where a new movement was about to break out.

> To our good fortune, as a magazine and as writers, all of a sudden there's this band called

Dr. Feelgood over there, and then Stiff [Records] started up, and then all hell broke loose and there was plenty to write about.

The moment it really all came together was when Kent got beat up at the 100 Club. Sid [Vicious] saw him and whacked him with that chain he wore around his neck.

As an English teenager at the time, I read the *NME* religiously, poring over the unfolding saga of the new punk scene every Thursday lunchtime at school. The most interesting stories always seemed to involve the interaction between these strange, exciting new bands and the writers covering them. The now legendary Kent-Vicious incident epitomized this.

"There was a *lot* of interaction," agreed Farren. "You see, the well-concealed secret, which pissed off all the labels and publicists who weren't signing was that. . ." Here he bent forward in a conspiratorial whisper: "There were only a hundred people. Just like the hippies starting up: 'There's only a hundred of us. Move around quick and maybe nobody will be able to tell.' It was all happening at this old gay bar, the Roxy, and initially there were hardly enough people to fill it."

Within a matter of months, punk rock had moved from a small clique of in-crowd musicians and writers into an entire national movement, and the *NME* had been in on the ground floor. The paper's circulation escalated accordingly—"like a Titan missile," Mick later wrote—outstripping all of its rivals, including the former top-seller *Melody Maker*. "It was fun at the time, because there was so much shit happening," remembered Mick. "It was kind of nice at the *NME*, because, although it was owned by IBC, in the office there was a good vibe about it—until [Tony] Parsons and [Julie] Burchill showed up and soured everything."

Often referred to as *enfants terribles*, Parsons—twenty-three-years-old at the time—and Burchill, just seventeen, were brought in to add some youth to the team, most of whom were either holdovers from the sixties Tin Pan Alley-beat music era or, like Farren, had come up through the radical underground papers. Young, hungry, provocative, and closely aligned with the burgeoning punk movement—or at least the bands that passed their personal purity test—the couple was often at odds with the rest of the *NME* staff. Parsons and Farren eventually came to blows after Mick had a brief affair with Burchill, and the atmosphere thereafter was fraught.

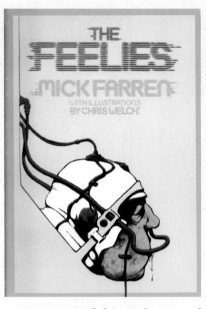

The Feelies (Big O Publishing, 1978)

However, with his newly renewed rock crit cachet, Farren was able to land some cushy book deals, dashing off text for quickies like *Elvis in His Own Words* (the first of many Presley-related works bearing his name), *Get on Down: A Decade of Rock & Roll Posters*, and *Rock 'n' Roll Circus*, a collection of rock tour photos.

Meanwhile he had not neglected his fiction writing. Tapping into the grim nihilism of punk, which he saw as a harbinger of "a world headed for cultural damnation," and stirring in some tropes from Huxley's *Brave New World*, he wrote *The Feelies* (1978).

Presciently, the book's premise anticipated not only virtual reality but also the rise of reality TV shows. In the book, "feelies" (a nod to *Brave New World*) are pod-like machines designed to immerse the user in an ultrasensory, virtual reality experience of their choice. However, the cost of a feelie experience is out of reach for most people, so only the wealthy could afford to partake, many of them choosing to opt out of their own reality for the alternative provided by the feelies. As Mick explains:

The secret was they fed them on intravenous Slimfast and they died after about four months. But the Corporation running it had an underlying philosophy that was some kind of eugenic Nazi idea that those who were capable of handling reality would, and those who couldn't wouldn't; they would retreat into fantasy and die very swiftly. So they kept the dying factor kind of quiet.

Phaid the Gambler (Ace, 1981)

The Song of Phaid the Gambler (New English Library, 1981)

Protectorate (Ace, 1985)

Farren regarded *The Feelies* as one of his stronger works, and although it wasn't a commercial success it was well-received among certain circles of the cognoscenti. Mick remarked:

Glenn Branca [New York City–based guitarist and avant-garde composer] says that *The Feelies* and some book by Orson Scott Card are the actual origins of cyber-punk, which to some degree it was—except there wasn't really very much about computers, because they hadn't really dawned on our horizon. But in every other respect it was a sort of nihilist punk blank generation novel.

*The Feelies* was republished in America by Del Rey in 1990 in a considerably revised form, updating details that the author felt had become anachronistic—"The Jules Verne Syndrome," he called it.

Meanwhile, with Mayflower/Granada dumping their entire publishing division, the late seventies were lean times for many science fiction writers.

After *The Feelies*, I very much felt like a lone voice crying in the wilderness. But I had a living to earn, so I went to New English Library, 'cause I knew a guy there who liked me. And, basically, he said, "Come back into the science fiction fold and you will be rewarded with large amounts of money."

With this in mind, his next work was a swashbuckling, futuristic affair, *The Song of Phaid the Gambler* (1981). "In many respects *Phaid the Gambler* is basically *The DNA Cowboys* dumbed down a bit, and sort of *Star Wars*-ized," he admitted. Nevertheless, it's an enjoyable read, full of his characteristic dark wit and with an interesting cast of characters and creatures.

By the time *Phaid* was completed, Farren had married and relocated to New York City, where his fiction output increased during the mid- and late eighties, with a series of books for Ace and Del Rey: *Protectorate* (1984), *Vickers* (1986), and *Their Master's War* (1987). *Vickers* also appeared as *CORP.S.E* for New English Library in 1986.

Mick explained:

*Protectorate* and *Vickers* and *Their Master's War* particularly—which, sadly, is the bestselling novel of the whole lot so far—were really almost a commercial retrenchment. Then cyberpunk came along, and *The Long Orbit* (1988) (UK title: *Exit Funtopia*) shows the most effects of that, though I'm always a bit squeamish about

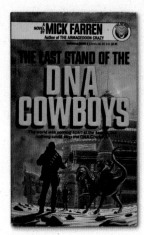

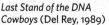

Last Stand of the DNA
Cowboys (Del Rey, 1989)

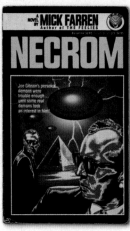

Necrom (Del Rey, 1991)

sticking bits of metal into my characters—and certainly not me—the whole implant idea.

While in New York, his science fiction output continued with *The Armageddon Crazy* (1989), inspired by the rise of Christian fundamentalism in America, and its role in the political arena.

That was real good fun, because it was really about the fundamentalists taking over. It was a very Reagan-era book. From when you had James Watt [Reagan's Secretary of the Interior] saying, "Don't bother about the trees because Jesus is coming back in about twenty minutes."

*The Last Stand of The DNA Cowboys* (1989) was followed by *Mars—The Red Planet* (1990), a bit of a sore subject for Farren, it turned out. "I'd just driven across the desert, going to Las Vegas, the scenic route up through 29 Palms and across where the Marines play war games, and I thought, 'I wanna write a book about Mars.'" Unfortunately, Farren decided to populate his red planet with a Soviet space colony. "I thought, this will all be jolly good fun, and then I think actually even before the book came out, the [Berlin] wall came down and... *whoops*! I thought the Soviet Union would take forty years to fall apart, not like five months!"

By this time, he had relocated to Los Angeles and was nearing the end of a particularly prolific run with no less than five books being published in 1989 and 1990.

The Del Ray situation got really peculiar, because I was writing books faster than they could publish them, and what I wanted to do was get ahead and then relax and do something that

was gonna be *Necrom* and was gonna be much longer. Then they started pumping these books out like every three months. They were selling reasonably well, but the titles were overlapping and people were missing them. The gross sales for the year were great, but they were divided between three or four titles. They were just shipping books like they were going out of fashion. The second half of *Necrom* never got written, and it was a great disappointment, really.

Scaled down or not, *Necrom* (1991) is anything but disappointing. A work of almost dizzying complexity, it's an interdimensional suspense thriller that grew out of a film script Mick had been working on. The movie never got made, but many of the ideas were channeled into what is one of his most impressive novels.

"The focus was really to try and create this masterpiece—a *Naked Lunch*, so to speak—*my Naked Lunch*. But there was the rapid discovery that, without actually risking death by various kinds of narcosis and overdose, writing *Naked Lunch* is a very hard trick to turn."

"But does any artist ever write their *Naked Lunch*?" I asked him. "After all, Burroughs probably doesn't even consider *Naked Lunch* to be *his Naked Lunch*."

"Well, that's the problem," shrugged Farren. "You only find that out after you're dead. So, fuck it, I'll write a vampire novel in the meantime."

Along with various musical projects, Farren's fiction writing continued through the nineties and into the twenty-first century with a series of vampire-themed novels—*The Time of Feasting* (1996), *Darklost* (2000), *More than Mortal* (2001), *Underland* (2002)—and the dystopian *Flame of Evil* series: *Kindling* (2004) and *Conflagration* (2006). Along the way, *Jim Morrison's Adventures in the Afterlife* (1999) was a humorous yet pointed fantasy about the Doors singer's journey through purgatory. Mick also continued to churn out nonfiction works at an impressive rate, most notably the autobiographical *Give the Anarchist a Cigarette* (2001). His final novel, *Road Movie*, was published in November 2012.

Eight months later, on July 27, 2013, Mick Farren died onstage while performing with a new incarnation of the Deviants. His science fiction writing was just one memorable aspect of the huge body of work he left behind.

**Mike Stax**

# Green Deaths and Time Warriors: *Doctor Who* Serials and Novelizations in the 1970s

Launched by the BBC in 1963, *Doctor Who* was an immediate success, with the time-travelling and space-hopping Doctor and menacing villains, such as the Daleks, soon becoming pop culture icons. *Doctor Who* was part of a new trend in television; one that keyed into generational change while appealing to those of all ages, in the process being unafraid to blend horror and other popular genres with science fiction to explore themes previously deemed as too heavy for children.

The point at which the show arguably tapped most into the political zeitgeist of the times was during the era of the third Doctor, played by Jon Pertwee, from 1970 to 1974. Although economic and social themes had been explored in previous seasons and would continue to be in the future, under the helm of producer Barry Letts, scriptwriters were empowered to bring them to fore. Whether in space or on earth, the need to counter the myopic, self-serving actions of politicians, militarists, and other elites and to find the way to peace and harmony was an overriding theme throughout the show in the early 1970s.

The demise of the British empire, internal anti-colonial agitation, and the impacts of colonization on Indigenous peoples were explored in various story-lines, including 1970's *The Siluarians*, 1971's *Colony in Space*, 1972's *The Mutants*, and *The Time Warrior* in 1973–1974. In 1974, *Carnival of Monsters* lampooned media-induced passivity. Out of touch, old empire-style authority figures and military officers got short shrift from the Doctor in 1970's *Ambassador of Death*, 1971's *Terror of the Autons*, 1972's *The Sea Devils*, and 1974's *Invasion of the Dinosaurs*, while disquiet surrounding entry into the European Common Market (later European Union) fueled 1972's *The Curse of Peladon*. Fascists, both contemporary and of the World War II variety, had clearly inspired the genocidal Daleks. Industrial and class conflict, referencing the 1969 and 1972 miners strikes, appears in 1974's *The Monster of Peladon*. Threats to existence arising from nuclear power, weapons of mass destruction, and superpower stand-offs were explored in 1971's *The Mind of Evil* and *Claws of Axos*, 1973's *Frontier in Space*, and 1974–1975's *Robot*, which marked the first appearance of Tom Baker as the fourth Doctor.

*Doctor Who and the Curse of Peladon* (Target, 1976).

Although many of these serials were clearly informed by progressive politics, they were male-dominated and tended toward the softer end of left-wing politics. Feminism was occasionally touched on, but women largely remained relegated to secondary roles. Notwithstanding extraterrestrial stand-ins and characters in comics, people of color barely existed in the *Doctor Who* universe until the series reboot of the 2000s.

The 1970s was also the period in which the novelizations of *Doctor Who* episodes really got rolling. Although a handful of titles had previously been turned into books, Target launched their long-running

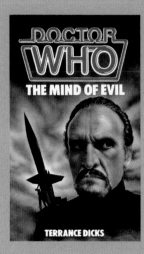
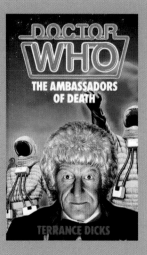

paperback series in 1973, with some titles also appearing in hardback via Allan Wingate and W.H. Allen & Co. By the end of the decade, fifty-two serials had been novelized, with over one hundred more to come.

The serial and novelization that perhaps most exemplifies the political, and occasionally radical, spirit of the third Doctor era is *The Green Death*. Originally aired in 1973, it was scripted by Robert Sloman and subsequently novelized by Malcolm Hulke in 1975. Tension breaks out at UNIT, the United Nations affiliated military organization the Doctor works with, after they are ordered to protect a petrochemical facility in Wales. Since economic rationalism has forced the closure of the town's mines, the local populace, made up of stereotypical salt of the earth Welsh folk, are initially keen to support a new employer, but suspicions grow after one of their number is struck down by a green fungus. While the brigadier (UNIT's leader) is initially all too keen

to blame a group of nearby commune dwellers, the Doctor's assistant Jo joins their crusade against the polluters.

What starts out as a relatively straightforward hippies versus the Establishment–type scenario soon takes on a number of bizarre twists including bullet proof mutant maggots chomping on humans and a mind-controlling computer called BOSS "processing" people into corporate automatons. With the earth threatened by the twin perils of a pollution-related "green plague" and computer-led dictatorship, even the straitlaced brigadier begins to question the role of multinationals and the wisdom of blindly following orders.

As a general rule, novelizations rarely live up to their source material, and the *Doctor Who* books varied widely in quality. In this case, Hulke, working for the first and only time on an episode not of his making, did a sterling job. The author often added

material and twists to the books he based on his own scripts and here brings extra depth to the characters and the plot of *The Green Death*, while retaining the feel of the original broadcast.

Hulke had joined the *Doctor Who* team in 1967 and fit neatly into the era. A lifelong socialist, he was a member of the Communist Party of Great Britain from the early 1950s to the late 1960s. Having worked with the Unity Theatre, he first had plays adapted by the BBC in the late 1950s and would write for television until his death in 1979, contributing to popular programs such as *The Avengers* and *Crossroads* and penning the seminal guidebook *Writing for Television* (1974). He wrote six story arcs for *Doctor Who*, all of which addressed themes concerning the environment, militarism, and racism to some degree.

**Iain McIntyre**

Above, left to right: *Doctor Who The Mind of Evil* (WH Allen, 1984). *Doctor Who and the Ambassadors of Death* (WH Allen, 1987). *Doctor Who and the Carnival of Monsters* (Allan Wingate, 1977). *Doctor Who and the Dalek Invasion of Earth* (WH Allen, 1977). *Doctor Who and the Destiny of the Daleks* (Target, 1979). *Doctor Who and the Doomsday Weapon* (Target, 1976). *Doctor Who and the Genesis of the Daleks* (WH Allen, 1976).

Below, left to right: *Doctor Who and the Sea Devils* (Target, 1979). *Doctor Who and the Giant Robot* (WH Allen, 1975). *Doctor Who and the Green Death* (Target, 1979). *Doctor Who and the Mutants* (Target, 1977). *Doctor Who in an Exciting Adventure with the Daleks* (Avon, 1967). *Doctor Who and the Time Warrior* (WH Allen, 1978). *Doctor Who and the War Games* (Target, 1979). *Doctor Who in an Exciting Adventure with the Daleks* (Armada, 1965).

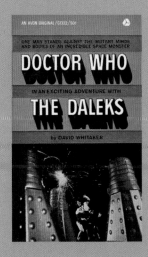

# A New Wave in the East

## The Strugatsky Brothers and Radical Sci-fi in Soviet Russia

Arkady and Boris Strugatsky

In Russia, no genre of fiction enjoyed greater popularity during the Soviet era than science fiction. The genre had come into being in Russia during the nineteenth century, but with the consolidation of communist rule in the 1920s, science fiction took off. It seems odd that a particular type of literature would evolve and flourish under a totalitarian system, but science fiction fit hand in glove with specific conditions that existed under the communist regime. When Vladimir Lenin became head of state, Soviet Russia existed, as Yvonne Howell states in her introduction to *Red Star Tales: A Century of Russian and Soviet Science Fiction* (2015):

> [A]t the margins of the industrialized world, belatedly undergoing a process that Leon Trotsky famously diagnosed as "combined" and "uneven" development. There was something inherently science fictional about this situation; during the Revolutionary decades before and after the Bolshevik coup in 1917, one detects a desire to jump from behind, over the present, directly into a radically more advanced future. Thus . . . many of the most renowned artists and intellectuals of the time produced works of fiction that consciously probed a revolutionary new premise: what if the unprecedented pace of scientific and technological discovery is

consciously harnessed to utopian ideals of social and even spiritual advancement, so that age-old dreams of peace, plenty, and even immortality are no longer the stuff of fairy tales, but the impetus for rational blueprints to shape the future?

This was a positivistic outlook the state apparatus endorsed, and it complimented the regime's push to increase literacy—a push that expanded the country's readership. All of these factors, along with the nation's social upheavals, could be explored and refracted by science fiction better than they could be by any other genre or by realist fiction.

In Alexey Tolstoy's *Aelita*, published in 1923 and filmed as *Aelita: Queen of Mars* by Yakov Protazanov in 1924, two Russians fly a rocket to Mars, where, to force the redistribution of wealth between the rich classes and poor, they start a revolution. Alexander Belyaev wrote a novel called *The Air Seller* (1929) about a crazed capitalist backed by rich Western imperialists who uses an air-sucking device to try to steal the world's atmosphere so that he and his cohorts can sell oxygen to people and control the world. At the book's end, the Red Army stops them. His story "Professor Dowell's Head" (1925) is about scientific attempts to transplant a preserved and living human head onto a body not its own. An editor's introduction at the time stated that the story was based on the type of scientific advancement not yet possible but that continued Soviet experimental work might one day make a reality. Optimism brimmed in these and other works, scientific predictions abounded, and capitalism came in for scorn. Without pressure from authorities, the writers themselves wrote story lines in tune with communist principles.

Two exceptions to this, and a harbinger of the subversive things to come in Russian science fiction, were Yevgeny Zamyatin and Mikhail Bulgakov.

Zamyatin's novel *We* (1921) posits a futuristic police state and is among the first satirical dystopian sci-fi novels ever written. Its picture of a conformist totalitarian state got it banned by the Soviet censorship board, and Zamyatin had to smuggle *We* out of Russia to get it published in the West. Eventually, in 1931, after writing a letter to Joseph Stalin requesting permission to leave the country, he went into exile.

Bulgakov's two mid-1920s novellas, *The Fatal Eggs* (1924) and *Heart of a Dog* (1925), use science fiction as a tool for satire, with scientists in each story engaging in projects that go completely awry. In *Heart of a Dog*, the Bolsheviks' preoccupation with transforming and perfecting human beings is satirized when a doctor gives a stray dog human testicles and a human pituitary gland. The surgeon's hope is to better the animal, but what results is a parody of the new Soviet man, a shambolic, self-centered person who, employed by the Soviet State, finds a low-level but satisfying job killing stray cats. *The Fatal Eggs* involves a zoologist named Vladimir Ipatyevich Persikov, whose similarities to Vladimir Ilyich Lenin cannot be missed. That an experiment Persikov does on one-celled organisms and frogs ultimately leads to Moscow being under attack from gigantic snakes can be read as an allegory of the destruction (as Bulgakov saw it) that Lenin and his Bolshevik cohorts unleashed on Russia as a whole.

Both these works were well-received by the Russian reading public, but Soviet critics frowned on them, and for the rest of his life, until 1940, Bulgakov could get almost nothing he wrote—books, stories, or plays—published or produced. A lot of his work, including his magnum opus *The Master and Margarita*, he read solely to his wife and trusted friends, and after his death that work stayed in drawers for decades, protected by his widow. The novel did not appear in Russia until it was serialized in *Moskva* magazine in 1966 and early 1967, and, even then, it came out in a censored version. A manuscript smuggled from the Soviet Union to Paris reached the YMCA Press, and that resulted in the first book edition of *The Master and Margarita*, in 1967. That same year the American publisher Grove Press did an English-language translation, as did Harvill Press in Britain. A complete version of the book in Russian did not come out in the Soviet Union until 1973, when the journal *Khudozhestvennaya Literatura* published it.

Mikhail Bulgakov's compositional secrecy, his decision to share his work with no one but confidants due to fear of reprisals from the government, was not something, of course, that would end with him. Decades later, it would apply to the most successful Soviet Russian sci-fi writers of them all, the brothers who had bestselling sales in the Soviet Union and achieved worldwide fame, Arkady and Boris Strugatsky.

They began their careers in the late 1950s, after the Stalinist era had ended. During Stalin's rule, science fiction had functioned within tight limits, its practitioners told to produce an art that served the state and the party. This meant reducing the scope of science fiction, detailing merely the near future in what the state prescribed as realistic terms, when Soviet-style socialism would be perfect or close to perfect. Attainable goals could be shown, but stories were not to be set on exotic worlds and certainly could not traffic in social satire. Not until Nikita Khruschev took control in 1953, instituting what was called "the thaw," could artistic expression loosen up. Science fiction blossomed again in the Soviet Union, beginning with the publication of Ivan Yefremov's *Andromeda*, published in 1957. In its otherworldly setting and with its emphasis on ideas, it had a momentous impact, and in how it portrayed a flourishing communist global civilization, it spoke to the last generation of Soviet Russian sci-fi writers with a genuine enthusiasm for communism. Boris Strugatsky himself would later write:

> The publication of *Andromeda* has become a symbol of the new era, its banner, in some sense. Without it, the new growth would have been an order of magnitude more difficult, and a thaw in our SF wouldn't have come until later.

The early Strugatsky brothers works, such as *Noon: 22nd Century*, from 1961 (translated into English in 1978), reflect the Yefremov influence. As critic Erik Simon says in his piece, "The Strugatskys in Political Context," in a special 2004 issue of *Science Fiction Studies* on the topic of "Soviet Science Fiction: The Thaw and After":

> The brothers' novels published before 1965 . . . share a common setting in a world which postulates not only the peaceful coexistence of different social systems . . . but also the gradual expansion of Communism because of its moral and economic superiority. The twenty-second century is imagined to be a global Communist utopia. Constant features of this future world include beneficial technological progress, general prosperity, and the ethos of scientific research (including contact with alien intelligence) as one of the most important human

activities. The decisive feature in all of these books, however, is the social design.

That design is complex in *Hard to Be a God*, their novel from 1964 (translated into English from a German-language edition in 1973 and from the original Russian by Chicago Review Press in 2014), and the tensions in the book reveal how its conception changed while the Strugatskys were developing it. As Boris notes in an afterword written after the fall of the Soviet Union, the book started "as a fun adventure story in the spirit of *The Three Musketeers*." This swashbuckling element remains in the final version, which tells the story of one Don Rumata who is sent from a future earth to a medieval planet called Arkanar. Rumata can sword fight, drink, brawl, and carouse with the best of them, but he is actually a kind of spy, sent from an earth where communism has been victorious. Earth, in effect, is a communist utopia, and Rumata's bosses there have instructed him to observe the life and feudal customs on Arkanar. The narrative contains loads of action and a great deal of fun, as Boris says he and his brother originally planned, but while they were conceiving the book, the political atmosphere in the Soviet Union darkened. Khruschev's thaw chilled. The significant moment occurred when Khruschev visited an abstract art exhibition in 1962. He loathed what he saw and was not subtle in expressing his loathing. A tightening over the arts occurred; back in full force were the government's censors. Boris Strugatsky says that from all this

> one thing became, as they say, painfully clear. We shouldn't have illusions. We shouldn't have hopes for a brighter future. We were being governed by goons and enemies of culture. They will never be with us. They will always be against us.

It was a "painful" insight, Boris says in his afterword, but a "beneficial" one. It led he and Arkady to see their story "in an entirely different light." Their hero Don Rumata is indeed powerful and competent, but his bosses on earth have given him instructions not to interfere with anything that happens on Arkanar. In that backward world, he is something like a god, but he can do nothing to combat superstition, fight disease, or advance knowledge. At this point, the Strugatsky's communism has a coldness and inflexibility not found in their earlier works. Don Rumata's mission dictates that he feel no pity for the suffering

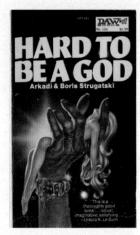

*Hard to Be a God* (Seabury Press, 1973)

*Hard to Be a God* (Daw, 1974)

people on Arkanar, because everything they are going through, all the horror, has to happen. It's part of what might be called "historical necessity." What began as a tale mixing Alexandre Dumas with the science fiction trope of a collision between two worlds, became, as Hari Kunzru puts it in his 2014 foreword to the book, "a much darker story about the fate of the intelligentsia under totalitarianism."

In the Strugatskys' next book, *Monday Begins on Saturday*, published in the Soviet Union in 1965 and in the West by DAW Books in 1977, the action is set on earth in the present, and there is no trace of a communist utopia. But the Strugatskys still lay out a Russia that seems tolerable to live in. People laugh a lot and go about their business without undue fear, tension, or suspicion. The novel centers around a young computer programmer, Sasha, and his time working at the National Institute for the Technology of Witchcraft and Thaumaturgy. Shortened, that's NITWit. Among its missions, Sasha finds, is to discover the essence of human happiness and perfect it. The book is more in the fantasy than the science fiction genre, but that doesn't prevent the Strugatskys from writing a story that is highly satirical, a send-up of how institutions operate. Rules and regulations serve no purpose, intellectual pomposity abounds, rivalries and jealousies fester, dysfunction reigns. In his afterword to the book, another one written after the Soviet Union's demise, Boris Strugatsky looks back at notes he and his brother jotted down for *Monday* and includes this one: "Show how annoying it is to work according to a dogmatic all-encompassing official theory." They do without question succeed in showing this, but they go about it in such a humorous way and with such an assortment of oddball characters—wizards, vampires, bureaucrats, shapeshifters, and fish and cats that talk—that the satire passes lightly. The Soviet reading public loved the book (and Russians have ever since), and, as Boris mentions in his afterword, "the censor did not assault this new story too much. It was a funny tale, and the cavils were funny as well." The easy time they had with the censor on this occasion would not be something they would experience often in the years to come.

Their troubles began in the late sixties, when the Strugatskys turned to work clearly satiric in intent. *The Snail on the Slope* (the book had

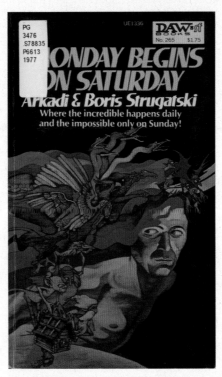

*Monday Begins on Saturday* (Daw, 1977)

a convoluted publishing history in the USSR, which makes it hard to pinpoint a precise publication date) is one such novel, alternating as it does between two plot lines, one set in the Administration world and one set in the Forest world. The two plots never come together, and in both strands, one absurd event after another unfolds, as if Kafka were having a science fiction dream. In the Administration sections, a man called Peretz yearns to visit the Forest, but he never gets closer than a cliff overlooking the Forest, and every effort he makes to achieve his objective meets with frustration, broken promises, and fruitless encounters. The Forest sections follow Candide, a man who crash landed in the forest and now lives a chaotic life among the somewhat primitive people who inhabit a landscape that is hazy and primeval. Logic is skewed in both worlds, talk between people ridiculous.

Here's an acquaintance of Peretz telling him how to listen to the Administration's director:

> "Write out the Director's Speech in a single line, excluding punctuation, and select words at random by throwing down imaginary dominoes. If two domino halves agree, the word is selected and written down on a separate piece of paper. If they do not agree, the word is temporarily

rejected, but it's left on the page. There are a few subtleties, associated with the frequency of the vowels and consonants, but that's a second-order effect. Do you understand?"

"No," said Peretz. "I mean, yes. I wish I had known about this method. So what did he say today?"

"It's not the only possible method. There's also, say the variable-stroke spiral method. This method is fairly cruel, but if only basic economic issues are under discussion, then it's very convenient due to its simplicity. There's the Stevenson-Zade method, but it requires the use of electronic devices. So I'd say that in the majority of cases, the domino method is best, while the spiral method is preferred in situations with a limited and specialized vocabulary."

"Thank you," Peretz said. "And what did the Director talk about today?"

"What do you mean?"

"What? . . . Uhhh . . . What did he talk about? W-What did he . . . say?"

As the Strugatskys conceived the novel, the Administration sections stand for the present, with all its maddening bureaucracy, and the Forest sections are the future, when humanity and nature, as they imagined it, would merge. The story is highly symbolic, open to myriad interpretations, but "the multitude of possible readings," to cite Boris's post-Soviet era afterword, "didn't do *The Snail on the Slope* much good. The novel didn't get destroyed per se, but for many years it was forbidden." Boris quotes one critic of the time who, before it was banned, wrote:

> The fantastic society depicted by A. and B. Strugatsky . . . is composed of people who live in chaos and turmoil, who are engaged in aimless, unnecessary busywork, and who carry out stupid laws and directions. Fear, suspicion,

sycophancy, and bureaucracy reign here.

The *Snail on the Slope* was unofficially published via clandestine samizdat methods in the Soviet Union, got to the West, and wound up being published in translation in Germany in 1972. In 1980, it was translated into English and published by Bantam Books. It took until 1988, during the reforming era of glasnost, for a publisher to release it in its complete form in the Soviet Union.

*Roadside Picnic* was written in 1971 and printed by the Russian literary journal *Avora* in 1972. After their satiric period and the trouble it caused them with publishers and censors, the Strugatskys wrote a book

*The Snail and the Slope* (Bantam, 1983)

about the aftermath of and reactions to a brief alien stop on the earth. It's a book that has little outright political content, which Andrei Tarkovsky helped make famous worldwide with his 1979 film adaptation, scripted by the Strugatskys. At home they were now on the censors' radar, and the brothers had difficulties with the novel. No book publisher in Russia would pick it up for eight years. During this period, the Strugatskys had to go through interminable editorial battles with it. The issue this time was not ideological or the result of them critiquing Soviet society; the Strugatsky's radicalism, as defined by the censors, was their use of coarse language and the failure to write comforting science fiction. They had lists of "vulgarisms" the editors and censors would order them to change, and no matter what changes they made, these lists would keep on coming, as would demands for further alterations. Once again, in a late career afterword, Boris is an invaluable source in describing their travails, saying of *Roadside Picnic*, along with *The Dead Mountaineer's Inn* and *Space Mowgli*, two thematically linked novels they were also looking to publish around that time (*The Dead Mountaineer's Inn* got a 1970 book release in the Soviet Union; Avora published *Space Mowgli* in 1971), "we're talking, essentially, about novels that have never caused a Big Ideological Disturbance,

about little stories that are completely harmless and even apolitical. It's just that the higher-ups wanted nothing to do with those Strugatskys at all."

The pattern is familiar. The Strugatskys loathed the version of *Roadside Picnic* that came out in book form in 1980, and it would not appear in Russia as they intended until the 1990s. By then, it had been published in nearly twenty countries. Macmillan first published it in English in 1977. The first United Kingdom edition followed in 1978, from Gollancz.

It must be said that the Strugatskys, once they realized that the censors would look hard at each new book they wrote, did not temper their vision. They had a strategy of writing where reality in their narratives would gradually cross into delirium. Their Russian readers liked this, judging by the brothers' sales, but no amount of distortion or grotesquerie could hide what the censors viewed as political criticism. In this, their frequent poking and jabbing, the brothers differed from other prominent Soviet and Eastern Bloc science fiction authors. Kir Bulychev, for one, made his major work the fifty-book children's series *Alisa Selezneva*, and, in Poland, Stanisław Lem put his primary focus on a wide array of moral and ethical questions. As Simon points out, Lem would sometimes allow himself "satirical barbs at socialist reality," but he tended to be "careful not to relate the two too obviously to each other."

*Definitely Maybe*, from 1977 (first published in English by Macmillan in 1978), is a vintage example of the Strugatskys taking on the reality around them. The novel is set in Leningrad in the seventies and was written soon after Boris Strugatsky got dragged into the Kheifits Affair, when the KGB arrested a historian named Mikhail Kheifits for circulating among his friends an essay he'd written about expelled Russian poet Joseph Brodsky. Boris had his first direct confrontation with the KGB—or, as Boris calls them, "our valiant competent organs"—and was summoned as a witness in the case. In his *Search for Predetermination*, released in Russia in 1995, he would describe this confrontation and the difficult challenge he faced making statements that satisfied the competent organs but implicated neither himself nor others. Not surprisingly, this ordeal left a deep impression on him, and, as Boris writes in his afterword to *Definitely Maybe*, it influenced the novel "in a completely specific way and with a completely specific tone."

That tone comes in passages like this, when the narrator is pondering how his life has abruptly mutated:

> I was realizing that just yesterday I was man, a member of society. I had my own concerns and worries, yes, but as long as I obeyed the laws created by the system—and that had become a habit—as long as I obeyed those laws, I was protected from all imaginable dangers by the police, the army, the unions, public opinion, and my friends and family. Now, something in the world around me had gone haywire. Suddenly I became a catfish holed up in a crack, surrounded by monstrous vague shadows that didn't even need huge looming jaws—a slight movement of their fins would grind me into a powder, squash me, turn me into zilch. And it was made clear to me that as long as I hid in that crack I would not be touched. Yet it was even more terrifying than that. I was separated from humanity the way a lamb is cut off from the herd and dragged off somewhere for some unknown reason, while the herd, unsuspecting, goes on about its business, moving farther away into the distance. I would have felt much better if only they had been warlike aliens, some bloodthirsty, destructive aggressors from outer space, from the ocean depths, from the fourth dimension. I would have been one among many; there would have been a place for me, work for me; I would be in the ranks! But I was doomed to perish in front of everyone's eyes. No one would see a thing, and when I was destroyed, ground to dust, everyone would be surprised and then shrug it off.

*Definitely Maybe*'s narrator Malianov is an astrophysicist holed up in his apartment, and, with his wife away on vacation, he plunges into the ever-continuing research he's doing, calling upon such considerations as Hartwig's function and Ragozinsky's arcs. He feels he is on the verge of a breakthrough, a discovery that will win him the Nobel Prize, but whenever his calculations fall into place, as if leading him to the answer he seeks, something interrupts him and prevents him from doing his work. He gets mysterious phone calls, a deliveryman brings him a crate of vodka and cognac—already paid for—and a seductive woman claiming to be his wife's old classmate knocks on his door and invites herself in. Then friends of his, scientists like him, also come over, and they reveal that they too keep bumping into work-hampering distractions. Their exchanges about what is happening are both hilarious and laden with anxiety. Events reach a nadir when a neighbor in the building is found dead, and Malianov becomes a suspect, an investigator telling him he might serve a long stretch in a prison camp. What is going on? It seems as if unknown forces are conspiring to stop Malianov and his fellow researchers from making headway in anything they do.

After much speculation, Vecherovsky, the mathematician in the group, proposes a concept they tentatively accept—the Homeostatic Universe. In a nutshell, it says that the universe tends toward equilibrium, the status quo, and that it needs to find a balance between disorder and "the development of reason." Because humans have reached the point where their discoveries can lead to supercivilizations (outdoing the universe, as it were), the universe is defending itself against those attempts, embodied in Malianov and his friends' work. By the end of the book, their "microrebellion" quelled by the obstructions created by the universe, everybody but Malianov abandons their work. The Homeostatic Universe is a brilliant theory devised by the Strugatskys, and it's a sly way to comment on the Soviet state itself. In Boris's words, the book delves into:

> The tormenting and essentially hopeless struggle of mankind to preserve the "right of primogeniture" against the dull, blind, persistent force that knows neither honor, nor nobility, nor charity, that knows only one thing—how to achieve its goals, by any means, without any setbacks.

But setbacks, over time, strike any force, regardless of how persistent it is. Even when the state appears to be winning, it may in actuality be failing. The brothers saw and wrote about this well before the Soviet Union collapsed, but the book they made their clearest exposition on the subject was one they considered too dangerous to publish. Its title says it all—*The Doomed City*.

Begun in 1969, the novel took three years for the Strugatskys to complete. They never before or after worked that long a book. The story is set in a city where the sun gets switched on and off every day, and its borders are an abyss on one side and a high wall on the other. The inhabitants comprise people taken from real life in the twentieth century, but the people come from different countries and eras. There's a British colonel from World War I, a German Soldier who fought in World War II, a Soviet man from the 1950s, and a 1960s American college professor. In a foreword to the book, author Dmitry Glukhovsky explains:

*Roadside Picnic* (Penguin, 1979)

> They all seem to speak the same language, but that language isn't Russian. Abducted from their own familiar earthly lives, times, and cultures, they have been transported to the City, where they have become the subjects of the Experiment, which has no beginning or end while its goal and its meaning are kept secret from the participants, who are constantly subjected to various trials. . . . The organizers of the Experiment look like ordinary people, just as officials of the Communist Party and case officers from the security services did—they smile just as gently and call for patience just as earnestly. And all the inhabitants of the City show patience.

Didn't Soviet citizens have to show patience for seventy years? In typical fashion, the Strugatskys employ subterfuge by making their metropolis a world metropolis, with aspects of both the East and West. The City is in an alternate world, not in the Soviet Union. But as Glukhovsky emphasizes, nothing could disguise the brothers' core idea of the endless Experiment done on living people.

For all their labor on the novel, the Strugatskys never tried to publish *The Doomed City*. In the wake of what they had seen and experienced in the Kheifits Affair, they did not think that submitting the book was advisable. Not unlike Mikhail Bulgakov decades earlier with *The Master and Margarita*, Boris and Arkady

stuck to reading the manuscript aloud to their closest friends inside their apartment. To make sure that more than one copy existed, Boris typed out three copies in total and delivered two of them to other people. He says in his afterword to *The Doomed City* that these were individuals "selected as being, on the one hand, absolutely and unimpeachably honest, above even the slightest suspicion, and, on the other hand, not obviously numbered among our closest friends so that if things took a turn for the worse, no one ought to come for them."

For years, one copy remained with them and one each with the people they had chosen as manuscript guardians. All three copies sat undisturbed in their hiding places until 1989. It was the last of their works to be published and did not appear in English translation until the Chicago Review Press put it out in 2016.

*The Doomed City* is a summing up work for the Strugatskys, and one can see what the authorities would have thought seditious about it. Boris discusses this. The book's main character, a devout Leninist-Stalinist, evolves into a "top-ranking bureaucrat, a smooth, lordly, self-indulgent, petty chieftain and arbiter of human destiny," and, throughout, there are comparisons drawn between the Experiment and communism and how the Experiment, despite the chaos and hardships it can cause, in essence, can never be wrong:

> "The Experiment is the Experiment," said the Mentor. "It's not understanding that is required of you but something quite different."
> "What?"
> "If only one knew. . ."

Later, after a mishap resulting in unexpected prolonged night in the City, we have this:

> "The Experiment has run out of control," the Mentor muttered, turning away.

"Run out of control…" Andrei repeated again. "I never thought the Experiment could run out of control."

The Mentor cast a sullen glance at him. "Well now. . .That is, in a manner of speaking. You could also look at it this way.… If the Experiment has run out of control, it is still the Experiment. Possibly something will have to be modified somewhat… recalibrated. And so in retrospect—in retrospect!—this 'Egyptian night'—will come to be regarded as an integral, programmed part of the Experiment."

Boris says that he and his brother understood the life trajectory sketched out in *The Doomed City*, and their entire generation also understood it. The book demonstrated "how, under the pressure of the circumstances of life, a young man's worldview radically changes, how he shifts from the position of unshakeable fanatic to the condition of a man, suspended, as it were, in an airless ideological void, without even the slightest purchase for his feet."

For readers of their generation, from the 1950s through the 1980s, the Strugatskys had the skill and fortitude to provide their own purchase.

As these pages indicate, the Strugatsky brothers, despite their ongoing conflicts and struggles with the Soviet censors, enjoyed decades of popularity among the Soviet reading public. And, as I've said, while the brothers were alive many of their books were published, in one form or another, in the West—in the United States and the United Kingdom particularly. This does not mean that they became household names among Western readers. During their years writing together, they never had the broad recognition of Stanisław Lem, by far the most famous Eastern Bloc Cold War era sci-fi writer in the West. Still, you can see from pieces published in response to the brothers' first English-language translations that fellow science fiction writers in the US and the UK held the brothers in high regard.

Theodore Sturgeon was an immediate Strugatskys supporter. *Hard to Be a God* was translated into English (from German) in 1973, and he wrote a review for *Galaxy Science Fiction* magazine in November of that year, calling the novel "one of the most skillfully written, heavily freighted sf novels I have ever read." He also wrote a preface to the first English-language edition of *Roadside Picnic*, which appeared in both

the 1977 Macmillan American edition and the 1978 Gollancz UK edition. Sturgeon was again positive, saying "The Strugatskys' deft handling of loyalty and greed, of friendship and love, of despair and frustration and loneliness [produces] a truly superb tale, ending most poignantly in what can only be called a blessing." Similarly, Ursula K. Le Guin praised *Roadside Picnic* when it came out, writing a glowing review in the July 1977 issue of *Science Fiction Studies*. In a foreword to an edition of the book printed years later, Le Guin mentioned this review and emphasized that what struck her in 1977, in the midst of the Cold War, was how the Strugatskys wrote "as if they were indifferent to ideology—something many of us writers in the Western democracies had a hard time doing. They wrote as free men write."

Endorsements like these and regular translations of their works throughout the 1970s and 1980s helped create and maintain, if not a wide Strugatskys readership in the US and the UK, at least a solid sci-fi fan base for them. Since then, their audience has only grown. If you pick up any recent edition of a Strugatskys novel, you'll see praise for their work from the *New York Times*, the *Chicago Sun-Times*, *Publishers Weekly*, the *Guardian*, and the *Times Literary Supplement*. You'll see accolades from writers like Jonathan Lethem, Kim Stanley Robinson, and Jeff VanderMeer. That there is a demand for the Strugatskys' books is evidenced by the many new English translations of their novels. Fresh translations of *Roadside Picnic*, *Hard to Be a God*, *Monday Starts on Saturday*, and *The Snail on the Slope* have come out in the US and the UK since 2010. The Chicago Review Press published them in the United States, and Gateway, along with Gollancz, published them in the UK. First time English translations of *The Dead Mountaineer's Inn*, from Melville House Publishing, and of *The Doomed City*, from the Chicago Review Press and Gateway, have also appeared. It is easier than ever to find the Strugatskys in English translation, and that is a wonderful thing.

**Scott Adlerberg**

# The Future Is Going to Be Boring

## The SF Present of J.G. Ballard

Take your pulp thrills, your space adventure, and either your blind optimism for a grand, shiny techno-future or your profound pessimism over a looming dark dystopia filled with ray guns and robot overlords and forget them all. According to English author J.G. Ballard, if the future will be anything, it will be able to be summed up "in one word: boring. The future is going to be boring."

Perhaps we should all be more concerned with the unending present instead? A present that seems to have somehow assimilated numerous futuristic SF gadgets, themes, and tropes back into itself. Rocket ships, colonization of alien territories, the breakdown of high-tech utopian communities, the cyborging of the human body, the psychological effects of techno-logical influence, the fluidity of online space—they are all already here. In fact, they've been with us for a long time, going back at least until the mid-1960s when Ballard decided that writing classic SF and even his his rich, distinct brand of dystopian "cli-fi" (as the now ubiquitous eco-apocalypse novels are often classified) was somewhat pointless, that journeys to outer space were far less interesting and relevant than journeys to inner space, that rich imagined alien worlds, or our very own planet transmogrified by some eco-collapse had nothing on the concrete-covered, media-saturated, cathode ray–illuminated world that you and I find ourselves existing in. "[N]either past nor future could change," Ballard wrote in 1965's *The Drought*, "only the mirror between them."

Even the earliest of Ballard's books and stories were never really traditionally SF outside of the con-trivances of their frequently apocalyptic scenarios. Ballard (1930–2009) was born to British parents in an international settlement in Shanghai that was subse-quently occupied by Japanese forces during World War II. He experienced firsthand a distinct and very real form of personal apocalypse early, one which appears to have powered his imagination. Later, as a medical student, he fell under the spells of surrealist art and psychoanalysis and abandoned medicine for fiction

writing, eventually penning stories that saw him at the forefront of 1960s New Wave SF, alongside luminaries like Michael Moorcock and Brian Aldiss.

While the New Wave was geared more toward literary experimentation than any kind of prognos-tication, Ballard honed his writing into a uniquely personal vision of the future, much of which feels not exactly timeless but still remarkably, disturbingly prescient. The futurism of short stories like 1963's "The Subliminal Man," which sums up much of Ballard's vision perfectly, was squarely aimed at the inevitabil-ity of the impact of technology and commercialization on societal and psychological change, as seen in this quote from that tale:

> Since the introduction of the "24-hour spend-ing day" the shopping complex was never closed. The bulk of the shoppers were discount buyers. Housewives contracted to make huge volume purchases of food, clothing and appliances against substantial overall price cuts and forced to drive around all day from supermarket to supermarket, frantically trying to keep pace with their purchase schedules and grappling with the added incentives inserted to keep the schemes alive.

The various ecological devastations of the worlds of early Ballard novels like *The Wind From Nowhere* (1961), *The Drowned World* (1962), *The Drought* (1964), and *The Crystal World* (1966) created environments that allowed the characters that populated them access to their imaginations and their pathologies and to bring both of these things forth upon the landscapes, trans-forming their surroundings into territories of personal freedom, exploratory spaces of either personal growth or regression, hotspots of violence and transcendence. Witness this from *The Drowned World*, in which the book's protagonist puts on his diving suit:

> It suits you ... you look like the man from inner space ... but don't try to reach the unconscious,

Kerans; remember it isn't equipped to go down that far!

It was in the late 1960s, however, that Ballard truly began fusing his desire to explore inner space with the then modern world. Ballard said:

> We live in a world ruled by fictions of every kind—mass-merchandising, advertising, politics conducted as a branch of advertising, the pre-empting of any original response to experience by the television screen. We live inside an enormous novel. It is now less and less necessary for the writer to invent the fictional content of his novel. The fiction is already there. The writes task is to invent the reality.

Casting away speculative doomsday scenarios, Ballard took SF tropes and stripped them of futurism—the rocket ship became the car, the alien landscape to be colonized became a hidden traffic island, the technological utopian outpost became a high-tech London apartment building. A menagerie of clinical and professional characters (doctors, architects, scientists) became the perfect astronauts to explore "reality," a landscape of confusion, a mass media–saturated territory blurring the lines between filmic fiction and the real, where our ability to relate to one another is contextualized by televisions and computers and the stylized, prepackaged worlds and existences presented onscreen. In the process, enabled by various technologies, these characters tapped into hidden parts of themselves—pathologies, fetishes, violent urges—that they acted out upon a territory terraformed by both their imaginative and literal explorations into worlds of their own making.

Ballard's protagonists, usually through a chance encounter with a technologically enabled act of shock or violence—a car crash or, in *High-Rise* (1975), the impact of living in "an architecture designed for war"—experience a strange kind of imaginative awakening that shakes their apathy and sloughs away what Ballard called "the death of affect." In the process, they reinvent the reality around them.

1973's *Crash*, one of the more notorious Ballard novels, follows James Ballard, a stand-in for a writer already blurring his imagined text with the reader interacting with it, who finds himself feeling both more embodied and oddly enlivened following a serious automobile accident. James describes the accident as

 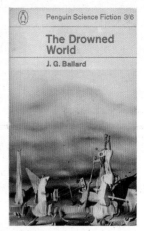

*The Wind From Nowhere* (Penguin, 1967)     *The Drowned World* (Penguin, 1965)

"the only real experience I had been through in years" and "almost a relief" after imbibing road safety propaganda year after year.

James and his wife Catherine perfectly demonstrate the extent of the emotionally evacuated landscape that Ballard the writer presents us. Prior to James's accident, the couple needed continuous stimulation from other sources to communicate and coexist. These "other sources" include the televised landscape and the fantasies that reside in each of their minds. Their marriage is a necessarily open one, for without the frequent extramarital affairs that they both engage in, the marriage would collapse into banal routine, the mundane conformity of everyday existence. Even when they have sex together, there is a distinct remoteness, a coldness between them, for it is not each other with whom they are truly engaging; it's the raw data of each other's extramarital sexual activities. Sex for the Ballards is only exciting when fused with input from outside, the fluids of their affairs acting as an aphrodisiac for the imagination:

> As we lay together we would describe a complete amatory encounter, from the first chit-chat at an airline cocktail party to the sexual act itself. The climax of these games was the name of the illicit partner. Held back until the last moment, it would always produce the most exquisite orgasms for the both of us. There were times I felt that these affairs took place merely to provide the raw material for our sexual games.

It doesn't end there. As well as the raw data of their affairs, they also need interaction with the technological landscape via the strobing eye of the television set. This portal into the glamorous mass media world (perhaps the only truly alien landscape) also becomes an integral part of their sex lives with flickering scenes of violence matching the rise of their inner perversities. The television makes scenes of atrocity banal, normalizing them, recontextualizing them as constant and acceptable parts of the world the Ballards inhabit up to this point:

> The beatings and burnings married in our minds with the delicious tremors of our erectile tissues, the spilt blood of students with genital fluids that irrigated our fingers and mouths.

Considering this, it is little wonder that when James is involved in a real act of violence via the crash that claims another human's life he doesn't dwell on the moral ramifications of causing a death. In fact, it's only moments after the crash that he states, "Already I felt isolated from the reality of the accident."

The crash is a catalyst, a moment of violent epiphany, unlocking within him a new way of seeing his own body and how it relates to the technological landscape. He immediately links his accident with sexual possibility. A sense of exhilaration refuses to leave James post-crash, as the traffic and the world around him now seems "threatening and super-real." Falling under the influence of Robert Vaughan, a former computer specialist turned "TV scientist" whose career was scuttled following a horrific car accident of his own, James and Catherine begin to explore their latent perversities in the cabin of Vaughan's Lincoln Continental— the same model President Kennedy was assassinated in.

Vaughan is compelling and dangerous. His body broken and scarred, signaling an open and willing retreat from the glamourous TV realms of which he was once a part. Marooned in our world now, in the eyes of his followers he takes on a kind of alien posthumanity, a creature designed for life in the blurred landscape existing somewhere in the intersection between their heads, the television screen, and the freeway. To capture the energy and liberation of celebrities who have died in automobile accidents is one of Vaughan's main aims and obsessions, made clear in his sexual exploits. His reenactments of accidents, such as the James Dean crash, are stepping stones to achieving this aim. They are also an attempt to understand his car crash, which left him disfigured and cast from the TV

 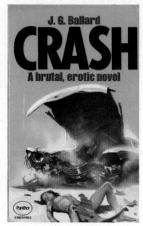

*Crash* (Jonathan Cape, 1973)  *Crash* (Panther, 1975)

landscape, stripping away even the perverse glamour that comes with a celebrity death. His endgame is apocalyptic, however—seeking "autogeddon," death, and a final merging with the mass media world via a head-on with Elizabeth Taylor.

With the automobile as their rocket ship, the characters of *Crash* travel not only along stretches of gravel and bitumen but also into the uncharted depths of their own minds. *Crash* is proto-cyberspace and proto-posthumanist in that the characters' desire to mingle with technology is at the book's heart, emerging in exploratory missions of eroticism, as well as violence, pushing latent desires outward from their minds onto their own flesh, the bodies of their cars, and the roads along which they travel.

Within the territory of the car, inner perversities are explored, released, and contained inside the steel womb of the automobile's cabin. Violence is also a compulsory component of sexual behavior in *Crash*. The violent meeting of two cars in a head-on collision is reenacted with the body. This often leaves sexual "partners" sore, beaten, scarred, as if they have just emerged from a collision, handprints and bruises replicating a bumper dent on a quarter panel.

The liberation, the rush and release that the car crash gives, is the only emotion the characters feel. It's an addictive cathartic rush, allowing them physical, moral, and imaginative freedom. As they reterritorialize their bodies with scars, cuts, and bruises, they further access the free spaces within their minds where room is granted for ever-increasing perverse experimentation. The car becomes a technology that allows the characters to realize their imagined spaces upon the physical landscape, morphing it from a confused,

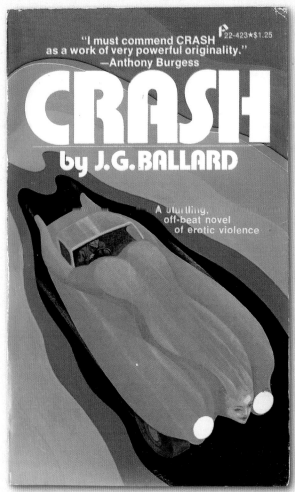

*Crash* (Pinnacle Books, 1974)

she emerged as yet another territorial site for the fantasies of both Vaughan and, in particular, James Ballard:

> This agreeable young woman, with her pleasant sexual dreams had been reborn within the breaking contours of her crushed sports car [which] had turned her into a creature of free and perverse sexuality, releasing within its twisted bulkheads and leaking engine coolant all the deviant possibilities of her sex. . . . Her strong face with its unmatching planes seemed to mimic the deformed panels of the car, almost as if she consciously realised that these twisted instrument binnacles provided a readily accessible anthology of depraved acts, the keys to alternate sexuality.

Having become "real" for the characters of the text only after becoming this compellingly odd cyborg figure, Gabrielle is hardwired to Vaughan's zeitgeist and, in many ways, is the harbinger of this crazed messianic figure's vision. Even her name has religious overtones—Gabriel was, of course, the messenger delivering the Word of God.

Gabrielle's posthuman body is a site where James Ballard's technological lust can be played out—their sex is rough, mechanical, and exploratory. Typical erogenous zones are ignored, and pleasure is found in exploring orifices and "wound areas" that their shared technological experience—the car crash—has created for them, and in the process James's intercourse with Gabrielle immerses him fully into Vaughan's apocalyptic imagined landscape:

> I visualised the injuries of film actresses and television personalities, whose bodies would flower into dozens of auxiliary orifices, points of sexual conjunction with their audiences formed by the swerving technology of their automobile.

Prefiguring cyberculture's sexual fascination with technology, disembodiment, and the feminine fluidity of the internet, *Crash* also has ties to that trailblazer of the cyberpunk movement, William Gibson's *Neuromancer* (1984). In Gibson's book, credited with creating the word *cyberspace*, protagonist Case uses the cyborged "Meat Puppet" Molly in much the same way that James Ballard uses Gabrielle—as a piece of technology to access something beyond the fixed landscape:

affectless realm into a nightmare world of sex, death, technology, and paranoia.

Not content to rewrite the rules of space travel in *Crash*, Ballard also puts his own spin on the cyborg, with the character of Gabrielle. The ultimate example of the aesthetic chased by Vaughan and his followers, Gabrielle is the offspring of a violent meeting of hardware and the body, what the cyberpunks would later call "wetware." She's the scarified subversion of the glamour as beauty myth perpetrated by the TV landscape. She's online sex and store-bought sex toy personified, a sexual creature, not despite but because of her abnormalities.

Gabrielle's post-crash "rebirth" unleashed a morally vacuous, pleasure-seeking posthuman, perhaps the first such being specifically designed to inhabit Vaughan's world. The crushed body of her sports car was essentially a metallic womb from which

She rode him that way, impaling herself, slipping down on him again and again, until they had both come, his orgasm flaring blue in a timeless space, a vastness like the matrix.

Vaughan and James Ballard's final meeting takes the form of a drug-fueled drive down a freeway, which under the influence of LSD and their shared imaginative space becomes a stretch of road made more of their minds than of gravel. The expressway becomes one created by Vaughan for James, a moment of transference of power from one to the other as James enters, for the very first time, the landscape created within their meshed mindscapes. For such an apocalyptic scenario, this final journey is through a landscape of beauty and wonder. James's wounds become "paradisial creatures." The landscape metamorphoses from a bleak, stark territory into one of glowing metallic creatures "soaring through the sunlight," and Vaughan himself is transformed into a creature with "scales of metallic gold . . . made beautiful by its scars and wounds." James, Vaughan, the car, and the world: all together at last.

James Ballard may still be cruising the fluid spaceways of the mind, but other J.G. Ballard characters find their own accidental ways to access inner space. So it is with Robert Maitland in *Concrete Island* (1973). Clearly echoing *Robinson Crusoe*, which both Ballard, in his introduction to the novel, and his protagonist explicitly reference, *Concrete Island* also thematically functions as a something of a Ballardian postcolonial SF novel.

With its space journey gone awry and an "alien" world in need of taming for its hero to survive, *Concrete Island* has the premise of many an SF tale, as exemplified in Andy Weir's 2011 hit novel *The Martian*. Clearly not leaving his roots behind, the book also features some of Ballard's most explicitly pulp references, smuggled into the text through its chapter headings. "Beast and Rider," "The Food Source," and "The Duel" all have a grandiose, pulpy ring of Golden Age SF about them, even though *Concrete Island*, at its most reductive, is just a little book about an injured man stuck on a traffic island.

Speeding back from a three-day rendezvous with his mistress to be

*Concrete Island* (Panther, 1976)

home with his wife and son, architect Robert Maitland loses control of his car, crashes off the road, and ends up on a spacious but neglected traffic island hidden below three intersecting motorways. Wounded and initially panicked, Maitland, like the protagonist of *The Martian*, is initially concerned with escape and rescue—attempting to signal other "vessels" passing overhead. However, Maitland soon begins to not only feel thankful for being "marooned" in a place that contains echoes of a familiar past now lost to modernity, but also sets out to make the island his own personal territory. Oscillating between the need to escape and the need to dominate, the space Maitland finds himself in draws forth not just the survival instinct but other lost parts of himself.

As he begins to explore his new world with its old relics from a world that no longer exists—payphones, air-raid shelters, old ruined cinemas—man and space begin to blur together, with the island "becoming an exact model of his head." It is not long before this identification of the island with himself leads to Maitland confusing its landmarks, "places of pain and ordeal," with "pieces of his body," a callback in many ways to Ballard's first novel, *The Drowned World*, whose character Strangman twisted John Donne's famous quote by offering, "Each man is an island unto itself."

Discovering that he's not alone on this Brave New World, Maitland's interactions with the "natives," Proctor, a giant, brain-damaged transient, and Jane Sheppard, a loopy, potentially dangerous young woman, are frequently confrontational, as he sways between the need to escape back to his former life and the desire to "dominate" his new neighbors and control his new "dominion." Proctor and Jane Sheppard also consider the island their turf and Jane specifically refuses to call for help on her nightly excursions back into the "real" world for food and money, even as she nurses Maitland back to health.

Domination and control are major thematic aspects of *Concrete Island*. As Maitland believes the island to be somehow a part of himself—going so far at one point as to believe, in a fevered delirium, "I am the island"—he considers Proctor and Jane Sheppard to be trespassers,

*High-Rise* (Holt McDougal, 1977)   *High-Rise* (Jonathan Cape, 1975)          *High-Rise* (Panther, 1977)

intruders in this solitary space in need of domination as much as is the island itself. For here, trapped on the resource-barren traffic island instead of cruising shared imaginative highways, there is only room for one.

As Maitland struggles to claim the traffic island for himself, somewhere out on a "mile-square of abandoned dockland and warehousing," two thousand people have isolated themselves from the world, occupying a technological and architectural marvel—a state of the art high-rise building. Filled with professionals of all sorts, atop this tower sits its architect Anthony Royal, a man recovering from a serious automobile accident of his own who unknowingly "constructed a gigantic vertical zoo, its hundreds of cages stacked above each other." This building is the setting of *High-Rise* (1975), a novel that takes *Concrete Island* and over-populates it and *Crash* but fixes the cars in place.

Like *Concrete Island* before it, *High-Rise* comes segmented with some playfully pulpy chapter titles. "The Vertical City," "Danger in the Streets of the Sky," "The Blood Garden," and the like all signal the book's playful intertextual mingling with the SF narrative space, even as its characters descend into a very "primitive" kind of savagery.

As the building's services and features begin to break down one by one—including elevator breakdowns and power cuts—an animalistic sort of modern "primitivism" slowly overtakes the building's occupants. The "modern primitivism" movement was popularized a decade or so after the book was published, with a blog sharing its name claiming that forms of ancient body modification were appropriated and updated to "meet this taste of the divine." While *High-Rise*'s

modern primitivism is less about the spiritual and more concerned with an end to a technologically imposed isolation via tribal bonds and clan warfare, the real movement's "strange juxtaposition of high technology and "low tribalism, animism, and body modification" appear as a utopian flipside of Ballard's nightmare vision.

The building itself is a distinct and fleshed-out character, anthropomorphized into a "huge animate presence" that seeds its own "intrigues and destruction." Inside the building, its reveling residents descend into splintered communities where "togetherness is beating up on an empty elevator" and, very soon, each other.

Seen predominantly from the viewpoint of two different characters, Doctor Robert Laing and documentary filmmaker Richard Wilder, the utopian technological outpost of the apartment building collapses into decadence, violence, and tribal warfare, as residents removed from the outside world turn the high-rise into a "Pandora's Box where a thousand lids were one by one inwardly opening" and headlines of discarded newspapers appear as though news "from another world."

Laing is the more passive observer of events in the building, coolly and clinically assessing the psychological shifts of both the tenants and himself. His conquering of the space comes with the decline in hygiene caused by the continual breakdown of services:

> The sweat on Laing's body, like the plaque that coated his teeth, surrounded him in an envelope of dirt and body odour, but the stench gave him confidence, the feeling that he had dominated the terrain with the products of his own body.

However, Wilder, like *Concrete Island*'s Maitland before him, sees the space as territory to be physically conquered; he's a "climber" at the foot of a man-made technological obstacle that he's compelled to scale at all costs. For both men—and many other residents—time away from the building, existing in the "real," becomes hazy, "dreamlike." The exterior world is forgotten as quarrels become skirmishes, skirmishes fights, and subsequent tribal warfare, classist in nature, inevitably overtakes the building. Based "on power, capital and self-interest," the upper, middle, and lower tribes each make up roughly a third of the building, with tribes vandalizing elevators and other amenities to advantage themselves and disadvantage (and provoke) their "enemies."

With numerous allegiances of both tribal and sexual natures shifting as the conflicts within the building escalate, it's worth noting the presence of "vagrant" tenants who wander around the building, sleeping where they can, an "invisible population" of troubled souls, one of whom is described as "endlessly climbing the service shafts," essentially the nervous system of the building, which "externalized an odyssey taking place within her own mind." These vagrants, characterized as living in "an interior world" within the building, are free to access their inner spaces with minimal interference from raiding parties of feuding tenants with floor numbers painted on their faces.

Where Wilder and others seek conquest and conflict, Laing seeks happiness through exploring latent "deviant impulses," and architect Anthony Royal seeks to preside over the battling creatures assembled below him. In contrast the vagrants seek self-discovery, spelunking their way up and down a technological climbing wall of their inner selves. The building caters to the real needs of all of these characters, even as it increasingly falters on a strictly operational level, representing the descent of all involved.

Over these three books, J.G. Ballard reconfigured the concepts of classic SF and brought them into the present, offering gleams of a future that, in many ways, has already arrived. Technology functions, as mentioned in *High-Rise*, as a model "of the world into which the future" carries us all, and Ballard's work challenges our relationships with it even more provokingly than the vast majority of modern SF is capable of. Underscoring it all is the notion that as we drive our cars and watch TVs in our apartments, "content to do nothing," the flipside of technology's ability to unlock inner space is its eventual creation of an extremely boring, passive, and numb future, one in which giving free rein to the darkest corners of one's psyche may well be the only path to freedom.

**Cameron Ashley**

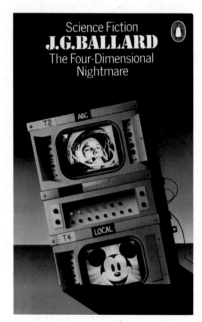

*The Four-Dimensional Nightmare*
(Penguin, 1977)

*The Terminal Beach* (Penguin, 1974)

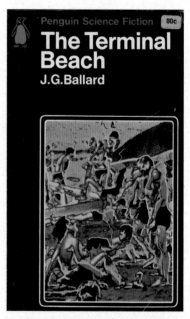

*The Terminal Beach* (Penguin, 1966)

# By Any Means Necessary: Revolution and Rebellion in 1960s and 1970s Science Fiction

*Commune 2000AD* (Bantam, 1974)

The period of social and political upheaval from the mid-1950s to the mid-1970s known as the "long sixties" was a time of revolution. Anti-colonial revolts swept the developing world, from Southeast and East Asia to the Middle East, Africa, and Latin America. There were failed uprisings against Stalinist control in Eastern Europe. From the mid-1960s, mass protest also gripped the West. Against this background, science fiction authors penned numerous revolution-themed works.

Influenced by the times, as well as the author's activism in the Socialist Labor Party of America, a reformist democratic socialist party critical of the Soviet Union, and one of the oldest socialist organizations in the United States until it dissolved in 2008, Mack Reynolds's *Commune 2000* (1974) is one example. In the year 2000, America has been saved from ecological and social breakdown by the emergence of technologically sophisticated, sexually permissive welfare society. It is also highly regimented, and information on citizens is kept in giant computers and used to assign those few individuals who do work their occupation and place in life. The exception is a growing commune movement that has moved out of the cities and is becoming self-sustainable and independent from the rest of society.

University student Theodore Swain is sent to research the communes. He visits the sexually themed Lesbos, an art commune, New Woodstock, and a nudist commune. The one commonality they share is a desire to escape from America's sterile and highly regimented society. Swain gradually realizes his study is a way for security officials to collect information on the communes, which they believe represent dangerous nonconformism. He falls in love with a female artist in New Woodstock and joins a revolutionary underground movement.

The idea of revolution against a supposedly benign society is also present in Scottish feminist Naomi Mitchison's *Solution Three* (1975). She depicts a feminist, eco-friendly, racially equal, post-aggression society in which homosexuality is the norm, and reproduction is undertaken by cloning. Her revolutionaries are a group of dissident women who want to procreate and raise their children via older methods.

Novels concerning humanity revolting against all manner of totalitarian regimes in near and far dystopian futures were common during the period: William F. Nolan and George Clayton Johnson's 1967 book *Logan's Run*, the basis for the 1976 film of the same name; William Tenn's *Of Men and Monsters* (1968), in which the human survivors of a brutal alien occupation plan insurrection; and British writer Susan Cooper's *Mandrake* (1964), about a dissident anthropologist who leads a revolution in an Orwellian Britain divided into destitute, fearful walled cities.

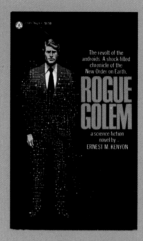

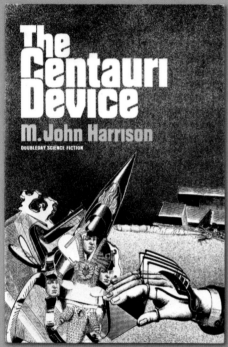

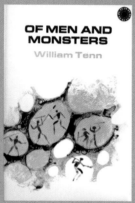

Clockwise from top left: *Mandrake* (Penguin, 1966). *1976 The Year of Terror* (Art Enterprises, 1961). *Rogue Golem* (Popular Library, 1977). *Sleep, Two, Three, Four* (Avon, 1971). *The Men in the Jungle* (Doubleday, 1967). *The Men In the Jungle* (Sphere, 1977). *Solution Three* (Warner Books, 1975). *The Premier* (Pyramid, 1964). *The Centauri Device* (Doubleday, 1974). *Of Men and Monsters* (Walker, 1968). *Solution Three* (Dennis Dobson, 1975). *Sleep, Two, Three, Four* (Harper and Row, 1971).

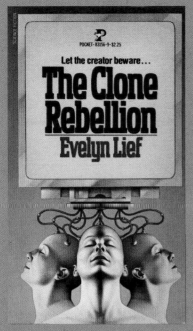
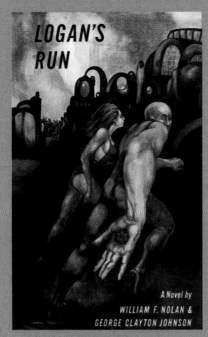

*The Clone Rebellion* (Pocket Books, 1980). *Logan's Run* (Dial Press, 1967). *Black in Time* (Paperback Library, 1970).

In young adult literature author John Neufeld's *Sleep, Two, Three, Four!* (1971), a ruthless administration has guaranteed itself lifelong rule by suspending the constitution and declaring permanent martial law. Thanks to the use of "black bag" operations in which government double agents randomly attack and rape citizens, this regime is supported by a white middle class frightened for its life and property. Blacks, Native Americans, and other so-called "minorities" are contained and dying out in festering slums labelled "Homogenous Zones." Anyone who challenges the system is jailed. Adolescents are sent to Maturity Centers to brainwash them in preparation for adult life, and any children deemed as subnormal or possessing precriminal personalities are shipped off to labor camps. The novel's teenage protagonists join a nascent but growing underground resistance involved in executing members of government terror squads. Following a bungled attempt to capture the sadistic leader of one of these, the teen team is forced to flee with a disabled brother and unwilling sister in tow.

John Jakes's *Black in Time* (1974) envisages a time machine sending a black militant and a white supremacist through time, both trying to alter history to reflect their political stance. In Earl Conrad's little known *The Premier* (1964), a talented and forceful black activist resists endemic racism by trying to establish a "Central US Negro Empire" in the middle of America.

In Norman Spinrad's *The Men in the Jungle* (1967), an ousted intergalactic dictator and con man, Bart Fraden, and his entourage turn their sights on ruling a planet known as Sangre. The vast majority of the inhabitants are terrorized by a small sect, the Brotherhood of Pain, devotees of the Marquis de Sade, who torture, rape, and cannibalize for pleasure. Fraden believes the planet is ripe for a revolution and begins to plan just that. First, however, he has to overcome hundreds of years of conditioned terror on the part of the inhabitants. How far is he prepared to go and will his ends justify his means? Underneath the pulpy gore, Spinrad draws parallels to the Vietnam War and failed revolutions, such as Che Guevara's attempt to export the Cuban Revolution to Bolivia.

**Andrew Nette**

# Performative Gender and SF

## The Strange but True Case of Alice Sheldon and James Tiptree Jr.

During the late 1960s, a blazing comet appeared in the world of Science Fiction. This new writer, appearing under the name of James Tiptree Jr., submitted short stories to genre magazines, then an accepted career path. These publications had begun early in the century as literal pulp but attracted

Alice and Huntington Sheldon, January 1946

increasingly sophisticated and stylish authors such as Theodore Sturgeon, C.L. (Catherine) Moore, and Ray Bradbury—not to mention charlatans like L. Ron Hubbard.

In his preface to Tiptree's 1973 short story collection *Ten Thousand Light Years from Home*, editor and writer Harry Harrison recalled the moment he spotted the new talent in the slush pile:

> I had a deadline. I was tired. I tried reading one more story; then I was no longer tired. Here was a story by a professional, a man who knew how to interest me, entertain me, and tell me something about the world and mankind's affairs all at the same time. I wrote at once, and was pleased to hear, some years later, that the word from me appeared just one day before a check from John W. Campbell. Now *that* is the way to start a career in science fiction.

Tiptree submitted in a golden age for science fiction writing, with guaranteed markets in both magazines and books and *Star Trek* and *2001: A Space Odyssey* on the screens. Moreover, contemporary social and political changes provided a milieu in which the present could be examined and reinterpreted through the lens of the future: environmentalism, colonialism, and feminism became prominent themes. These topics were precisely the areas where the new writer Tiptree excelled.

Even climate change appears in Tiptree's work: "Tell them...*the winters grow*" (the last lines of the 1973 short story, "Love Is the Plan, the Plan Is Death"). Moreover, the stories emerging from the typewriter in suburban Washington, DC, were written with tremendous verve, intensity, intelligence, wit, and subversion.

Consider the 1971 "And I Awoke and Found Me Here on the Cold Hill's Side," the title from Keats, but the Belle Dame Sans Merci being not fay but truly alien, the theme being xenophilia. In this dark mirror, colonialism is refracted weirdly:

> "Ah, Jesus, don't you see? Everything going out, nothing going back. Like the poor damned Polynesians. We're gutting Earth, to begin with. Swapping raw resources for junk. Alien status symbols. Tape decks, Coca Cola and Mickey Mouse watches."
>
> "Well, there is concern over the balance of trade. Is that your message?"
>
> "The balance of trade." He rolled it sardonically. "Did the Polynesians have a word for it, I wonder?"

Tiptree, while eschewing the public meeting places of SF, the editor's offices and the conventions, garnered a reputation, increasingly appearing in magazines and selected for Year's Best anthologies. "The Last Flight of Doctor Ain" was a finalist for the 1969 Nebula ballot: two thousand brutally effective words on plague, ecocide, and the Gaia theory. "Love Is the Plan, the Plan is Death" won the Nebula in 1974, the same award bestowed on the very stylish "The Girl Who Was Plugged In":

> Listen, zombie. Believe me. What I could tell you— you with your silly hands leaking sweat on your growth-stocks portfolio. One-ten lousy hacks of AT&T on twenty-percent margin and you think you're Evel Knievel. AT&T? You doubleknit dummy, how I'd love to show you something.
>
> Look, dead daddy. I'd say. See for instance that rotten girl?

In the crowd over there, the one gaping at her gods. One rotten girl in the city of the future. (That's what I said.) Watch.

Tiptree stories had a tendency to grab the reader by the throat and not let go. "The Girl Who Was Plugged In" was no exception, being a spirited and savage depiction of capitalism, complete with vat-grown, remote-controlled humans and icons setting consumer trends. It was a direct and influential precursor of cyberpunk.

The most awarded Tiptree work was the 1976 novella *Houston, Houston, Do You Read?* SF in the 1970s was a wild and crazy place, but even so the story was an unusual award winner. It begins with that iconic 1960s figure, the astronaut, but on drugs. So are the rest of the crew, comprising a jock pilot and a religious fundamentalist captain. Their vessel has passed through a singularity, emerging in the future. They are rescued by a spaceship with a female crew intent upon hiding from them the fact that plague has wiped out all males. All three men voice misogyny, so all hell breaks loose, including an unforgettable description of an ejaculation in free fall.

The main character, a scientist and self-confessed beta male, asks, "If you take the risk of giving us equal rights, what could we possibly contribute?" The question is rhetorical, the implied answer being: nothing. Almost the last words of the story are:

"what do you call yourselves? Women's World? Liberation? Amazonia?"

"Why we call ourselves human beings. . . Humanity, mankind." She shrugs. "The human race."

Compare that with Harrison's use of the word *mankind*.

A previous story, "The Women Men Don't See" (1973) was withdrawn from awards by Tiptree. It dealt with a first contact in which two women prefer exile with aliens to life on earth with males. The narrator is a middle-aged male, ex–secret service. After a plane crash, he finds himself in an exquisitely awkward scenario, camping out with a woman determined to keep him at a distance:

The woman doesn't mean one thing to me, but the obtrusive recessiveness of her, the defiance of her little rump eight inches from my fly— for two pesos I'd have those shorts down and

introduce myself. If I were twenty years younger. If I wasn't so bushed. . . But the twenty years and the exhaustion are there, and it comes to me nicely that Mrs. Ruth Parsons has judged things to a nicety. If I *were* twenty years younger, she wouldn't be here. Like the butterfish that float around a sated barracuda, only to vanish away the instant his intent changes, Mrs. Parsons knows her little shorts are safe.

Radical feminist speculations were not unprecedented in SF, with Murray Constantine's (Katharine Burdekin's) *Swastika Night* from 1938 (think: a Nazi *Handmaid's Tale*). Tiptree contributed to a second-wave feminist surge within SF, which included some very distinguished and formidable authors: Ursula K. Le Guin, Suzy McKee Charnas, and Joanna Russ, among others. In this company Tiptree seemed a fellow traveler, even being invited to join a 1975 symposium on Women and SF in the fanzine *Khatru*. There Tiptree wrote:

I think we can take it for granted that women are human beings who have been drastically oppressed, deprived, and warped out of shape by our male-dominated and largely lunatic culture. So are men, to a lesser and less personally destructive degree.

The only other male name in the symposium was Samuel R. Delany.

During this fruitful period of writing, nobody in SF had actually met Tiptree. Writers concealing their identities to write SF was not unusual, with "Cordwainer Smith" being in real life psychological warfare expert and US government advisor Paul Linebarger. It did not stop friendly letters passing between such authors and their editors, letters to other writers and fans, even appearances in fanzines, such as *Khatru*. Tiptree soon had a large epistolary network, some of the greatest names within SF. As Tiptree's star rose, so did the speculation as to what sort of person this very private writer was.

Tiptree stoked the fire with some guarded but tantalizing admissions, as in the fanzine *Phantasmicon* in 1971:

Well, I was born in the Chicago area a long time back, trailed around places like colonial India & Africa as a kid (and by the way, I knew in

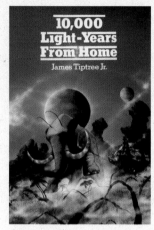

Alice Sheldon, aka James Tiptree Jr., with Kikuyu people, Kenya, in the 1920s

*Ten Thousand Light-Years from Home* (Methuen, 1975)

*Up the Walls of the World* (Berkley, 1979)

my bones that they weren't going to stay "colonial" any more than I was going to stay a kid, but nobody ever asked me). I'm one of those for whom the birth and horrendous growth of Nazism was the central generation event. From it I learned most of what I know about politics, about human life, about good and evil, courage, free will, fear, responsibility and What To Say Goodbye To… And, say it again, about Evil. And guilt. If one of the important things to know about a person is the face in his nightmares, for me that face looks much like my own.

Other things revealed by Tiptree were time in the army, academe, and the Pentagon, a knowledge of firearms and male sexuality. In his Introduction to Tiptree's 1975 collection, *Warm Worlds and Otherwise*, Robert Silverberg imagined the author was a "man of 50 or 55, I guess, possibly unmarried, fond of outdoor life, restless in his everyday existence, a man who has seen much of the world and understands it well." He added, "It has been suggested that Tiptree is female, a theory that I find absurd, for there is to me something ineluctably masculine about Tiptree's writing." That final remark would become one of the most famous last words of literature.

By the mid-seventies, Tiptree had an established reputation within SF; and the onerous, heartbreaking task of looking after an aging mother. This fact was confided via letters to a now wide circle of correspondents, as was the inevitable parental death, in late 1976. In Tiptree's grief, more information was confided than necessary, sufficient to send people to the obituary columns. One Mary Hastings Bradley of Chicago seemed the likeliest candidate, but the obituary listed only one child, a daughter: Mrs. Alice Sheldon.

James Tiptree Jr. proved to be the woman nobody saw, Alice Sheldon, née Bradley, nicknamed Alli. Born Chicago, in 1915, she had travelled widely with her parents, who were big-game hunters and explorers, worked in intelligence during World War II and afterward, and earned a PhD in experimental psychology. She had been married for over thirty years to Huntington (Ting) Sheldon, who was older, supportive of her writing, and a senior CIA official. As Tiptree wrote: "Everything but the signature is me." She had not lied but intentionally misdirected, with the pleasure of having a secret life.

Now she could write more directly about herself, as in *Khatru*, 1978: "Alice Sheldon. Five ft 8, 62 years, remains of a good-looking girl vaguely visible, grins a lot in a depressed way, very active in spurts."

She also recalled her introduction to SF pulps. Her family accumulated "Uncles," bachelor friends, and one of these arrived with reading matter, serious publications like the *New York Times*—with one noteworthy exception:

Out of his bundle slipped a 7 by 9 magazine with a wonderful cover depicting, if I recollect, a large green octopus removing a young lady's brassiere. We stared. The title was *Weird Tales*.

"Ah," said Uncle Harry. "Oh. Oh yes. I, ah, picked this up for the child."

"Uncle Harry," I said, my eyes bulging, "*I am the child*. May I have it, please?"

"Uh," said Uncle Harry. And, slowly, handed it over.

And so it all began. He would slip them to me and I would slip them back... We never discussed them; it was just Our Secret. But I'll tell you one thing: you haven't read fantasy or sf until you have retired with a single candle, to your lonely little cabin in the woods, far from the gaslights of the adult world; and set your candle-stub up in a brass basin... And then, just as you get to where the nameless THING starts to emerge, the last shred of candle gutters out, leaving you in the dark forest. And a screech-owl, who has silently taken up position on the roof above, lets loose with a nerve-curdling shriek.

*That's* Tales of Wonder as they should be read, man.

Alli Sheldon had fought all her life with expectations about what women should be, from the perspective of a privileged and very unusual upbringing which made her a perpetual outsider. She was an only (surviving) child in an era when boys were the ideal offspring. When she wrote as Tiptree, it was through a literary persona, the man her parents would have preferred. Small wonder the likes of Silverberg found her male voice so convincing.

When Tiptree began to gain critical plaudits for his depiction of women, Alli created a second persona, Raccoona Sheldon, based in Wisconsin. The two personas even had their own distinct signatures. As Tiptree's biographer Julie Phillips notes, a raccoon is an animal with a mask. Tiptree even recommended Raccoona to his editors. Here could be diverted the radically feminist stories, such as "The Screwfly Solution," in which men set out to exterminate women, which appeared in the June 1977 issue of *Analog*. It was written shortly after Mary Bradley's death and before the revelation and won a 1978 Nebula award under the Raccoona Sheldon name.

This game of personas ended after Mary Bradley's death, for the consequent revelation meant that Tiptree and Raccoona died too. The pair had functioned as the mediums through which Alli wrote, and without them she was triply bereft. It did not help that as a writer she was just making the jump from short to long fiction. The long-expected novel *Up the Walls of the World* (1978) was well-received but ultimately lacked the power and intensity of the shorter fiction. She shone at shooting-star lengths—that was her métier and also a summation of her career.

Editor Gardner Dozois wrote to her:

I'm afraid that if you abandon the Tiptree name entirely you may also lose "your tone of voice"—this is a very subtle, almost mystical, matter, but I think it is a real thing[, a] projection of sub-conscious functions, and if it can't "be" Tiptree anymore, it may go away and not come back.

Tiptree did go and never returned. So did Raccoona, that lesser but still fiery persona. By the 1980s, Tiptree was again caring for the aged, this time her beloved Ting. She had health problems herself, heart surgery and something that was a continual presence throughout her life, depression. She still wrote, turning the couple's travel into articles, and an Arkham Press collection, *Tales of the Quintana Roo* (1986). Huntington developed Alzheimer's and lost most of his sight. The couple's situation became increasingly desperate: Alli wrote a suicide note in 1979, waiting for the opportunity to use it.

Tiptree had three great themes, love, sex, and death, in fiction and in life. Alli told various people she did not intend to survive her husband's death and, in the end, took the initiative. In May 1987, she shot Ting as he lay sleeping in bed, rang her lawyer, then lay down beside her husband and shot herself. Love was her plan, and that plan was death. She was seventy-one.

Such was the SF field's shock at Tiptree's death that a commemorative panel was not held at the World SF Convention in Brighton, August 1987. Nonetheless writers Karen Joy Fowler and Pat Murphy set up the Tiptree Award for works of speculative fiction exploring and expanding notions of gender. It began in 1991, the initial funding raised, with deliberate irony, from bake sales and cookbooks. Indeed, the award took the form of a chocolate typewriter. The Tiptree is awarded annually at Wiscon, a feminist SF convention held in Madison, Wisconsin.

Though the author was dead, the plaudits continued: posthumous publication led to a Locus and World Fantasy award for *Tales of the Quintana Roo*. *Meet Me at Infinity* (2000) collected much of her nonfiction. Collections of her poetry and some of the correspondence (including with Russ) have appeared, as well as an anthology of tributes, *Letters to Tiptree*, published by Twelfth Planet Press for her centenary.

In 2006, Julie Phillips's biography *James Tiptree, Jr.: The Double Life of Alice B. Sheldon* appeared, a meticulously researched account that bridged the gap between genre and literary readership. It won awards, including the prestigious National Book Circle Critics' award. The book revealed much about Tiptree: that the family treks around Africa and Asia became books by Mary Bradley, for which her daughter was subject matter; that she had been addicted to prescription drugs; that she was profoundly shy, with her greatest accumulation of friends being as Tiptree, via his correspondence, varied with phone calls. Very few met Tiptree in person, but those who did found a vivid, charismatic woman, devoted to her husband and still flirtatious in her sixties. Yet she told Russ in a 1980 letter:

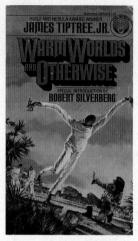

*Warm Worlds and Otherwise,* featuring the Triptee stories, 'Love is the Plan, the Plan is Death' and 'The Girl Who Plugged In' (Del Rey, 1975)

> It occurred to me to wonder if I ever told you in so many words that I too am a Lesbian—or at least as close to one can come to being one never having had a successful love with any of the women I've loved, and being now too old and ugly to dare try. Oh, had 65 years been different! I *like* some men a lot, but from the start, before I knew anything, it was always girls and women who lit me up.

Julie Phillips has opined that writing both sides of the gender war, as in "The Women Men Don't See," caused "psychic damage" to Alli Sheldon. Maybe, but she was already damaged. What she could write with genuine power was something she could never resolve in life. It is precisely this balancing act, expressed in fluid, angry, precise prose, that makes her work enduring.

Though Tiptree's stories would seem ideal for the screen, only two have been filmed, both for television anthology series: "The Girl Who Was Plugged In" (*Welcome to Paradox*, September 1998) and "The Screwfly Solution" (*Masters of Horror*, 2006). Currently in process is a documentary called *Tip/Alli*, by US filmmaker Rox Samer, and a television series interspersing Tiptree's life and her fiction, by Australian director Jennifer Kent (*The Babadook*). Kent comments in a Sundance 2019 interview:

It's not a straight biopic; so aliens from her stories inhabit her true world, and then she will be in the world of her stories, and it's so exciting to me. It's science fiction, which I love. I came across that because I was being given a lot of science fiction scripts. And I thought, "Where are the female science fiction stories?" So I Googled "female science fiction," and I came across her! It was so hard to get the rights. And then I got all the rights to these stories, so it's just meant to be.

More recently, in late 2019, the Tiptree Award got renamed, as a result of internet activism. As SF has become more diverse in its practitioners and audience, attention has been drawn to some great names from its past. They have been weighed in the balance of modern opinion and found wanting primarily for reasons of racism, as with H.P. Lovecraft and editor John W. Campbell. Consequently, their names and images have been removed from awards that originally honored their achievements.

Tiptree was not racist—anything but—however the last act of her life, the murder-suicide, *is* deeply problematic. It certainly fails the test of "expressivist objection," a recent term from disability activism. Because Huntingdon Sheldon was disabled by dementia, he could not consent to his wife's actions. An internet furor began, outrage that the award was named after someone so morally unjustifiable—although Alli Sheldon herself can be perceived as disabled by depression and health issues.

The Motherboard of the Tiptree Award initially resisted change, then with profound apologies for causing offence agreed to rename the award. It is now known as the Otherwise Award, the title derived from the Tiptree collection *Warm Worlds and Otherwise.* Yet just as Lovecraft might be personally repugnant while casting a pervasive cultural shadow, it could be argued Tiptree the persona and wordsmith is similarly separate from Alli Sheldon. The works are not the person but rather the best part of the person. Bones and flesh decay, but words endure.

**Lucy Sussex**

# Coming of Age between Apocalypses

## Young Adult Fiction and the End of the World

Everywhere was the shadow of death...
    No witchcraft, no enemy action had silenced the rebirth of new life in the stricken world. The people had done it themselves.
—Rachel Carson, *Silent Spring* (1962)

The advanced technology and advanced anxiety of the Cold War period provided a rich source for end of the world scenarios. These included nuclear war, environmental disasters, and plague pandemics; often these disasters are depicted as bleeding together, with one following another. While these narratives were informed by the rise of globalism and the political unrest of the era, they were also influenced by a new wave of millennialism, with religious apocalypse and savior figures prominently featured in many works of the latter half of the twentieth century.

Two *nonfiction* bestsellers of the era provide insight into the rise of these issues in the popular consciousness: Rachel Carson' s *Silent Spring*, published 1962, about the ongoing and systemic consequences of pesticide use in modern life; and Hal Lindsay's *The Late Great Planet Earth*, published 1970, a feverish interpretation of current events as biblical end-times. That both of these books were bestsellers suggests a literary climate ready to be mined for stories about worlds that are already doomed but can perhaps be saved in a new, better, reformulated version.

The young adult titles from this time period can be broken down into three distinct eras: those focused on the immediate postwar anxiety, new globalism, and life in the shadow of the atomic bomb; those that were written during the Vietnam War era, dealing with ongoing world and domestic political unrest and (in the United States) often informed or inspired by the Nixon presidency; and the late Cold War novels, focused specifically on the USSR, the nuclear arms race, and Ronald Reagan's America.

Apocalyptic narratives for the young adult market ran the gamut from straightforward post-nuclear coming-of-age stories (*After the Bomb*, Gloria D. Miklowitz,

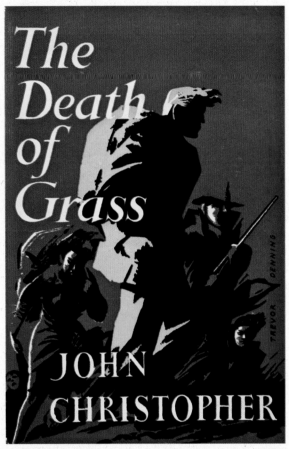

*The Death of Grass* (Michael Joseph, 1956)

1985) to baroque doorstops in which teenagers both good and evil fight for the upper hand in a nightmarish near future (*Swan Song*, Robert McCammon, 1987).

Published in Great Britain in 1956, *The Death of Grass* (published the following year in the United States as *No Blade of Grass*) got the jump on Rachel Carson's dire predictions of environmental disaster by a full six years. Written by Samuel Youd under his sci-fi pseudonym John Christopher, it depicts slowly mounting dread in postwar London, as news comes of an agricultural virus discovered in China that ravages the rice crop, with famine and the resulting political mayhem devastating the Asian continent. It centers

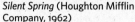

*Silent Spring* (Houghton Mifflin Company, 1962)

*No Blade of Grass* (Pocket Books, 1965)

on two middle-class families, the Custances and the Buckleys, who learn from their government connections that the situation is much worse than has been revealed to the general public: the government is going to bomb its own population centers in order to thin the herd.

The families resolve to make the journey to the Custance family farm in Westmorland, which is protected by a valley that can be turned into a fortress, to farm potatoes, one of the few crops that remain out of the virus's reach. While the traveling party quickly learns that there is not much keeping a gentleman from turning into a savage when it comes to food and family, and citified John Custance must prove he has what it takes as a leader, Christopher also focuses on the teenage members of the party and the unique contributions they have to make as the generation Custance is trying to save. This is especially true of young David Custance's schoolmate, the aptly nicknamed Spooks. Taken in at the insistence of Mrs. Buckley, after being abandoned by his parents and teachers at their boarding school, Spooks proves himself uniquely suited to the challenges that lay ahead. But the immediate changes in British society also embolden characters like Pirrie, the gun shop owner that Custance and Buckley encounter on their journey out of London, who arms the party and provides the much-needed survival skills the Londoners never learned; however, Pirrie also doesn't think twice about coolly killing his own wife when she makes a pass at John nor of taking a teenage farmgirl as his "bride" less than twenty-four hours later, reasoning that he can "look after" her much more capably than any young man under the present circumstances. Even as the elected leader, John

can only look on, passively observing that "It had been silly … to imagine this world was a world in which any kind of innocence could be preserved."

In Miklowitz's *After the Bomb*, set in the suburbs of Pasadena, California, before and in the immediate aftermath of the accidental detonation of a Soviet nuclear weapon over Los Angeles, Philip Singer is another teen dealing with awkwardness and insecurity in the shadow of his popular, athletically gifted older brother. With his father away and his mother and older brother injured, Phil has to step into the role of leader and turn his own scant talents into strengths to save his family. Miklowitz loads environmental disaster on top of nuclear catastrophe, as Phil's mother notes the seasonal wildfires that have been burning in the background all summer, foreshadowing how they will complicate the struggle for survival.

While Phil Singer and *The Death of Grass*'s teenagers suggest that it is the most ordinary of characters who must find what is extraordinary within themselves to ensure survival, a second strain of postapocalyptic teenagers was seemingly born exceptional, with the end of the world revealing them as humanity's destined leaders. *This Star Shall Abide* (Sylvia Engdahl, 1972; published in the United Kingdom as *Heritage of the Star*) is set in the far distant future on a generally hostile planet. It is hinted that it is inhabited by the survivors of the human race who depend on technology for their very existence. Sullen teenager Noren rebels against the expectations of the strict religious-scientific caste system he has been born into. Facing a dead-end future in his primitive agricultural society, he rashly speaks out against what he assumes is a baseless "prophecy" passed down from on high by the Scholars and enforced by the Technicians through a number of complicated purification rituals. First imprisoned, then escaping an attempted lynching before he can be tried, he undertakes a journey to the fortress-like City, where he challenges the Scholars to prove the legitimacy of the prophecy. His rebellion and survival prove his exceptionalism, and he has the Truth revealed to him, learning how the Founders deftly turned science into religion, ensuring the survival of the settlers, while only buying time until the same catastrophic end comes to this new world as well. With this knowledge bestowed upon him, Noren must take up his rightful place as the society's reluctant savior.

An even more explicitly religious figure, Sue Wanda "Swan" Prescott, the savior of humanity in

McCammon's *Swan Song*, is a little girl who has constantly been ostracized due to her supernatural attenuation with nature. When she and her single mother escape their trailer park and the mother's abusive boyfriend just ahead of the nuclear holocaust, every adult she encounters is given the instructions to "protect the child," for she is the only one who can save humanity.

While the vast majority of the teenage saviors rely on collective action, democracy, and a gentle touch, ten-year-old Lisa in *The Girl Who Owned a City* (Dell, 1975) takes a more hard-nosed approach. As the book opens, we learn that a plague has killed off everyone over the age twelve. Struggling for survival with her younger brother in the ruins of suburban Chicago, Lisa never abandons her highly developed Ayn Rand–style libertarian values in the face of the mushy-headed socialism advocated by her friends. The world needs a strong individual to show people what to do, and Lisa knows that she was born to be that leader.

Stephen King, always popular with teenage readers, deals with teenage characters and postapocalyptic scenarios in a number of his early works, including *The Stand* (1978) and *The Long Walk* (as Richard Bachman, 1979). The most reluctant of the genre's reluctant saviors, the appropriately named John Smith (*The Dead Zone*, 1979) awakens from a four-and-a-half-year coma to find that the slight psychic ability he had as a child has become alarmingly acute: with a mere touch he has startling visions of a person's future. As a lark he starts meeting as many political candidates as he can as they pass through New England in the wake of Richard Nixon's 1974 resignation; it becomes a curse when he shakes the hand of former Bible salesman and populist congressional candidate Greg Stillson and has a vision of the future President Stillson starting World III. John, a high school teacher in his first year out of college as the book opens, is in his early twenties, his character appealingly idealistic, and the physical and psychic trauma induced by his accident constituting a kind of coming of age, by which King echoes the background of disillusionment in a post-Nixon America.

In all of these stories, the world has reached a point of no return because of the failures of older generations. Whether political, social, scientific, or religious, the looming disasters are laid at the feet of the adults in the room. And while these novels reflect the contemporary society in which they were written, the era's forms of protest are frustratingly ineffectual in the face of these looming threats. The "No Nukes" rallies, the progressive approaches to current events in the classroom, and the willing wartime tightening of belts are completely inadequate responses to the realities of survival in a post-plague, post-famine, post-bomb world.

Instead, a big part of survival is dependence and willingness to react with violence. Phil Singer's parents in *After the Bomb* consider themselves progressive types: his mother is thinking about running for public office, declaring "if women were running the world there'd be no wars." She also dutifully protests nuclear armament. His father is an engineer who doesn't talk about his work building things "like bomb silos." Neither does the family discuss the air raid drills the teenagers are still performing at school or the state-of the art fallout shelter in the backyard. His parents have left Phil woefully unprepared for the chaos his neighborhood is thrown into: as a child he vowed to never touch a gun again after a classmate killed a bird with a BB gun. When his family's survival depends on him, he finds himself accepting a pistol from an elderly survivalist couple and wondering if he will be able to pull the trigger if the time comes.

Parents have failed Lisa and the other children in *The Girl Who Owned a City* by all dropping dead, leaving no instructions or guidance. She explicitly rejects her friend Jill's communal overtures and basic democratic principles, declaring ownership of the fortified high school as her "city" and equating voting with slavery: "I know you like to share things, but it just doesn't work out the way you'd like it to. Call me selfish all you like, but I don't want to own anybody. I don't want anyone to own me, and that's what a sharing group wants to do." Lisa instead draw inspiration from a real-life 1972

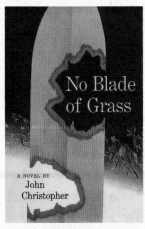

*No Blade of Grass*
(Simon and Schuster, 1956)

*No Blade of Grass*
(Avon, 1967)

incident in which a libertarian group briefly claimed a South Pacific coral reef as the Republic of Minerva, transforming a historical footnote into an overarching philosophy. Unlike her friends, the communally-minded Jill and the pacifist Craig, Lisa shows no hesitation in taking up arms (by liberating the armory of the local police station) to defend her city, guided by the wisdom of an unnamed source:

> Then one day she made a lucky discovery—a single book with words and ideas she could understand because they applied to her life. They made sense to her. She never spoke about the book to anyone; it was her private treasure. She kept it safe behind a panel in the tower chamber. She was finding that it wasn't easy running a city, but the special book helped her.

When threatened by a band of juvenile delinquents from a neighboring street, Lisa eagerly turns to violence, raining down kettles of boiling oil upon the attackers.

Traditional government and its figureheads are also depicted as doomed and ineffectual. As *Swan Song* opens, the unnamed President of the United States, a former astronaut, is paralyzed with inaction, staring into the flame of a match and ruminating on the lost promises of science and technology, with the world at the brink of thermonuclear war. Great Britain's government is less passive but no less destructive in dealing with the impending international crisis in *The Death of Grass*. The story includes a public relations hack for the Ministry of Productivity, Roger Buckley, pumping out racist propaganda claiming that the Western world

*After the Bomb*
(Scholastic, 1985)

*Swan Song*
(Pocket Books, 1987)

is on top of the agricultural catastrophe, dismissing the death of two hundred million mainland Chinese as "due as much as anything to the kind of failure in thoroughness that might be expected of the Asiatic."

Traditional religious beliefs also offer no relief in the face of modern disasters. While *The Dead Zone* protagonist John Smith's mother prayed for him for nearly five years and credits the emergence from his coma as a certified miracle, the experience also derails her mainline Protestantism, giving way to progressively weirder beliefs involving UFO cultists and other fringe groups (King specifically name-checks *The Late Great Planet Earth*). John must struggle against his own mounting dread that his mother is right, and that he is humanity's lonely savior.

At one point in *The Death of Grass* Roger Buckley comments, "The scientists have never failed us yet. We shall never really believe they will until they do," a sentiment that applies equally to imperiled world of *This Star Shall Abide*, in which science is disguised as religion. As the story opens, Noren is a classic smug teenage atheist who holds his peasant-like family and fellow villagers in contempt for their unquestioning acceptance of the ritual blessings and purifications performed by the higher-caste Technicians and Scholars. After he is driven out of society as a heretic, the Truth is revealed to him: a small band of survivors escaped from a distant galaxy when their home world's sun turned supernova and the system of rituals was developed to force their ancestors into compliance with the technology required to make the new world survivable. Noren learns that the population is not being manipulated by a false prophecy but by one that is terribly true: the Technicians and Scholars are buying time, trying to save humanity before the supernova reaches this galaxy too.

While *This Star Shall Abide* literally takes place between apocalypses, the concept plays out in more figurative ways in other books. King very specifically starts John Smith's *Dead Zone* coma in the fall of 1970; before his accident at the forefront of his consciousness are: "The marches, the cops in their crash helmets and gas masks, the mounting attacks on the press by Agnew, the Kent State shootings, the summer of violence as blacks and radical groups took to the streets." When he awakens nearly five years later, it is into a changed world and different political climate (he has a bad moment when his parents inform him that Nixon had resigned and he imagines life in Spiro Agnew's

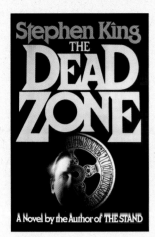

*The Dead Zone*
(Viking Press, 1979)

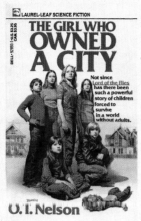

*The Girl Who Owned a City*
(Dell-Laurel Leaf, 1975)

America); it is a climate so strange that a psychotic ex–Bible salesman can win a congressional seat and have his eye on the presidency sooner rather than later.

When a Soviet nuclear bomb detonates over Manhattan in *Swan Song*, the climax of what the press had come to term "the grim summer" of worldwide political upheaval, it is above a Times Square that was two-thirds of the way to Armageddon already. McCammon describes a nightmarish version of the city, overwhelmed by crime, crack, pornography, homelessness, and failing infrastructure. When Sister, the middle-aged bag lady-turned-prophet, emerges from a collapsed subway tunnel, the last structure remaining standing is the Empire Theater, showing the docu-snuff film *Face of Death 4*.

This level of commentary is in keeping with *Swan Song's* generally superficial treatment of contemporary issues: the bad guys literally put on Nazi uniforms and start exterminating survivors marked by keloid scars that they term the Mark of Cain. McCammon's only specifically African American major characters in the book's sprawling ensemble are Josh Hutchins, a former pro-wrestler who serves as Swan's chief protector, and Glory, the widow of a small-town minister. While both are on the side of good, they are not deep characterizations, existing solely to suffer nobly and protect Swan, the blonde, blue-eyed savior of humanity.

Roger Buckley's opinions on the "Asiatic" races and their reaction to the Chung-Li agricultural virus invite a more critical eye from the reader. Early on, Roger comments, "Thank God for not being reduced to cannibalism as the Chinese were," but just months later as the families escape London for the north country, the party is hijacked by a group of Yorkshire famers with just that on their minds. Even in the "civilized" Western world, the distance between "Keep Calm and Carry On" and cannibalism is only about forty-eight hours.

With the major exception of Lisa, the Nietzschean Übermädchen of *The Girl Who Owned a City*, postapocalyptic scenarios tend to treat female characters—the moms, wives, girlfriends, and sisters that serve as satellites to the male heroes—as chattel or prizes to be won: morally pure but physically weak. The breakdown of society in *Swan Song*, *After the Bomb*, and *The Death of Grass* makes rape an ever-present threat to the women in the party, and women are typically sidelined, injured, or too physically or mentally frail to function as leaders.

All of these works set up conflict between the individual and the collective and portray danger as laying in large groups untethered by man's law: fearful, brutish, and violent. The faceless mob serves as the villain, even when it rallies behind a figurehead: the danger isn't just Congressman Stillson, it is the frustrated populace in their mid-1970s malaise who are ready to send him to White House; it is the frightened and ignorant villagers who drive Noren out of society; it is the looting mobs in search of guns and medical equipment in the well-tended California suburbs.

And when the mobs do congregate around a leader, it tends to be those who were marginalized in the "before" who in the "after" seize power and become cruel and sadistic tyrants. We see this in Stillson in *The Dead Zone*, in the delinquent Chidester Gang in *The Girl Who Owned a City*, in cuckolded Pirrie in *The Death of Grass*, and most of all in *Swan Song*, in which McCammon represents the forces of evil as including a teenage Dungeons & Dragons–playing computer nerd, a former Vietnam POW gone to seed, an escaped serial killer, a disgraced televangelist, and, in the final word on the subject, Satan himself, played as an angsty gorehound, still bitter about having fallen out of Daddy's good graces.

These books represent a small slice of coming of age literature in an era of advanced technology and advanced anxiety, showing how such work commonly turned to biblical, mythical, and supernatural responses, serving as genre window dressing for simple stories about turning teenage differences into adult strengths.

**Molly Grattan**

# Crowded Worlds and False Dawns:
# 1970s Dystopian Science Fiction

The world was always ending in 1970s science fiction.

Influenced by New Wave narratives that shifted the focus from space travel and laser gun–wielding aliens toward real-world problems and anxieties, writers had plenty of material to work with: the war in Indochina, growing corporate power, pollution and global population growth, and unease over the impact of technological innovation and computerization.

In Martin Bax's *The Hospital Ship* (1976), the nuclear-powered vessel *Hopeful* traverses the seas, stopping to pick up the wounded and sick from an unidentified and nameless catastrophe. Cut off from outside communication, the ship's medical staff are unclear as to what is going on, perhaps a war, maybe even several. Other terrors stalk the world. From their ship they watch machine gun–toting men overseeing mass crucifixions. "What should the doctors in their

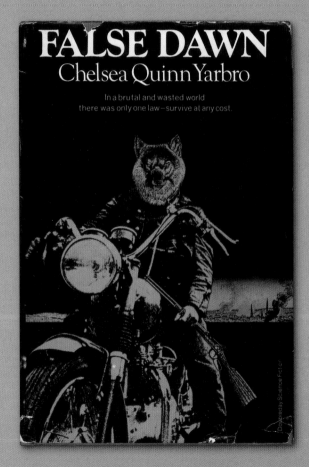

ship do? Could they intervene or should they just watch? It was a role they knew well—one of sustained helplessness."

Some patients suffer from strange psychological conditions, which one of the ship's doctors treats with experimental therapies; others rebel and demand greater participation in their treatment. Meanwhile, the crew oscillate between depression and the kind of free love party atmosphere that was common in a lot of 1970s science fiction. A none too subtle take on inactivity in the face of carnage in Vietnam, the book has a detached, free-flowing style, with discursions into quotes from unrelated books and topics, including the history of African Americans and the US Navy and a report to shareholders of a corporation.

Another New Wave dystopia is Norman Spinrad's *The Iron Dream* (1972). In an alternative world, Hitler emigrated to the US after World War I to escape a successful communist revolution in Germany. He ekes out an existence as a hack science fiction writer, editing the popular fanzine *Storm*, before finding success with a postapocalyptic fascism infused tale *Lord of the Swastika*. Underneath Spinrad's pulp hijinks is a critique of machismo in classic science fiction and authoritarian politics generally, his metafiction reinforced by the inclusion of a faux scholarly afterword by a university professor, lauding Hitler's book as a work of heroic fantasy.

No doubt influenced by the dire predictions in American biologist Paul Ehrlich's nonfiction blockbuster *The Population Bomb* (1968), overpopulation and its consequences became a key theme of seventies dystopian science fiction. Population pressure and compulsory birth control turned a future New York into a hellish dystopia in Thomas M. Disch's *334* (1972). Robert Silverberg's *The World Inside* (1971) is set on a massively overpopulated earth in the year 2381. War and hunger have been eliminated and humans live in giant skyscrapers, with no privacy or outdoor travel. Society is ruled by a religious belief in reproduction as the highest form of human endeavor, and it is illegal for women to refuse sex (a plot point, one can speculate, that owes more than a little to Silverberg's pre–science fiction days writing smut

Clockwise from bottom left: *False Dawn* (Doubleday, 1977). *334* (MacGibbon & Kee, 1972). *The Hospital Ship* (New Directions, 1976). *Empty World* (Dutton Books for Young Readers, 1978). *The Iron Dream* (Panther, 1974). *If You Believe the Soldiers* (Doubleday, 1974). *The Lathe of Heaven* (Charles Scribner's Sons, 1971). *False Dawn* (Warner, 1979).

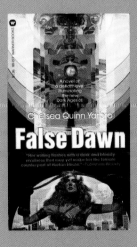

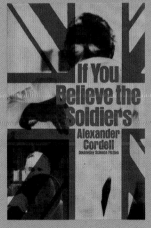

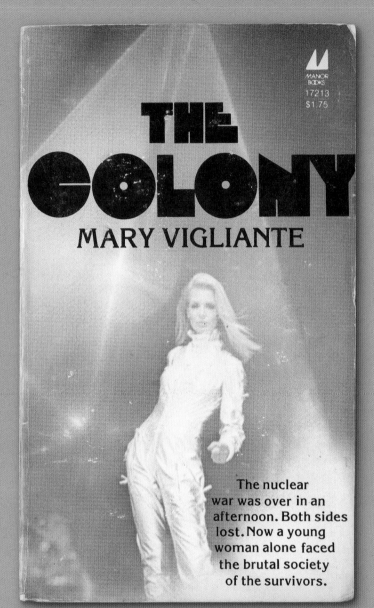

THE COLONY

MARY VIGLIANTE

The nuclear war was over in an afternoon. Both sides lost. Now a young woman alone faced the brutal society of the survivors.

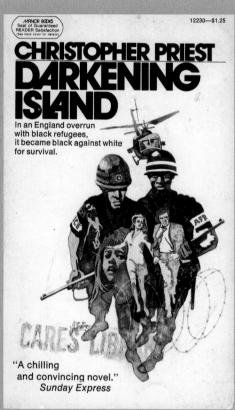

MANOR BOOKS
Seal of Guaranteed
READER Satisfaction
(See back cover for details)

12230—$1.25

CHRISTOPHER PRIEST
DARKENING ISLAND

In an England overrun with black refugees, it became black against white for survival.

"A chilling and convincing novel."
Sunday Express

Clockwise from top left: *The Colony* (Manor, 1979). *Darkening Island* (Manor, 1972). *Where Late the Sweet Birds Sang* (Arrow, 1984). *The Long Walk* (Signet, 1979). *The Shockwave Rider* (Ballantine Books, 1976). *Kampus* (Bantam, 1977). *The World Inside* (Panther, 1978). *The Iron Dream* (Pocket Books, 1982). *On Wheels* (Warner Books, 1973). *On Wheels* (Warner, 1973).

SLAUGHTERHOUSE FIVE...DUNE...AND NOW...
ON WHEELS
THE POWERFUL AND PROPHETIC NOVEL OF TOMORROW'S WARRIOR OF THE HIGHWAY
BY JOHN JAKES

JOHN JAKES
ON WHEELS
A terrifying vision of America's future by the master novelist of America's past

TIMESCAPE
BANNED IN GERMANY—BURNING INTO HISTORY
ADOLF HITLER'S BEST SCIENCE FICTION NOVEL!
THE IRON DREAM
NORMAN SPINRAD

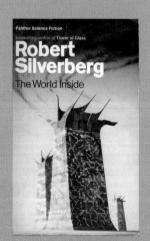

Panther Science Fiction
bestselling author of Tower of Glass
Robert Silverberg
The World Inside

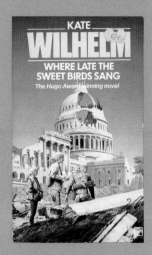

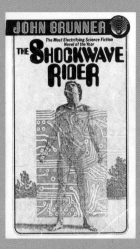
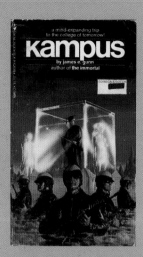

pulp). In Christopher Priest's *Fugue for a Darkening Isle* (1972) or *Darkening Island* as it appeared in America, a man tries to protect himself and his family in a near future England decimated by government collapse and an influx of refugees fleeing nuclear war and famine in Africa. The story, which jumps between time periods, was praised by some and criticized as racist by others.

Alternative histories focused on the emergence of totalitarian political systems were another rich theme. *The Long Walk* (1979) by Richard Bachman (a pseudonym for Stephen King), depicts an authoritarian America in which young teenage boys are selected to take part in a grueling walking contest where they must maintain a certain speed or face execution. *If You Believe the Soldiers* (1974), by Alexander Cordell, a pen name for Welsh-born author George Alexander Graber, is a grim tale set in a near future Great Britain under fascist rule. John Brunner's proto-cyberpunk novel *Shockwave Rider* (1975) offers perhaps the most prescient view of the future. America in the twenty-first century is dominated by criminal oligarchs who use access to individual computer data to track and subjugate the population, and people consume drugs to numb the stress of dealing with rapid technological change. The main character, a young man who escapes a government-run school for gifted children after he realizes it is involved in horrific experiments uses his computer skills to assume various identities and hide from all-pervasive state surveillance.

Other authors focused on postapocalyptic dystopia. Kate Wilhelm's *Where Late the Sweet Birds Sang* (1976) sees a future America devastated by social and environmental collapse that has killed off most of the population and the rendered the remainder sterile. A group of survivors begin cloning humans in the expectation that the clones will be able to revert to traditional methods of biological reproduction. Once grown, however, the clones lose interest in natural human procreation and the older humans find themselves the minority in an emerging new order.

In Chelsea Quinn Yarbro's *False Dawn* (1978), a crossbow-wielding mutant, Thea, wanders a North America rendered part *Mad Max*, part Cormac McCarthy's *The Road* by complete environmental and social collapse. Survivors barricade themselves in makeshift fortresses, while caravans of horribly mutated people, known as Untouchables, roam the countryside. Preying on both are a gang known as "the Pirates," particularly dedicated to wiping out mutants. Thea reluctantly teams up with another mutant, Evan, the ex-leader of the Pirates, to search for safety. In addition to the Pirates, who will stop at nothing to kill their ex-leader, they have to deal with wild animals and homicidal religious fundamentalists. The duo's day-to-day struggles are depicted in unrelenting detail. Thea is raped by a drifter early in the novel, a trauma that echoes in a very believable way throughout the story, particularly in regard to her relationship with Evan.

**Andrew Nette**

# Cosmic Bond, Super Lover

## William Bloom's *Qhe!* Series

William Bloom in the 1970s (courtesy of William Bloom)

By the 1970s, the popularity of genres of crime and espionage fiction was long-established and showed no sign of abating. Nevertheless, change was afoot, and alongside private investigators and suave superspies came new heavyweights in the world of thrillers: vigilantes, assassins, and black-operations agents carrying out secret, personal, and vengeful wars against wrongdoers big and small. Often fueled by a backlash against the progressive values and political approaches broadly associated with the 1960s, "Men's Adventure" novels helmed by embittered tough guy, such as the Executioner, Penetrator, Destroyer, and Killmaster, proved wildly popular, spawning series that in some cases have run to hundreds of instalments.

In part responding to changing tastes, and in part driven by the insatiable need for plot variation, the more audacious adventure writers began mashing up genres, bringing in elements from sci-fi, martial arts, occult, horror, and disaster novels and films. Soon spies were battling Amazon woman warriors aligned with North Korean agents in the actual Amazon and fighting

killer aliens, killer apes, killer ants, and killer bees in locations near and far. In the seventy-one-part *Death Merchant* series, a raisin-munching assassin serving "The Cosmic Lord of Death" mulled over then trendy topics such as the lost city of Atlantis, extraterrestrial interference in human matters, and the mysteries of the Bermuda Triangle—with footnotes to boot. And all this amid forensically detailed descriptions of sidearms and gratuitous accounts of blood-soaked maiming.

Alongside such outré heroes and antiheroes came the character of Mendep Bramhen Qhe!, Auren Bando of Pashman, 43rd Dragon King of the Land of the Floating Clouds in the Heavens of Infinity and Lord of the Seven Stars. Written by the mysterious W∴W∴, and with its protagonist touted on the cover of 1973's debut *The Taming Power* as "the divine ruler of the world's smallest, richest state, cosmic Bond and super lover," the series proved relatively short-lived in comparison to its competitors, running to only four novels between 1973 and 1976. In many ways, the prose and focus of these novels conformed to genre requirements: tough guy slaughters enemies in a hundred ways; tough guy screws his way out of trouble; tough guy faces impossible odds, yet we know he's never really going to lose; and so on. Where the *Qhe!* series differed massively from the pack was in its immersion in mysterious entities, occult magic, Eastern spirituality, and lost kingdoms from an unabashedly countercultural perspective, as well as its stridently left-wing politics. Very few mainstream thrillers of the time—or ever for that matter—would feature a bisexual person of color as a hero, with an aristocratic Englishman as his manservant, on a mission to steal weapons of mass destruction in order to force power-crazy governments of all stripes to keep their hands off the Third World.

Just as importantly, the series, which also included the enigmatic sage conquering the power of LSD, explaining the principles of numerology, and leading anti-war demonstrations, all while exposing the inability of "humanitarian" military interventions to bring peace and pushing the message that love conquers all, made for a wild and entertaining read. While mysticism and the occult are very much front and center, there were also elements drawn from classic science fiction adventure tales, including evil scientists, space missions, and deadly, cutting-edge technology, alongside mind-warping psychic machines and astral journeys into cosmic realms.

W∴W∴ was the pseudonym of one William Bloom. At the age twenty-five, the *Qhe!* series allowed him to coalesce many elements of his life up until that point, including a deep immersion in writing, mysticism, radical politics, and the associated British counterculture of the 1960s and 1970s. Growing up in a middle-class family in Earl's Court, his mother was a photographer who ran various charities, and his father was a doctor. Both were survivors of Japanese prisoner of war camps in Singapore, and their politics were left-leaning and humanist. Beyond this influence, living in the center of London during the early 1960s gave Bloom access to a wide range of life-shaping stimuli. As recalled in an interview with the author of this chapter in 2020:

> From the age of about eleven or twelve, I started to range around London on my own. I found Speakers Corner, which was full of weird people giving speeches of various kinds and I also found a folk club in Earl's Court. I think they let me in because it was interesting to have a kid there. Across the road from the folk club there was a café run by a pacifist, anti-nuclear campaigner. I used to go there too. So from that age I was hovering around bohemians, because I'd just sniffed them out. I also had a political outlook from a young age and was aware that there was a different way of looking at things: more compassionate, an expanded consciousness.
>
> Then, around sixteen or seventeen, I started smoking dope, taking acid, and just naturally

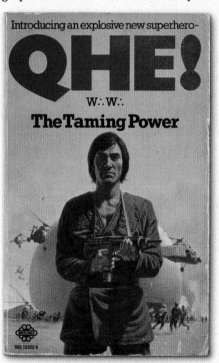

*The Taming Power* (Mayflower, 1974)

gravitated toward where the other Freaks were. Living in central London meant that "swinging London" was right in front of me. The whole package of the counterculture, the psychedelic consciousness, the need for social justice, etc. It just fitted my needs, my psyche, my character.

Having written fiction from a young age, Bloom first began working in the book trade at seventeen. After being kicked out of public school, he initially worked as a tea boy/assistant for the Leslie Frewin Organisation, a public relations firm and publisher based in Mayfair. Taking over a desk from Andrew Oldham, who'd moved on to other hustles, including managing the Rolling Stones, the discipline of writing press releases and blurbs every day meant that within twelve months Bloom had become, in his words, "a hack, a professional writer." For a time, he had considered going into the music industry but says that "it was so full of criminals and hustle that I didn't and moved toward book publishing."

Bloom also began to establish himself as a novelist. By the age of twenty-two he had his debut novel, *Softly Children, I'm Coming* (1970), published in hardback by Joseph. The company would publish two more, *A Canterbury Tale: A Game for Children* (1971) and *Getting There* (1973), with the former also published in paperback by Macmillan in 1973, as well as in France. Asked about these commercial titles now, their author is derisive:

> You know, there's a part of me that doesn't even want to think about them (laughter). Those novels reflect the entrepreneurial, slightly aggressive, slightly hustly aspect of my psyche. There was a lot of sex in them, some violence.... Although I'm slightly dismissive of them now, they were getting reviews in the *Sunday Times* and whatever, and I was considered a rising young mainstream literary novelist.

In the late sixties, Bloom and other counterculturalists gravitated toward the "Freak" end of what had become known as the British "underground." Freaks represented the more unruly, in-your-face, sussed, outrageous, piss-taking, and radical end of the scene, whereas, in Bloom's words, "hippies were love and lentils and laid back and fractionally thick." The London Freak scene's heartland laid in areas like Ladbroke Grove, Notting Hill, Chalk Farm, and Camden, with members involved in organizing free festivals and turning on others via newspapers, comix, and magazines, including *International Times, Nasty Tales, Friends/Frendz,* and *Oz.* Beyond freaking out the straight world with its lifestyle, political action centered around squatting, welfare and housing rights, anti-censorship actions, resisting drug busts, and other issues central to the underground community. For many, there was also a continuing push, rhetorically, at least, for all-out revolution at home and overseas.

Other than rubbing shoulders with anarchist direct actionists the Angry Brigade—who carried out a series of bombings between 1970 and 1972 against Tory cabinet ministers, banks, the Miss World beauty pageant, and other targets, targeting property rather than persons—the scene is perhaps best known today for what were then referred to as "people's bands." These played a pivotal role in terms of providing righteous entertainment, as well as outreach and fundraising via an endless stream of benefit gigs and free open-air shows. Key acts included Hawkwind (who performed and cowrote material with SF doyen Michael Moorcock) and the Edgar Broughton Band, both of whom had releases that made the pop and album charts. Others included the Pink Fairies and their predecessors the Deviants, whose singer Mick Farren, in a 1998 interview with music writer Richie Unterberger, summed up the approach of many Freaks in terms of the band "trying to push it in simultaneously a more demented and more intelligent direction."

While operating among the Freaks, Bloom differed from many others in the scene by taking his cues from the lighter end of the Yippies and pranksterism. For the most part he found that:

> The politicos were not a joyful crew. There had to be very loud music and drugs before they'd get up off their arses and have some fun. And I was always up for having fun. I found life really entertaining. I was a prankster. I'd go to places and give out acid and help create situations. I identified as a situationist prankster; that was my energy; that was the kind of person I was. What I liked to do was create situations that woke people up. It was affectionate but cheeky; there wasn't a lot of safeguarding involved.

The White Panthers [a UK offshoot of the US group, who to some degree represented the political side of Freakdom] thought I was a capitalist pig, because I had this mainstream publishing job going, was being published by mainstream publishers, and, therefore, had a bit of money compared to them. And anyone who had a little bit of money, even if they had earnt it themselves as I had, was considered very dubious. I was also considered too clean, too much of a meditator. Perhaps it was also because I'd been to a public school. Even though I'd failed and been thrown out, I may have still had that aura about me.

Bloom contributed to the British underground in a number of ways. Grassroots information services were a key part of the milieu, and in keeping with this he helped found Advise, the UK's first twenty-four-hour-a-day immigration support service. Involvement in publishing, however, was always central. In 1971, a particularly busy year, he not only saw his second novel come out but also began commissioning books for a new imprint at Macmillan called Open Gate. Over the next two years, Open Gate would publish a collection of Don McCullen's photojournalism titled *The Destruction Business* (1971), Jerry Hopkins's *Elvis* (1972) biography, which gave Macmillan its first chart-topping bestseller in years, and *The Essential Lenny Bruce* (1973), an anthology of the groundbreaking American comedian's work. In terms of UK subcultures, Bloom also commissioned Mick Farren and Edward Barker's call to arms Freak manifesto *Watch Out Kids!* (1972) and Jamie Mandelkau's biography of the Hells Angels All England Chapter's leader *Buttons: The Making of a President* (1971), which was later republished in paperback by Sphere. Thanks to friendships forged through his involvement in the Angels, Bloom would be made an honorary member of the Hells Angels and regularly ride with them during the 1970s. Alongside books on magic, Open Gate also published a second book by Bloom's sometime housemate Mandelkau, *Harmony Farm* (1973), a novel about an American commune that becomes the target of violence. As Bloom recalls:

I originally went to Macmillan as a publicity assistant for their general publishing list. I did the blurbs for book jackets and press releases and that kind of thing. Because I'd had a novel of my own published and was zeitgeisty, Alan MacClean, who ran Macmillan at the time and was the brother of the Cambridge spy Donald MacClean, recognized I had some talent. Not only that, but I also had a lot of energy as well. I was a workaholic, driven.

I brought into Macmillan a very prestigious academic book about the politics of utopian thinking and proposed to them that, given what was happening in London, they should have a countercultural imprint. I was then made the commissioning editor of what was their attempt to keep up with the times and modernize.

The books that I brought in made money, so they trusted me. I have to give them a stroke, as there were very posh gents and ladies running the place, but they were absolutely relaxed about eccentrics and bohemians and very kind to me. Over those years, I had three older gents in publishing who really helped me. When I went off to do my two-year retreat in the spring of 1973, I tied up all the bows, but there wasn't anyone to step into my place so the imprint folded.

In 1971, Bloom Publications became the official publisher of *International Times* (*IT*), with its name first appearing in the editorial section of the seminal underground newspaper's one hundredth edition. *IT* would fold in 1974, but, in 1971, it was still a fighting concern, in part thanks to an intercession from Bloom:

[With *International Times*] it looks as though I was more involved than I was. Through Jamie Mandelkau I came to hang out with the people at *Oz* and *IT* and wrote for them occasionally. *IT* had a financial crisis, and the only person who would save them was a bloke called Ronan O'Rahilly, who was running [pirate radio station] Radio Caroline.

They needed rescuing. My mum had a little publishing firm which had gone defunct but on paper still existed as a Limited Company called Bloom Publications. She transferred it to me, and we then put *IT* underneath it legally so that all the debts and problems related to [the

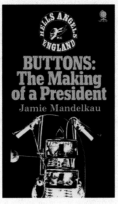
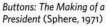

*Buttons: The Making of a President* (Sphere, 1971)

*Watch Out Kids* (Open Gate Books, 1972)

newspaper] were released to its previous legal entity. Radio Caroline did not suck *IT* into its orbit, and it could carry on as before. I didn't want any influence and just moved on. It was a very clean transaction. I got a bit of kudos from appearing to publish it, but, really, I just did them a favor.

By the early 1970s, Bloom was feeling seriously burned out and, at twenty-two, was prescribed the tranquilizer Librium to help with the stress. Although being "well-accustomed to taking drugs" he didn't like its effects so soon stopped taking the medication and instinctively turned to a self-generated form of meditation to "self-soothe." Six months into the daily practice, he found he was becoming connected to a broader force, one he didn't yet understand, and so he plunged further into study of the metaphysical.

One of the elements of the counterculture that I was very threaded into was the renaissance in British culture of Aleister Crowley type magic, Tibetan approaches to Yoga and meditation, the resurfacing of paganism and Wicca, the beginning of interest in Tai Chi and Qi Gong, all that stuff. It was bubbling.

From my teens I'd been having psychic experiences. I was interested in supernatural phenomena, many of which I witnessed, and not just when I was on acid. My parents' model was completely straight, and I was having all these experiences, which according to them meant I was mentally ill. But I was stable, so I went into two years of psychoanalysis with Edward Glover [one of the therapy's founders], who was eighty-four, to check out whether I was bonkers. And I wasn't, I was just having these multidimensional experiences.

I was reading loads of stuff about the Western Mystery Tradition, Sufis, the Egyptian Book of the Dead, the Tibetan Book of the Dead, Rudolf Steiner, Theosophy, etc. After years of meditating, I reached a point at twenty-five where all the novels, Open Gate, and the success, it all seemed meaningless and hollow. So I thought, "Well I'm not a dilettante, I'm interested in spirituality, so let's just fuck off for a while."

"Fucking off for a while" involved Bloom leaving in a VW camper to undertake a six-month ritual in the mountains of Morocco, the diary of which was published as *The Sacred Magician* in 1992. Such a journey required financing. Thus Qhe! was born:

I wrote the first two books in the mountains in order to keep some money coming in. I couldn't write a thriller as fast as George Simenon, who could write a book ready for publication in a week. I could do a thriller ready for publication in six weeks. [Initial Qhe! publisher] Mayflower were very easy, and the books were always ready to go to print; they needed very little subbing. Looking back, I'm very grateful that I could write. It was very important to do those two years offgrid. I could just bring an ordinary typewriter and make enough to live off.

I didn't realize at the time that Qhe! fitted into a genre, I was just mixing James Bond with magic, really. [My agent] was Desmond Elliot. Desmond was a stocky, short gay Irishman in Mayfair, and he suggested something like "Why don't you write a spy series with some of your weird magic shit in it?"

Because of the nature of my other novels it was absolutely clear from a publisher's point of view that it wouldn't make sense to put the Qhe! books out under [William Bloom]. The W∴W∴ bit came out of the way Crowley and the Golden Dawn people used to sign off on things, and I just thought it would look "occult."

And occult it was. Qhe's 1973 debut, *The Taming Power*, opens with brief contemplations on the metaphysical nature of good and evil before rapidly segueing into the hijacking of a French nuclear bomber by a barefoot man "dressed in what appeared to be loose-hanging violet pyjamas, a white gauze scarf wrapped around his face." The action then shifts to the Kingdom of Pashman. Situated on the edge of Tibet, it has isolated itself for centuries from the rest of the world. Aware of the unhappiness and inequality that exists elsewhere, its inhabitants have long performed rituals to prevent matters from declining even further.

However, with pollution, starvation, and nuclear Armageddon threatening all of existence, Pashman and its allies, including a shadowy mystic organization known as the Holy Brotherhood and a very proper English martial artist replete with an umbrella named Willard, are forced to take action. Through the use of submarines, magic, and brute force, Pashman's warrior king Qhe goes on to appropriate further nukes from Russia and the US. These are then used to hold the major powers to ransom and force them into peaceful coexistence. This is not only for the sake of the world's people but also so that Qhe and company can concentrate on fighting cosmic threats far greater than nation-states. In the process, the hero engages in wild sex with a female Soviet sea captain, endures torture under the influence of LSD, and teaches the idiotic rulers of the world and their minions that the new, non-imperialist order is here to stay.

In 1972, a sequel, *White Fire*, was published. With the help of his sadistic aristocratic British assistant and an army of zombified albino slaves, a mad scientist named Veiss is perfecting devices that torture people to the point of death but do not kill them. Channeling the accumulated dark energies from their base in a former Mayan temple, the conspirators are increasingly driving the people of Central America insane. The aggressive and confused behavior that ensues only serves to further build the power of their cruel technology.

The effect of this increasing chaos and disturbance on the stock market, combined with localized social breakdown, has led key industrial and military powers into a trap. With UN peacekeepers deployed and the use of deadly violence about to explode at the center of the maelstrom, Veiss gleefully awaits the final "unit of throbbing chaos and death" he needs to ascend to godlike power and fully warp the world.

Veiss, who incidentally has a penchant for crushing Chihuahuas, has not, however, reckoned on having to deal with Qhe. Pulled off a hunt for a Yeti stalking the peasantry of his kingdom, the mystic master witnesses at first hand the swirling confusion and impending

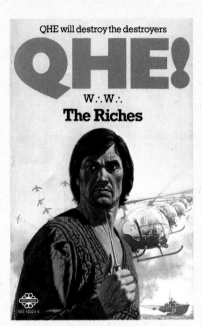

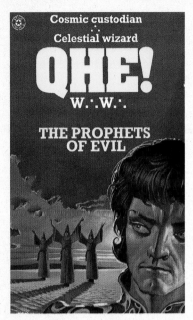

White Fire (Mayflower, 1974)

The Riches (Mayflower, 1975)

The Prophets of Evil (Star, 1976)

sense of doom created by Veiss's infernal machines. Along the dark and winding road to the heart of darkness, he utilizes the I Ching, the power of ley lines, and his own mystic abilities to dispel pain, damage, and weariness, as well as to control the minds of others. In the process, he also gets to indulge his love of "any activity involving speed" by flying a few jets. Most importantly, he discovers and teams up with a lost Mayan community to fight bedlam and hatred with the help, yes, of blow darts, but ultimately by drawing, with Zen-like calm, on the power of love.

Although Bloom shared an agent with Adam Diment, the creator of hash-smoking, groovy sixties Carnaby Street–style spy Philip McAlpine, featured in thrillers like *The Dolly Dolly Spy* (1967), and had read Michael Moorcock's Jerry Cornelius books, whose countercultural protagonist shared much of Qhe's taste for the mystic, Bloom doesn't believe that either exerted much influence. Ian Fleming's James Bond novels and the "clean and tight" writing of Mickey Spillane helped shape the style and approach of the series, but he claims that for the most part the books just flowed out of him. Similarly, rather than deliberately seeking to create a thriller series that could be enjoyed by the counterculture and turn on the straights at the same time, he claims he had no set agenda.

I didn't read a lot of fantasy fiction, although I did read some sci-fi. Writing the *Qhe!* books I wasn't in any way consciously referencing the rules of any genres. I wasn't reflecting on my style. I was not reflecting on my plot. I was just being creative and telling a story. [Che Guevara] was not a conscious part of it. I never had a Che poster or t-shirt.

The character of Qhe reflected aspects of me, [in terms of] being a hippy, Freak, social activist, hanging out with Hells Angels, all that blends into those thrillers. I never once reflected on the fact that he's a man of color; it never occurred to me that it was radical or unusual. I didn't have any kind of meta-narrative going on at all.

[Qhe] was in some ways a persona that I wanted to be. . . . I'd read all these books about magic in the Himalayas by Victorian travelers like Alexandra David-Neel, who had observed monks up in the mountains in the snow naked but drying wet towels with the heat of their bodies and young runners who could bound twenty yards at a time.

Willard, the butler, was modelled on my boss at Macmillan, who'd been very kind to me. I transposed him into this character who is very supportive of Qhe, but in a butlering role.

It was fun to write the books. At the same time, looking back several decades on, they are sexist in so much as [Qhe!] goes off on his travels to save the world while his wives are left behind praying in star formation for him. The gender politics are embarrassing.... He's a boy hero.

Having returned to the UK in the mid-1970s, Bloom soon became fully committed to what he describes as a "downwardly mobile" life focused upon spirituality. Nevertheless, he still had two Qhe! novels left in him. Duly, *The Riches* came out through Mayflower in 1975. By this point, Qhe's geopolitical interventions appear to be paying off, as the world's major powers have combined forces to launch a mission that will survey all of the earth's mineral resources from space before dividing them up in such a way as to ensure prosperity for all. Not everyone is in favor of this development, and the delicate balancing act required to pull the operation off is soon upended after one of the astronauts is hypnotized and sends his compatriots and their valuable data hurtling back to an unknown destination.

Having, in their bureaucratic shortsightedness and fear of failure, failed to heed obvious warning signs and head off the plot, the various military and intelligence factions involved in the project soon fall back into pursuing sectional ends after the resource secrets are put up for auction. Pulled away from a mission to end ivory hunting in the African nation of Tanzanayka, Qhe, the previously mollycoddled Tanzanaykian king, and Willard are forced to draw out the evildoers via a massive ruse.

This time around, the key evildoer is a street level gangster turned corporate oligarch who, despite surrounding himself with bodybuilding champions and former beauty queens, can only get his rocks off by concluding massive business deals. With the future of extractivism at risk, the theft of the mineralogical data looks to be the ultimate deal of them all. Having been involved, just for kicks, in looting various archaeological digs, the plotter is also under the influence of an unspecified dark power. While Qhe has to survive days of acupuncture-based torture, and the Kingdom of Pashman a UN-sanctioned British invasion, spiritual power and love, as well as machine guns and the threat to expose various governments dodgy dealings via "whitemail," once more sees the world set to right.

After *The Riches*, Mayflower passed on a fourth novel. Although the details remain hazy, Bloom recalls that the series' "mixture of magic, political awareness plus James Bond didn't find a market. It wasn't making money." Among his friends and peers, "the stoners thought they were funny. My literary friends were slightly sardonically amused by the fact that I wrote thrillers."

A new publisher, in the form of Star Books, was quickly found, and *The Prophets of Evil* came out in 1976. In this instalment the warrior king tackles what, on the surface, appears to be a Mafia-linked religious scam, the cult of the Prophets of the Prophet. Surviving multiple attempts by hitmen and "psychic hooligans" to rub him out, Qhe is assisted in peeling back layers of deception by a cast that includes Willard and a pair of French journalists, as well as the combined spiritual efforts of the entire Pashmani population. Along the way, we also meet a celestial Adept who is taking a direct role in guiding economic matters on earth. Having been teased with hints of it in previous books, the wider cosmic battle that Qhe plays but a small part in is brought front and center, as he and three of his best warriors infiltrate the purple clad Prophets. Previous attempts to get near their life-sucking leader saw double agents suffer psychological meltdowns, but none of these had been Pashmanis. Yet even a spiritual figure as accomplished as Qhe struggles in the face of such immense demonic power, a force that must be simultaneously vanquished on both the material and astral planes. Qhe ultimately exploits the vanity and conceit of both the Prophet and the Mafia, bringing them all to heel. In doing so he also hijacks the devotional power of two million would-be followers of the Prophet to force their godlike guru to become, against his will, a messenger for peace and equality.

Although a little rushed toward the end, the novel proved, like its predecessors, to be an enjoyable romp. All the more so for its continuing denigration of corporate masters, military men, officious bureaucrats, and oxymoronic intelligence agencies caught up in destructive petty power games. Nevertheless, after this mighty battle the *Qhe!* series was laid to rest. The public still weren't showing great interest, and Bloom had lost his enthusiasm. Indeed, he wouldn't write fiction again. Instead he has devoted the best part of fifty-odd years to writing about, teaching, and applying spiritual practices, as well as pursuing social justice causes. He has more than a dozen nonfiction titles to his name, with 1997's *Psychic Protection* translated into multiple languages and reprinted numerous times. All of which I'm sure Qhe would heartily approve.

**Iain McIntyre**

# Feminist Future

## Time Travel in Marge Piercy's *Woman on the Edge of Time*

Building on H.G. Wells's *The Time Machine*, not as the first of its kind but as a seminal text, the popularity of time travel narratives saw a drastic increase during the twentieth century. Despite the prevalence of time travel in popular culture, it is a genre that Marge Piercy rightfully described in 2016 as one that is hogged by "affluent white males," both as authors and characters—a group she termed as one that would not be "the sort of visitors" she would prefer if she were part of "a future good Society." By contrast, *Woman on the Edge of Time* serves as an intersectional feminist intervention in a genre saturated with homogeneity. Countering this lack of diversity, Piercy provides readers with an alternative time traveler: Consuela Ramos, a thirty-seven-year-old Mexican-American woman incarcerated in a New York mental hospital, who journeys between the possibilities of futures both better and worse than her present. Because of her social position, Ramos is incited to act against the oppressive power structures of the present. Consequently, Piercy's novel creates a time traveler imbued with the ability to change the course of history.

Time travel stories following the Wellsian tradition are based on preexisting hierarchies relating to gender, race, and class that benefit the white male time traveler. Conversely, in *Woman on the Edge of Time*, Ramos's experiences of discrimination as a poor Latina woman with a history of institutionalization shift the rules commonly associated with time travel; in this novel, varying degrees of discrimination toward marginalized people create a motivation to change the course of the future that socially privileged (white, male, heterosexual, wealthy, and healthy) time travelers do not have. *Woman on the Edge of Time* challenges the moralities and conventions of the present, thus provoking community and solidarity across temporal divides. Unlike time travelers in so many popular time travel narratives written and propagated by white men, who relate to time travel purely as an as an entropic disruption of capitalist progress, which disproportionately benefits Caucasian males who have some degree of economic security, Piercy's feminist classic reverses

Marge Piercy (reprinted with permission of author)

the polarity of those discussions by framing time traveling as a politically mobilizing and agency-creating mechanism.

Time travel often exposes the grim determinism of the future and reinforces structures of oppression embodied by contemporary society. Piercy's novel, instead, provides a scenario in which time traveling is productive, enabling, and inspiring, because minoritized, underprivileged individuals are presented with the power to change the future. As a seminal text in the cultural revival of the utopian imagination that occurred toward the latter half of the twentieth century, *Woman on the Edge of Time* has received a large amount of critical attention. Yet much of this research primarily focuses on Piercy's text as an example of a feminist utopia—highlighting the ways that the imagined future functions as a space where individuals can confront issues of gender embedded in the patriarchal present. Despite her popularity, there has been less focus on the use of time travel in *Woman on the Edge of Time*, and consequently much of the critical work that has been done does not discuss the implications of Ramos as a female time traveler at the intersections of many forms of discrimination.

The critical attention that Piercy's time traveler has received, specifically as a time traveler, is embodied by

Elaine Orr's 1993 article "Mothering as Good Fiction: Instances from Marge Piercy's *Woman on the Edge of Time*," which briefly draws attention to the protagonist Ramos as being specifically chosen as the "most likely candidate for time travel" because of her role as a mother. Orr argues that the significance of choosing Ramos as the individual most suitable to time travel is underpinned by the fact that she has been deemed an unfit parent despite her nurturing disposition. Yet the novel problematizes the role of the mother as one that is imposed on the female characters of the present and works to broaden the definition so that in the future mothering will be a communal activity. Ramos is initially disgusted by the new concept of motherhood, because it disrupts the emotional connection that only occurs between a mother and her biological children. However, the future presents an opportunity for Ramos to regain her role as a mother that has been denied to her in the present. I agree with Orr that Ramos is depicted as the ideal time traveler who "recommends herself to the future" and broaden her argument to add that Ramos is presented as the ideal time traveler, because her role in the revolution is built from the intersecting layers of discrimination that provide her with motivation to fight for a better future. As a result, the future represents a chance for Ramos to fulfill her personal desires, as well as the desires of the community. Thus, the introduction of a minority time traveler shifts the way that time travel functions in the novel by portraying it as an instigator of united revolutionary action that delivers motivation to change the trajectory of the present—something vastly dissimilar to the traditional time travel narrative.

Because it was originally published in 1976, these intersections of discrimination reflect the fact that *Woman on the Edge of Time* is a literary artifact of American cultural concerns regarding minority groups that were percolating in contemporary discourse. As such, *Woman on the Edge of Time* epitomizes the shift from second-wave feminism to intersectional feminism. In the 2019 collection *The Global 1970s: Radicalism, Reform, and Crisis*, Duco Hellema argues that "there is, perhaps, no other decade that has evoked such divergent and even contradictory images" as the 1970s. In 2016, Piercy described this period as a "time of great political ferment and optimism" among those who "longed for a more egalitarian society with more opportunities for all people, not just some of them." In *The Hidden 1970s: Histories of*

*Radicalism*, Dan Berger writes that, historically, the 1970s was a decade "rife with contingency," filled with a sense of hope to break down systemic hierarchies of oppression. The decade has been characterized as a space of "fierce contestation" brought forward by "radical social movements" that have been traditionally cast off as "irrelevant." Significantly, in the 2012 article "Transmuting Grammars of Whiteness in Third-Wave Feminism," Rebecca L. Clark Mane noted that the women of color involved in the development of intersectional feminism sought to expose the fact that the "ideas of middle-class white women," upon which the first and second wave were founded, "were masquerading as concerns of the universal woman in feminism." Commenting on the period, Berger argues that white, liberal, second-wave feminism moved toward the more inclusive form of intersectional feminism, meaning American women, particularly women of color, witnessed "an array of revelations and changes in social, political, and public thought and policy" throughout the 1970s. These initial social transformations inspired minority groups to fight against the discriminatory "limits of American government." Confronting vast social inequality, activists worked to use radical political action to build a society on the pillars of "insurgency, solidarity, and community." Significantly, the revolutionary responses to oppression in the 1970s seem "to inform the current era," while also "reappearing in it," marking the fact that equality has not yet been achieved.

Given this context, revisiting Piercy's classic novel in this time of extreme political division is especially important. Based in the revolutionary social movements of the 1970s, *Woman on the Edge of Time* serves as a critical analysis of the intersections of inequality affecting minority populations. In the novel, Piercy depicts numerous forms of discrimination, representing the inherent systemic inequalities embedded in the present. Ramos's social standing forces her to live in a "dirty world" that has determined her fate from birth. The space of the novel's present is saturated with varying levels of inequality, so as to ensure that the perceived social hierarchy will be maintained. Ramos recognizes that one of the ways for her to move up in society would be to apply for a job as a typist, but the hiring agencies "liked to use the younger women" and, as somebody "with a police record and a psychiatric record," she is trapped in her current position of oppression. In this example of intersectional

*Woman on the Edge of Time* (Fawcett Crest, 1977)

language lacks gender-neutral terms to refer to people, which ensures that gender is always considered, with the categories of male and female represented in binary opposition. Mattapoisett, by contrast, has removed gender-based language. Pronouns like her and him have been replaced with the all-encompassing "per," creating a sense of equality between the genders.

Likewise, in Ramos's present, issues of race are still prevalent, and the social structure privileges individuals of Caucasian descent over people of color. Mattapoisett's social structure works to value racial diversity, ensuring that the children are born "multi-colored like a litter of puppies without the stigmata of race and sex." As a result, people are presented with many skin tones that do not necessarily have any connotation of race and, in turn, they are presented as equal, despite their physical differences. The world is structured to ensure that there is "no chance of racism again."

Finally, the society of Ramos's present favors youth over age, particularly in relation to women. By contrast, in Mattapoisett, the elderly are treated with deep respect. Instead of being considered feeble and a burden on the rest of society, "old people" retain "an ongoing strength," because they are "useful." Throughout Mattapoisett there is a sense of harmony; the residents are shown in social situations debating "heatedly, laughing and telling jokes" in a space where everyone is accepted. The relationships between members of the population are often shown as pleasant, but more importantly they are given equal opportunity to speak—eliminating the forced voicelessness of the past's minority population. And so, in *Woman on the Edge of Time*, time travel exposes a future defined by its potential to become better than the world of the present, advancing the idea that equality is possible, and discrimination is not a natural occurrence that must be put up with.

However, this future is not presented as inevitable, placing the eventuality of Mattapoisett in jeopardy. Alternative futures in *Woman on the Edge of Time* are shown as "equally or almost equally probable," which presents a malleability inherent to the timeline that "affects the shape of time." The world of the future that Ramos is initially drawn into is "struggling to exist" against the possibilities of other futures. In other words, the future has the possibility to become better than the present, but it is also possible that it may become far worse. Piercy contrasts Mattapoisett with an alternative

discrimination, Piercy uses Ramos as a conduit to examine problems entrenched in American culture, exemplifying the experiences of some of the most marginalized members of society. The narrative thus evaluates the position of the minority figure embodied by Ramos: "a fat Chicana aged thirty-seven without a man" and "without her own child." In doing so, *Woman on the Edge of Time* critically investigates intersections of discrimination in relation to gender, race, physical appearance, and age put into place by contemporary power structures.

While the present is characterized by broad social inequality, the future exposes the potential for a better world, free from discrimination. Ramos travels into the future world of Mattapoisett, which is characterized by complete equality—each layer of discrimination that Ramos faces in the present is confronted and broken down in the future. In the present, the English future shown to Ramos later in the novel as a means to expose the risk of inaction. Women in this alternative future are "cosmetically fixed for sex use" to be sold in businesses called "knockshop[s]." In other words, females are reduced to mere bodies to please men in power—they are commodities rather than people. When Ramos arrives in this version of the future, Gildina, one of the women she first meets, is scanned and determined to have the "mental capacity" of a "genetically improved ape." Women are thus presented as naturally inferior to men, lacking the intellect to be treated as human; any female figure willing to speak for herself is considered a "dud" not "functional" enough to be used in society as a sex slave, although she is owned by the overarching "corporate body" either way. Ramos is, therefore, exposed to the consequences of allowing the power structures of the present to continue, as they are set to be exaggerated in the future.

Given that time travel has provided Ramos with a new perspective on the future's certainty, she understands the risks of allowing contemporary social hierarchies to continue. Building on what Sam McBean calls a "connection to her contemporary moment" in the 2014 article "Feminism and Futurity: Revisiting Marge Piercy's *Woman on the Edge of Time*," I argue that Piercy offers a "critical distance on the present's inevitability" that demonstrates the significance in the role of the individual in changing their society. Similar to 1970s activist groups, the characters in the novel are imbued with the ability to modify their living conditions and change the course of the future accordingly. The comparison between temporal spaces in Piercy's novel exposes the fact that the hierarchal constructs of the present are not naturally occurring, and there is always the potential for change. While time travel offers a possible answer to the problems of the text's present, the solution does not rest only in the unattainable future. Rather, *Woman on the Edge of Time* works to argue that in order to ensure the world becomes better rather than worse, people must actively rebel against what is considered to be unjust. Ramos's identity as a minority places her in a position where her experiences of discrimination serve as a form of provocation to change the trajectory of the present to ensure a better future.

Therefore, a knowledge of the potential that rests in the future is not enough to guarantee change will occur. Rather, Piercy's novel emphasizes the importance of the individual in determining the timeline's trajectory. The present is shown to be a temporal space that is on the crux of determining whether the future will be better or worse—pivoting on the figure of Ramos. Within the novel, inaction ensures that the future will be worse than the present, placing the lives of minority figures in jeopardy, which makes achieving the utopian society of Mattapoisett a critical venture. Ramos's exposure to "the other world that might come to be" solidifies her place in the revolution, because it allows her to question the principles that inform the makeup of the present. Through the act of describing a new design and shared practices in the space of social institutions, Piercy offers the potential to apply revolutionary ideas to the real world—a dangerous but crucial venture. Building on the risks of revolution, Claire P. Curtis argues in the 2005 article "Rehabilitating Utopia: Feminist Science Fiction and Finding the Ideal" that the quest for utopia often "justifies violence," presenting fighting as a necessary tool in ensuring that a better future will occur, and, in line with this, Ramos is incited to violent revolution to change the world for the better. As a result, time travel allows Ramos to find her place in the "war" for Mattapoisett that she considers herself to be "enlisted in" as a moral duty. Therefore, Ramos is presented as a pinnacle figure in the revolt against the social structures of the present, working to "deny" her "oppressor" her "allegiance" in the continued discrimination against minority groups. In other words, time travel presents an "opening to fight back" against the current conditions to ensure that they will not get worse.

*Woman on the Edge of Time* is imbued with the language of violence—presenting opportunities for those "without power" to find "ways to fight." Within the novel, power is equated with violence. For Ramos to ensure that the future becomes better, her only option is to fight against her oppressors. Inspired by the rules of Mattapoisett, where the population elects to "kill people who choose twice to hurt others," Ramos revolts against the oppressors of the present who continue to allow social injustices to occur. Thus, violence is presented to Ramos as the only means to ensure that the future will become a better world than the present. This can be seen in the mental hospital when Ramos prevents the implantation of a mind control device in her brain by poisoning the coffee pot with parathion: a chemical so potent that it was illegal to "possess" without "a license." Ramos justifies killing six people, because they "are the violence-prone" and "theirs is

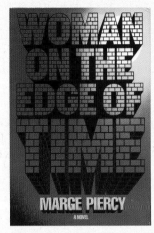

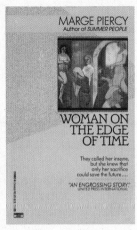

*Woman on the Edge of Time*
(Alfred A. Knopf, 1976)

*Woman on the Edge of Time*
(Fawcett Crest, 1976)

the money and power," making them the first enemy casualties in the war. Although Ramos recognizes that it is not "right to kill them," their murder is presented as an essential act to push for the future existence of Mattapoisett. In other words, Ramos acknowledges that murder is morally wrong but considers it a necessary act, which, from her perspective, makes it the most righteous decision. Hence, Ramos is incited to action by the risks of her current layers of oppression continuing into the future, which makes it necessary for her to face the violent dangers of revolutionary change to achieve a better world. Thus, time travel in the hands of a minority figure disrupts conventional moralities that, if adhered to, will perpetuate a status quo of oppression.

Piercy's novel demonstrates that violence is often necessary for revolution to occur, despite the fact that Ramos's violent revolt against the systemic injustices of her time ultimately ends in her demise. Nevertheless, the novel places emphasis on the decision to fight against society's tyrants as being the true success of Ramos's actions. After killing her oppressors, Ramos recognizes that she is a "dead woman now too," because she knows that she will be caught, despite her attempts to hide her crime. Although Ramos will likely be imprisoned and potentially given the death sentence, her actions are presented as heroic, because she has pushed against the power structures of her time. The beginning of a revolution is inherently linked to Ramos's actions, because she "tried," which presents the possibility of change occurring in the future. Ramos's attempt allows her to play a fundamental role in the possibility of inciting change by revolting

against the society of the present as a means to ensure a better future.

Throughout *Woman on the Edge of Time*, revolution is presented as a communal activity inspired by the oppressed. Within Mattapoisett, the population is still fighting a war for the continued existence of their utopia. The world of the future is formulated around an idea of strength spurred by working toward a shared goal, reinforcing "how good" it is "to fight beside" other members of the community. This statement implies a sense of connection between individuals who stand together for the same cause. Furthermore, joining the struggle is not merely presented as a moral choice but rather a shared responsibility in fighting against inequality to ensure that the future continues to be better than the past. Every able member of the population is conscripted into the army to provide "defense" in order to fight an ongoing battle to sustain their existence. Although war prevents the people of Mattapoisett from living in a world of peace in which they are able to "push all energies into what people need and want," this violence is considered necessary to prevent their extermination—showing that a world of equality is something that must be continually fought for. Revolution is presented as a community-based action that pushes forward hope for a better future. Consequently, by centering a poor Mexican woman as time traveler, the novel positions time travel as more than an entropic disruption of what the most privileged members of society consider to be positive advancement. Ramos's experience—both in the futures she encounters and in her present—challenge the concept of progress as necessarily positive and different from the past. More simply, by exposing Ramos to both possible futures, the science-fictional aspects of the text enable a critique of progress by exposing its inherent subjectivity.

Through time travel, Ramos becomes a member of Mattapoisett's community, which makes her actions in the present a necessary continuation of the war of the future. Time travel thus creates possibilities for the formation of unlikely communities. As such, the rebellion does not end with Ramos's eventual death, because the knowledge of the future's potential has been passed on to other characters, thereby enlisting minority populations in the fight to build a better world where they will not be discriminated against. Piercy's novel incites revolution through time travel, because it is within the vision of future potential that humanity can be inspired to change.

During her stay in the hospital, Ramos speaks to Sybil, another patient who is also set up for brain surgery. In a similar spirit, Sybil is willing to do "anything to stop them." Building on this inner yearning for revolt, Ramos informs Sybil that the present is a "war" that she has to "fight" in, reminding her to "hate" her oppressor "more than" she hates herself so that she will "stay free." The idea of freedom has dual meaning in this passage, referring to an ensured freedom in the present but also to an extended freedom in the future that has been built on revolution. In the 1980 essay "The Dialectics of Power: Utopia in the Science Fiction of Le Guin, Jeury, and Piercy," Nadia Khouri argues that "the desire for utopia," no matter how many times it is "reiterated and emphasized" within the novel, may not "lead to a utopian outcome." This is reflected in *Woman on the Edge of Time*, which concludes with Ramos waiting on death row.

Despite the fact that Ramos tried to ensure a better future, she could only lay the foundation for others to continue the revolution. Through an emphasis on the human power to shift the trajectory of the timeline, Piercy reasons that knowing the future is not inevitable can incite change in both the reality of the novel and for readers. Therefore, the importance of community activism within the text is a commentary on the importance of community activism when the book was written and published. Duco Hellema noted in her 2019 collection *The Global 1970s: Radicalism, Reform, and Crisis* that several new social movements, including the women's movement, the gay movement, and racial equality movements converged to dominate the 1970s "political arena" with left-wing radicalism and activism in a way that would not have been possible without cross-cause collaboration. *Woman on the Edge of Time* is a product of these movements' combined efforts to change the lives of minoritized individuals within the United States.

Notwithstanding the fact that Ramos, as a minority time traveler, finds that the future's potential provides the necessity for revolution, there is a large amount of doubt within the text about the reality of the events. Donna Fancourt's 2002 article "Accessing Utopia through Altered States of Consciousness: Three Feminist Utopian Novels" takes on the concept of changed consciousness as providing access to utopian visions, while also "creating a new" form of "consciousness." The concept of utopia is relatively inaccessible; to properly imagine the concept of a perfect society, there must be an altered state of consciousness. Fancourt asserts that the utopia depicted in *Woman on the Edge of Time* is constructed in Ramos's mind and is thus presented as a state of mental "temporality." She notes that the novel places Ramos in a mental hospital, which ultimately links "utopian vision" to "madness." This is significant, because the novel presents Ramos's perspective and, as such, the events seem to occur within the perceivable reality of the text.

While I concede that the veracity of the narrative is called into question by the fact that Ramos is in a mental hospital because of her "deteriorating" mental state, I argue that labeling her as mad creates another layer of discrimination, especially since the history of mental illness is deeply intertwined with the social position of minority figures. In the 2006 article "Women and Madness: Teaching Mental Illness as a Disability," historian Kim Hewitt argued that people already experiencing issues of inequality related to "race, class, and gender" are further marginalized by the diagnoses of mental illness. Often, the forced institutionalization of those diagnosed with mental illness leads to imprisonment within an asylum system that denies the individual power to make decisions pertaining to their own lives. Hewitt notes that women in particular have been "oppressively categorized, socialized, and pathologized" by mental institutions, which often labeled women as mad when they did not adhere to the gender roles imposed on them by society. In other words, there has been a long-standing legacy of diagnosing, or even misdiagnosing women as a means of controlling dissent. Furthermore, in her 2010 book *Madness: An American History of Mental Illness and Its Treatment*, Mary Young notes that the American Psychiatric Association has acknowledged that "racism and racial discrimination" have led to "mental health care disparities" within the context of the psychiatric hospital. Class likewise plays an important factor in relation to mental health, with a "historic overrepresentation" of impoverished people "institutionalized" in US asylums. Sociologist Frank Furedi argues that the majority population, including health care professionals, "will shift the line between sanity and madness" to "medicalize the social expressions" in minority groups. As a result, those who are already discriminated against by intersecting layers of injustice, such as Ramos, are often diagnosed with mental illness and institutionalized as means of controlling those who endanger current social hierarchies.

MARGE PIERCY
WOMAN
ON THE EDGE OF TIME

sf

'One of the most important novelists of our time'
ERICA JONG

*Woman on the Edge of Time* (Women's Press, 1987)

Within the "excerpts from the official history of Consuelo Camacho Ramos" provided at the end of novel, the clinical summary states that Ramos has been diagnosed with paranoid schizophrenia. Ramos's perception of reality is described as impaired, which presents time travel within the novel as possibly mere hallucination. This is supported by the fact that it is unclear if her time-travelling companion from Mattapoisett, Luciente, can be seen in the present, while Ramos is fully visible to the people of the future. The implication of this difference is that it rationalizes why only Ramos can perceive the instances of time travel, pointing to the possibility that it may be occurring due to mental illness. In addition, throughout Ramos's stay in the mental hospital she is administered a cocktail of drugs, including "Thorazine," "Prolixin," and "Artane," meant to manage her mental state. When Ramos first receives visits from Luciente, even she seems to be uncertain

as to if the events are real or if they are linked to the "dope," which she claimed was "really powerful." As such, the worlds of the future are depicted as potentially existing only within Ramos's imagination.

Yet building upon the knowledge that Ramos is a minority figure, the mental hospital functions as a continuation of forced voicelessness. The mental hospital in the novel is a prison that holds women who are not necessarily mentally ill but, rather, who do not conform to the social roles thrust upon them. For this reason, labeling Ramos as schizophrenic is a continuation of society's oppression of minority groups. It is meaningful that Ramos's time travel remains real to her, despite any doubt on the part of the reader. Hence, Ramos's utopian vision manifests from an altered state of consciousness or a form of mental time traveling, which I would argue does not mean that the experience is insignificant. Time travel, whether real or imagined, inspires Ramos to rebel against her oppressors to achieve a better world and ensure that the problems of the present do not get worse. Different temporal spaces within *Woman on the Edge of Time* are accessed through altered states of consciousness, which implies that the mind works as the time machine through which visions of the future provoke violent resistance. Throughout the text, time travel exposes the role of human action in affecting the timeline even as the hoped for better future remains only as a possibility. As such, I argue that Ramos's time travel is real, or, in any case, significant.

Furthermore, when writing, Piercy spent a large amount of time doing research inside mental hospitals. In the acknowledgments Piercy references the individuals that she "cannot thank by name who risked their jobs to sneak" her "into places," such as mental hospitals, so that she could get an inside perspective. Piercy also acknowledges that there were a number of "past and present inmates of mental institutions who shared their experiences" with her. This engagement with the stories of those within the asylum demonstrates that Piercy acknowledged that there was value in the narratives of those diagnosed with mental illness—something that is often overlooked.

In the introduction to the 2004 anthology *The Feminist Standpoint Theory Reader*, Sandra Harding argues that feminist standpoint theory posits the notion that feminist issues cannot be restricted to "what are usually regarded as only social and political issues, but instead must be focused on every aspect of natural and social order, including the very standards for what counts as objectivity" and "rationality." As such, it is imperative that readers see what is presented as madness in the novel as perhaps merely another way of producing and receiving valuable knowledge. So, while the book, like society, places the validity of Ramos's time travel in question, I argue that we too are meant to find value in the narrative. Whether or not the events actually transpire as Ramos describes, readers are meant to listen, as Piercy did, and learn from the story being told that the future has the potential to improve if we act collectively against systems of oppression.

To sum up, within Piercy's novel *Woman on the Edge of Time*, time travel in the hands of a minority figure incites an awareness of the potential for a better future and draws attention to the fact that social forces are denying their citizens access to this better world. The sense of urgency within the text rests in the fact the future is not presented as static but as malleable—containing both utopian and dystopian potential. As an intersectional feminist text, temporal spaces work to examine the overlapping layers of discrimination in the present and situate this discrimination as fuel to inspire minority figures to push back against oppression. As such, the novel parallels two versions of the future as potential outcomes to the present, situating hope for the future in a state of reliance on human action. Designating multiple possibilities for the individual to construct a better future thus constitutes a call to united revolutionary action.

The representation of time travel in the form of mental transportation between timelines works as a lens through which the present can be compared to the future. *Woman on the Edge of Time* argues that the individual has the potential to modify the future by inciting collective resistance. Therefore, in following the experiences of a minority figure, Piercy's novel provokes revolution through time travel; it is through the vision of future potential that humanity can be inspired to change. Piercy argued that "creating futures" allows people to imagine a better world and "maybe do something about it." Yet, despite the call to action embedded in *Woman on the Edge of Time*, Piercy claimed in a 2016 introduction to the novel that since the text was written

> inequality has greatly increased—more people are poor, more people are working two or three jobs just to get by, more people have seen their

savings and their future wiped out by bad health or lost jobs. The homeless are everywhere, not just the single man or woman down on their luck or the shuffling bag lady but whole families with their children. There are fewer chances for the children of ordinary people to go to an ordinary college; if they can go, they will then have to drag huge debt through much of their adult lives. Many working-class jobs that paid people enough to buy and pay for a house and to hope for an even better life for their children have been shipped overseas. There, people even poorer will do the work for pennies. Unions that protected workers have lost much of their clout and represent fewer workers each year.

In other words, there are still many things that people should be fighting for to ensure there is a future better than the present. We are all on the edge of time.

**Kirsten Bussière**

# Who Are the Beasts? Animals in Science Fiction

Animals went into space long before people. Uncertain about the impacts of space flight on the human body, scientists on both sides of the Cold War initially tested it on animals. The first of these, Albert I, a rhesus monkey, was launched in a V-2 rocket from White Sands, New Mexico, on June 11, 1948. Many more primates, as well as mice, rats, rabbits, tortoises, and dogs followed, sometimes on one-way trips, including most famously Laika, a stray from the streets of Moscow, who became the first animal to orbit the earth in 1957. No doubt influenced by their role as real-life space explorers, as well as their appearance in fairy tales and books, such as H.G. Wells's *The Island of Doctor Moreau* (1896), anthropomorphic animals and interspecies communication have been a major theme in science fiction.

In John Crowley's *Beasts* (1976), a young orphan woman, Caddie, indentured to work in a remote bar, is sold to a strange humanoid lion creature, Painter. Painter is a "leo," the result of genetic experiments conducted before an unspecified civil war that ravaged America. Fearful of what they had created, the authorities exiled leos to remote preservations. Now a central government is trying to reassert control and, influenced by the technocratic Union of Social Engineering, wants to hunt down and exterminate them.

Caddie and Painter travel deep into the forest. She becomes his lover and the first of a "pride" of people to gather around the charismatic leo, who slowly transforms from outcast to freedom fighter. Crowley introduces a large ensemble of additional characters: Meric a filmmaker who wants to document the world of the leos; Loren a ethologist who loses his government funding to research hawks and has to make ends meet by becoming a tutor to Gregorius, the leader of the emerging central government; the scheming fox/human leo Reynard. A blend of science fiction and fantasy, the book is not an easy read. Characters come, go, and reappear again over various timelines. Little is explained about the civil war, just brief references to America simply falling apart, or why the leos came into being. But their fraught relationship with

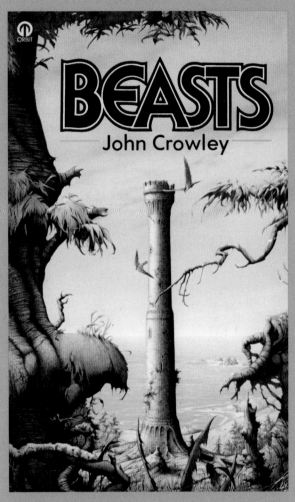

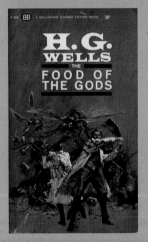

*Beasts* (Futura, 1978). *Food of the Gods* (Ballantine, 1962). *Slave Ship* (Four Square, 1973).

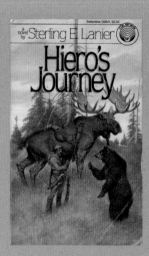

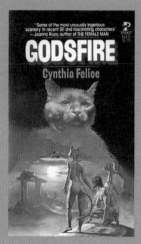

humans is brilliantly handled. Crowley also pens what must be one of the most sensitively handled and realistic human/animal hybrid sex scenes put on paper.

In a similar vein to George Orwell's iconic *Animal Farm* (1945), much animal-themed science fiction has political, class, and racial allegories. Human-animal communication is a given in Frederik Pohl's 1956 novel *Slave Ship*, a parable about the French conflict in Vietnam, in which a soldier is sent to infiltrate the base where an enemy is developing a deadly new weapon, the result of animal research. Explorers end up on a planet ruled by intelligent apes in Pierre Boulle's 1963 novel *La Planète des singes*, published as *Monkey Planet* in the UK and *Planet of the Apes* in America, the basis for the very different 1968 film of the same name. In Russell Braddon's *The Year of the Angry Rabbit*, published in Britain in 1964, a new strain of myxomatosis causes giant flesh-eating rabbits to run amok in Australia. An intelligent lab rat saves earth from an animal rebellion in *Doctor Rat* (1977), William Kotzwinkle's protest against animal experimentation. In Cynthia Felice's *Godsfire* (1978), Homo sapiens are the slaves on a planet ruled by cat people.

Animals also feature in postapocalyptic science fiction. In Sterling E. Lanier's *Hiero's Journey* (1973), a warrior priest leaves his closed community to explore the wilderness of the United States five thousand years after a nuclear holocaust. His companion is a mutant moose, with whom he communicates telepathically. They are joined by other companions, including a telepathic black bear. A sequel, *The Unforsaken Hiero*, was published in 1983.

Another example is Vonda McIntyre's Hugo award–winning *Dreamsnake* (1978). A young woman, Snake,

part of a mysterious group of healers, wanders the wastelands of earth hundreds of years after nuclear war. Her ability to heal disease is reliant on three snakes with whom she has a close bond: Grass, a small viper, Sand, a Diamondback rattlesnake, and Mist, an albino cobra. Grass is particularly important, an incredibly rare "dreamsnake" whose venom lulls a patient into a torpor while the venom of the other two serpents create an effective vaccine. When Grass is killed by a fearful villager, Snake's healing powers are compromised, and she has to try find another dreamsnake. Her quest involves her going to a far city that may be in contact with "Otherworlders," aliens who might be able provide her with a replacement.

The central question posed in nearly all these books is who exactly are the real beasts? The answer is nearly always those that walk on two legs.

**Andrew Nette**

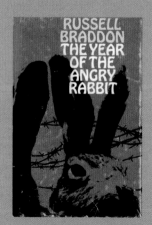

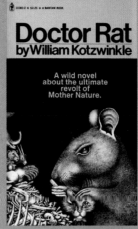

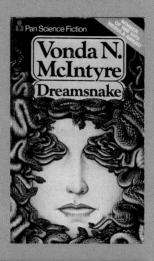

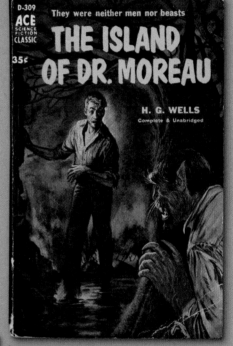

Clockwise from top left: *Hiero's Journey* (Del Rey, 1973). *Hiero's Journey* (Chilton, 1973). *Hiero's Journey* (Panther, 1976). *Godsfire* (Pocket Books, 1978). *Dreamsnake* (Houghton Mifflin, 1978). *Doctor Rat* (Bantam, 1977). *Dreamsnake* (Pan, 1979). *The Island of Dr. Moreau* (Ace, 1963). *Slave Ship* (Ballantine, 1975). *Monkey Planet* (Penguin, 1966). *Beasts* (Doubleday, 1976). *The Year of the Angry Rabbit* (Heinemann, 1964).

# The Moons of Le Guin and Heinlein

There have rarely been two books so closely related, so superficially similar, and so different in thrust as Robert Heinlein's *The Moon Is a Harsh Mistress* (1966) and Ursula K. Le Guin's *The Dispossessed* (1974). Both books use the idea of a colony of exiles on a moon, where a parent planet plants her undesirables and essentially

Ursula K. Le Guin

Robert Heinlein (left), L. Sprague de Camp, and Isaac Asimov, Philadelphia Navy Yard (*Navy Yard News* periodical, August 9, 1944)

lets them run things as they wish. The societies that develop under these circumstances are "anarchist"—they function without law or government. Both books have strong didactic intentions, teaching, explaining, moralizing, and exemplifying in favor of their own versions of "anarchism." Both books radically redesign family structures, allowing freedom to fulfill individualized needs for love, sex, bonding, and stability. Both books give children and teenagers complete sexual freedom. Both books deal with the issue of language change. Both books have strong male protagonists whose sensibilities are shared by the reader. Although both colonies are hostile to their planets of origin, both main characters make the trip there and back again under uncertain and difficult conditions. Both men despise the parent societies and yet are tempted by them. They resist the temptation and joyfully return home to the land of exile.

The similarities are impressive. Why then does Heinlein's book inspire some readers to run out, buy a gun, and vote Republican, while Le Guin's book opposes such behavior (nonviolently, of course) on every point? How can two books be so different and so alike?

The invented societies of Le Guin and Heinlein are based on the same contrivance: a colony of exiles on a separate orbital body. New social patterns develop as

a result of selective immigration, a new environment, and enforced isolation from the parent society. The artifice has a direct historical analog in the exile of British prisoners to the American colonies in the seventeenth and eighteenth centuries, and, later, when the American Revolution made this impossible, to Van Diemen's Land in Australia. Settlement by transported convicts tends to leave an area with a tradition of perverse pride in its misfit ancestors. The myth of descent from the toughest, most individualistic, least compliant fraction of society becomes part of the civic identity that glues the heterogeneous young society together.

On the premise of lunar exile, both books build an experimental sociology of how a society might work if certain philosophical principles were put into practice. ("Experiments of the imagination," Le Guin calls this process in her 1989 essay collection *Dancing at the Edge of the World*.) For Heinlein, the principles might be described as "masculine," individualist, libertarian, laissez-faire capitalist, anarchist, and based on Christianity. For Le Guin, the governing principles might be described as feminist, communal, centrally coordinated, anarchist, and Taoist. The governing principles drive the plots both from behind: What historical background would be needed to force these ideas into practice?—and from in front: Where would these ideas take a society? The ideas drive the stories of the individual characters, as well as those of the societies.

*The Moon Is a Harsh Mistress* is a "masculine" book, masculine in a pre–women's liberation sense that has never heard of Robert Bly (the American poet whose 1990 book *Iron John* called for new rites of passage to produce what he saw as a "balanced" masculinity) and upholds the most traditional virtues of the male-dominated world. The principal leadership roles—except family leadership—are filled by men, although there is one token woman, Wyoming Knott, who is skilled at emotional rhetoric, who contributes "beauty" in the summary of "talents and experience" possessed by the leaders of the revolution, who on the day of the revolution is sent out to get the children off the streets, and who is "terribly nervous at being left to hold the fort alone" while the men are negotiating on earth. The male narrative voice relates events in a colorful, telegraphic idiom reminiscent of military slang, supplying us with interpretations, comments, and moralizing in favor of "masculine" values. This includes frequent generalizations about the nature of women, and, yet, amid unabashed willingness for the female role to be defined by the male, Heinlein states contradictorily that "women are scarce and call the tune." But what does this "calling the tune" extend to? Not to politics or power. So what are the tunes that a woman can call? She can control who she has intercourse with. Women are safe from rape in Luna, because men protect them from it by their willingness to kill rapists quickly. The family organization of Mannie, the man and the narrator whose viewpoint the reader must share, is run by the wives, behind the figurehead of the senior husband. In the press of crisis, women are free to die and kill patriotically.

In this traditional masculine framework, victory and freedom are attained by military action that involves skillful and brave use of weapons to kill and intimidate a clearly defined external enemy. When the day of the revolution finally comes, Mannie simply longs for violent action. The hero hungers to shed blood for his tribe, and so is able to save his people.

Heinlein's is a masculinist book by a male writer who was educated at the United States Naval Academy, an institution famous for instilling the traditions and values of the phallocentric weapons culture. The book was first published in 1966, at a time when these traditional values were sorely threatened by the peace movement. (It is perhaps no coincidence that the bad

*The Dispossessed*
(Harper and Row, 1974)

*The Moon Is a Harsh Mistress*
(G.P. Putnam's Sons, 1966)

guys are called "Peace Dragoons.") *The Dispossessed* is a feminist book by a female writer educated at Radcliffe College, a traditional women's institution, which, when Le Guin attended, had recently dealt with the issue of integrating women and men into the same classes. Her book was first published in 1974, the middle of the decade of the resurgence of feminism.

The feminism of *The Dispossessed* does not represent women struggling to attain social equality. The calm acknowledgement of physiological gender variations (such as pregnancy hormones) gives evidence of a world in which human equality is not threatened by differences. Le Guin even ventures to allow characters to express sexist stereotypes. In her utopia, neither gender differences nor gender stereotyping have disappeared. They simply are not given much importance. On Anarres, women have already attained equality and are now undistractedly living the productive lives that their talents, tastes, and values dictate. This freedom to live authentically is contrasted with the limited, manipulative, wasted lives of women like Vea on Urras. The contrast both emphasizes the strength, freedom, and social value of the free woman and connects the novel to the contemporary world of the reader, who will certainly recognize in Vea something close to the ideal woman of present cultural reality. Shown Vea's limitations in her distant world, to which we owe no allegiance or attachment, the reader is brought closer to seeing objectively the limitations of Vea's sisters on earth, where conditions frequently become too customary to be noticed. Familiarity breeds invisibility far more often than it breeds active contempt.

The feminist position of *The Dispossessed* is manifest in female characters free to live lives of positive accomplishment, such as Odo the philosopher, Takver the artist and biologist, and Gvarab the physicist, but it is also shown in those women who have used their freedom to choose painful limitations that are generally associated with men in our society. Shevek's emotionally frozen, career-driven mother Rulag is the most poignant picture of this darker side of freedom. After her sacrifice, or abandonment, of her son, she comes to him as an adult and tries to make contact. She offers to help him professionally and lays her connections at his feet, in much the same way that a conventional contemporary male parent might avoid contact with offspring during the messy, needy years of early childhood, and yet later expect alliance and affection from the young person who hardly knows him.

Besides portraying the positive and negative choices available to women in a nonsexist society, *The Dispossessed* demonstrates the enrichment of men's choices in such a society. Shevek uses a full palette of emotions. He is a faithful nurturing parent to Sadik and Pilun, especially when Sadik is persecuted in school for her parents' political independence. As women are not despised, there is no need for men to hate and fear homosexuals. The absence of homophobia extends all men's options regarding how to show love and creates a world in which the "pretty definitely homosexual" can live without shame.

In showing not only what women stand to gain in a nonsexist society but also what men will gain, *The Dispossessed* recasts the feminist struggle from a polarized "war between the sexes" to a movement toward human liberation that benefits all.

If gender politics are one axis on which the two books can be compared, communality vs. individualism is another. *The Moon Is a Harsh Mistress* strongly embraces individualism. Heinlein's colony is grounded in individualism: individual criminals, transported for individual crimes. "Tanstaafl," the motto of Luna, is a crisp acronym for individual responsibility: "there ain't no such thing as a free lunch," an exhortation to accept without evasion the cost or consequence of every action. The Loonie victory over the earth invaders is attributed not to coordinated group effort but to the fighting spirit of individuals. Although the individual berserk patriotic fighting adds up, in effect, to a species of group solidarity, the independence movement has a hard time getting people to do work, to do the boring, repetitive, and ongoing jobs of preparedness. The book expresses profound impatience with and distrust of group decision-making processes. Politicians are called "yammerheads."

On the other hand, Le Guin's colonists on Anarres were exiled in a body for a group-crime, the crime of dissident "Odonianism." In place of Heinlein's assertions of the impotent silliness of group decision-making, Le Guin portrays democratic group process as unwieldy and strenuous but ultimately effective.

Le Guin shares with Heinlein the high valorization of individual self-responsibility. "[O]nly the individual, the person, had the power of moral choice," thinks Shevek, as he considers his interrelated responsibility toward his talents and his community. Heinlein's Professor puts the same concept differently:

A rational anarchist believes that concepts such as "state" and "society" and "government" have no existence save as physically exemplified in the acts of self responsible individuals. He believes that it is impossible to shift blame, share blame, distribute blame . . . as blame, guilt, and responsibility are matters taking place inside human beings singly and nowhere else. . . . My point is that one person is responsible. Always. If H-bombs exist—and they do —some man controls them. In terms of morals there is no such thing as "state." Just men. Individuals. Each responsible for his own acts.

Although for both authors individual responsibility is central, for Le Guin, it is centered in the faith in the possibility of an organically healthy society, while, for Heinlein, it is centered in the belief in the inescapable foolishness of humans acting in groups. For Le Guin, it is individual responsibility that makes true community possible. For Heinlein, it is the impossibility of community that makes self-responsibility necessary.

In the place of tanstaafl, the guiding principle of the Anarresti is "Odo's Analogy": a healthy society as a healthy body, with well-functioning cells working together in well-functioning organs working together in well-functioning systems serving the benefit of the whole, all completely interdependent in literal fact. When Anarres faces its great crisis of survival (significantly, not masculine military attack but a famine, a failure of nourishment), the Odonians are saved by their sense of community:

> The old tag of "solidarity" had come alive again. There is exhilaration in finding that the bond is stronger after all, than all that tries the bond...
> "We'll see each other through," they said, serenely.

Heroism rests not on brief berserk patriotic passion but on fidelity to hard, sustained work, like mining or driving trains, which is essential to the survival of the whole.

The different attitudes of these two books toward centralized economic planning are probably corollaries to their differing attitudes toward individualism. *The Moon Is a Harsh Mistress* goes to considerable lengths to set forth attractively the charms of laissez-faire capitalism. Entrepreneurs sell schooling, life insurance, judicial services, air—whatever is needed. None of the main characters live in poverty. No mention is made of the possibility (high probability) of the rise of thug-enforced price-fixing, monopolies, exploitation of labor, or despoliation of the environment in a developing anarchistic society, though in the prison society that exists before the revolution Mannie deals with monopolistic price-fixing by stealing water and power. If these classical abuses of capitalism were to become a problem after the revolution,

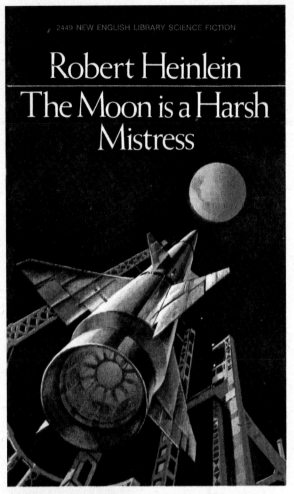

*The Moon Is a Harsh Mistress* (New English Library, 1969)

*The Dispossessed* (Panther, 1979)

one can extrapolate that the Loonie solution would be similarly direct, if the society is to remain faithful to its foundational anarchist principles.

Le Guin directly confronts the disadvantages of her chosen economic form. Although she offers centralized administration as the only way to deal successfully with the limited resources of barren Anarres, she deals explicitly with the problems it causes. Her "PDC" (Production and Distribution Coordination unit) is set up to prevent self-interest from gaining the upper hand. It is run by volunteers who are selected by lottery and serve short terms. In spite of an organizational design that is supposed to prevent hierarchy from developing, power tends to concentrate at the center, and bureaucrats like Sabul gain more and more control, unless conscious revolutionaries like Shevek, Takver, and Bedap say nay. When someone rocks the boat in this manner, their social position is threatened but, in this basically humane society, the cruder methods of political repression, such as disappearance, assassination, and physical coercion, do not occur. The absence of these brutalities does not seem to be because the author is ignoring their possibility, like Heinlein ignores the possibility of the abuses of capitalism, but because in the unalienated society that Le Guin postulates, it is unlikely that humans would be so damaged as to inflict coldblooded violence on each other, although violence in hot anger is not out of the question.

Both *The Moon Is a Harsh Mistress* and *The Dispossessed* are deeply marked by systems of spiritual and ethical belief. The capitalist economic values of Heinlein's book are driven by a kind of male-dominated monotheism, while the more diffuse nontheism of Le Guin's work motivates an entirely different set of values.

Christianity exerts a very definite pull on Heinlein's moon, although the religious presence in the book is not of the explicit doctrinal sort. It is not comprised of stated propositions, such as "Jesus died for your sins, rose from the dead on the third day, and rules now in Heaven." It is found on the level of the explicit belief's presuppositions: that God exists, is outside and separate from the self, is male, and sanctions human stewardship of the universe-as-exploitable-resource. The fact that Heinlein's religious content is not explicit in no way means that it is not important. In fact, unstated religious presuppositions often have pervasive social significance, because, while the explicit doctrinal tenets of a religion are stated, evaluated, and consciously accepted or rejected, the implicit presuppositions of doctrine are rarely examined at all. They provide the unconscious ground for many of the political consequences of religions that cannot be

*The Left Hand of Darkness*
(Ace, 1969)

*The Left Hand of Darkness*
(Futura, 1983)

explained by explicit creeds—which are often quite benign. Heinlein's religious ideology is intimately entwined with his capitalism.

God is present in Heinlein's utopia, and the Judeo-Christian Bible is mentioned. Some of the first words that Mike the computer utters in the book are from Genesis. God is referred to in the creole language of Luna by his Russian name, Bog. Most of the mentions of Bog in the book are curses or exclamations, but by the end of the book, Mannie uses the word in heartfelt, although casual, prayer: "You listening, Bog? Is a computer one of Your creatures?" Mannie, the Loonie everyman, conceptualizes a God that is external to himself and knows the answers to the "Great Questions" that Man is not able to answer for himself.

The virtue of humility, central to Christian ideology, is stressed in the character of Mannie, who repeatedly asserts that he is not very smart, stumbled into his job, and bumbles along, more or less accidentally doing the right thing at every turn. Mannie is tempted in the wilderness of earth: "He took me up on that high mountain and offered me the kingdoms of Earth. Or of Luna." The Christian paradigm of martyrdom is the path of heroism in this book, which a good many follow selflessly: Shorty Mkrum, the Professor, Ludmilla, and Mike himself. Many of the most emotionally charged scenes of the book are drawn around these self-sacrifices. "Greater love hath no man than that he lay down his life for his friends." (John 15:13) Besides the consummation of martyrdom, Mike bears a suspicious resemblance to a Christ figure in other dimensions. He is born by immaculate (to say the least) conception. He has an unusual childhood. He is at the center of a cadre of loyal followers who teach and proselytize and end up changing the world. He dies for his people. His death is ambiguous, and no one knows where his remains lie.

On the other hand, Le Guin's book makes no reference to the Bible or to any concept of a god that exists outside of humanity. Religion is seen as a human "capacity, a relationship man has with the cosmos." The purpose of life seems to be life itself, and the "higher good" that inspires ethical behavior is the organic community of humans. The path of heroism in this book does not involve self-abnegation as much as being faithful to the self, although that fidelity might sometimes entail sacrifice: "Sacrifice might be demanded of the individual, but never compromise."

In *The Dispossessed*, the model offered is not the Christian martyr but the Taoist sage. The sage is the person who understands the Tao, the way in which the universe works, the order of nature. Shevek the scientist devotes his life to expressing a Unified Field Theory—in other words, to understanding the Tao. Like a good Taoist, he tries to model his life on the Tao as he comprehends it. Intellectually, he believes that "chronosophy does involve ethics." Emotionally, his understanding of his science affects his experience of his life: "So, looking back on the last four years, Shevek saw them not as wasted, but as part of the edifice that he and Takver were building with their lives. The thing about working with time, instead of against it, he thought, is that it is not wasted. Even pain counts." Shevek does not separate his science—the way he understands the Tao—from his ethical life. His spiritual understanding leads not to martyrdom but to a long and fruitful life. He is physically healthy. He does his work well. He parents well. He maintains the proper balance between himself and his society, between his inner life and his outer life.

Shevek and his society live by the aphoristic "Sayings of Odo," just as the Taoist lives by the collected aphoristic wisdom of Lao Tzu and other classical philosophers. Odo tells her followers, "True voyage is return," while in the *Tao Te Ching* Lao Tzu's Tao "causes all things to undergo a process of cyclic change." Even the name Odo iconographically suggests cyclic return: a circle at the beginning that returns to a circle at the end, passing through a half-circle on the way. The complex double structure of the plot, Anarres to Urras and Urras to Anarres (with two circular maps sketched at the head of every chapter in some editions)

takes Shevek on the complete Taoist cyclic journey out and back.

Like a good Taoist, Shevek is comfortable with ambiguity and paradox. "You can't assert two contradictory statements about the same thing," Dearri protests when Shevek views time as both sequency and simultaneity. (What is light? Particle or wave?) Lao Tzu's *Tao Te Ching* points at truth using similar ambiguities and contradictions.

One of the paradoxes of Taoism is that the submissive and the weak are held up for emulation, because they are able to overcome the hard and the strong. Where the weak overcomes the strong, it becomes strong in its turn and is fated to be overcome by the weak that follows after it. This cyclic sequence of short-lived victory for the submissive, soft, and weak is understood by Shevek when he comprehends that Odonianism has become institutionalized and anarchism has become bureaucratic. He not only understands but willingly accepts that this revolution, this cycle, can never be won definitively for all time. Each generation must live the revolution for itself.

The evanescence of revolutionary victory forces the conclusion that positive utopia and stability are mutually exclusive. (Interestingly, Heinlein reaches the same conclusion.) For Odonian society to maintain its integrity requires continuous revolutionary challenge from individuals within the society who are striving to live ever more authentic lives according to their own light.

Heinlein agrees that the minute you think you have attained liberty, there it goes. Small minds, creeping bureaucracy, and, his ultimate dirty word, "government" spring up like weeds and begin to choke out independent thinking. But his solution is different. *The Moon Is a Harsh Mistress* has the form of a memoir written some fifty years after the events it chronicles. In the years following the revolution, the Loonies set up a government "that never adopted any of [the Professor's] ideas." At the end of his story, Mannie, shifting to the present tense, turns his mind to the next frontier: "Since the Boom started quite a few young cobbers have gone out to Asteroids. Hear about some nice places out there, not too crowded. My word, I'm not even a hundred yet." For "Boom" perhaps we should read "Gold Rush" and we will have an idea of Heinlein's solution. The continuing physical presence of frontier, of wide-open spaces for that small minority of strong men with the initiative to go and carve out a place in the wilderness where they can conquer and live by their own Light, that is the only hope for Eden—in other words, expansionism.

Finally, it is necessary to discuss a point on which the two books seem to agree: anarchism. Both books seem to espouse it, but based on different understandings of nature.

Heinlein's hopeless hope is in a kind of pseudo-Darwinian survival of the fittest. Although in his view the "unfit" will always eventually outnumber the "fit" and redesign society for their convenience and comfort, frontier conditions can fleetingly nurture wholesome societies. Heinlein sees environmental danger and interpersonal violence as positive forces for weeding out misbehaviors ranging from gangsterism to bad manners. He assumes that, without meddlesome laws, violence will be used appropriately, falling primarily on those who deserve it. It is this unregulated but basically just violence that, along with public opinion, can guarantee social order. The National Rifle Association would be very comfortable with Heinlein's assumptions about violence. (Although he is very specific about cheap and easily available alcohol in Luna, he never engages the problem of alcoholic violence.)

Le Guin's anarchism is different. Le Guin seems to truly believe that in a healthy society humans, undeformed by anomie, will actively want to cooperate and associate. She believes that well–cared for children can be educated away from the patterns that make cooperation difficult. She tells us that humans innately like to work together and care about each other. Freed from interference, they will do these things. Her interpretation of human nature is equally based on assumptions about biology, but she focusses less on humans as animals subject to the laws of natural selection and more on humans as cooperative social animals. Punishment is not the primary maintainer of social order, although it becomes a factor when the society stagnates.

Another point on which these two versions of anarchism differ is in the distribution of goods. Heinlein, in a way which parallels some of the tenets of Ayn Rand, trusts absolutely that where a need is felt, an entrepreneur will appear to fill that need at a reasonable cost. He does not deal with the issue of poverty. Le Guin trusts that people of goodwill—and all people are people of goodwill if they are not deformed by greed and class society—are able to plan and execute just sharing, even of limited resources.

So, although the two authors share the position that life without laws is possible and desirable, they have different assumptions, or faiths, underneath. Heinlein trusts in public opinion, the ability of an unregulated frontier society to punish misdeeds, and the free market, while Le Guin trusts in the cooperative nature of humans and in the ability of groups to plan and work together effectively.

The opposition between the moons of Le Guin and Heinlein is not just of interest from a literary standpoint. The dialogue between these two books illuminates how ideas about right government and right economics and right relationships—political ideas—are transmitted by fictional texts. These books can be seen as representatives of two trends in our society, one that looks backward for its ideal to a time when men were men, only the strong survived, and there was plenty of room to go west, young man, go west. The other looks forward to a future that has not yet existed, a crowded, interdependent global village where socially responsible people live modestly and share work and resources evenly. These two visions, in one form or another, stand behind many of the choices that individuals and communities must make today.

**Donna Glee Williams**

# Black Star

## The Life and Work of Octavia Butler

In America—especially when it comes to intellectual endeavors—race matters. Black folks are often thought of as being less smart than their white counterparts and, therefore, their work is labeled less important. In the world of literature, fiction by black authors is rarely required reading in public schools. Many young people of all races don't realize that black writers exist until they either discover them on their own or take a higher education class that introduces them to the works of Langston Hughes, Zora Neale Hurston, Richard Wright, Lorraine Hansberry, James Baldwin, and countless others. Still, these writers are rarely "important" enough to be part of the canon that values William Shakespeare and Emily Dickinson over August Wilson and Ntozake Shange.

Octavia Butler, 1980s

While the rules of the game have changed slightly in both academia and the real world, in the twentieth century the literary landscapes were so marginalized that even aspiring scribes of color might've believed that black writers didn't exist, and, even if so inspired, it was impossible to become one. This marginalization was even more pronounced in the world of genre writers, especially with science fiction, where editors and writers were often more comfortable with characters that were Martians and slimy space creatures than they were with other races.

Staffed and written by white men, diversity wasn't an issue that concerned them. Hell, even most science fiction films didn't have any black characters and basically erased the race from the future. Of course, as editor Sheree Renée Thomas pointed out in her seminal collection of black science fiction *Dark Matter: A Century of Speculative Fiction from the African Diaspora*, that exclusion never stopped black people from being fans of the genre, be it books, magazines, films, or the four-color pages of DC and Marvel comics.

Years before the term "Afrofuturism" became just another marketing label or TED Talk, early twentieth-century "colored" writers, most notably Pauline Hopkins's serialized novel *Of One Blood* (1902–1903), W.E.B. Du Bois's 1920 apocalyptic short story "The Comet," and George S. Schuyler's satirical book *Black No More* (1931), one of best novels of the Harlem Renaissance, were practitioners of the form.

Yet unlike H.G. Wells, Mary Shelley, or the pulp generation published in the pages of *Astounding Stories*, edited for decades by the notoriously racist John W. Campbell (who, in 1968, said he didn't think his readers "would be able to relate to a Black main character"), the speculative works of the black writers remained obscure for years. It wasn't until the Ace published Harlem native Samuel R. Delany's debut *The Jewels of Aptor* in 1962 that the genre got its first black star writer.

Only nineteen when his book hit the shelf, Delany would go on to become a Nebula and Hugo award–winning author whose work inspired, influenced, and taught the next generation. Published in 1975, Delany's novel *Dhalgren* has been compared more to James Joyce than to Robert A. Heinlein and serves as just one example of the genre's possibilities. Along with Thomas M. Disch, Harlan Ellison, Michael Moorcock, and J.G. Ballard, the Sugar Hill kid was a part of the "New Wave" writers who attempted to tell different kinds of stories utilizing various literary techniques and styles.

There was also *New Worlds*, edited by Moorcock and published in England, and, later, the shorted-lived *Quark*, edited by Delany (with his then wife, poet Marilyn Hacker). The New Wave writers not only brought modernism/postmodernism to old-fashioned futurism, but they were also impactful in breaking the down racist/sexist walls of oppression, making way for Ursula K. Le Guin (*The Left Hand of Darkness*, 1969), Joanna Russ (*And Chaos Died*, 1970), and Sonya Dorman, whose short story "Go, Go, Go, Said the Bird" was published in Harlan Ellison's landmark *Dangerous Visions* anthology (1967). Other writers included in that classic collection included Phillip K. Dick, Fritz Leiber, and Samuel R. Delany.

Meanwhile, the same year *The Jewels of Aptor* was published, on the other side of the country, in Pasadena, California, a young "Negro" teenager named Octavia Estelle Butler was scribbling stories in notebooks and plotting the complexities of her own future-world novels. Butler, having turned fifteen that June 22, was already jotting down ideas that would become her book *Mind of My Mind* more than a decade later. Published in 1977, the novel was the second in her *Patternist* series that began with *Patternmaster* the year before. She had started writing a few years before, stories about horses and white men who smoked too much, but at the ripe age of twelve she slipped into science fiction after a bad B-movie experience. In an oft-told story, it was the Brit flick *Devil Girl from Mars* that sent her scurrying toward the stars and the textual worlds of Robert Heinlein, Theodore Sturgeon, and John Brunner.

Certainly, as proven by the innovative stories and novels she'd write a few decades later that incorporated African spiritualism and major characters of color, the absence of blackness within the genre would not deny her dreams or force her to give up. Refusing to be written off, Octavia Butler wrote herself into the narrative. "When I began writing science fiction, when I began reading, heck, I wasn't in any of this stuff I read," Butler said in 2000. "The only Black people you found were occasional characters or characters who were so feeble-witted that they couldn't manage anything, anyway." That same year she told PBS interviewer Charlie Rose that science fiction allowed her freedom, "Because there were no closed doors, no walls."

Born under the astrological sign of Cancer, she was a stubborn girl/woman when it came to her writing. Coming from a working-class family, Butler didn't have much, but she held on to the one thing she owned outright: her talent. Butler's father Laurice James Butler was a shoeshine man who died when she was seven. "He was a huge man who ate too much, drank too much and died young," Butler told NPR's commentator in

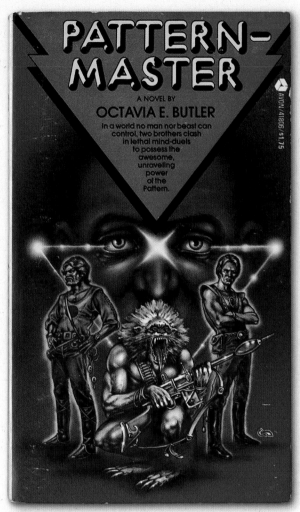

*Patternmaster* (Avon, 1979)

1993. She was raised by her religious mother, who was also named Octavia, and attended Baptist church services. The elder Octavia, who had come to Pasadena when she was a child, had been pregnant four previous times with sons, but her daughter was the only one who survived. She was her mom's miracle baby, a fighter from the womb.

After her father's death, Octavia was sent to live on her grandmother's chicken farm in the High Desert town of Victorville, California, for a year. Her grandmother had worked hard cleaning houses and saved money to buy property. Years later, Butler cited her mother and grandmother as her main inspirations. After Butler moved back into her mother's home, the elder Octavia took in retired roomers to help pay the bills. Octavia, who was intensely shy around other kids, got along better with the elderly roomers, including an aged woman, a carnival mentalist that she told her stories to. Like a scene from a Ray Bradbury novel, you could easily imagine the two sitting on the Pasadena porch trading tall tales on moonlit nights.

In 1965, at seventeen, Butler left the church and graduated from John Muir High School a few weeks before the Watts Riot. Having enrolled at Pasadena City College, she became active in the black student union. According to biographer Gerry Canavan, her experiences at the school contributed to ideas Butler put into her most famous novel. Caravan wrote:

> Kindred was largely influenced by from her time at college where Butler was exposed to the Black Nationalist Movement (1950–1970) and the ideas of fellow African Americans in regards to the discrimination they faced in the past and present. Many of these ideas played a large role in influencing the creation of Kindred.

Throughout her life, whether working minimum wage jobs or publishing novels, Octavia looked after her mother, who worked as a domestic and had bought the child a Remington typewriter. A few of the older people in her community tried to discourage Octavia. A shy, often sad child, teachers labeled her "slow," and her Aunt Hazel famously told Butler her dream was impossible. In her 2018 medium.com essay on Butler, Kodi Vonn/Destiny Bezrutczyk wrote, "[U]pon learning of her niece's intention to become a writer, she tried to break it gently to the young, dark, complicated girl, saying, 'Negroes can't be writers.' Butler didn't stop. She had a compulsion — a drive she would later instill in her human and alien characters." After finding a copy of Writer magazine on the bus, she read their marketplace section and began submitting her stories to editors.

In 2016, a year-long celebration of Butler's life called Radio Imagination involved a series of events, lectures, and performances. It also published a catalogue edited by Janet Duckworth and Savannah Wood featuring notes, journals, mantras, and pictures from the writer's archive located in Huntington Library in San Marino, California. A reprinted school photo showed a sad-faced girl, a young woman taller than her peers and often bullied for her otherness, staring blankly into the world, as though dying to escape the planet and the cruelty of other kids.

"I wanted to disappear. Instead I grew six feet tall," Butler told Across the Wounded Galaxies (1990)

Kindred (Garden City, 1979)     Clay's Ark (St. Martin's, 1984)

editor Larry McCaffery. Gabrielle Bellot noted in a 2017 essay: "Her voice was deeper than that of the girls around her. Its gentle rumbling tone and pitch varying from androgynous to masculine, and students teased her mercilessly. Some of them called her a boy, others a lesbian. [However] Butler did not identify as gay." Butler seemed to have been as asexual as she was asocial. Like many outsiders, she found refuge in old movies and the library, where she'd been "hiding out" since she was a youngster.

"After I got out of the Peter Pan Room, the first writer I latched on to was Zenna Henderson," she explained to McCaffery. "[She] wrote about telepathy and other things I was interested in, from the point of view of young women." Though Henderson is an absent name in current science fiction discussions, her novels Pilgrimage: The Book of the People (1961) and The People: No Different Flesh (1966) had an impact on Butler's writing in the Patternist series.

Written out of chronological sequence, those often depressing and scary books, along with Survivor (1978), Wild Seed (1980), and Clay's Ark (1984), made up the connected Patternist novels that served as her introduction to the world of science fiction; Butler's tales were fantastic, but they felt so real. Octavia was more than a writer, she was, as she wrote in her journal in 1987, "a wordweaver and a worldmaker."

Though these books were written during the latter part of the New Wave era, Butler's work lacked the experimental styling and intellectual hijinks of her peers. One might say she was her own "wave," writing books that were more earthy and grounded. Sometimes it felt as though one needed PhDs in philosophy, semiotics, and post-structuralism to get through Delany, while Butler wrote in a way that was more wise than

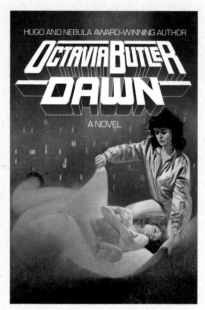

*Adulthood Rites* (Warner, 1987)　　　*Mind of My Mind* (Doubleday, 1977)　　　*Dawn* (Warner, 1987)

intellectual and could be grasped by a working-class person on his/her lunch break at the factory.

In her 2006 essay "Parable of a Writer," journalist/director Dream Hampton wrote:

> The Patternist series, which culminates in the 1980 magnum opus *Wild Seed*, features one of literature's most terrifying villains, the body-snatching Doro. He tracks Anyanwu, a shape-shifter and healer hundreds of years old, to 18th-century Africa. There he forces her to spawn his progeny. She becomes his great love and the only protection her generations of children have from his merciless appetite for fresh flesh. Anyanwu, most at home in her early-twenties body, is beyond fierce: Imagine a Pam Grier who makes the middle passage both as a slave and a dolphin.

During that same era, Butler, not a fan of writing short stories ("Trying to do it has taught me much more about frustration and despair than I ever wanted to know," she wrote in 1995), also published "Speech Sounds" (1983), winner of the 1984 Hugo Award for best short story, and "Blood Child" (1984), which won the 1984 Nebula and the 1985 Hugo for best novelette. While "Blood Child" was an otherworldly slave narrative set on an unnamed planet where human men were impregnated by the Tilic creatures, the brilliant "Speech Sounds" was an earthbound tale of the end of world kind about a deadly virus, a familiar theme

in Butler's work, that takes away mankind's ability to communicate and, in the case of more than a few, lowers their intellect considerably.

The main protagonist Rye, after losing her family to the disease, headed to Pasadena in search of her brother. Travelling by one of the rare buses, she's twenty miles away from her final destination when her world goes haywire. Butler, who never learned to drive, knew a lot about the bus lines in her city. In "Speech Sounds," society was broken and became worse when people were killed, riots erupted, and trust became a synonym for wishful thinking. Still, somehow, Butler managed to bring a tad of unexpected hope to the climax. Both "Speech Sounds" and "Blood Child" were published in *Asimov's Science Fiction Magazine*. "Octavia draws a picture of an all-but-destroyed society that is so vivid that you will find yourself living in it," editor Shawna McCarthy wrote in the introduction.

Under McCarthy, according to a history of *Asimov's* written by Sheila Williams, the magazine "acquired an edgier and more literary and experimental tone." McCarthy also published work by women writers Connie Willis, Kit Reed, Nancy Kress, and Ursula K. Le Guin. McCarthy won a Hugo for Best Professional Editor in 1984. Years later, Octavia Butler's friend and former teacher Samuel R. Delany, who met her in 1970 when he taught her for a week at the six-week Clarion Writers Workshop in Pennsylvania, cited those stories as her "most important works." While that critical

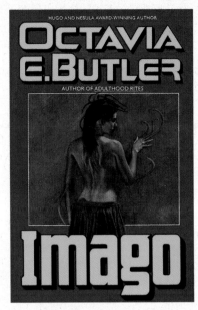

*Imago* (Warner, 1989)          *Survivor* (Doubleday, 1978)          *Survivor* (Signet, 1978)

conclusion is debatable, there's no denying the power of her lean prose in the short form.

It was Butler's "controlled economy of language and . . . strong, believable protagonists, many of them Black women," that brought diverse readers back for more. Still, in the years before Butler was Delany's student and later peer on equal standing, it was Harlan Ellison who was Butler's first mentor. According to the *Modern Masters of Science Fiction: Octavia Butler*, by Gerry Canavan, the two met in 1969 when Butler "took a class through the Screen Writers Guild of America 'Open Door' Workshop—a program intended as outreach to Black and Latino writers in L.A.—run by Harlan Ellison, himself a brilliant short story writer, editor and television writer since the 50s."

As a devoted *Star Trek* fan, it would've been difficult for Butler to turn down the opportunity to study with the man who wrote the famed 1967 "The City on the Edge of Forever" episode. Ellison wasn't much impressed with Butler's skills as a screenwriter but saw her potential as a storyteller and invited her to Clarion. In addition, he loaned her part of the tuition funds and helped her buy a new typewriter. Coming at a time when fiction programs were relatively new, Clarion began in 1968 and would go on to become the premier sci-fi/fantasy writers workshop in the country.

Cultural critic Carol Cooper, who was friends with both Butler and Ellison, also studied at Clarion with the famed writer. She recalled:

Most of us were terrified Harlan would rip us a new one, and yet he was generous, clever, rigorous, fearless, and incredibly funny. He read us stories, told us jokes and anecdotes, and shredded our wannabe stories in the workshop circle to make them better. He never forgot any of us. His memory was spooky. As was his energy level. People don't realize how many people he personally got into Clarion, because he believed in their talent. He bought their stories for his anthologies or recommended his students to other editors.

In 1970, the year that Butler attended Clarion, her classmates included future Marvel Comics/*Law & Order* scripter Gerry Conway and Vonda N. McIntyre, who would go on to write the Hugo and Nebula award–winning novel *Dreamsnake*. "Everybody knew her as Estelle," McIntyre wrote in 2010. "She was tall, quiet, dignified and very shy." Conway, who too would become a successful writer, said in 2016, "It was obvious even in those early days that her star would burn bright." In addition to Harlan Ellison and Samuel R. Delany, their instructors included James Sallis, Joanna Russ, Fritz Leiber, Kate Wilhelm, Damon Knight, and Robin Scott Wilson.

"When she turned in her first story," McIntyre continued, "it was clear from the first page that she was an extraordinary writer as well as an extraordinary person. Over the course of the six weeks of the workshop, her talent and range impressed her fellow workshop members as well as her instructors." Ellison, known as one of the more prolific writers in science fiction, a term he hated, preferring "speculative fiction," expected his students to write a story a night, a speed that was frustrating for Butler. Still, she stuck it out.

"When I was at Clarion, Harlan Ellison said if anybody can stop you from being a writer, then don't be one," Butler told the *New York Times* in 1997. Before leaving the workshop, Butler sold two stories. "Crossover," which isn't exactly a science fiction tale, but does have a *Twilight Zone* creepiness, was sold to Damon Knight for the *Clarion* (1971) collection, while the novella "Childfinder" was bought by Harlan Ellison for the *Last Dangerous Vision*, the infamous anthology that was never published. These were Butler's first sales, and she was excited, as is to be expected.

The novella "centers on a woman who senses latent psionic power in children and works to sequester them from an aggressive organization of psis," essayist Carl Abbott wrote in "Pasadena on Her Mind: Octavia E. Butler Reimagines Her Hometown," published by the *Los Angeles Review of Books* in 2019.

> Set in a seedy bungalow court that could have matched dozens of places in Butler's familiar quadrant of the city, the story's conflict mirrors the racial tensions that Butler experienced in childhood: the "child finder" and the young girl she hopes to protect are African Americans and the Organization are whites. At the story's climax, several psi-active Black children band together to protect the child finder and form a racially separate psi-active group.

Though Ellison told Butler in 1970 that publication in his book would launch her career, since the book never materialized the story would remain unpublished until 2014 when Butler's *Unexpected Stories* was published. Still, they stayed close friends. Ellison blurbed the 2003 edition of *Kindred*, calling it "that rare artifact... the novel one returns to, again and again."

Growing up, Butler was a geeky science fiction and comic book fan, but she was also coming of age in a militant era of the Black Panthers, the Watts Riots, Angela Davis, the Black Arts Movement, and *Sweet Sweetback's Baadasssss Song*; it all awakened a rebellious spirit within her. While Butler's work wasn't considered literary in the way of her more mainstream peers, she was still connected in feminist spirit with

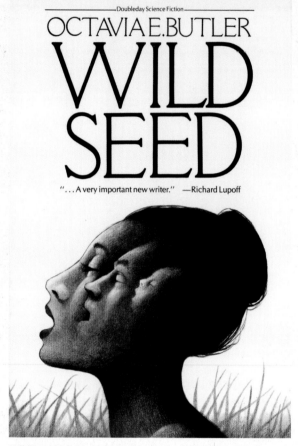

*Wild Seed* (Doubleday, 1980)

writers Toni Morrison (*The Bluest Eye*, 1971), Alice Walker (*Meridian*, 1971), and Toni Cade Bambara (*Gorilla My Love*, 1972), who a few years later became a friend, a critic, and a pen pal. Butler even invited Bambara to contribute to *Black Futures*, an anthology she was coediting with Martin Greenberg (who died in 2013) and Charles Waugh that was never completed.

"Childfinder" was a precursor to the psi-powered people with their "telepathy, telekinesis, precognition, and other parapsychological activity" in *Patternmaster* and *Mind of My Mind*. Just as psi powers connect many of Butler's novels, the apocalyptic landscape motif and urban breakdowns of "Speech Sounds" manifests in *Clay's Ark*, as well as in her bestsellers *Parable of the Sower* (1993) and *Parable of the Talents* (1994). Still, while her wild books were praised by the science fiction community, it wasn't until her stand-alone time travel slave narrative *Kindred* was published in 1979 that she began developing an audience beyond the limitations of speculative fiction fandom.

With the exception of *Survivor*, a book she denounced and refused to have reprinted, all of Butler's books are still in print, and her stature in various communities, including LGBTIQ, feminist studies, Afro-pessimists, and black nerds (blerds), continues to grow. While Butler dismissed *Survivor*, those who've read it weren't offended. Carol Cooper said:

> *Survivor* was my first purchase in 79, and had been her first published novel. I loved the *Patternist* series and thought it evolved brilliantly. I found it very psychologically accurate in how it portrayed contemporary Black and white people. My favorite single book was *Mind of My Mind* followed closely by *Wild Seed*.

Butler often played music when she wrote, and friend and fellow writer Tananarive Due recalled visiting her and hearing Motown songs blaring. She also wrote herself positive affirmations of becoming a best-selling author, getting on the bestseller list, and not worrying if she had enough money to eat *and* pay the rent. One of the highlights of the *Radio Imagination* catalogue was the "interview" section "Free and Clear" that journalist Lynell George constructed from Butler's autobiographical fragments and pieces of memoir. "I understand that writing is my fulfillment and my life, that anything else—any other job—is emotional torture." Even when Butler didn't have to work those jobs, her nocturnal nature stuck, and she continued to compose her novels after midnight.

In a 1989 *Essence* magazine essay, "Birth of a Writer," she spoke of her perseverance as a "positive obsession." Toward the end of that autobiographical piece, Butler wrote:

> At the time nearly all professional science fiction writers were white men. As much as I loved science fiction and fantasy, what was I doing? Well, whatever it was I couldn't stop. Positive obsession is not about being able to stop just because you're afraid and full of doubts. Positive obsession is dangerous. It's about not being able to stop at all.

Ten years before publishing that essay, Butler released the novel *Kindred*, the book that transported her from the science fiction ghetto to a more mainstream audience, including the women who read *Essence*.

Set in 1976, the two hundredth anniversary of the America, when the airwaves were overflowing with bicentennial tales of brave white men and the declaration they signed that declared everyone except black people free, *Kindred* told the story of a modern day black writer named Dana Franklin who, on the same day she moved to a new house with her white husband Kevin, began being zapped through time into antebellum Maryland, back to the slavery days when it was illegal for black people to read, let alone write. For some, this was when America was great; for others it was a nightmare that only ended in escape or death.

Butler told the *New York Times*:

> One of the books that I read when I was doing *Kindred* was a book called *Slavery Defended*. It was a wonderful addition to my research, because you don't read very much about the defenses of slavery these days. And there were a lot of them. One of them said blatantly that it was necessary that the poorest class of white people have someone that they could be better than.

On Dana's first jump she saved a drowning boy named Rufus and, minutes after getting the kid to dry ground, had the barrel of a rifle aimed at her face. No doubt the pale-faced man holding the gun thought she was a runaway slave, but Dana jumped back into her own era before he could blow her head off. It soon becomes apparent that repeatedly saving Rufus from a disastrous end was her mission in order to make sure her own bloodline began.

Afterward, each jump back and forth through time became more brutal and difficult, especially so when her Caucasian husband is also flashed back with her. In her 2013 book *Afrofuturism: The World of Black Sci-Fi and Fantasy Culture*, Ytasha Womack wrote:

> Forget the scariness of a dystopian future, the transatlantic slave trade is a reminder of where collective memories don't want to go, even if the trip is in their imagination. The tragedy that split the nation into warring factions has effects that can be felt in politics of the present.

Coming two years after the *Roots* "television event," a 1977 miniseries based on the book by *Playboy* interviewer and *The Autobiography of Malcolm X* collaborator Alex Haley that helped make slavery part of mass discussion, *Kindred* was rooted in the fantastic and magical, while simultaneously depicting a raw reality. Butler, however, didn't consider it a sci-fi novel.

Butler told Joshunda Sanders in 2004:

> If you're going to write science fiction, that means you're using science and you'll need to use it accurately. At least speculate in ways that make sense, you know. If you're not using science, what you're probably writing is fantasy, I mean if it's still odd. Some species of fantasy…people tend to think fantasy, oh Tolkien, but *Kindred* is fantasy because there's no science. With fantasy, all you have to do is follow the rules that you've created.

In 2017, comic book artist John Jennings teamed with writer Damian Duffy on a brilliant graphic novel of *Kindred* that received the 2018 Eisner Award for Best Adaptation from Another Medium.

Octavia Butler followed the rules that she created for herself and her writing. Throughout the 1970s, she scrimped, scraped, sacrificed, and submitted her work and was finally becoming the writer she'd always wanted to be. In 1980, the brilliant *Wild Seed* was published. This was after achieving literary success with *Kindred*, a success she'd long wanted not just for personal gain and fame but also to be able to take care of her mother.

In 1981, Butler began working on a new novel that she hoped would be her bestseller. Titled *Blindsight*, she envisioned it as a commercial blockbuster that would find a place at the top of the *New York Times* bestsellers list. Unfortunately, even after much writing, rewriting, and with two completely different drafts, Butler was unable to sell the book. In the 2017 text *Luminescent Threads: Connections to Octavia E. Butler*, edited by Alexandra Pierce and Mimi Mondal, biographer Gerry Canavan wrote about the shelved project in his essay "Disrespecting Octavia."

> *Blindsight* is Butler's lost thriller, a novel more in the mood of Stephen King (whom she admired and envied) than any other works. It tells the story of a boy born blind, but with strange psychic powers, who becomes the leader of a cult-like religious movement.

Though Canavan declared *Blindsight* a good book, as it had been sent out to and rejected by several publishers, Butler abandoned the book in 1984, the same year the bleak *Clay's Ark*, the last *Patternmaster* book, was published.

For the next few years, Butler would plan and plot her *Xenogenesis* series, with the first book *Dawn* published in 1987. Into the 1990s, Butler would have her biggest successes with the publication of *Parable of the Sower* (1993) and *Parable of the Talents* (1998). In 1995, she was the recipient of the MacArthur Grant, also called "the genius award," and received $295,000 over five years.

In 1999, Butler moved to Seattle—more specifically to Lake Forest Park, Washington—where she wrote her vampire novel *Fledging*, which was published in 2005. Butler was dealing with high blood pressure and the prescribed medicine made her foggy. Her writing was going slowly, if at all, and the third *Parable* book, which she had begun before *Fledging*, was stalled. Indeed, it was a long, bumpy road from Pasadena to prosperity, from writing in notebooks at her mother's kitchen table to sitting behind a typewriter in her own apartment, from collecting rejection slips to composing classic texts, from working as a dishwasher or warehouse cog and waking up in the middle of the night to write to being hailed a genius and as gifted a couple hundred thousand times in the process.

Butler came into science fiction as the first black female writer, but her work has inspired a speculative-minded sisterhood of scribes that includes Sheree Renée Thomas, Nalo Hopkinson, Nisi Shawl, Ytasha Womack, Walidah Imarisha, adrienne maree brown, Nnedi Okorafor, N.K. Jemisin, and legions of others we haven't heard of yet. In life, her influence was strong, and since her untimely death on February 24, 2006, it has gotten that much stronger.

Butler died after she fell and hit her head. Some sources claimed her fall was caused by a stroke that, in the end, killed her. She was fifty-eight. Though her life was short, her legacy roars on. In Butler's lifetime, she tore down walls and destroyed barriers, so that others could have their literary freedom. As N.K. Jemisin wrote in her 2019 introduction to the *Parable of the Sower* reissue. "We weren't asking for much from our fellow writers: just more than European myths in our fantasy, and more than token representation in the future, present, and past." Somewhere beyond the stars, Octavia Butler was smiling.

**Michael A. Gonzales**

# Herland: The Women's Press and Science Fiction

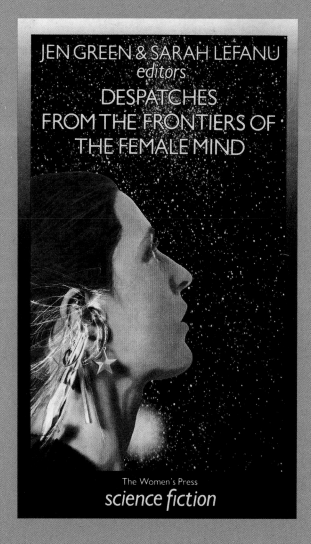

Responding to longstanding inequities and discrimination and reflecting the "doing it for ourselves" feminism of the time, a number of independent publishers emerged from the women's liberation movement during the 1970s. One of the most successful and enduring was London's Women's Press. Founded in 1977, its first foray into science fiction came two years later with the UK publication of Marge Piercy's *Woman on the Edge of Time*, a book they reprinted four times. Following *Woman on the Edge of Time*, the Women's Press released Sandi Hall's *The Godmothers* in 1982 and Elizabeth Baine's *The Birth Machine* in 1982, before launching a dedicated science fiction imprint in 1985.

As a keystone novel by a leading feminist writer, it was unsurprising that a reprint of Joanna Russ's *The Female Man* kicked off this new venture. Originally written in 1970, but not published by Bantam until 1975, the novel is a trenchant critique of patriarchy from the perspectives of four women, or four facets of the same woman, from different places and timelines in earth's past, present, and future. Its depiction of various realities, including one in which men no longer exist, primarily served to underscore the crippling and repressive nature of prevailing gender roles and sexual norms. The book also espoused the transphobic positions common among some radical feminists at the time of its writing. This was something Russ openly regretted in later life, stating in an interview with Samuel R. Delaney in 2006 that "it's almost as if my life has arranged itself to disabuse me of one prejudice after another. And all of these have gone because none of them were real, really."

The incisive and absorbing nature of Russ's novels and short stories was matched by her work as a critic. Ignoring admonitions regarding the interrogation of the politics of science fiction, she was an avid reviewer and produced key works about literature, including 1983's *How to Suppress Women's Writing*.

*Herland* (Women's Press, 1986). *Russ The Female Man* (Women's Press, 1985). Despatches *From the Frontiers of the Female Mind* (Women's Press, 1985).

Dedicated to exposing and countering homophobia and misogyny in the field, she maintained a belief that sci-fi ultimately held great liberatory potential.

These sentiments were echoed in the 1988 nonfiction book *In the Chinks of the World Machine: Feminism and Science Fiction* by Sarah LeFanu, a then senior editor at the Women's Press. She argued that although it was not without precedent, the work of women writers such as Russ, Sally Miller-Gearhart, and others in the 1970s and 1980s had brought about major changes in science fiction's form and direction. This shift was in part possible because the genre was innately "feminism-friendly," due to its basis in speculation. LeFanu argued that change also came out of "the possibilities opened by an important strand … that is in opposition to the dominant ideology, that, rather than celebrating imperialistic and militaristic glory, is subversive, satirical and iconoclastic."

Of the eighty or so sci-fi novels and books of related criticism that the publisher would release in

its lifetime, more than thirty-five came out from 1985 to 1991 as Women's Press Science Fiction titles. All of these featured a distinctive design, with original artwork devoid of SF clichés from a variety of female artists, housed initially in a grey border and spine, and later white borders with a black-and-white-striped spine. Many titles also bore a preface that read:

> Our aim is to publish Science Fiction by women and about women; to present exciting and provocative feminist images of the future that will offer an alternative vision of science and technology, and challenge male domination of the Science Fiction tradition itself.

This imprint certainly did that. Alongside reprints of feminist utopian tales, such as Charlotte Perkins Gilmore's 1915 novel *Herland*, and more recent groundbreaking books like Naomi Mitchison's 1962 novel *Memoirs of a Spacewoman*, Octavia Butler's 1979 novel *Kindred*, and Miller Gearhart's 1980 anthology

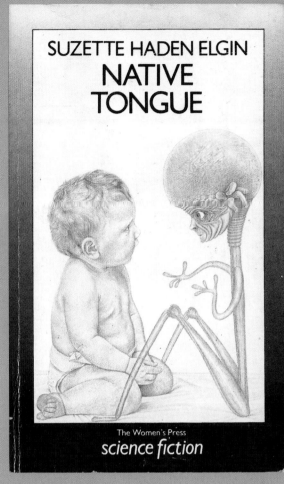

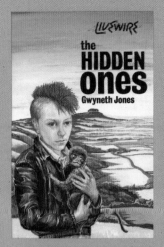

*Wanderground* came a slew of original titles. Some of these were UK editions of recent works by established writers like Russ and Suzette Haden Elgin, while others, such as Carol Emshwiller's *Carmen Dog* (1988) and Lorna Mitchell's *The Revolution of Saint Jone* (1988), appeared in print for the first time. The Women's Press also delved into sci-fi for young adults, with two entries in its Livewire series, Melisa Michael's *Skirmish* (1987) and Gwyneth Jones's *The Hidden Ones* (1988). Although its main imprint for the genre was wound up in the early 1990s, sci-fi remained a key part of the publisher's work over its remaining ten years, with further reprints and original work appearing from Suzy McKee Charnas, Katherine V. Forrest, Patricia Grace, and others.

**Iain McIntyre**

Clockwise from top left: *Kindred* (Women's Press, 1988). *Passing for Human* (Women's Press, 1986). *The New Gulliver* (Women's Press, 1988). *The Incomer* (Women's Press, 1987). *Native Tongue* (Women's Press, 1985). *The Hidden Ones* (Women's Press – Livewire, 1988). *I, Vampire* (Women's Press, 1986). *Wanderground* (Women's Press, 1985). *The Watcher* (Women's Press, 1986). *The Travails of Jane Saint* (Women's Press, 1986). *The Planet Dweller* (Women's Press, 1985). *Queen of the States* (Women's Press, 1986).

# Acknowledgments

In addition to our contributors, the editors would like to acknowledge the following people for their help in sourcing front cover scans of many of the hard to find titles presented in this book: Jim Stokes, Richard McKenna, Jonathan Knighton, Joachim Boaz, Ron Clinton, Tim Kitchen, Alison Sinclair, Roy Nugen, Will Errickson, Kurt Reichenbaugh, Dave Owen, Natalie Conyer, Jules Burt, Jeanette Sewell, Lindy Cameron, Steven Sheil, Evan Pacewicz, Mark Hodgson, John Englehart, Margaret Creagh, Peter Riley and Josh McPhee. Particular thanks to Wendy Comeau at the science fiction specialty store DreamHaven books, in Minneapolis.

"Imagining New Worlds: Sci-Fi and the Vietnam War" was originally published in 2011 in *Overland* no. 202. "Sextrapolation in New Wave Science Fiction" was originally published in 2006 in *Science Fiction Studies* 33, no. 2. "Feminist Future: Time Travel in Marge Piercy's Woman on the Edge of Time" was originally published in 2019 in *MOSF Journal of Science Fiction* 3, no. 3. "The Moons of Le Guin and Heinlein" was originally published in 1994 in *Science Fiction Studies* 21, no. 2.

We also acknowledge the invaluable work done by the Encyclopedia of Science Fiction (http://www.sf-encyclopedia.com), the Internet Speculative Fiction Database (http://www.isfdb.org) and the Luminist Archives (http://www.luminist.org/) in collecting bibliographies, images, and other information.

Andrew Nette would like to thank Angela and Natasha for their support throughout the process of putting this book together. Iain McIntyre thanks his family for all their support during the editing, writing, and compilation of this collection, as well as the Riverton Library for granting him access to the works of Le Guin, Ballard, Silverberg, and many others during his teenage years.

# Contributors

**Scott Adlerberg** is the author of four books, including *Jungle Horses* (2014), a novella that blends fantasy and noir, *Graveyard Love* (Broken River Books, 2016), a psychological thriller, and *Jack Waters* (Broken River Books, 2018), a story of revenge and revolution on a Caribbean island in the early twentieth century. He contributes pieces regularly to *Criminal Element, Crime Reads*, and *Mystery Tribune*, and every summer he hosts the Word for Word Reel Talks film series in Bryant Park in Manhattan. His essay on Chester Himes had a place in the book *Sticking It to the Man: Revolution and Counterculture in Pulp and Popular Fiction from 1950 to 1980* (PM Press, 2019). He lives in Brooklyn.

**Cameron Ashley** lives and works in Melbourne, Australia.

**Rebecca Baumann** is the head of public services at the Lilly Library, the rare book and manuscript library of Indiana University. She is also adjunct associate professor in the Department of Information and Library Science at Indiana University, teaching courses in Rare Book Librarianship, Rare Book Curatorship, and the History of the Book: 1450 to the Present. She was the curator of the 2018 exhibition *Frankenstein 200: The Birth, Life and Resurrection of Mary Shelley's Monster* and author of the accompanying catalogue, published by Indiana University Press. Her research interests include the history of pulps and paperbacks, the history of book collecting, and the horror, science fiction, crime, and romance genres. Her own collection of pulp paperbacks is featured on social media @ arkhamlibrarian.

**Kirsten Bussière** is a doctoral candidate and part-time professor in the Department of English at the University of Ottawa. She holds a Bachelor of Arts with Honors in English and a Master of Arts in English and Digital Humanities from Carleton University. Her most recent scholarly publications include: "Digital Humanity: Collaborative Capital Resistance in Doctorow's *Walkaway*," in *Vector: Future Economies* 288; "Feminist Future: Time Travel in Marge Piercy's *Woman on the Edge of Time*," in *MOSF Journal of Science Fiction* 3, no. 3; and "Beginning at the End: Indigenous Survivance in *Moon of the Crusted Snow*," in *Foundation* 49, no, 136. Her current research, funded by the Social Science and Humanities Research Council of Canada, examines representations of space, time, and memory in contemporary postapocalyptic fiction.

**Kat Clay** is an award-winning crime and horror author from Melbourne, Australia. Her short story "Lady Loveday Investigates" won three prizes at the 2018 Scarlet Stiletto Awards, including the Kerry Greenwood Prize for Best Malice Domestic. In 2017, she was long-listed for the CWA Debut Dagger award for her unpublished novel *Victorianoir*. She is the author of weird-noir novella *Double Exposure* and has published in *Aurealis, Weird Fiction Review, SQ Mag*, and *Crimson Streets*.

**Daniel Shank Cruz** grew up in New York City and Lancaster, Pennsylvania. He is a graduate of Goshen College (BA) and Northern Illinois University (MA, PhD). He is the author of *Queering Mennonite Literature: Archives, Activism, and the Search for Community* (Penn State University Press, 2019), and his writing has appeared in venues such as *Crítica Hispánica, Mennonite Quarterly Review*, the *New York Times*, and several book collections.

**David Curcio** is a Boston-based artist and writer. In 2001, he received his Master's in Fine Arts from Pratt Institute in Brooklyn, New York. He is a certified master printer who has worked in numerous studios in Florence, Italy, and has studied Japanese woodcut in Kobe, Japan. David has written extensively on film, literature, boxing, and horror and is currently writing a book on boxing and cinema and the ways in which the boxing film holds up a mirror to more than a hundred years of race, crime, and culture in the United States (working title: *Cinema Pugilistica: A Century of Race, Crime, and Culture in the Boxing Film*).

**Rjurik Davidson** is a writer, editor, and public speaker, who has published the novel *The Stars Askew* (Tom Doherty Associates, 2016). *Chicago Review of Books* recommended it as one of the best ten SF novels to read over the summer, and *Pop Mythology* says, it "fleshes out his wonderfully bizarre world, a world that blends familiar elements of history and mythology in unique ways." *Sci Fi Now* claimed his novel *Unwrapped Sky* (Tor Books, 2014) could "go toe-to-toe with China Miéville's best." *Kirkus Reviews* called it "Impressively imagined and densely detailed." His screenplay *The Uncertainty Principle* (cowritten with Ben Chessell) is currently in development. Rjurik is a former associate editor of *Overland* magazine. He can be found at www.rjurik.com and tweets as @rjurikdavidson.

**Michael A. Gonzales**, from Harlem, is the coauthor, with Havelock Nelson, of *Bring the Noise: A Guide to Rap Music and Hip-hop Culture* (Harmony Books, 1991). He has been a senior writer for *The Source*, writer-at-large for *Vibe*, and a regular contributor to *The Village Voice*, *Essence*, *Wax Poetics*, and *Newark Bound*. A former book columnist ("The Blacklist") at *Catapult*, his literary essays have appeared in the *Paris Review*, *Longreads*, *Afropunk*, and *CrimeReads*, while his music journalism has appeared in *Pitchfork*, Soulhead.com, *New York* magazine, *Contact High: A Visual History of Hip-Hop* (Crown Publishing Group, 2018), edited by Vikki Tobak, and *Best African-American Essays* (Random House, 2009), edited by Gerald Early. His fiction has appeared in *Black Pulp* (Pro Se Press, 2013), edited by Gary Phillips, theroot.com, *The Darker Mask* (Tom Doherty Associates, 2008), edited by Gary Phillips and Christopher Chambers, *The Global Village: Tell Tales Volume 4* (Peepal Tree Press, 2009), edited by Courttia Newland, *Bronx Biannual*, edited by Miles Marshall Lewis, and the Brown Sugar erotica series, edited by Carol Taylor.

**Molly Grattan** grew up in Brockport, New York, and has turned a longtime fascination with vintage teenage social-problem novels into the long-running young adult fiction and pop culture blog, mondomolly.com. Her nonfiction work has also appeared in *Sticking It to the Man: Revolution and Counterculture in Pulp and Popular Fiction, 1950 to 1980* (PM Press, 2019); *Girl Gangs, Biker Boys, and Real Cool Cats: Pulp Fiction and Youth Culture, 1950 to 1980* (PM Press, 2017); and *Spaceout: Memory* (Space Heater Gallery, 2017). In 2020, she presented the Made in Ridgewood film series in partnership with the Greater Ridgewood Historical Society. She holds a degree in Film and Media Studies from the City University of New York, Hunter College, and teaches film studies and journalism to middle school students in New York City. She lives in Queens.

**Brian Greene** writes short stories, as well as feature pieces on books, music, film, and visual art. His work has appeared in more than thirty publications since 2008. Brian's on Twitter @greenes_circles.

**Rob Latham** is the author of *Consuming Youth: Vampires, Cyborgs, and the Culture of Consumption* (Chicago University, 2002) and the editor of *The Oxford Handbook of Science Fiction* (Oxford University, 2014) and *Science Fiction Criticism: An Anthology of Essential Writings* (Bloomsbury, 2017). He is currently completing a book on the science fiction of Robert Silverberg, as well as a larger study of New Wave SF of the 1960s and 1970s. For two decades, he served as a senior editor for the journal *Science Fiction Studies*.

**Nick Mamatas** is the author of several novels, including *I Am Providence* (Night Shade Books, 2016) and *Sabbath* (Tom Doherty Associates, 2019). His short fiction has appeared in *Best American Mystery Stories*, *Year's Best Fantasy & Science Fiction*, and dozens of other venues—much of it was recently collected in *The People's Republic of Everything* (Tachyon Publications, 2018). His fiction and editorial work has been nominated for the Hugo, Locus, World Fantasy, Shirley Jackson, and Bram Stoker Awards.

**Maitland McDonagh** is a writer, editor, publisher, film critic, and longtime collector of vintage gay adult novels, who founded 120 Days Books in 2012 to republish forgotten gay erotic titles of the 1970s. Now partnered with Riverdale Avenue Books, the 120 Days imprint represents novels whose bold depiction of the realities, aspirations, and fantasies of gay men anticipated decades of political and social change and remain strikingly relevant today.

**Iain McIntyre** is a Melbourne-based author, musician, and community radio broadcaster who has written and edited a variety of books on political activism, history, and music. Recent PM Press publications include: *Sticking It to the Man: Revolution and Counterculture in Pulp and Popular Fiction, 1950 to 1980* (2019) *On the Fly: Hobo Literature and Songs, 1879–1941* (2018), *Girl Gangs, Biker Boys, and Real Cool Cats: Pulp Fiction and Youth Culture, 1950 to 1980* (2017), and *How to Make Trouble and Influence People: Pranks, Protest, Graffiti & Political Mischief Making from across Australia* (2013). He is also a regular contributor to activist resource website commonslibrary.org and the author of *Environmental Blockades Obstructive Direct Action and the History of the Environmental Movement* (Routledge, 2021).

**Andrew Nette** is a writer of fiction and nonfiction. In addition to two crime novels, *Ghost Money* (Crime Wave Press, 2015) and *Gunshine State* (Down & Out Books, 2018), he is coeditor of *Girl Gangs, Biker Boys, and Real Cool Cats: Pulp Fiction and Youth Culture, 1950 to 1980* (PM Press, 2017), and *Sticking it to the Man: Revolution and Counterculture in Pulp and Popular Fiction, 1950 to 1980* (PM Press, 2019). His writing on film, books, and culture has appeared in a variety of print and online publications. You can find him on Twitter at @Pulpcurry.

**Kelly Roberts** is editor in chief of We Are the Mutants, an online magazine focusing on the history and analysis of Cold War era genre, pulp, cult, occult, subculture, and dissident media.

**Erica L. Satifka** has published short fiction in *Clarkesworld*, *Shimmer*, and *Interzone*. Her Philip K. Dick–inspired novel *Stay Crazy* won the 2017 British Fantasy Award for Best Newcomer, and her rural cyberpunk novella *Busted Synapses* will be released soon by Broken Eye Books. She lives in Portland, Oregon, with her husband Rob and several adorable talking cats.

**Mike Stax** is a writer and rock 'n' roll historian. Since 1983, he has edited and published *Ugly Things* magazine, covering the best overlooked music of the 1960s and 1970s. He is the author of several books, including *Swim through the Darkness: My Search for Craig Smith & the Mystery of Maitreya Kali* (Process Media, 2016) and has written the liner notes for numerous reissues. He's also the lead singer for the psychedelic garage rock group the Loons. He lives in La Mesa, California, with

his wife Anja and son Philip. For more about Mike's work, see ugly-things.com.

**Lucy Sussex** is an Honorary Fellow at Federation and La Trobe Universities. She has abiding interests in women's lives, Australiana, SF, and crime. Her writing includes five collections of short stories, and she has taught at Clarion West. She has won various SF awards, been short-listed (as editor) for the World Fantasy award, and her *Blockbuster: Fergus Hume and The Mystery of a Hansom Cab* (Text Publishing Company, 2015) won the 2015 Victorian Community History Award. Currently she is cowriting a true crime/crime fiction biography of Mary and George Fortune with Megan Brown.

**Nicolas Tredell** has published twenty-one books and over four hundred essays, articles, and reviews on authors ranging from Shakespeare to Zadie Smith and on key issues in literary, cultural, and film theory. His recent books include: *Anatomy of Amis: A Study of the Work of Martin Amis* (Paupers' Press, 2017), the most comprehensive account so far of the work of Martin Amis; *Conversations with Critics* (Verbivoracious Press, 2015), an updated edition of his interviews with leading literary figures; *Shakespeare: The Tragedies* (Macmillan International Higher Education, 2012); and *C.P. Snow: The Dynamics of Hope* (Springer, 2012). He is consultant editor of the *Essential Criticism* series, published by Red Globe Press (formerly Palgrave), which numbers eighty-eight titles so far, eight of which he produced. He was a judge of the Geoffrey Faber Memorial Prize for poetry in 1994 and of the English and Media Centre Close Reading Competition in 2016, and a co-organizer of the Literary London Society Annual Conferences in 2018–2020, which attracted distinguished speakers from across the globe. He formerly taught literature, drama, film, and cultural studies at Sussex University and now gives live and video lectures and presentations and leads discussions at a wide range of school, university, and public venues in England and abroad. His website is http://nicolastredell.co.uk.

**Donna Glee Williams** is a poet, editor, scholar, and writer of literary fantasy and science fiction. She makes her home in the mountains of western North Carolina, but the craft societies in her novels *The Braided Path* (Hades Publications, 2014) and *Dreamers* (EDGE Science Fiction and Fantasy Publishing, 2016) owe a lot to the time she's spent in Mexico, Spain, Italy, Israel, Turkey, India, Wales, Ireland, and Pakistan. Her forthcoming novel, *The Night Field*, is based on the work she did in India on a Fulbright Senior Environmental Leadership Fellowship in 2008. As a finalist in the 2015 Roswell Awards for Short Science Fiction, her short story "Saving Seeds" was performed in Hollywood by Jasika Nicole. Her graceful speculative fiction has been recognized by Honorable Mentions from both the Writers of the Future competition and Gardner Dozois's Best of the Year collection. These days, she earns her daily bread by writing and helping other writers as an editor, but in the past she's done the dance as turnabout crew (aka "maid") on a schooner, as a librarian, as an environmental activist, as a registered nurse, as a teacher and seminar leader, and for a long stint as a professional student.

# Index

## ABOUT PM PRESS

PM Press is an independent, radical publisher of books and media to educate, entertain, and inspire. Founded in 2007 by a small group of people with decades of publishing, media, and organizing experience, PM Press amplifies the voices of radical authors, artists, and activists. Our aim is to deliver bold political ideas and vital stories to all walks of life and arm the dreamers to demand the impossible. We have sold millions of copies of our books, most often one at a time, face to face. We're old enough to know what we're doing and young enough to know what's at stake. Join us to create a better world.

**PM Press**
**PO Box 23912**
**Oakland, CA 94623**
**www.pmpress.org**

## FRIENDS OF PM PRESS

These are indisputably momentous times—the financial system is melting down globally and the Empire is stumbling. Now more than ever there is a vital need for radical ideas.

In the years since its founding—and on a mere shoestring—PM Press has risen to the formidable challenge of publishing and distributing knowledge and entertainment for the struggles ahead. With over 450 releases to date, we have published an impressive and stimulating array of literature, art, music, politics, and culture. Using every available medium, we've succeeded in connecting those hungry for ideas and information to those putting them into practice.

*Friends of PM* allows you to directly help impact, amplify, and revitalize the discourse and actions of radical writers, filmmakers, and artists. It provides us with a stable foundation from which we can build upon our early successes and provides a much-needed subsidy for the materials that can't necessarily pay their own way. You can help make that happen—and receive every new title automatically delivered to your door once a month—by joining as a Friend of PM Press. And, we'll throw in a free T-shirt when you sign up.

Here are your options:

- **$30 a month** Get all books and pamphlets plus 50% discount on all webstore purchases

- **$40 a month** Get all PM Press releases (including CDs and DVDs) plus 50% discount on all webstore purchases

- **$100 a month** Superstar—Everything plus PM merchandise, free downloads, and 50% discount on all webstore purchases

For those who can't afford $30 or more a month, we have **Sustainer Rates** at $15, $10, and $5. Sustainers get a free PM Press T-shirt and a 50% discount on all purchases from our website.

Your Visa or Mastercard will be billed once a month, until you tell us to stop. Or until our efforts succeed in bringing the revolution around. Or the financial meltdown of Capital makes plastic redundant. Whichever comes first.

## Girl Gangs, Biker Boys, and Real Cool Cats: Pulp Fiction and Youth Culture, 1950 to 1980

Edited by Iain McIntyre
and Andrew Nette
with a Foreword by Peter Doyle

**ISBN: 978-1-62963-438-8**
**$29.95    336 pages**

*Girl Gangs, Biker Boys, and Real Cool Cats* is the first comprehensive account of how the rise of postwar youth culture was depicted in mass-market pulp fiction. As the young created new styles in music, fashion, and culture, pulp fiction shadowed their every move, hyping and exploiting their behaviour, dress, and language for mass consumption and cheap thrills. From the juvenile delinquent gangs of the early 1950s through the beats and hippies, on to bikers, skinheads, and punks, pulp fiction left no trend untouched. With their lurid covers and wild, action-packed plots, these books reveal as much about society's deepest desires and fears as they do about the subcultures themselves.

*Girl Gangs* features approximately 400 full-color covers, many of them never reprinted before. With 70 in-depth author interviews, illustrated biographies, and previously unpublished articles from more than 20 popular culture critics and scholars from the US, UK, and Australia, the book goes behind the scenes to look at the authors and publishers, how they worked, where they drew their inspiration and—often overlooked—the actual words they wrote. Books by well-known authors such as Harlan Ellison and Lawrence Block are discussed alongside neglected obscurities and former bestsellers ripe for rediscovery. It is a must read for anyone interested in pulp fiction, lost literary history, retro and subcultural style, and the history of postwar youth culture.

Contributors include Nicolas Tredell, Alwyn W. Turner, Mike Stax, Clinton Walker, Bill Osgerby, David Rife, J.F. Norris, Stewart Home, James Cockington, Joe Blevins, Brian Coffey, James Doig, David James Foster, Matthew Asprey Gear, Molly Grattan, Brian Greene, John Harrison, David Kiersh, Austin Matthews, and Robert Baker.

## Sticking It to the Man: Revolution and Counterculture in Pulp and Popular Fiction, 1950 to 1980

Edited by Andrew Nette and Iain McIntyre

**ISBN: 978-1-62963-524-8**
**$34.95    336 pages**

From Civil Rights and Black Power to the New Left and Gay Liberation, the 1960s and 1970s saw a host of movements shake the status quo. The impact of feminism, anticolonial struggles, wildcat industrial strikes, and antiwar agitation was felt globally. With social strictures and political structures challenged at every level, pulp and popular fiction could hardly remain unaffected. While an influx of New Wave nonconformists transformed science fiction, feminist, gay, and black authors broke into areas of crime, porn, and other paperback genres previously dominated by conservative, straight, white males. For their part, pulp hacks struck back with bizarre takes on the revolutionary times, creating vigilante-driven fiction that echoed the Nixonian backlash and the coming conservatism of Thatcherism and Reaganism.

*Sticking It to the Man* tracks the changing politics and culture of the period and how it was reflected in pulp and popular fiction in the US, UK, and Australia from the 1950s onward. Featuring more than 300 full-color covers, the book includes in-depth author interviews, illustrated biographies, articles, and reviews from more than 30 popular culture critics and scholars. Works by science-fiction icons such as J.G. Ballard, Ursula Le Guin, Michael Moorcock, and Octavia Butler, street-level hustlers turned bestselling black writers Iceberg Slim and Donald Goines, crime heavyweights Chester Himes and Brian Garfield, and a myriad of lesser-known novelists ripe for rediscovery, are explored, celebrated, and analyzed.